NO PLACE IN
TIME

NO PLACE IN
TIME

The Hebraic
Myth in Late-
Nineteenth-Century
American
Literature

SHARON B. OSTER

WAYNE STATE UNIVERSITY PRESS
DETROIT

ISBN 978-0-8143-4582-5 (hardcover); ISBN 978-0-8143-4583-2 (ebook)

Library of Congress Control Number: 2018941783

An early version of chapter 2 was first published in *ELH* 75.4 (2008): 963–92 and is reprinted with permission by Johns Hopkins University Press.

Wayne State University Press
Leonard N. Simons Building
4809 Woodward Avenue
Detroit, Michigan 48201-1309

Visit us online at wsupress.wayne.edu

IN LOVING MEMORY OF Jeannine Ida Gomby Oster and Morris Oster

CONTENTS

ACKNOWLEDGMENTS

THE FUTURE OF THIS book is ineluctably connected to those who helped shape its past, whose intellectual and social engagement contributed to its making.

Having evolved over time, this book has accrued many debts and I'm keenly aware at the outset that discharging them with gratitude—no matter how sincerely felt—is, at best, inadequate remuneration, a poor dividend on generous investments of time, effort, and friendship. Still, I would like to acknowledge individuals who have played a significant—and, in some instances, recurring—role in shaping both the project and my approach to it. By example, they have instilled in me the pleasure of literary recovery and the responsibility of grappling with what are, at times, difficult histories and discomfiting ideas. Always generous with her capacious archival knowledge, masterful critical skills, and lifelong dedication to the critical canons of James and Wharton, Martha Banta has provided core inspiration and support for this project from the start. Vince Pecora has shaped my sense of intellectual history from Hegelian dialectics through postsecular thought, and that fundamental influence is visible in this book. Kenneth Reinhard has helped me to form a Jewish philosophical framework for this project, and to sustain the infectious love of ideas and of learning that he, himself, exemplifies. Exacting in language and rigor of thought, Sharon Cameron challenged me always to go deeper, and deeper still, with Henry James. The late Janet Hadda introduced me to Yiddish literary culture; her quiet brilliance awakened in me a deep appreciation for that culture's impact on American literature and aroused my own commitment to its academic stewardship. The late Barbara Packer, whose recitation of Milton once brought me to tears, exemplified scholarly rigor, the joy of interpretive reading, and professional generosity—and above all with grace and impeccable taste. Her scholarship epitomizes how one might bring even the most sophisticated philosophical and theological ideas to heel with stunning clarity. Max and Estelle Novak have encouraged me to think more profoundly about Abraham Cahan's work and Jewish literature generally. Joe Bristow helped me to organize my book's overarching argument at a critical juncture. Chris Looby sharpened my scholarship and thinking by exposing them to the provocative conversations for which UCLA's Americanist Research Colloquium is—for a generation of Americanist scholars from across the nation—almost a rite of passage.

Many colleagues read various parts of this book—some more than once—and I am grateful for their generous questions, responses, and suggestions. Eric Sundquist has provided unfailing support and mentorship, inspiring in me my very best work. Jen Fleissner had faith in this project early on; her groundbreaking work, scholarly example, and valued friendship have had an immeasurable influence. Passionate interlocutor, astute reader, and loyal friend, Greg Jackson has helped me refine my thinking about this project in crucial ways over the years. I am also indebted to Michelle Chihara, Aaron DeRosa, Bert Emerson, Rebecca Evans, Paul Gilmore, Eric Hayot, Tom Koenigs, Greta LaFleur, Michele Currie Navakas, Lindsay Reckson, Sarah Rivett, Stella Setka, Caleb Spencer, Kyla Wazana Tompkins and our colleagues who are, or were, members of the Southern California Americanist Group. From that group, Mark Eaton has been a dedicated colleague and friend, and Stefanie Sobelle deserves special mention for the astute feedback she offered in our treasured one-on-one exchanges. For inviting me into the community of scholars in Jewish literary studies that she has helped to build, and modeling utmost scholarly generosity, I am deeply grateful to Victoria Aarons.

For their unfailing encouragement, passionate intellectual exchange, and years of friendship at the Huntington Library, I thank Will Fisher and Kadin Henningsen. Our daily conversations over lunch, often in the brilliant company of Juan Gomez and Penny Geng, were central to the writing process. I have enjoyed countless hours writing in the Huntington Library's Ahmanson Reading Room, and wish especially to thank Mona Shulman for her friendship, patient ear, and nurturing kinship. I am grateful to my colleagues at the University of Redlands, above all in the English Department and in the Johnston Center for Integrative

Studies, for the intellectual culture that they and our students foment on a daily basis. I especially thank Lorenzo Garbo, Claudia Ingram, Daniel Kiefer, Bill McDonald, and Judy Tschann for their provocations that have stretched my thinking about key themes in this project, and for the richness of conversations from which I never fail to profit. Every marathon is measured by the spirit of the final sprint, so I am indebted to those colleagues and friends from many academic corners who nurtured my fortitude through the toughest stages of revision and, finally, production: J. K. Barret, Juliette Cherbuliez, Hilary Earl, Kathy Feeley, Hilene Flanzbaum, Valerie Hébert, Dorene Isenberg, Carla Mazzio, Camille Serchuk, and Ivonne Vailakis. Julie Townsend has been with me the length of this journey, exchanging ideas and providing constant friendship and company. From the Huntington and beyond, Tiffany Werth has been a solid rock. Cherished friend and colleague, role model, and so much more, Monica Varsanyi has enriched my ideas, diminished my doubts, and joyfully celebrated each and every small victory.

This book came into being with the support of several institutions. Fellowships from UCLA and UC Irvine funded early stages of research. For resources to complete the project, I'm indebted to the Faculty Research Grants Program at the University of Redlands; to College of Arts and Science deans over the past few years Barbara Morris and Kathy Ogren for sabbatical and travel support; and to my current dean Kendrick Brown for providing funds and course release to see the book through press. Redlands' Sandy Richey always seemed to work magic, materializing hard to get books and articles. My profound thanks to many intrepid research assistants over the years, especially Brighid King and Andrew McLellan in early stages of drafting, Sofia Munoz and Jessica Castanon more recently, and Bret Talbert for his careful labor on the bibliography.

An early version of chapter 2 appeared in *English Literary History* 75, no. 4 (2008): 963–92. I'm grateful to the editors and to the anonymous readers.

Kathryn Wildfong, editor-in-chief and interim director at Wayne State University Press, ushered this project through the review process and to press with thorough care and a steadfast commitment to the book's subject and cross-disciplinary nature. The book has benefitted greatly from Sandra Judd's careful copyediting and from the efforts of Kristin Harpster and the editorial team who brought this manuscript into print. The keen insights and suggestions of the three anonymous press readers helped me sharpen my arguments and better pace the book's claims. For their efforts, I pledge myself to paying forward that heroic act of generosity.

My oldest and heaviest debts are, of course, to family: I could not have done any of this without the steadfast love and guidance of my brilliant sisters, Stephanie Oster and Deborah Oster Pannell, who have believed in me all along. Mark Lee's unfailing curiosity and wit buoyed my spirits. I thank the Ketsios family for their unconditional love and support and the Gersten family for providing me a West Coast home when I was still building my own. A loving nod to my nephew Josiah Pannell, whose courage and confidence continue to inspire me. I thank my chosen family, my dear friends, for knowing when not to ask me about my book. Last, but hardly least, for the ever-replenishing source of love and support, for their patience and quiet sacrifice during the years and months it has taken to complete this book, my deepest obligation and gratitude go to George Ketsios and Leo Oster Ketsios: my morning, day, evening, and night, who give joy and meaning to every minute in between.

Introduction

A Figure Out of Time: The "Hebraic Myth" and Christian Typology

Among the principal criticisms leveled against the merchants was the charge that their profit implied a mortgage on time, which was supposed to belong to God alone. For example, we have the following remarks of a lector-general of the Franciscan order in the fourteenth century concerning a disputed question: "Question: is a merchant entitled, in a given type of business transaction, to demand a greater payment from one who cannot settle his account immediately than from one who can? The answer argued for is no, because in doing so he would be selling time and would be committing usury by selling what does not belong to him."

> —Jacques Le Goff, *Time, Work and Culture in the Middle Ages* (1980)

. . . in all matters pertaining to their religious life that tinges all their customs, they stand, these East Side Jews, where the new day that dawned on Calvary left them standing, stubbornly refusing to see the light. A visit to a Jewish house of mourning is like bridging the gap of two thousand years.

> —Jacob Riis, *How the Other Half Lives* (1891)

AFTER LIVING ABROAD FOR twenty years, Henry James returned to the United States from 1904 to 1905, to find his birthplace in New York City dramatically transformed, a jarring experience he recorded in his travelogue,

The American Scene (1907).[1] His youthful picture of "old New York," he lamented, was "violently overpainted"; a once familiar landscape no longer yielded recognition in this uncanny return to a familiar yet foreign place (7). Mere blocks from his childhood neighborhood in Washington Square, the Lower East Side was altered by tenements, the cacophony of foreign tongues, the desperate poverty of immigrants, and communities in the flux of assimilation and resistance to it. No immigrant group absorbed James's interest more or received more attention from his pen than the "inconceivable alien" of the city's Jewish communities.[2] In the crowded stretch of city blocks between Broadway and the East River, and Canal and Fourteenth Streets, James's alienation was heightened, his attention especially arrested in the "dense Yiddish quarter" by a "swarming that had begun to thicken," a scene that "bristled, at every step, with the signs and sounds, immitigable, unmistakable, of a Jewry that had burst all bounds."[3] As if in an aquarium with water to the housetops, he describes how "innumerable fish, of over-developed proboscis, were to bump together, for ever, amid heaped spoils of the sea," so that "multiplication of everything, was the dominant note . . . multiplication with a vengeance" (100). For James, immigrant Jews on the whole were monstrous, a physical, excessive, accumulative mass, with the "strength" of their "race" somehow embodied in each individual part, like "snakes or worms . . . who, when cut into pieces, wriggle away contentedly and live in the snippet as completely as in the whole" (99–100).

James's debasing metaphors for Jewish people—snakes, worms, large-nosed fish—certainly sound an antisemitic note, and have provoked among James scholars considerable critical debate since the 1990s, including concerted efforts to redeem his apparent genteel antisemitism in relation to the Jewish "other."[4] These efforts are well justified, since James also seemed to express fascination, even wonder, with denizens of the Jewish quarter. He was struck, for example, by the rich Old Testament history he imagined the Jews transported to America, comparing the "denizens of the New York Ghetto" to "splinters on the table of a glass-blower," each carrying the "whole hard glitter of Israel," with its "gathered past . . . mechanically pushing through" each visage.[5] What I want to emphasize here is the synecdochic pattern formed by this assemblage of images, how each individual person is thought to carry a collective Hebraic past, one of redemptive cultural value. Despite the incessant construction, the droning noise of human bustle, the patchwork of streets alternating between dust and deep mud, and the increasing verticality of the buildings that reduced humanity to a closed-in, "ant-like population," unlike the "dark, foul, stifling Ghettos of other remembered cities," James goes so far as to declare that this "Ghetto," with its "far-spreading light," may yet be the "city of redemption," the "New Jerusalem on Earth" (101). This last phrase requires a second look: *Is* it really about redemption? Or was James being ironic, invoking theodicy to underscore the hopelessness of modern poverty and abject suffering? Critics have certainly, perhaps exhaustively, debated James's attitude toward Jews. I begin with this moment, however, to illustrate something different, the key premise of this book: that when reading for affect, we might overlook something less obvious, how this moment captures the palimpsestic, temporally layered quality of typological rhetoric about Jews in a Protestant-centric culture. Much critical attention has been given to antisemitic literary stereotypes, yet less to the "philosemitic" ones, those that suggest feelings of appreciation or affection for Jews and Jewish culture. This book will attend to the latter, with the caveat that we set aside the affective, binary framework of "antisemitism" and "philosemitism"—that is, the variously negative, positive, and often coincident attitudes adopted by Gentile writers or communities toward Jewish people. Instead, in what follows, I read philosemitic discourse as fundamentally about time, pervading the writing of even the most prolific literary realists of the era.

No Place in Time contends that following the onset of 1880s Jewish immigration, realist writers such as Henry James, Abraham Cahan, Edith Wharton, Mary Antin, and Anzia Yezierska struggled to transform into reality what I'm calling a "Hebraic myth," an inherited philosemitic version of the "Jew": the noble biblical "Hebrew." From the seventeenth-century Puritan jeremiad through nineteenth-century poetry and religious novels, the trope of the noble Hebrew, though certainly more "positive" than other tropes of Jewishness, served a particular temporal function: to buttress Protestant providential narratives as a metaphor for the pre-Christian past, since, according to Protestant typology, the Old Testament prefigures the New Testament. Just as with Native Americans, who were also depicted in the popular imagination as mythic and relegated entirely to the past, the Hebraic myth rendered the Jew a figure *out of time*.[6] Jewish traditions long provided the basis of Christian typology, but unlike Native Americans, who were racialized and then exterminated, Jews in this modern moment—though still suspect, dangerous—were being absorbed, in the process of becoming citizens, their messianic and prophetic teachings transformed into a normative, Anglo-Protestant vision of the American nation and its destiny.[7] Confronting modern Jewish people perceived as a social, national "problem," as alien figures of religious or "racial" difference, yet with particular contemporary experiences and potential futures, realist writers needed to write the "Jew" *in time*. Their efforts to do so reveal a telling paradox of historical coexistence and simultaneity: if the Hebraic myth helped seventeenth-century Puritans to equate themselves with noble, ancient tribes of Israel, to authenticate their self-definition, and to insert America into redemptive history, in nineteenth-century literature the "noble Hebrew" persisted alongside other figures—the Arnoldian Hebraic "philistine" or, worse, the avaricious "Jew," petty pawnbroker, or international financier—as a stubborn, atavistic holdover from the pre-Christian past. These competing tropes, commonly thought to indicate authorial affect—hatred, love, or ambivalence toward Jews in the face of a "Jewish Problem"—in my account signal temporal coincidence, incompatibility, and serve as an index of the radical flux of modernity. In the pages that follow, I propose to shift our understanding of the Jewish place in American literature away from the reigning models of affect and assimilation, in which literary Jewishness "reflects" degrees of relative acceptance or absorption of Jews into a larger Protestant nation. Instead, I provide an account of how seminal realist authors, both Jewish and non-Jewish, facing the upheavals of modernity, reconfigured a philosemitic Hebraic myth that imagined Jews outside of time, by trying to place them in it as guarantors of a promising American future.

To read late-nineteenth-century American literature through the lens of religious notions of time—nostalgic, perhaps, but also messianic, typological, providential, eschatological—is to reveal how sacred discourse and thought permeate and shape purportedly secular literature. But this lens also reveals that literature with a Protestant-centric temporal structure cannot readily contain the insertion, or simple incorporation, of Jewishness without that structure itself becoming fractured. James's reference to the "New Jerusalem on Earth," after all, is doubly allusive: to the Hebrew biblical book of Ezekiel—whose prophetic vision centers on a future messianic kingdom of God, the "World-to-Come," a paradise on Earth where all nations will come to worship in a rebuilt holy (Jewish) temple— but also, simultaneously, to the Christian book of Revelation, which describes a different eschatological future, a dawning of eternal paradise based on the Second Coming of Christ.[8] It therefore opens up contested imagined futures. A key allegorical trope of Protestant millennialism (a movement that flowered in the nineteenth century), the image of the "New Jerusalem" invokes as it erases a foundational Jewish past, at once ancillary and obsolete, as well as a competing messianic Jewish future, in order to assert a superior Christian double.

James's use of the trope illustrates the extent to which his mind is not only in the fluctuating grip of both alienation and familiarity but also, and more importantly, of both past and future, and of different versions of each, depending upon one's theological point of reference. His version of the Jewish Ghetto—simultaneously a grotesque manifestation of industrial modernity and home to the ancient biblical elect—illuminates the doubling logic of typology, and the literary problem of anachronism that the Hebraic myth creates. The connection between new and old holy cities may be broken by fire escapes that give "the whole vista so modernized and appointed a look," but that technology only serves to dramatize what the comparison bridges, "the distance achieved from old Jerusalem."[9] Even the impoverished Eastern European Jews seem to link Jerusalems old and new. Victims of Russian pogroms and czarist oppression, these utterly modern figures appear to have stepped right out of the past, recent Old World history and distant biblical myth alike. James knows about typology, and how his Protestant forbears accordingly read themselves into the Bible's sacred history as the *Kairos*—the "in-due-time" fulfillment—of God's plan, the heirs of his first "chosen" children. The "New Jerusalem on Earth" signals the logic by which Protestant America unfolds and fulfills a divine plan that would, in turn, render Judaism obsolete. Living Jews thus seem atavistic, persistent remnants of Old Testament culture and of a race James's elder contemporary, Henry Wadsworth Longfellow, had pronounced a half century earlier as a "dead nation" never to rise again.[10] Except that they are rising everywhere James looks, from Ellis Island, from the stairwells and alleys of tenements, like a return of the typologically repressed, to disrupt the American Protestant narrative of rebirth.

I dwell on James's example because it points to something literary critics rarely discuss, which is how talking and writing about Jewishness often happens in the language of time: whether of the usurer who sells the time of others, according to Jacques Le Goff, or as representing time itself, a premodern, often mythical Hebraic past that must be overcome to ensure a Christian providential future. James may avoid the hackneyed racist stereotypes of his day even though his metaphors point to a pattern in late-nineteenth-century literature, a bifurcated vision of "the Jew," embodied in figures like the greedy Shylock or the noble Hebrew. Harold Fisch dubbed this vision the "dual image": the Jew excites "horror, fear, hatred," but also "wonder, awe, and love."[11] Fisch's formulation provides a key point of departure for this project, which diverges fundamentally from an emphasis on the affective nature of the dual image. In what follows, I both narrow Fisch's scope and widen the interpretive lens. I focus on a necessarily limited selection of American literary realist and naturalist works in the late nineteenth and early twentieth centuries, but read them beyond the frames of affect or assimilation in order to reveal the Judeo-Christian temporal framework that grounds and shapes such texts, one that they (and we) seem to take for granted. If, according to Christian typology, Old Testament Hebraic culture provides the prophetic, allegorical foundation for the New, but in its own right is to be superseded, then, accordingly, both religious and secular Jews in one's midst, as the literature depicts them, are persistent, medieval, backward, perhaps quaint—in a word, anachronistic. They are figures out of time.

The role of the Jew in American literature through the late nineteenth century has been in a sense *Christianized*—that is, set within a necessarily Christian, or more specifically Protestant, temporal framework. The chapters that follow bring Jewish writers into conversation with their non-Jewish contemporaries to trace the Hebraic myth as the aesthetic manifestation of this contested framework, of the dependence of Protestant American narratives upon what Kathleen Biddick calls "the Christian typological imaginary" that fundamentally cuts off a new Christian "this is now" from an old Jewish "that was then."[12] The crucial, relatively unnoticed work performed by the Hebraic myth in supporting normative Protestant visions of American belonging creates what I call a "typological aesthetic." Traditional Christian typology in American writing from the Puritans through Melville depended upon the supersession of Jewish history and thought, biblical Jewishness serving as the temporal marker of "then," Christianity's own point of departure. The surprising thing is how American realists—writing at an altogether different industrial, demographic, and economic moment in American life, when time itself felt fractured—recuperate Hebraic "pastness" symbolically, whether to gain access to a more stable, religious, premodern relationship to time or to imagine a viable future. As illustrated by James, the typological aesthetic creates this pattern of temporal doubling, a layering of unresolved rhetorical palimpsests. Reading for such patterns allows us to shift focus from questions of Jewish ethnic "identity" as "represented" within a Protestant American literary culture, or of attitudes about the Jewish "other," and toward the vicissitudes of time that complicate a Protestant American temporal trajectory, allowing us to see the typological aesthetic as a crucial literary response to modernity. *No Place in Time* moves the Hebraic myth from the margins to the center of American literary study, attending to a critical lacuna regarding religious conceptions of time, both Protestant typology and Jewish "collective memory," to deepen conversations about literary Jewishness—Jewishness not as an alien thing to be absorbed but as already a basic part of, and inherent challenge to, the very temporal logic of American literature.[13]

A second, historically newsworthy example may help to crystallize the paradoxical thinking and the constitutive temporal binary that inform the typological aesthetic, dealing with a series of events with which James's readers would have been familiar. In June 1877, Joseph Seligman—German-Jewish millionaire, international banker, and former financial advisor to Presidents Abraham Lincoln, Ulysses S. Grant, and Rutherford B. Hayes—was denied entry to the prestigious Grand Union Hotel in Saratoga Springs, New York, by Judge Henry Hilton.[14] Hilton reasoned that he did not "consider Mr. Joseph Seligman a Hebrew" because, years ago, Seligman "threw overboard the Hebrew-Bible and Moses" and had joined "the Adler set of

Liberals," recently immigrated German reformed Jews.[15] Hilton disliked the "ostentatious," "vulgar," "disgusting" class of whom he regarded Seligman its representative—"Jews" in the "trade sense of the word," "repulsive to the well-bred"—but he revered the "Orthodox Hebrew Church," and old New York Sephardic families like the "Hendricks and Nathans," who were "welcome everywhere."[16] By "Jews" he meant the *nouveaux riches*, too new, too loud, too modern. "Hebrews," by contrast, were old—old-moneyed and old in tradition and biblical history. We can hear Hilton's class snobbery, perhaps anxiety—after all, he, too, was newly wealthy by Old New York standards. But we also see a clear attempt to separate pernicious "Jews" as a race from noble "Hebrews" as a religious group using the temporal distinctions of "new" and "old."

On the surface, Hilton's comments seem expressions of ambivalence toward Jews, veering between the affective, ideological poles of antisemitism and philosemitism. By adopting this framework, however, we might not notice how Hilton's comments, though they imbricate attitudes about racial, class, and religious differences, also rest on a trenchant, binary logic of Christian typology that, by theological definition, cannot be resolved. Critical race theorists have gone far to establish the complex inseparability of feelings, cultural appropriations, and uses of negative, racist stereotypes.[17] The temporal lens I use here sheds similar light on the Jewish "case," but complicates conclusions about Hilton's "attitude," or feelings, toward real Jewish people, since the Hebraic myth fundamentally relegates the "best" of Jewish culture to an ancient, mythic past and renders Judaism's faithful "Israelites" abstract ideas—obsolete, antiquated at best, and in any case antithetical to modernity. By invoking the Hebraic myth, non-Jews like Hilton could maintain respectability by praising with one hand what they denigrated with the other—that is, by divorcing a celebrated, noble Jewish past from their living Jewish neighbors in the present. Taken together, then, these two moments illustrate the anachronism created by the Hebraic myth and mark the multiple trajectories of literary Jewishness this book explores—across time, from history and culture to literature, and from journalism to literary realism. They help frame the book's story of how, as we will see, modern literary realists, Jewish and non-Jewish alike, negotiated persistent, popular concepts of the Jewish relation to time as they struggled to write a Jewish place *in* time, the present time, that often looked not just back but also ahead to the future. This story, in turn, reveals a rich multiplicity of temporalities in American literature of this period.

The chapters that follow are arranged according to a rough chronology of the publication of key texts, involving historical shifts in literary genre (from journalism and local color writing through high literary realism to naturalism), which coincide with shifts in the discourse of Jewishness more broadly. Starting in the next few pages, I hope to demonstrate that I have less interest in attributing causality between literature and history, or in proving a specific direction of influence between text and context, than in illustrating by way of significant literary texts and the historical phenomena they reference a constellation of temporal modes of articulating Jewishness that reverberate across boundaries of secular, sacred, poetic, fictional, political, and journalistic writing. After defining the key terms of this study, in particular "philosemitism," I will trace a brief history of Christian philosemitic ideas that reflects the theological basis of a typological aesthetic, which I hope will contribute to the recent "postsecular" phase of American literary study.[18] I will first show the prevalence of the Hebraic myth from the 1840s to the 1900s, Northeast to Midwest; in poetry by Henry Wadsworth Longfellow and Oliver Wendell Holmes; and in the literary and cultural criticism of Matthew Arnold. In later chapters, we will see the enduring legacy of Christian typology in journalism and naturalist fiction, but also, for different reasons, how even Jewish immigrant writers evoked the Hebraic myth, envisioning America as their own "Promised Land," as the title of Mary Antin's famed autobiography suggests. Within this broad literary and cultural context, the texts at the center of this account—Abraham Cahan's *The Imported Bridegroom* (1898), James's *The Golden Bowl* (1904), Edith Wharton's *The House of Mirth* (1905), Antin's *The Promised Land* (1912), and Anzia Yezierska's *Salome of the Tenements* (1923) and *Bread Givers* (1925)—while seeming to negotiate an antisemitic-philosemitic antinomy, confront the aesthetic challenge posed by a persistent view of Jewishness as backward, antiquated, unmodern, even mythical, in order to place "the Jew" back in time. James redeems the Jewish pawnbroker as a noble arbiter of precapitalist and modern economic values; Wharton's Jewish Wall Street speculator promises to reconcile aesthetic value with the only viable future; Cahan transforms the Hebraic myth of the past into a figure of messianic hope; Antin rewrites the Protestant conversion narrative to reclaim an American Jewish future; and Yezierska, critiquing both Jewish patriarchy and Protestant progressive reform, confers redemptive status onto her Jewish heroines. *No Place in Time* challenges the notion that these texts produce historical "Jewish" types that reflect feelings about Jews or that confirm or challenge the logic of Jewish assimilation. Rather, this book contends that, in their collective negotiation of the typological aesthetic, these texts show how Jewish literary figures mediate the temporal vicissitudes and fractured values of modernity in order to open up ways of envisioning an American future.

The Jewish Problem: Race and Religion

The "Seligman-Hilton Affair," as we now understand it, encapsulates key aspects of what was discussed in the American periodical press from the 1870s through the decades leading up to World War I as the "Jewish Problem." This debate of increasing social importance centered on a key issue that dominated immigration politics, not that of Jewish citizenship or political freedom but of cultural assimilation: could Jews become fully American—that is, loyal, English-speaking Americans, stripped of any and all past national affiliations? For Jews in an Anglo-Protestant culture, this inherently raised the problem of religion, since the logic of cultural assimilation presumes and is arguably predicated on that of religious conversion. This religious problem distinguishes the first major prose writings by Jewish immigrants like Cahan and Antin: To participate in liberal American society, did Jews have to renounce the practices of Jewish faith as well as of language and culture?

It is well known that, unlike in the United States, in Europe the "Jewish Question" centered on Jewish political emancipation, the proper civil and legal status of the Jewish minority, given modern, liberal models of citizenship—first in Great Britain, then in France following the French Revolution of 1789, then debated in Germany in such influential essays as Bruno Bauer's *Die Judenfrage* (1843) and Karl Marx's response, "Zur Judenfrage" (1844).[19] Yet imbricated with these political concerns was the implication that Jews in the religious sense were a backward, medieval, expressly unmodern people. As Amanda Anderson puts it succinctly, "The Jewish Question interrogates the limits of modernity."[20] German-Jewish leaders had confronted these perceptions of Jewish backwardness in the early decades of the nineteenth century. Philosopher Moses Mendelssohn, father of the eighteenth-century *Haskalah*, or Jewish Enlightenment, most famously broke with rabbinic tradition as he tried to reconcile the schisms and conflicts of Jewish particularism, tradition, and culture with a broader project of universality, conceived as fully modern.[21] Likewise, in 1819, Leopold Zunz had founded the *Verein für Kultur und Wissenschaft der Juden* (The Society for the Culture and Science of the Jews) in Berlin, which undertook a "science of Judaism" in order to resist religious assimilation by proving the significance of Jewish history and culture for modernity.[22]

In the United States, the "Jewish Problem" arose somewhat later, during the postbellum era of mass immigration, of East European Jews in particular, toward the century's close. It was also the era of Reconstruction, racial segregation, and increasing Jim Crow violence. Debates about American national identity thus emerged across a fundamental black-white racial divide, given longstanding commitments to white supremacy in the United States. In this context, debates about "the Jewish Problem" of cultural assimilation, a secular version of efforts at religious conversion, began to take on a racialized, antisemitic tone. 1880 was a powerful year in Jewish American history: it witnessed the onset of this concentrated period of East European Jewish immigration to the United States and the subsequent rapid growth of Jewish immigrant communities in East Coast enclaves like Boston's North and West End and New York's Lower East Side. The appearance of so many uncouth, impoverished Ashkenazim was uncomfortable even for assimilated "older" American Jews. Old-moneyed Sephardim, descendants of seventeenth-century colonial settlers, and newly established, reformed, German-speaking "uptown" Jews alike were scandalized by the perceived medieval Orthodox practices of these highly visible, often poor newcomers, seemingly untouched by modernity, much less the Enlightenment. Writers like Jacob Riis and Abraham Cahan illustrated the unprecedented level of squalor in the densely populated pockets of immigrant life in turn-of-the-century lower New York City, out of which immigrant Jews strove to pull themselves economically.

The vast majority of Jews already living in the United States by the 1880s, though, were hardly ancient relics, with religious reformers like Rabbi Isaac Mayer Wise in Cincinnati having worked for decades since the 1850s to find ways to accommodate ancient religious practices to modern American life.[23] As in Germany, France, and England by then, political liberalism in the United States offered Jews essential equity before the law, and freedom from the kinds of cruel violence Russian Jews in the Pale of Settlement were facing and then fleeing. Consequently, whether 1880 represented a radical demographic shift in American Jewry or simply a quantitative extension of what had begun earlier, as Hasia Diner argues, the intensification of ethnic Jewish visibility was dramatic in the transition from largely German and Sephardic to East European Jews; from wealthy urban to poor rural Jews; from educated, secular, and enlightened to uneducated, pious Jews.[24] Jewish religious and cultural life in the United States also began to move from private institutions and religious societies to the streets, so that whole neighborhoods were now visibly, ethnically Jewish, Yiddish-speaking, and openly religious. The establishment of Jewish and other distinctive ethnic immigrant communities gave rise to arguments about inassimilable "races" and destabilized the very idea of "Americanness" as a unified concept.[25] By the 1890s, the United States consequently witnessed a massive spike in nativist nationalism, xenophobia, and anti-immigrant legislation, including the Immigration Act of 1891, expanding the list of excludable classes of immigrants.[26] Even though US Civil Service commissioner Theodore Roosevelt argued in 1894 that in America "all citizens, Protestant and Catholic, Jew and Gentile, shall have fair treatment in every way," he also maintained that where immigrants "cling to the speech, the customs, the ways of life, and the habits of thought of the Old World which they have left, they thereby harm both themselves and us."[27] In other words, religious tolerance had its limits, articulated in terms of mandatory cultural and ethnic assimilation, providing the basic tenets of the budding progressive reform movement. "True Americanism," according to Roosevelt, demanded that immigrants admitted to the United States (Jews being among the largest of religious groups) assimilate fully, which meant merging "Old World religious race and national antipathies," or prejudices, "into love for our common country" (28).

As the discourse of the Jewish Problem slowly transformed from one of stubborn religious affinities to that of innate biological, racial differences, Muckraker Burton Hendrick asked, in a 1907 piece not so subtly titled "The Great Jewish Invasion": "Is [the Jew] assimilable?"[28] For Hendrick, it was now a question not just of whether Jews could accommodate themselves to secular (implicitly Protestant) American culture—and, in effect, be modernized—but also if they could intermarry with Gentiles and biologically "assimilate" away their threatening, degenerative, racial differences. As lawyer and soon-to-be Supreme Court justice Louis Brandeis argued in a 1915 speech to the Eastern Council of Reformed Rabbis, the Jewish Problem had morphed into one of modern antisemitism.[29] Registering these shifts, in scholarship of the late 1990s anthropologist Karen Brodkin and historian Matthew Frye Jacobson reshaped the conversation about Jewishness by arguing that successful Jewish assimilation in the Progressive Era was predicated on Jewish immigrant whiteness. The value of these developments in critical race theory for thinking through American Jewishness cannot be overstated, but one consequence is that religion as an analytic category has become subordinated to the more historically trenchant categories in the hierarchy of race.[30] It is thus unsurprising that Jewishness is often addressed in discussions of assimilation and race, nation and homeland, with Jews figuring as the "other" that disrupts these traditional categories, as Jonathan and Daniel Boyarin suggested.[31] Here, however, we will take a different approach. We will consider how the "Jewish Problem," even as it was reinterpreted under the banner of emerging modern antisemitism, never lost its essentially theological origin: about how to account for the continued existence of Judaism as a religion and of Jewish people within the unfolding of Christian time. Within an American Protestant worldview, heirs to the Puritan project of divine settlement, this problem begins with typology, for which the living, breathing Jew is a disruption, an anachronism. Examined through the lens of a religious framework turned poetic convention, the problem for Protestant realist writers was as much one of time as it was of place.

PHILOSEMITISM AND TEMPORALITY

While the literary discourse of this era contains its own formal patterns and logic, its meaning is inextricable from the set of historical circumstances, such as mass immigration, that brought writers like Cahan, Antin, and Yezierska from Eastern Europe to the United States in the first place. These circumstances, as we will see, also brought them into New England and New York literary scenes shaped by the likes of James and Wharton, of periodical editors William Dean Howells and Philip Cowen, and of Progressive journalists like Riis, Steffens, and Hutchins Hapgood. These writers' lives and careers overlapped; they lived in the same cities, ran in similar circles, and in some cases socialized and read each other's work, their fiction published in many of the same magazines for a shared genteel readership. As I show in chapter 1, reading these authors' works together, and in the context of a shared history, illuminates this scene and, more importantly, the shared concepts by which Jewishness was understood and written about within it. Exploring the temporal dimensions of these literary works in relation to one another, I hope, will provide a new and interesting window onto the key role of the Hebraic myth in literature of this period, as well as illuminate a web of connections among these texts and the historical contexts of Jewish immigration, religious discourse, and the cultural and social concerns expressed in debates about the "Jewish Problem."

What "counts" as "antisemitic" in Anglo-American discourse can be controversial enough, the subject of numerous scholarly books over the last century.[32] But what constitutes the less appreciated, yet enduring phenomenon of "philosemitic" language and expression, a central lens for this story, is even less clear. When historian Oscar Handlin described the 1890s as an American decade "uniquely marked by philo-Semitism"—at times inflected through the sacred history of "God's chosen people," at others through imputed Jewish virtues like "superior intelligence, economic acumen, ethnic loyalty, cultural cohesion, or familial commitment"—he meant the idealization of Jews.[33] In a recent collection dedicated to the subject, however, Adam Sutcliffe and Jonathan Karp suggest that the term "philosemitism" is not so simple, as problematic even as "antisemitism." Together these inseparable concepts express, rather, an "intricate ambivalence," the most common feature of non-Jewish constructs of Jews and Judaism, a tension inherent in the term's etymology.[34] Coined in 1880 by German antisemites as a clear antonym to their favorite coinage, antisemitism, "philosemitism" was meant as a term of derision, intended to both embarrass and caricaturize the political agenda of their opponents.[35] The Greek prefix *philo* (denoting a liking for something, derived from the Greek *philos* for "loving") was meant by antisemitic antagonists as a kind of hyperbole to exaggerate their opponents' social and political positions (as in the insult "Jew lovers"). Therefore, even those who opposed antisemitism rigorously eschewed the tainted "philosemitism" label, preferring to describe their position as not pro-Jewish so much as against all forms of radical prejudice. They regarded "philosemitism" with suspicion, a kind of "counterfeit benevolence" that was no more than the flip side of the antisemitic coin, a one-dimensional and exceptionalist view of Jews and Judaism.[36] While these terms seem to create a clear binary, Sutcliffe and Karp warn against such "analytical reductiveness," the tendency to see philosemitism as either the celebratory opposite of antisemitism or just another form of it.[37] Mitigating this binary, Zygmunt Bauman suggests the term "allosemitism," from the Greek *allos* for "other": "the practice of setting the Jews apart as people radically different from all the others, needing separate concepts to describe and comprehend them and special treatment in all or most social intercourse."[38] "Allosemitism" is a useful term, in that it exposes the continuity of the paired concepts, if not dialectically overcoming their tensions. But allosemitism is also essentially "attitudinally ambivalent," and thus the concept more fully enshrines what it describes, an affective sense of radical Jewish distinction, of essential Jewish otherness.[39]

These tensions over terminology are mirrored in the problem of affect itself, with its muddied boundaries. What is murky on the levels of both feeling and etymology, however, when regarded from a theological point of view becomes clear. Christian philosemitism makes explicit the very division informing the underlying logic of these affective terms: the temporal, structural binary of Christian typology. Beneath the rhetoric of tolerance or ambivalence, or feeling at all, that is, Christian philosemitism relies upon the use of allegorical doubling to rewrite Jews and Judaism and render them necessary players in a temporally structural, yet subordinate, stage in the larger unfolding of Christian time, meaning, and destiny. Given the historical parameters and context of this book, just following the close of a century that witnessed the spread of Christian support of

Jewish resettlement, or "Christian Zionism" so-called, it is worth considering the temporally vexed assumptions of Christian philosemitism.[40] Sutcliffe and Karp insist that Christian philosemitism—Christian Zionism among American evangelicals in particular—has long been motivated by a "conversionist desire" that would "erase Jewish distinctiveness altogether."[41] To offer a contemporary example, leading a tour of 160 evangelicals on a tour of Christian holy sites in Israel in 2010, former Baptist minister and politician Mike Huckabee expressed his great enthusiasm for Jews, the progenitors of Jesus: "I worship a Jew!" Huckabee said. "I have a lot of Jewish friends, and they're kind of, like, 'You evangelicals love Israel more than we do.' I'm, like, 'Do you not get it? If there weren't a Jewish faith, there wouldn't be a Christian faith!'"[42] Huckabee clearly loves the Jew in Jesus. But what he neglects to mention is how evangelical Christian Zionism is part of a long Christian messianic tradition about Jews' real purpose in history: to return to the Land of Israel as a preparatory stage for the Second Coming, "the return of Jesus of Nazareth to earth."[43]

The theological doubling and resultant temporal tensions inherent in Christian philosemitism like Huckabee's are the hallmarks of the typological aesthetic. In the pages that follow, I bring historical thinking and a variety of theoretical formulations of temporality to bear upon the practice of literary close reading, in order to name the Hebraic myth and elucidate the ways in which it functions as yet another trope not for marking feeling about Jews or Jews' perceived assimilability but as a metaphor for irreconcilable orders of time in modern, realist literature—biblical and modern, sacred and secular, Jewish and Christian. That trope, as we will see, mediates the traversal across modern, realist portraits in all their purportedly historically situated specificity by such mythical temporal narratives as the Christian supersession, absorption of, and superiority over Judaism, or that of messianic redemption in the Jewish "World-to-Come." The Hebraic myth simultaneously reveals the disruption, and finally the impossibility, of the Protestant typological narrative through the contingencies of realist plot and character, as it also disrupts realism's own historicity, particularly when adopted by Jewish writers to envision the future. A mythical antecedent appearing as realist type, the Hebraic myth thus mediates time for modern readers—the biblical past, the living memory of what has been overcome, and that past's persistent intrusions into the present. A brief history of Christian philosemitic expression allows us to see the full complexity of this logic. I will follow this with some poignant literary examples to illustrate how, when considered outside the binary logic of its moniker, philosemitism relies upon and perpetuates the temporal paradoxes of the Hebraic myth. As it did for Hilton, the logic of the Hebraic myth is often used to justify antisemitism, illustrating the fluid interweaving and continuity of antisemitic and philosemitic discourse. Given their shared religious roots and temporal links, it is no surprise that these twinned ideologies appear in both Jewish- and non-Jewish-authored literary texts. A careful practice of historically and theoretically informed close reading, however, reveals the Hebraic myth to be neither a simple character type of historical referentiality with significance for plot or ideology—the noble Hebrew—nor the affective attitude of its author, but rather the mark of a perhaps obvious, yet somehow ignored, temporal structure of typological thinking that shapes literary realist texts.

THE TYPOLOGICAL AESTHETIC: A WORD ON METHODS

Christian philosemitism has been a shaping feature of American literature since the Puritan era, when the boundaries of sacred and secular, religious and literary writing, were perhaps more fluid. Jews were admired as the "chosen" descendants of, and heirs to, the biblical tradition—miraculously preserved, antiquated "people of the Book"—but also resented for their refusal to acknowledge Christ as the prophesied Messiah. The Hebrew language was foundational for Puritans seeking the "original meanings" of scripture to justify the new settlement, given how early American colonial Protestants saw themselves as Hebraic doubles, the new chosen people, a covenantal nation, as epitomized in Cotton Mather's widely read colonial history, *Magnalia Christi Americana* (1702).[44] In spite of ongoing conversion efforts, a "grudging tolerance" for Jews remained in colonial America, based on practical, economic grounds and the opportunities and privileges Jews enjoyed as white people. This meant that a recalcitrant Judaism never went away.[45] By the nineteenth century, the early Reformed Calvinist view of the Jew as having a special providence apart from the Christian faith—but "chosen" nonetheless for having been the "source" of

Jesus—began to give way to popular new beliefs that Jewish conversion would mark the beginning of the millennium.[46] Though many of these views persisted side by side, with Jews and Protestants living more or less harmoniously in America, the conviction that a law-exacting (often simply coded as "legalistic") Judaism found its fulfillment in a humanistic Christianity, and that the "New Israel" superseded the "Old," remained fundamental to nineteenth-century millennial belief.[47] Secular history—not to mention reality—thus marched on in tension with religious ideologies, according to which Judaism posed an ongoing temporal contradiction to, and disruption of, Protestant time.

Dating from the Christian exegesis of the apostle Paul, who recast Judaism within an eschatological schema prefiguring the coming of Christ, the doubling logic of typology allowed seventeenth-century Puritans and their descendants to equate themselves with ancient tribes of Israel, thus authenticating their reformation theology and drawing both early colonial Calvinists and American geography into redemptive history.[48] Indeed, the Hebraic myth informed the very founding narratives of American culture: when Cotton Mather exclaimed in 1690, "How Goodly are thy Tents, O New-England, and thy Tabernacles, O thou American Israel!" he sounded the familiar refrain of John Winthrop's "city on a hill," of the Puritan settlers as God's new chosen people.[49] As Sacvan Bercovitch has most famously argued, America was built on this sense of sacred mission, an "errand of pilgrimage" leading "from promise to fulfillment: from Moses to John the Baptist to Samuel Danforth; from the Old World to the New; from Israel in Canaan to New Israel in America; from Adam to Christ to the Second Adam of the Apocalypse."[50] "The newness of New England," he contended, "becomes both literal and eschatological, and . . . the American *wilderness* takes on the double significance of secular and sacred place."[51]

The overtly typological temporal rhetoric of the settlers' mission survived, as we shall see, in more and less subtle forms in nineteenth-century culture. Whereas other Protestant millennialists of their time understood the relation between Old and New Israel as a spiritual one, this generation of Puritans uniquely applied the doctrine of the National Conversion of the Jews (1662) literally and historically to their venture. They expected a mass conversion of Jewry, and complete restoration of Israel to its former glory before the Second Coming, when God would reclaim the Jews, then everyone, a controversial interpretation that provoked a widespread messianic Zionism.[52] As the Great Awakening extended into the early nineteenth century, especially with the great religious revivalism in the 1830s and 1840s, Joseph Smith's Mormon followers went even further to claim themselves the New Israel, the "latter-day Hebrews," and America a temporary Zion, the real Zion to be restored with the dispensation initiated by Christ's return.[53] Likewise, Christian typology turned the Hebrew Bible into an allegorical precursor to the New Testament, with "Hebrews" presaging the Christian salvific future, rendering the Jewish supporting role one of planned obsolescence.[54]

Millennialist Zionism constituted a key strain of Christian philosemitic belief, but was itself stirred by early Jewish messianic activity of the Shabbatai Zvi in the 1660s. In fact, a number of Jewish millennialist groups for whom the Jewish return to Palestine was a precondition to the Messiah's arrival emerged in the seventeenth century.[55] Jewish theologians from Rabbi Akiba to Rashi, to Maimonides, to Menassah ben Israel had prophesied Israel's restoration and preached a widespread messianic Zionism, prompting debates about millennial speculations. This led Protestant ministers to learn Hebrew and adopt Hebrew versions of apocalyptic thinking from the Zohar, the main text of Jewish mysticism, the Kabbalah.[56] In their eyes, the Jews were continuers of the biblical Israel, heirs to the Abrahamic covenant, and their return to Palestine was the first step in the "advancement of the messianic timetable."[57] Christian Zionism, as both idea and political movement, "resurfaced with a vengeance" in the early nineteenth century.[58] In 1831, William Miller, a memorable "end times prophet," informed followers that Christ would "return in 1843, gather the faithful, living and dead, and destroy the unbelievers and the world in a holocaust."[59] For this to pass, the world's Jews needed to be restored to Palestine and converted. As late as 1891, American evangelical and Christian Zionist William Blackstone petitioned President Benjamin Harrison to convene an international conference to build support for granting Palestine to the Jews.[60] More than four hundred American governmental, business, and religious leaders signed the "Blackstone Memorial" petition to do so.[61] Although President Harrison declined, we see the persistent level of commitment among apocalyptic evangelicals to Jewish restoration, revealing not just the subordinate, yet necessary, role Jews were thought to play in this Christian plot of salvation and redemption but also the way this belief took shape politically. Christian Zionism thus constituted a multifold betrayal that revealed a key paradox. If this love of Jews was "philosemitic," it was largely self-serving. The Christian dependency on the Jews amounted to using their very biblical prophesies against them to convert them and write them out of both the American nation and its redemptive history. Viewed among such conversion efforts, Christian appropriations of Jewish "chosen" status, and the continued work among Christian Zionist evangelicals to restore Jews to Palestine, Progressive Protestant reforms focused on Jewish assimilation seem to perpetuate an ongoing pattern of efforts to eliminate the Jewish anachronism in the United States altogether.[62]

These temporal tensions and conflicts in theological discourse form the symbolic basis of what in literature we are calling a typological aesthetic, which depends upon and recirculates a seemingly benign "philosemitic" Hebraic myth. From the Puritan jeremiad to Smith's *The Book of Mormon* (1829), to Protestant evangelical tracts and immensely popular *fin de siècle* religious novels, the Hebraic myth has loomed large in American literature, whether through different eschatological equations between present-day Christians and ancient Hebrews or as the antecedent for a more progressive Christianity. The irreconcilable binary of typology, with its temporal contradictions, moreover, manifests the pernicious flip side of the Hebraic myth: a religious antisemitism rooted in claims not only that Jews crucified the Messiah, whose coming their holy books prophesied, but also that the persistent Jewish holdout for the Messiah was a willful, irrational refusal to reassess the likelihood that after two millennia, Jesus of Nazareth had indeed been the long-awaited Christ.[63] Accordingly, throughout the nineteenth century, Sunday school literature and religious books like *An Illustrated History of the Holy Bible* (1868) referenced "perverse Jews" who magnified their crime by a blind and entrenched faith.[64] Jews were commonly depicted as "narrow people, bigoted by nature," wed to a tribal religion and a harsh, cruel God, Yahweh. Some writers capitalized on the general fervor of the great religious revivals early in the century, when missionary efforts with Jews took on great intensity. Others, like the

Reverend Joseph Holt Ingraham, emphasized the "*decadence* of Hebraic power."[65] Ingraham's 1855–1860 biblical trilogy showcases "the grandeur of Hebraic history," only to emphasize the dramatic fall of King David, "Prophet, Priest, and King, and type of Him," that is, to make way for the culminating crucifixion of Jesus Christ.[66] He dedicated these immensely popular novels, selling over five million copies, to "the American Hebrews" in hopes that they would see the light of the cross.[67] Actual Jews may have been marginal figures in society, but the "Hebrew" loomed large in the literary and cultural imagination.

Beliefs in the Jewish role in the Crucifixion and in the Jewish refusal to acknowledge Jesus as the true Messiah (themes that justified early antisemitism) find their common basis in the typological contradiction posed by unregenerate Jews as the source of Christianity. This logic then persisted into so-called philosemitic modern literature in the form of the Hebraic myth. Among nineteenth-century poets, for example, Henry Wadsworth Longfellow evoked the myth to eulogize the oldest Sephardic community of American Jews in "The Jewish Cemetery of Newport" (1854), a poem I take up in the Coda to this book, as a sleeping "race" on "The long, mysterious Exodus of Death."[68] Similarly, Oliver Wendell Holmes was deeply informed by the Puritan typological view that the American nation was the "Chosen People." In "The Pilgrim's Vision," Holmes appropriated Jewish biblical primacy to illustrate the heroism of the first American settlers, the perishing, "scattered remnant" who rise again to face the "'bloudy Salvages'" in "The light of Heaven's own kindling," the "chosen tribe that sought this Western Palestine!"[69]

Holmes's "At the Pantomime" (1874), in particular, exemplifies the typological aesthetic, as a Christian speaker accepts the status of the Chosen People by discursively converting the figure of the Jew into a mirror reflection of Christ himself.[70] Sitting amid a crowd of "Hebrews not a few, / Black-bearded, swarthy,—at their side / Dark, jewelled [*sic*] women, orient-eyed," the speaker describes on one side a "beak" that "Betrayed the mould of Abraham's race" (lines 10–12, 19–20) and on the other a "second Israelite!" (line 24). Racial slurs and Shylockian avarice abound, as the speaker "stabbed in turn with silent oaths / The hook-nosed kite of carrion clothes / The snaky usurer, him that crawls / And cheats beneath the golden balls" (lines 27–30). The speaker decries the unregenerate "cursed, unbelieving Jew!"—the "Spawn of the race that slew its Lord," evoking the familiar "Christ-killer" charge (lines 22, 32). The poem rehearses stereotypes like Christian children being sacrificed to the "ducat-sweating thieves" (line 37) until the speaker spots "A fresh young cheek" and "Soft, gentle, loving eyes" (lines 49, 53), beautiful because "so looked that other child of Shem, / the Maiden's Boy of Bethlehem!" (lines 55–56). Like Christ himself, the fair Jewish boy suddenly becomes sympathetic in the speaker's eyes: "From thee the Son of Mary came, / With thee the Father deigned to dwell,—/ Peace be upon thee, Israel!" (lines 75–80).[71] He becomes tolerable for Holmes's speaker as the progenitor of, and palimpsestic double for, Jesus Christ, the New Adam.

For James Russell Lowell, the youngest of the New England Brahmins (also known as the Fireside Poets), the "Jew" embodied decadent class mobility, a "symbol of the diseased, crass, and parvenu society" displacing his own patrician class.[72] As descendants of Puritan settlers, with their sense of divine mission, Michael Dobkowski suggests, the patricians "saw themselves and their children being gradually eclipsed by the new industrial barons and immigrant populations" of the mid-nineteenth century, "with their denigration of the genteel virtues" (114). A minister's son and learned philologist, Lowell nevertheless retained the Puritan admiration of the Old Testament "Chosen People," taking great pride in his own Hebrew fluency, as the founders of Harvard College did before him, even as he believed that, since the Middle Ages, the Jew "had come out of the ghettos as a wretched, usurious, street hawker."[73] The dual image obsessed Lowell: he tried to trace influences of Semitic ancestry on Knickerbocker families, all the while insisting that, like the Rothschilds, all bankers, brokers, and financiers were Jewish. Another great example of the antisemitic-philosemitic continuity rooted in typological thinking, Lowell chided Jews around him while at the same time claiming to have Hebrew blood in his own veins. In the last years of his life, he even likened his whole generation to the Jews, "pariahs in their own nation," a "new Diasporic people, the expatriate Brahmin Wandering Jew."[74] Lowell's seemingly schizophrenic, obsessive love-hate for Jews points to how persistent typological thinking cathected broader anxieties about social mobility and a swelling financial economy, as well as uncertainty and discomfort over expanding Jewish social and political realities at various levels of American society.

Popular nineteenth-century religious novels certainly shared with the Fireside poetic tradition this pattern of sympathetic, yet symbolic Jewish figures that yet refuse to recognize the superiority of Christian morals and values, especially if they do not completely convert.[75] Yet this characteristic recalcitrance is figured in terms of time, a purported willingness to forsake the future to regress into a past of severe, anachronistic Talmudic and Old Testament culture.[76] In his bestseller, *Ben Hur, A Tale of Christ* (1880), to name the most prominent example, Lew Wallace glorified Hebrews for producing Christ, but also saw them as servants of the law. In Christian socialist utopian fictions like Edward Bellamy's *Looking Backward, 2000–1887*, the avarice of "Jewish" capitalism (read now as service to Mammon) was at best to be overcome by Christian socialism, charity, and love; at worst, to be eliminated through selective breeding, as in Alexander Craig's *Ionia; Land of Wise Men and Fair Women* (1898).[77] For Reverend Jesse H. Jones, whose heroine in *Joshua Davidson* (1903) is "a Jewess," a "Gentile and Israelite Christian combined," Christians were "latter-day Jews whose relationship to God is fulfilled through the agency of Jesus."[78] And Joachin Miller's *The Building of the City Beautiful* (1893) features Miriam, a "strange woman of the old world," "a Jewess . . . as Mary, the mother of Christ, was a Jewess," harking back to Holmes's poem.[79] These utopian fictions together perpetuate the Hebraic myth in the service of Protestant eschatological plots, offering new "Edens" to complete the providential narrative of America as the "Promised Land." Jews, meanwhile, figured as trapped in medieval superstition, were living anachronisms who not only resisted Christ's teachings but were "shackled and blinded . . . from modernity" itself.[80] As an overwhelming number of immigrant Jews found their place in America, their own Promised Land, these utopian authors tried to reconcile the fundamental temporal contradiction they posed by imagining places in the future from which Jews could be excluded, overcome, and their legacy rendered obsolete—where they simply disappeared.

Nineteenth-century secular writers and cultural critics also reproduced the logic of typology. Perhaps most famously, Matthew Arnold named two Western cultural traditions, but also two warring impulses in each of us, in his essay "Hebraism and Hellenism."[81] Western culture, he argued, had become too Hebraic: Hebraistic "strictness of conscience"—a focus on duty, moral rules, and obligation—dominated English society, and Hellenistic "spontaneity of consciousness"—a concern for knowledge, beauty, and the free play of ideas—needed more sway (128). Even the good critic must relax the sway of Hebraistic law, limited to obedience to tradition, to "right acting," as opposed to Hellenistic "right thinking" (128, 127). The Hebrew notion of felicity, Arnold claimed, "pursued with passion and tenacity . . . would not let the Hebrew rest till, as is well known, he had at last got out of the law a network of prescriptions to enwrap his whole life, to govern every moment of it, every impulse, every action" (128). In short, for Arnold, Hebraism is archaic; Hellenism is modern. The nineteenth-century "Hebraising revival" placed in check the modern, intellectually superior, Hellenistic impulses of the Renaissance and signaled a return of Reformation obedience and duty, strictness of conscience, and slavish reentrance into the so-called prison of Puritanism (135). Arnold saw Protestantism as a typological extension of Judaism that bore the chains of its servitude in a new form. The shift he described from Hellenism to the Renaissance was predated by an earlier shift when Jesus Christ was born: Hebraism then became "altogether . . . unprofitable" and "could not but be, the later, the more spiritual, the more attractive development of Hebraism. It was Christianity." Christianity was progressive and Hebraic values, regressive. "Hellenism is of Indo-European growth, Hebraism is of Semitic growth; and we, the English, a nation of Indo-European stock, seem to belong naturally to movement of Hellenism" (135–36). Characteristic of the typological aesthetic, Arnold praised a Hebraic myth abstracted from Jewish people while showing antisemitic disdain for racialized, backward Jews, both of whom impede British cultural progress. Secular redemption through high culture is possible, he argued, but only by overcoming an atavistic Hebraic past.

One last exemplary case of the typological aesthetic in secular writing is Hutchins Hapgood's *The Spirit of the Ghetto* (1902), a sympathetic chronicle of turn-of-the-century immigrant Jewish life in New York City.[82] In it, Hapgood praised Orthodox Jewish scholars' love "for the remote" and "pathetic passion to keep the dead alive," lending them "a nobler quality than what is generally associated with the east side."[83] His admiration for Jews was genuine, but his emphasis on their "pastness," their antiquated, quaint quality, is palpable. What Hapgood cast as nobly tragic, however, the Protestant reformer Jacob Riis saw as a spiritual offense, expressed as an explicit problem of typology: the way in which East Side Jews stand "where the new day that dawned on Calvary left them standing, stubbornly refusing to see the light."[84] Despite their contrasting feelings about Jews, Hapgood's secular commentary shares with Riis's conversionist argument the sense that Jews are, for better or worse, unchanging, recalcitrant pre-Christians, un-Christian and therefore also unmodern. As Frank Felsenstein contends, "defying the ecumenical sentiments of those who would prefer that it were otherwise, the roots of Judaism and Christianity continue to be fed by a common soil."[85] For Christians seeking self-definition, then, religious Jews could be regarded only as "stiff-necked in their inability or refusal to recognize in Jesus the true Messiah."[86] Even generous accounts of Jewish life like Hapgood's participated in this rhetoric of stubborn anachronism, according to which religious Jews were not just culturally different but also, however noble, unmodern. The Hebraic myth, with its power and persistence, registers this constitutive place of the noble, unmodern Hebrew in the American imagination.

I've been gathering these so-called philosemitic observations about Jews under the banner of the "typological aesthetic" to provide an alternate conceptual framework for identifying language that, in its various iterations, helps us to see Jewish literary figures functioning as ready indices of the modern fracturing of time. Where noble "Hebraic" values and practices would ground time in a pre-Christian, premodern past, they are also too antiquated, retrograde, or unmodern, or are otherwise obsolete. At the same time, the noble Hebrew marks the disruptive return of that past, complicating narratives of Protestant redemption in anticipation of alternate futures. More properly than any given literary "type," the stock in trade of realist fictions, this temporal fracturing signals the formal and aesthetic markers of the rapidly changing conditions of modernity. This book does not try to offer a comprehensive overhaul of American literary realism, nor is it intended as a radical critique of Jewish American literary critical methodology along the lines of, for example, Benjamin Schreier's recent

The Impossible Jew (2015), which presses for a genuinely self-reflexive "Jewish critical studies" over one built upon a nation-based "identitarian" politics of literature "about Jews."[87] Neither does it entirely follow the pattern of such recent influential books in Jewish studies as Dean Franco's *Race, Rights and Recognition* (2012) or Jonathan Freedman's *Klezmer America* (2008), which, as if anticipating Shreier's clarion call, explore texts that break down the rigidity of racial discourse itself, reading Jewish literature as imbricating a broad spectrum of ethnic, religious, and national formations in Freedman's case, and, in Franco's, creating what he calls literary "relations of torsion" that challenge our recognition and reification of conventional racial categories.[88] What it does share, I hope, with these invaluable studies is an effort to avoid essentializing critical tendencies and instead to contribute to what the Boyarins once called "the New Jewish Cultural Studies," which term, though not so "new" anymore, still applies. Above all, this book brings the critical categories of religion and temporality to the table, uniquely placing Jewish and non-Jewish American literature about Jews into conversation, to unearth the overlooked aesthetic patterns of temporal logic that cross over among sacred and secular, literary, journalistic, and even literary-critical writings.[89]

In the chapters that follow, I weave detailed close readings of the language of time in key realist and naturalist texts of this study—for example, providential time, labor time, chronographic time, sidereal time—with contemporaneous conceptions of Jewishness on the one hand. On the other, I read these details through, at times, ahistorical, nonlinear, theological, and theoretical concepts to name and elucidate the patterns they create. Svetlana Boym's notion of "reflective nostalgia," for example, is central to my claim that Cahan rejects nostalgic literary and cultural formations as the basis for Jewish history and memory.[90] Cahan's brand of realism is inherently forward-looking, messianic, attentive to the "World-to-Come" in ways that transcend secular realism's temporal loop, which becomes a cyclical frozen past like that of the cyclorama and the nostalgia it generates. Each chapter situates a key text within the broader historical contexts of Jewish immigration, literary production, and the discourse about Jews and Jewishness specific to late-nineteenth-century literary culture. But each also provides a conceptual, theoretical framework for narrating a meaningful story about the literary negotiation of time, given theories of nostalgia by Boym; of Jewish memory and history by Joseph Hayim Yerushalmi and Pierre Nora; of the temporal framework of gift economies by Emile Durkheim and Marcel Mauss; of religion, gambling, and chance by Jackson Lears and Maurice Lee; and of messianic time by Walter Benjamin, to name a few. In doing so, I hope to show how a reading practice viewed through the lens of religious, sacred time, from both Jewish and Christian perspectives, allows us to tell a new story about American literature.

It may seem obvious to point out that late-nineteenth-century realist writers were not publishing in a vacuum, that they shared the field with religious literature and culture surrounding them. However, the notion that the novel is essentially a secular genre, or literary realism a secular cultural formation, its rise coinciding with that of the Enlightenment, has only recently been critiqued.[91] Here I want to acknowledge the important work of scholars who have challenged the "secularization thesis," such as Vincent Pecora (2006), Charles Taylor (2007), Talal Asad (2003), and Tracy Fessenden (2007).[92] "The core of the secularization idea," Pecora contends, "is the claim that overt belief and participation in religion are abandoned as Enlightenment science, technological modernization, and the fragmentation of social life into separate and autonomous spheres of endeavor are embraced."[93] Secularization has most often been understood as a "one-way street," he notes, which leads to notions like those of Jürgen Habermas, for whom modernity is still an "unfinished project" (30). But we have also come to question this narrative, Pecora argues, including the idea that religion has simply disappeared. We have instead seen a renewed interest in the account of secularization that claims, "the emotional and psychological energies formerly exercised in religious activity simply migrated elsewhere" (26). We can thus speak of religiosity, or "sublimations of what was once called religion," or of what Charles Taylor calls "fullness," a moving or inspiring experience, particularly in literature.[94]

In British and American contexts, such logic has informed powerful challenges to the secularization thesis in literary studies of the novel, even though they maintain a largely Christian-centric focus. Such studies as Pecora's *Households of the Soul* (1997) and Pericles Lewis's *Religious Experience in the Modernist Novel* (2010) allow us to read religion as an aesthetic category, and modernist novels as formal efforts to seek out and create alternative sacred communities, the texts themselves enchanted objects of potentially sacred value.[95] Collectively, such work overturns the long-standing assumption that the novel, as Georg Lukács wrote in 1916, is "the epic of a world that has been abandoned by God."[96] Challenging this notion of secularization in late-nineteenth-century American literature from a historical-formalist approach, Gregory S. Jackson expands the genre of realism to include writers like Jacob Riis and Louisa May Alcott. Jackson uniquely traces in their work a homiletic tradition of pedagogical realism that encouraged a particular reading practice, fostering "spiritual sight," which dates back to the eighteenth- and nineteenth-century sermons of Jonathan Edwards, Henry Ward Beecher, and others.[97] In doing so, Jackson also critiques histories that conflate secularization with modernity, offering a new version of literary realism that accounts for the everyday interpenetration of sacred and secular forces, of the worldly shot through with otherworldly meaning. The current study takes up what Jackson might describe as a "bifurcation" of time, the sacred and secular temporal splits in late-nineteenth-century texts, but it rethinks these splits in terms of the simultaneous Jewish centrality to, yet erasure within, this temporal schema: that of a Christian present and future superseding a mythical Hebraic past that engenders and disrupts it.[98] Where this study departs from Jackson's and others' is in its account of the persistent aesthetic legacy of Protestant typology and the temporal dimensions of the Hebraic myth that shadow and shape otherwise secular realist texts.

This book is also indebted to a recent spate of American literary-critical studies of temporality, so it is important to take a moment to situate it within what Cindy Weinstein, in her own fascinating account of temporal grammars in Poe and others, recently called "the temporal turn."[99] This project may not share Weinstein's laser-sharp eye for tracking time and tense, Elizabeth Freeman's focus on queer temporality in her groundbreaking study *Time Binds* (2010), or Dana Luciano's focus on the temporality of grief.[100] However, it does share an effort to "think against the dominant arrangement of time and history," as Freeman puts it, in order to explore "nonsequential forms of time" in literature: nostalgia, anticipation, hope, chance, promise, and reciprocity.[101] Freeman suggests that queer time "overtakes both secular and millennial time," to generate a "discontinuous history of its own" (x–xi); here, however, we will actually pause and dwell on the formative impact of millennial (and other forms of sacred) time that provide an imagined "longue durée" for secular fictions of this period. I take this latter notion from Wai-Chee Dimock's crucial rereading of American literature as part of world literature, *Through Other Continents* (2006). Dimock creates unlikely pairings of authors and genres across time, space, and, in particular, national, continental, and linguistic boundaries, to resituate American literary history and chronology within the "longue durée" of geology, or of astronomy.[102] Dimock is interested in "alternative durations" across national literary traditions, but also how the "long durations" of other cultures get threaded into the relatively short US chronology through literature, a "double threading" that "thickens time, lengthens it, shadowing in its midst the abiding traces of the planet's multitudinous life" (3). Unlike the typically linear formulations of modernity, this phenomenon of "deep time" involves "loops of relations" that move in multiple directions at once, across time and space, and uniquely in literature, "the home of nonstandard space and time" (4).

Although I choose to confine the current study within US national and literary history, and largely to the late nineteenth century, Dimock's formulation of "deep time" allows us to think about the "thickening" and "lengthening" of literary time enabled by the transhistorical Jewish and Christian eschatologies that reconfigure and "pluralize" literary time, to use Lloyd Pratt's term. Pratt's *Archives of American Time* (2010) has transformed the way we think of American national time in literature by successfully challenging two reigning temporal models: Benedict Anderson's notion of national simultaneity and Walter Benjamin's oft-cited "empty, homogeneous time." Pratt argues that nineteenth-century writing by Frederick Douglass and others supplemented "the orders of time that emerged from industrial manufacture, slave economies, and the like with the anachronistic temporalities that any literary genre (re)introduces into the present."[103] His work has helped me formulate the possibility that reading Jewishness in terms of the typological aesthetic, the anachronism of the Hebraic myth, and the underlying tensions between Jewish and Christian versions of providence certainly opens up thematic patterns and plot devices *about* time, but it also exposes the formal, shaping forces that pluralize literary temporality from a particularly theological perspective. I aim to build upon these collective critical attempts to excavate alternative temporalities mediated by literary realism by turning on the religious switch, to reveal the sacred temporal structures of the literary form most often considered historically bound in secular, linear time.

Speaking to this final point, because Fredric Jameson's influential recent study, *The Antinomies of Realism* (2013), approaches the whole question of literary realism from the angle of temporality, it would seem a fitting theoretical source for the current project; yet this is not the case. In spite of others' previously unsuccessful efforts to do so, Jameson not only defines literary realism in temporal terms, he asserts that it is born of a "dialectical experiment" at the intersection and tension between two temporalities—"destiny and the eternal present."[104] The "twin sources" of these temporalities are, respectively, narrative and affect, which exist in an "irrevocable antagonism," a "ceaseless muffled battle" that can be reconciled only in dialectical "symbiosis" between narrative's "tripartite temporal system of past-present-future" and affect's "eternal present" (10–11, 19, 26). For Jameson, narration is temporal in a traditional sense, rooted in the practice of storytelling that moves through linear time like history, thus giving the novel its form. The realm of "affect," meanwhile, formed by description, disrupts narrative; in the "painterly moment" of "ekphrasis," narrative is "suspended" (7–8). Narration and description thus constitute realism's "chronological endpoints," so that when grasped simultaneously, a "new concept of realism" emerges (10).

Jameson's formula, parsing as it does the binaries of narration and description, telling and showing, illuminates exceptionally well the dynamic nature of realism's temporality. As Goran Blix notes, the scenario of an "unresolved tension between pure story-time and this extraorbital present" is appealing; "it gets at the hybridity of the realist novel and accounts for the unstated clash between social prescription and utopian possibility that strains its internal machinery."[105] In chapter 3, I draw upon this notion of temporal hybridity in order to describe a similar tension in *The House of Mirth*, between fate and chance, that plays out in the novel's narrative structure. Yet, that said, it remains unclear why Jameson so starkly opposes description to narration, the latter always in the past and the former in the "eternal" present.[106] Furthermore, for all that Jameson thinks about "destiny" or "fate" in narrative, as narrative form's "deeper philosophical content," his definition of "destiny" is not only confusing, it also expressly eschews sacred time. Jameson wants nothing to do with providence. Here, however, we will concern ourselves unapologetically with such notions of religious time. If modern time is not homogeneous but fractured, for better or worse Jewish anachronism figures at the fault lines. The current study thus uniquely accounts for the religious roots of the story of Jewishness as a "problem," exploring how realist writers adopted and negotiated views of the Jew as the disruptor of Christian destiny in order to imagine viable futures for both Jews and non-Jews in America.

Chapter 1 begins with the newspaper and periodical culture in which the key novelists of this study were writing and found their careers interconnected. Thus we see early Howells as not only friend to Henry James but also editor, purveyor of "local color" writing and socialism like Cahan's; Cahan's socialist politics, activism, and newspaper apprenticeship under Protestant reformer and police reporter Jacob Riis; Riis, Hutchins Hapgood, and Lincoln Steffens, progressive muckrakers who take up the anachronistic "Hebrew" for their own projects; Cahan introducing Hapgood, Steffens, and Howells to the Yiddish East Side; Mary Antin and Anzia Yezierska engaging with settlement house progressive reform; Emma and Josephine Lazarus engaged in immigrant aid societies; and various feature stories in *Harper's New Monthly* and *Century Magazine* that satisfied consumer appetites for the novelty of "local" New York Jewish life in ways that James would explore in *The American Scene*. This broad literary culture reflects a multivalent temporal discourse veering between portraits of the "noble Hebrew" and the "avaricious Jew" that subordinate carefully crafted versions of Jewishness to both sacred and secular Protestant narratives. This discourse applied even to authors like Abraham Cahan, who, entering this scene as a writer himself, struggled to create, evaluate, and translate forms of Jewish culture for American readers and American culture for immigrant Jewish readers. Although Cahan began his English-writing career with journalism and socialist political activism, as one of Howells's first literary protégés, Cahan was launched as a local colorist of the Lower

East Side who could speak authentically as a living noble Hebrew. His literary career in English thus partakes in a crucial transitional moment in American literary history when ethnic self-representation—marketed now as authentic "local color"—became the mark of "the real" that separated a Jewish writer like Cahan from the emerging canon of largely Protestant realists, like James, Howells, and others, whose work was evaluated on moral and aesthetic principles. It marks the emergence, in other words, of early identity politics.

Chapter 1 subsequently focuses on Cahan's work because, given his own struggles with the marketplace—between a commitment to socialist principles and gritty reportage and the expectation that he produce "Jewish" local color, between English and Yiddish languages, American and immigrant status—it effectively coordinates these debates. His predicament puts the paradox of the Hebraic myth in relief as he talks back. Working within and against the confines of the literary market, I argue, Cahan challenges the characteristic nostalgia of local color. His novella *The Imported Bridegroom* (1898) is particularly useful in this context because it critiques the secular, backward glance of nostalgia, and ultimately looks forward to a sacred, messianic "world-to-come," an inspired, if uncertain, future, the anticipation of which disrupts the traditionally linear trajectory of the realist novel. Through a clever metaphor comparing the East European *shtetl* to a "cyclorama"—a key modern form of nostalgic popular culture—Cahan satirizes nostalgia for the "Old country," as featured in writings by Hamlin Garland and other local colorists. He also critiques immigrant desire for a specific Jewish place in historical time—even in its future, Zionist forms—as a futile *trompe l'oeil*. The cyclorama captures the illusoriness of returning to the past, but also, I argue, metaphorizes the linear time of literary realism itself, which creates a future nostalgia for the present it engenders. Cahan's story instead ends with the cyclical time of ritual reading and messianic anticipation, linked less to linear progress than to an eschatology of collective Jewish history that stabilizes modern, diasporic Jewish experience. With its structural challenge to local color, the realist subgenre to which Cahan was relegated, and its invocation of Judaic time within the secular novel form, *The Imported Bridegroom* illustrates realism's limitations for capturing more than a Hebraic myth or Jewish "type": that is, for rendering Jewishness on its own temporal terms.

If Cahan was writing at the margins of the literary market, chapter 2 takes us with Henry James to its center, plunging into a highly theorized literary realism, where we find, paradoxically, the figure of "the Jew." My reading of James breaks the critical impasse regarding his purported ambivalence toward "the Jew" in his late works by rethinking this figure through the logic of cosmopolitan detachment, diasporic mobility, and the temporal expectations of the gift economy. It traces how the forms of social and economic exchange enacted by liminal Jewish characters in James's work produce dynamic, contingent forms of value (economic, aesthetic, social, moral) and expose the concealed links between sacred and secular economies and temporalities. If in *The American Scene* we see, in James's view, a spatial and temporal displacement of Jews now returned en masse from the biblical past to haunt the Lower East Side, and perhaps to redeem Protestant America, James chooses this figure as the pivotal character for his next major novel, *The Golden Bowl*. Here James redeems the avaricious Jewish pawnbroker who, both central and marginal, best captures the position of the modern cosmopolitan writer at the nexus of capitalist and gift exchange. James's choice of the pawnshop for the locus of the literary in modernity is one that places the key metaphor for the art of the novel in Jewish hands, and not those of a sentimental pawnbroker but (by the novel's end) an omniscient, ethical, modern noble Hebrew. This figure mediates and collapses two distinct, yet overlapping orders of time (secular and sacred) structuring the novel's plot, but he is no mere throwback to the biblical past. Rather, James modernizes the "noble Hebrew" as a dynamic figure who enables the reconciliation, and hence the future, of the novel's central married couple. If the pawnbroker allows James to reclaim friendship over business, the noble Hebrew of ethical modernity comes from Jamesian realism into naturalism as Wharton takes up what James doesn't address: intimacy and intermarriage with "the Jew."

In chapter 3, I argue for the mutual interdependence of two orders of time in literary naturalism: the inexorable linearity of naturalist determinism and the unpredictable futurity of gambling and financial speculation that disrupts it. In my reading, these competing temporalities reproduce the tension I trace throughout this book between the secular and the sacred, one that, in Wharton's novel *The House of Mirth* in particular, converges in the pivotal figure of "the Jew." If her novel's secular time is driven by rational calculation, and the sacred by the providential workings of chance, it is the Jewish character Simon Rosedale who mediates this tension and promises its resolution. That this promise is left unfulfilled, I argue, shows that naturalism cannot contain the Jew "in time." At key moments, Rosedale, with his wealth and power, holds the fate of Wharton's heroine, Lily Bart, in his hands, promising her, through marriage, a financially stable, viable future. Lily struggles to escape the "great gilt cage" and its structured social time that, with Rosedale's financial support, is tainted by market time and, for her, his Jewishness. She longs for "the republic of the spirit," an eternal, aristocratic time of freedom, chance, and spontaneity. Lily's poor timing, missteps, missed trains, missed opportunities, and actual aging, however, show that by the laws of naturalist determinism, she is fated to die by falling, literally, out of time. That Rosedale *could* rescue her, *could* stabilize time for Lily through marriage (and in turn, she could, with her old-moneyed pedigree, stabilize his value), and that Wharton holds out this possibility but lets Lily die instead, positions Rosedale, I argue, as the genre-buster of naturalism, to which the story of Jewish intermarriage just doesn't hew. The tragic decline of Jews according to the Hebraic myth is belied by Rosedale's rise; instead, it is the WASP leisure class that's in decline. As in Frank Norris's *McTeague* (1899) and *The Octopus* (1902), and Harold Frederic's *The Market-Place* (1899), also novels of speculation and risk, determinism and chance alternately control the plot structure of *The House of Mirth*. But in Wharton, these mutual disruptions pivot explicitly on the figure of the Jew. Rosedale may be least vengeful, in fact, kindest to Lily, but, for Wharton, intimacy through intermarriage with "the Jew" poses her heroine the greatest risk, because it is predicated on trust. The tragedy is that the two characters are aligned but they don't meet; Rosedale's calculated time could resolve the temporalities of risk and chance for Lily, but in a future Wharton rejects. As the novel shows glimpses of this future, however, Rosedale exceeds the story of Jewish duality, challenging the inherited binary—the secular, avaricious "Jew," the sacred, noble

"Hebrew"—and leaving open the question of how this story of "the Jew" in time can be told.

In Theodore Roosevelt's 1894 essay "True Americanism" and Israel Zangwill's 1909 play *The Melting Pot* (dedicated to Roosevelt), the future for American Jews lay in cultural assimilation and intermarriage, respectively, arguably a cyclical repetition of the demand for religious conversion from centuries earlier, but now in secular form. Chapter 4 looks at this future from a Jewish female perspective, through the writings of Mary Antin and Anzia Yezierska. Whereas Wharton rejects intimacy with the male "Jew," Mary Antin's famous autobiography, *The Promised Land* (1912), is narrated from the perspective of a Jewish women already married to a Gentile man. Like Antin's autobiography, the many novels of this era that feature intermarriages of choice—as opposed to those arranged from within the ethnic clan or religious community—propound an ideology of progress and liberation from restrictive, antiquated traditions. In writing these fictions, literary authors engaged in broader debates over the relationship between religion and American cultural citizenship, "racial" family and nation, their narratives mediating the Jewish past with the American future. By contrast, Anzia Yezierska, in *Salome of the Tenements* (1923), thwarts religious intermarriage. Yezierska's heroine, Sonja Vrunsky, realizes the dream of full individualist freedom and self-worth not in a melting-pot marriage plot but by fashioning herself as a noble Hebrew, delivering the world from dirt and dinginess with beauty. In *Bread Givers* (1925), Sara Smolinsky finds no more recourse in the past than Cahan's Asriel Stroon did. Rather, through public education, she navigates between an inescapable prison of the Jewish past—that of female sacrifice and ignorance—and a more open future within a Protestant culture that, yet, demands she become Americanized and marry. If, in one novel, Sara's freedom, like Lily Bart's, is posed as a culturally specific temporal trap, in the other novel Yezierska shows that a viable Jewish future, neither religious and patriarchal nor assimilationist, lay in modernist aesthetics. These works illustrate the limitations of the "assimilation" model for understanding American literary Jewishness, here worked out as a series of temporal negotiations.

A brief coda looks at the work of Emma Lazarus, the first American Jewish poet of note, whose work and life illustrate a profound combination of

Hebraic myth and Jewish history. In the 1880s, as an activist for oppressed Jewish refugees, Lazarus embraced Zionist nationalism, a political alternative to both immigrant nostalgia and Jewish providential messianism. Unlike that of her elder male peers—German poet Heinrich Heine, whose "Hebrew Melodies" she translated, and the American, "philosemitic" Fireside Poets discussed above—Lazarus's poetic work reshapes the typological aesthetic she inherited. As the surge of East European immigration brought to the fore the obvious gulf between mythical "Hebrews" and a vital Jewish people, Lazarus poeticized not more Hebraic myths but real, impoverished immigrants in "The New Colossus," and became an international activist for a viable social and political Jewish future. She thereby revised an inherited tradition of contested Christian identity by rescuing Hebraic Jewishness from typological absorption and reclaiming it to protect an imperiled Jewish future. Whereas Longfellow eulogized the oldest Sephardic community of American Jews on "The long, mysterious Exodus of Death" in "The Jewish Cemetery at Newport" (1854), Lazarus honors a glorious, living legacy with her poetic response, "In the Jewish Synagogue at Newport" (1867). Lazarus puts forth a Hebraic Jewishness that, in its Zionist fulfillment, is not dead, but vital and distinctly modern.

Tracing this persistent problem of religious anachronism, *No Place in Time* aims to deepen the conversation about literary Jewishness by including religion in the critical study of literary and cultural formations. It shines a spotlight on the Jewish relation to time, the Jewish disruption of Protestant time, and how the religious, temporal role Protestants take Jews to play in their own redemptive narratives has shaped and provided a symbolic foundation for American literary culture.

1

The Cyclorama Effect
Nostalgia, Memory, and Jewish Time

The rottenness of capitalistic society inevitably lends color to
every work of realistic fiction.

—Abraham Cahan, "Realism" (1889)

He sees things with American eyes, and he brings in aid of his
vision the far and rich perceptions of the Hebrew race.

—William Dean Howells,
"New York Low Life in Fiction" (1896)

THERE IS PERHAPS NO more iconic Jewish "place" than the East European or Russian Jewish *shtetl*. These little Jewish towns in the midst of
Gentile cultures have long been perceived as resistant to time: hermetically
sealed loci of "Old World" Jewish life and medieval backwardness, but also
of generations of precious Jewish tradition, learning, music, and culture. In
the wake of their destruction in the Nazi genocide, *shtetls* became a primary source of postwar nostalgia, taking on a mythical status all their own.
In the late nineteenth century, however, actual *shtetls* were hardly pristine
places; they were already compromised by the surrounding modern, urban,
Gentile culture. For East European Ashkenazic Jews, in fact, the modern
era opened in the eighteenth century with the "controversies, conflicts and
schisms" created by the dawning of the *Haskalah*, or the Jewish Enlightenment.[1] The *maskilim*, the secular intellectuals who broke with rabbinic
tradition and partook in the explosions of science and philosophy around
them, started a revolutionary Jewish *Kulturkampf* that crystallized into a
full-blown movement by the century's end, influencing Jewish thought for

centuries to come.[2] Associated with Jewish scholar Moses Mendelssohn, the *Haskalah* was centered in the German cities of Berlin and Königsberg. By the end of the nineteenth century, however, as debates over Jewish emancipation, citizenship, nationalism, and diaspora evolved into a full-blown social "Jewish Question," *Haskalah* activity manifested in Eastern Europe as well, particularly among a new generation of secular Yiddish literary writers.[3]

In response, Enlightenment enthusiasts and urban sophisticates like Shalom Rabinowitz (Sholem Aleichem, 1859–1916), one of the founders of modern Yiddish literature, and S. Y. Abramovitsh (Mendele Moykher-Sforim, 1835–1917, also known as "Mendele," the founder of modern artistic prose in Yiddish and Hebrew), invented the *shtetl* as a literary site of religious and folk burlesque.[4] Among many Lithuanian radical *maskilim* seeking to bridge Enlightenment and Jewish beliefs, and to mediate the ancient and the modern, from the 1860s through the first decade of the 1900s Sholem Aleichem, Mendele, and other writers of modern Yiddish and Hebrew classics fictionalized the pastoral *shtetl* in the image of a provincial locale that was purely Jewish, "the nucleus of a besieged civilization" that was nonetheless harmonious. They did this in order to satirize it, whether nostalgically or more critically, as a world in need of reform were Jews to integrate into larger, gentile society.[5] In the 1920s and 1930s, however, anthropologists and ethnographers in the United States mistakenly read Mendele's work, though it was fiction, as ethnography proper, taking his satirical representations of the *shtetl* for the real thing—in other words, viewing Yiddish literary works as historical museums of Jewish life.[6] Mark Zborowski and Elizabeth Herzog's classic study of "salvage ethnography," *Life Is with People: The Culture of the Shtetl* (1952), is a key example, reifying "the shtetl" as the timeless, anthropomorphized embodiment of East European Jewish life, the book a paragon of postwar Jewish nostalgia. Real Jewish "little-towns," meanwhile, were subject to history and, eventually, genocidal extinction.[7]

Among the Lithuanian radical *maskilim*, Abraham Cahan was a Yiddish- and later English-language author who treated with equal satire another iconic Jewish place, the "New York ghetto." Read within the cultural trajectory of the *shtetl*, Cahan's fictions can be said to contribute to, but also to challenge, our ongoing postwar nostalgia for desecrated Jewish places that he, like his Yiddish literary contemporaries, treated with irony and mock sentimentality. Although less acclaimed than his first novel, *Yekl: A Tale of the New York Ghetto* (1896), *The Imported Bridegroom* (1898) certainly sealed Cahan's fate as a "Ghetto storyteller."[8] But if, like its protagonist Asriel Stroon, its readers expected the *shtetl* it depicts to recuperate the past, perhaps offer an enchanted panacea for capitalist anomie, and reveal the "genuine Judaism" for which Asriel longs, they were to be disappointed. One of the first English-language stories to feature both the ghetto and the *shtetl* as sites of Jewish memory, rather than mimetic correspondence, the story's imaginative geography forms what David Roskies calls a "structure of remembrance," a fabrication, or recycling, of ancient myths that constitutes just one of many competing versions of a Jewish "usable past."[9]

As *The Imported Bridegroom* tries to imagine a Jewish future independent of place, it mediates different orders of time. The story begins with an identity crisis: facing middle age, immigrant Asriel Stroon tries desperately to reclaim his forgotten past, but also his forsaken Judaism. Like a Yiddish Rip Van Winkle, the aging landlord seems to have slept through thirty-five years in the New World, when one day, after hearing a fiery sermon by a new rabbi at his temple, he awakens to find himself "very wicked, . . . as full of sins as a watermelon is of seeds."[10] Although he had thoughtfully stashed his "earthly title deeds" away in his fireproof safe, preserving his earthly future, he had disregarded "such deeds as would entitle him to a 'share in the World-to-Come'" (98). Guilty for the past and afraid of his future, he converts to Jewish Orthodoxy. Its redemptive promises will provide order and meaning to his life of material gain and will compensate for years of spiritual neglect. His worldly successes might seem less empty within a broader frame of providential experience that Jewish history structures, between the biblical past and the messianic future. Like a good businessman, Asriel resolves to settle these spiritual debts and earn future spiritual credit by returning to Pravly, the Polish *shtetl* of his youth, the *place* from his past he most associates with "genuine Judaism" (90).

Between the *shtetl* and the ghetto, the story's most significant locations, and Cahan's emergence onto the American literary scene as a "local color" writer himself, a critical focus on location in this story would make sense; yet the problem the text raises is as much about time as it is about place. For one, Asriel's pilgrimage to the Old World *shtetl* fails as a scene of homecoming, when he finds the place far worse than memory allows. Nostalgic fantasy is at play, but so is the linear time of modern progress, bespeaking the story's realism—time passes, things decay, there is no return, only loss. But further, *The Imported Bridegroom* actually pronounces the death of the iconic Jewish *shtetl* and any remaining nostalgia for it. As Asriel arrives in Pravly, readers might expect a religious revelation, a spiritual homecoming, but unlike in his enchanted memories, he finds the *shtetl* mean, shabby, ravaged by time: "All the poetry of thirty-five years' separation had fled from it, leaving a heap of beggarly squalor" (111). The passing of the *shtetl* is nowhere better captured than in an easily overlooked metaphor for Asriel's confrontation between reality and nostalgic fantasy, surprising for its source in US popular culture: "everything was the same as he had left it; and yet it all had an odd, mysterious, far-away air—like things seen in a cyclorama" (103). With this curious image, we will see, the story shatters the nostalgic fantasy of the past and reinscribes memory in and *as* fiction. It does so by spatializing time's "mysterious" passage: an uncannily "far-away" aesthetic replica substitutes for the quintessential Jewish place of the past.

As a metaphor for Asriel's imagined lost childhood, the cyclorama-*shtetl* becomes visually symptomatic of temporal failure, of a spiritual quest the character cannot realize in time: a return home from the modern New World of Gentile materialism. Immanuel Kant was first to note that homesickness longs for a lost *time*, youth itself, to which no return is possible, a symptom of modernity; likewise, Cahan's cyclorama-*shtetl* displaces the "remembered" past place as an object of nostalgic longing, suggesting a tale not of local color but of deterritorialized exile.[11] Were Cahan's tale a Jewish diasporic narrative of *homecoming*, then the *shtetl* might have fulfilled its mythical function, as in the correspondence between "place" and what Zali Guravitch and Gideon Aran refer to as the "Place" in the Zionist uotipan imaginary, *Eretz Yisroel*, the utopian, redemptive space of collective exile.[12] But Cahan disrupts this myth: no more does Asriel's return recuperate his loss than, we can assume, will his decision to live out his days in the actual "Land of Israel" at the story's end. The cyclorama metaphor thus registers how one cannot *both* create *and* enjoy the illusion of unmediated access to the past, much less locate it in space; no one can be both the Wizard and

Dorothy at once. With his vision shattered, Asriel's failed homecoming undoes the narrative thematic of return that local color promises.

Like many fin de siècle *maskilik* narratives, *The Imported Bridegroom* is critical of nostalgia for places of origin. As a Jewish tale, it fails to recover a pre-exilic Eden; and as an American immigrant tale, it fails to recover the immigrant's authentic homeland. This geographic and spiritual displacement of the *shtetl* by the cyclorama instead contributes to what Sidra Dekoven Ezrahi calls a shift in the "relative place of place" that we see in contemporary Yiddish literature, but here within a "particularly American diasporic agenda."[13] The cyclorama image gestures toward this vexed Jewish relationship to place, and simultaneously demonstrates realism's vexed relation to time: its inability to satisfy nostalgia, to recuperate the past by reproducing an original, pristine place in the modern novel. The Jewish doubling of place and Place—whether Zionist longing for a perpetually deferred homeland or messianic longing for an Edenic paradise in the World-to-Come—illuminates this problem as it shifts our view from a locatable past to a placeless, redemptory future. Read through this lens, *The Imported Bridegroom* reveals an allegorical doubling that rewrites the doubling of Christian typology to open space for a redemptive Jewish future. As a realist tale of individuals passing through historical time and space, it also gestures toward the collective Jewish history transcending any one individual's fate, mediating a crucial temporal heterogeneity. The simultaneous temporal planes that structure the story's Jewish experience challenge the assumptions of homogeneous secular time that situate the best of Jewish life in the past and that have, until recently, shaped our understanding of the late-nineteenth-century novel.

THE "NEW STAR OF REALISM": CAHAN'S JOURNALISTIC BEGINNINGS AS A LOCAL "HEBREW"

A brief look at Cahan's biography illustrates that he, himself a Jew, was misread within a Protestant-centric culture by an array of writers who seemed to take typological thinking as a matter of course. Born to a devout Lithuanian family in 1860 and raised as a Talmudic scholar groomed for the rabbinate, Cahan ultimately renounced the religious calling to embrace revolutionary politics. A socialist and political refugee, Cahan immigrated to the United States in 1882 to begin an English writing career. Although perhaps best known for his novel *The Rise of David Levinsky* (1917) and as founding editor for a half century of the *Jewish Daily Forward*—the first, most successful Yiddish-language paper in the United States (still in print and online today)—it was with his publication of the novella *Yekl: A Tale of the New York Ghetto* (1896) that Cahan emerged as the first Jewish immigrant novelist in late-nineteenth-century America.[14]

The former rabbinical student turned socialist, labor leader, and cultural mediator for Yiddish-speaking immigrants understood the need for collective Jewish memory in the face of displacement, secular progress, and laissez-faire capitalism. Treated by fellow American writers and editors as a local "Hebrew" with insider authority on the exotic Jewish immigrant community, however, Cahan made his place in American literature by inventing presumed "authentic" American Jewish places for readerly consumption. When he first entered the American literary scene with *Yekl*, William Dean Howells, the famed arbiter of literary value, hailed Cahan as "The New Star of Realism."[15] For a fledgling novelist—indeed, for an immigrant author of Jewish stories—this assessment was unprecedented. Animating that crucible of immigrant life, New York's Lower East Side, *Yekl*, a paradigmatic tale of cultural conflict, assimilation, and the world of the "greenhorn," justified this praise. The first American Jewish immigrant novel of note, *Yekl* actually put the Jewish ghetto on the American literary map, even though Manhattan's Lower East Side was hardly a place of popular romance. In 1882, the *New York Tribune* complained of "Hebrew immigrants" crowding the quarter in their "filthy condition"; the *New York Herald* reported that Jews "were accustomed to taking only one bath a year"; and the *New York Times* warned of Jewish "thievishness."[16] Cahan's fictions transformed this image, rendering the streets, tenements, and sweatshops picturesque literary locales, key landscapes in the American literary scene.

Cahan began his English-language career as a chronicler of a particular kind of literary realism rooted in progressive journalism. By the time he assumed the editorship of the *Forward* in 1902, he had transformed Yiddish journalism: didactic socialist pieces written in baroque Germanic Yiddish became, in Cahan's hands, a popular press in colloquial Yiddish. His stories mirrored readers' everyday experiences, offering socialist solutions to common problems, and his column, *Der Proletar-ishker Maggid* (the proletarian preacher), merged Jewish folk-religious discourse with socialist principles.[17] Like a traditional Lithuanian traveling preacher, Cahan opened his columns with a biblical portion of the week, or *Sidra*, to discuss current, practical, social issues—here, too, bridging the past and the present.[18] In this role, he was discovered by Howells, champion of the common man, of realist rhetoric, "democratic egalitarianism," and by the 1890s, of local color fiction.[19] In 1893, Cahan translated into Yiddish and published Howells's socialist utopian novel *A Traveler from Altruria*, illustrating their mutual influence, political idealism, and shared taste for ethically engaged literature that defined the early stages of American realism.[20] Embroiled in politics, Cahan came to see realism as the primary aesthetic means for working out "the relationship between literature and social problems," the form of art whose "power . . . arises from the pleasure," or "thrill," we derive from "recognizing the truth."[21] These ideas had coalesced in a March 15, 1889, lecture he delivered to the New York Labor Lyceum, entitled "Realism," where he defined realism against high aestheticism, challenging the "fallacious proposition that the sole end of art is to afford pleasure and has therefore to be limited to the province of the beautiful."[22] Depicting class difference, suffering and oppression superseded beautiful landscapes designed for bourgeois consumption, a gritty version of what Phillip Barrish calls the "really real."[23] Cahan called it "socialist realism," with Howells as his foremost American example, not a socialist in the Russian sense—as Jewish immigrants would have understood it—but a man whose writing laid bare "the fictitiousness of American equality."[24]

For Cahan, "local color" derived not from locale or dialect but out of a dialectic between material and economic tensions and their imagined resolutions: as he put it, "[t]he rottenness of capitalistic society inevitably lends color to every work of realistic fiction."[25] Howells, however, viewed Cahan less as a socialist realist than as an embodiment of "the real" itself—of class struggle and immigrant ethnicity. In 1895, Howells's wife Elinor discovered Cahan's tale "A Providential Match" in the magazine *Short Story*.[26] At her behest, Howells sought Cahan out, invited him to dinner, and told him, "[the tale] isn't really a serious thing. But it convinced me that you must write. It is your duty to write."[27] That initial meeting formed the providential match of their friendship and literary patronage, just when Howells had begun to embrace, and launch literary careers for, authors of regionally based local fictions.[28] While Cahan praised Howells for his politics, however, Howells praised Cahan for his ethnic, but specifically "Hebraic," authenticity, as the new voice of the Jewish immigrant ghetto. Cahan's writing thus emerged from this nascent split between aesthetic and identity-inflected literary categories in the United States, as a deracinated, bourgeois realism of style and principle gave way in the 1890s to ethnic local color and "gritty" naturalism. Howells promoted Cahan as a "realist," in other words, but the "real" he was expected to—and did—depict was limited to the immigrant world of the Lower East Side.[29] When Cahan completed *Yekl* in 1895, however, no mainstream magazine publisher would take it, a sign of ongoing backlashes against the impropriety of Zolaesque naturalism and immigrant encroachment upon American culture. In his dismissal of *Yekl*, the *Harper's Weekly* editor asked Cahan if Yekl had a "beautiful soul": "our readers want to have a novel about richly dressed cavaliers and women, about love that begins in the fields while they're playing golf. How can a novel about a Jewish immigrant, a blacksmith, who became a tailor here and whose wife is ignorant interest them?"[30] He summed up the problem as one of historical inaccuracy: "You portray only Jews. According to your book one could believe that in America there were no other people but Jews" (67).

Such seemingly antisemitic reactions to Cahan's subject matter suggest that when local color reached its apogee in *fin-de-siècle* America, its appeal was bound up with the postbellum rise of a new high social class and its voracious drive for cultural consumption. Influential literary organs—*Atlantic Monthly, Harper's New Monthly, McClure's, Scribner's Monthly, Century Illustrated Monthly*—were the regnant venues for high culture, and their taste for the gritty, regional, realist writing emerging in the 1880s helped codify local color's appeal to the Gilded Age "imagination of acquisition."[31] But as the *Harper's* editor made clear, readers preferred consuming upper-class cultural capital to working-class cultural critique. Howells, by contrast, saw in Cahan himself a living ethnic commodity, with his unique temporal perspective and ability to shape the local and modern through a biblical, Hebraic lens. Howells finally took *Yekl* to his own publisher, R. Appelton and Company, after urging Cahan to revise its title from "Yankel the Yankee" (which seemed "all right for vaudeville") to *Yekl*, to capture this unique story of exotic Jewish urban realism.[32] "Yekl" had "the right ring," and the subtitle, "A Tale of the New York Ghetto," promised readers whose taste for the real of urban immigrant poverty had been shaped by reformer-journalists like Jacob A. Riis, Stephen Crane, Walter Wyckoff, B. O. Flower, and Helen Campbell a further glimpse into exotic Lower East Side slums.[33] When Howells then hailed Cahan as "the new star of Realism," he singled out his unique Hebraic perspective: "He sees things with American eyes, and he brings in aid of his vision the far and rich perceptions of the Hebrew race."[34] Howells's apparent philo-semitic lens results in a temporally double vision of Cahan and his brand of realism, emphasizing how it yoked the modern, urban slums to the noble Hebraic, biblical past. Only after Howells's glowing review did magazine requests begin to pour in for stories by the new local colorist.[35]

As the now sanctified, noble Hebraic voice of gritty immigrant Jewish culture, Cahan inadvertently—and, he noted, regrettably—helped to pioneer a literature encouraging not the eradication of immigrant poverty but greater fascination with it: summering's flip side, urban "slumming."[36] Slumming was the unwanted stepchild of progressive journalism, where Cahan's English-writing career began. As early as 1884, he contributed sketches of New York's Jewish Quarter to the *New York Sun*.[37] When he brought them in person, "with pounding heart," to the chief manuscript editor, Erasmus Darwin Beach, the latter enthusiastically demanded more. But as Cahan was leaving his office, Beach asked a startling question: "Pardon me . . . You use a word about which I must ask. What is a ghetto?"[38] Cahan was "astonished"; he had assumed every educated, "well read" man had heard of the medieval Jewish ghettos of Venice and Rome.[39] His metaphor—the New York slums as reminiscent of the medieval ghettos—lost its figurative status, and the temporal disjuncture he implied was flattened, read as realistic. His "New York Ghetto" became a cultural milestone in the articulation of Jewish American immigrant experience, a powerful metaphor for displaced placeness, but for an audience upon whom the reference to the past place was lost, the metaphor collapsed.

In short, his figurative place begot a new realism; and his realism a new place.

After publishing *Yekl* in 1896 with little success and his story "Circumstances" in the *Cosmopolitan* in April 1897 for a fee of fifty dollars, Cahan, beset with financial concerns, turned once again to the American press for livelihood.[40] As a staff writer at the progressive venue *Commercial Advertiser*, Cahan's priorities shifted from socialist realism, as he understood and valued it, to creating Jewish local color for a largely Gentile readership.[41] Although his first assignment there was to write a description of the Jewish holidays, Sukkot and Simchat Torah, Cahan tried to write a polemical socialist portrait of Tammany Hall's Republican New York City mayoral candidate in 1897, Benjamin V. Tracy. His effort was in vain, as editor Harry J. Wright refused to publish it. From then on, Cahan, an avowed socialist, refused to take on political assignments, so concentrated instead on "human interest sketches" of various quarters and portrayals of its Jewish types.[42] *The Commercial Advertiser* rarely appeared in actual Jewish neighborhoods, but when Lincoln Steffens assumed its editorship from 1897 to 1901, it was soon staffed by sympathetic philosemites fascinated with Jewish culture, such as the Harvard academic Hutchins ("Hutch") Hapgood, who would go on to author the extensive philosemitic study of the Jewish Lower East Side, *The Spirit of the Ghetto* (1902), discussed in the introduction.[43] Cahan was a "natural inclusion" in the "elite circle" of the paper's new writers.[44] Steffens's bold move in hiring Cahan, Hapgood, and "only college men with literary ambitions," rather than seasoned journalists, was part of his ambition "to have [New York] reported so that New Yorkers might see, not merely read of it, as it was: rich and poor, wicked and good, ugly but beautiful, growing, great."[45] Cahan's "eminence and worldliness" also "gave him a position of influence on the paper out of proportion to his duties there."[46] In other words, Steffens's reformist goals for the paper required a blend of reporting and inventing, creating yet another iteration of literary realism, which, in this case, meant renditions of Jewish life suffused with Hebraic mythology. For example, Steffens sent Cahan to apprentice under *Sun* chief police reporter Jacob Riis on his Mulberry Street beat, the "Bend," one of the most poor, violent, immigrant quarters in the area.[47] Cahan trod through these lower Manhattan slums, acquiring a lifetime of socialist realist material and honing the skills of detailed realism that distinguished writers who began their literary careers in journalism, such as Theodore Dreiser and Stephen Crane (another local color writer and Howells protégé). As Steffens describes, "I soon had my writers reporting in their daily news stories such close and correct observation of the details of demeanor that artists and professional men began to take notice. William Dean Howells . . . once said that no writer or artist could afford not to read the *Commercial Advertiser*."[48] Cahan's experience at the *Advertiser* helped shape his literary career, yet the writing expectations placed on him still stemmed largely from Steffens's own infatuation with Jewishness.[49]

Typical of the philosemitism of the day, and of a broader reliance upon a typological aesthetic among religious and secular writers, Steffens saw Jewish life as a picturesque, irreconcilable admixture of "the Old Testament days of hundreds of years B.C." and "the children of the streets of New York today."[50] For Steffens, the "Jew" was both atavistic biblical remnant and modern ghetto denizen—a far cry from the racialized Jews of popular antisemitic portraits, but still fetishized for temporal transcendence. Among the new writers on staff, Cahan thus seemed exceptional: he was not a "Harvard man," he was the only published novelist, and above all, he was the only Jew. Steffens therefore expected Cahan to translate Jewish culture for the paper's readers, his own Jewishness equally fascinating. In turn, Cahan played for his colleagues the Russian intellectual and Lower East Side ambassador, touring Steffens and Hapgood around Lower East Side haunts.[51] He "brought the spirit of the East Side" into their "shop," and this cosmopolitan prestige "flowed over into [Steffens's] newspaper." Cahan's "interest in the picturesque Ghetto" also increased the paper's cachet, its circulation, and "broadened the minds of the staff and of [its] readers."[52] There is deep irony in this celebration of Cahan's Jewishness, given the literary shift toward located, regionally specific forms of the American "real" in the 1890s. This shift, after all, distinguished Jewish immigrants from Anglonormative literary Americanness and the realist canon, so that readers might see Jewish immigrant fiction as little more than a repository of quaint, marginal relics for a future past, records of a place most immigrants would soon leave behind as they transcended their humble beginnings.

Steffens's philosemitism went beyond hiring practices and heated intellectual discussions in the *Commercial Advertiser* office; he actually tried to adopt a culture that, for him, bridged not just Old and New worlds, but also ancient and modern ones. Carrying on the typological aesthetic this book has been tracing, Steffens expressed his reverence for anachronistic biblical "Hebrews" of passionate East Side Jewish culture, those often disparagingly contrasted with their wealthier, more refined "uptown" German coreligionists. Yet even in such "philosemitic" moments, Steffens fetishized the quaintness of antiquated Jewish culture, as when, in this piece about a synagogue fire and funeral service for the *Post*, he wrote, "They fascinated me, those old practices, and the picturesque customs and laws of the old orthodox Jews from Russia and Poland. . . . I read up and talked to funny old, fine rabbis about them, and about their conflicts with their Americanized children. . . ."[53]

A midwesterner already taken with city life, and now exposed to New York's immigrant Jewish enclaves, Steffens began to attend Jewish religious services regularly. In the *Post*, he describes Jews celebrating their holidays as showing "[a] queer mixture of comedy, tragedy, orthodoxy, and revelation" that "interested our Christian readers" (243). When an assimilated German-Jewish woman complained that the *Post* was giving too much space to the "ignorant, foreign East Side Jews and none to the uptown Hebrews," Steffens welcomed the opportunity to inform her "about the comparative beauty, significance, and character of the uptown and downtown Jews" alike (243). Steffens became so enamored with the East Side, East European Jewish life and Yiddish culture that he describes fancying himself "almost a Jew":

> I had become as infatuated with the Ghetto as eastern boys were with the wild west, and nailed a *mazuza* [*sic*] on my office door; I went to the synagogue on all the great Jewish holy days; on Yom Kippur I spent the whole twenty-four hours fasting and going from one synagogue to another. . . . My friends laughed at me; especially the Jews among them scoffed. 'You are more Jewish than us Jews,' they said.[54]

Like the "wild west" for some, Judaism became Steffens's boyish mythology. Even as he embraced Jewish religious practices, however, there is little sense that he grasped their purpose for fostering collective Jewish memory. His obsessive enthusiasm for all things Jewish even came between him and his less tolerant wife, Josephine Bontecou Steffens, though a cosmopolitan in her own right, their personal conflict mirroring the public debates of the historical moment.[55]

Steffens's philosemitism is worth looking at in some detail, not just as a curious, extensive case of the power of Hebraic mythology but also for his mutually influential relationship with Cahan, his apprentice and a soon-to-be famous Jewish novelist. Neither their friendship nor the journalism about actual living Jewish immigrants could temper Steffens's tendency to fetishize the noble Hebrew as a miraculous atavism. This mythology shaped Steffens's writing explicitly. In "Yom Kippur on the East Side," published in the *Post* on September 17, 1896, he describes men in the synagogue "swaying gently, earnestly, back and forward as they mumbled, reading the book of prayer, and tapped their breasts."[56] He later describes stories about the New York Ghetto as "heart-breaking comedies of the tragic conflict between the old and the new, the very old and the very new. . . . Among the Russian and other eastern Jewish families in New York it was an abyss of many generations . . . between parents out of the Middle Ages, sometimes out of the Old Testament days hundreds of years B.C., and the children of the streets of New York today."[57]

For all of his veneration of the Jewish people, Steffens thus perpetuated a typological aesthetic that imagined the best aspects of Jewishness as outside the present time. When in 1896 Steffens wrote for *Chap-book* a short sketch called "Schloma, Daughter of Schmuhl," he fictionalized his romantic notions of Jews and became, in effect, just the kind of local colorist who encouraged literary slumming.[58] "Schloma," a picturesque tale of intergenerational conflict between a Jewish daughter and father, in theme anticipates Cahan's *The Imported Bridegroom*, complete with Yiddish language dialect (albeit in the transliterated Germanicized Yiddish that Cahan rejected).[59] Its seeming ethnic authenticity is wrapped up in the sort of middle-class moral judgment of the poor that would appeal to genteel, and Gentile, readers. Although it reflects some knowledge of Jewish tradition, its one-dimensional characters and forced motivations reveal its author's reliance upon the typological version of an antiquated, "legalistic" Judaism. Schloma, a good but "frivolous" girl who works in her father's tenement sweatshop sewing clothes, likes to gaze out the window and, when her father is not around, to sing, which, according to Orthodox tradition, women are forbidden to do. Neither did medieval rabbis traditionally appreciate any music that lacked an "edifying objective"; passionate music was condemned, and "listening to female singing voices" was part of this prohibition.[60] Schloma's transgression is thus doubly reprehensible, for she not only sings aloud but "[t]hey were Schickse [sic] (Christian) songs too."[61] Schmul's neighbors blame him for his daughter's problem: he educated her in the New World for so long, they believe, "that with the English she had acquired the Christian love of pleasure" (128).

Schloma's reckless singing is also coded in sexually transgressive terms, as if she were engaging in musical miscegenation. Neighbors repeatedly warn Schmuhl to "pass auf" (or "be careful" in Germanicized Yiddish), as one prays, "Let her labor long and be silent, that her son's sons may sing songs" (128). In other words, she should sacrifice her personal pleasure for the future survival and posterity of the Jewish people. With legalistic parochialism, the Jewish community renders Schloma's otherwise innocent singing a mark of infidelity, creating a cautionary tale for readers. She becomes an outcast, with the entire community calling her names in the street like "Schickse, Schickse—Nafke! Pfui!"—"schickse" being the derogatory Yiddish term for a Gentile woman and "nafke" for a "whore."[62] Singing "schickse" songs—let alone learning English, or otherwise culturally assimilating—in the eyes of Steffens's Jewish characters is as bad as sleeping with Gentile men.

So Steffens's Jews are anti-modern, resistant to Gentile culture and to change. But at the same time, they are greedy modern capitalists. Schmuhl's punishment of his daughter exemplifies this, invoking the pecuniary Jewish stereotype as he loads a pile of clothes onto her back, cruelly punishing her with excessive labor. Yet, as she recedes down the stairs with her burden, singing about the money she will earn for him, her song suggests at once defiance, adaptability to Gentile life, and her Jewish social death:

> "Zwelve in der bundle, done in a' Tag; achtzig cent. In sex
> Tag' four dollar' achtzig. Der week, also, a' dollar forty,

sechzig—wenn Schloma's good, dann a dollar eighty to capital. Ach!"

Schloma was singing again. Her cheerful voice came back from the dark stairs like a blow to his heart. He threw up his hands in despair.

"Ach, wei d' Schuh, wei d' Schuh!" he cried.

"Will mein' Dochter be bat? Weh, Schloma, Schloma, mein Kind, mein Kind!"

The old man sank into a chair and buried his face in his hands, weeping. (129)

"Woe is me," Schmuhl cries, as he exploits his "good" daughter's cheap labor. Finally ostracized, like Crane's Maggie three years earlier, Schloma gives in to the "street girls" who rightfully earn that epithet, as Schmuhl gives up his daughter to a life of tragic sin: "'Schma b'ni,' muttered the neighbors. 'Schloma, the daughter of Schmuhl, is bad. Let the women work and be silent that our sons' sons may be glad.'" As if his daughter has died, Schmuhl, "the aged, wept and rent the hem of his shirt, crying 'Ei wei, wei d' Schuh! Mein child is' a' Schickse, a' Nafke! Pfui!'" (132). An outcast convert of sorts, Schloma becomes a noble martyr in a way that probably rang true for Steffens's readers: the ghetto may cause young "good girls" to go astray, but the story's real problem is how they are driven out by narrow-minded, Old World Hebraism, with its legalistic, Arnoldian "strictness of conscience."[63]

True to Steffens's aims, the story combines observation and imagination, the latter of which, in his case, was limited to common Hebraic myths. In spite of his fascination with working-class Jews of the Lower East Side, Steffens arguably had more in common with his uptown, assimilated German Jewish critics than he cared to admit. As much as he admired the "funny old, fine rabbis," he remained a well-educated, genteel college boy from the West who acquired no small degree of prestige from his status as an expert on the Jews.[64] He may have thought himself a philosemite and even, perhaps facetiously, an actual Jew, but from this story it appears he idealized the image of a rarefied, if rigid, "Hebrew" of Talmudic devotion—itself a fictional invention—over that of actual working-class, East European immigrants. Jacob Riis, as we will see, also believed that immigrant Jews would do better to abandon their petty, money-worshipping ways and their Hebraic religion alike, hoping for the secular conversion through social reform of the denizens in the place he dubbed "Jewtown."

How "The Jew" Lives

As noted earlier in the introduction to this book, Oscar Handlin described the 1890s as a decade in American history marked by "distinct philo-Semitism."[65] Yet we have seen how Steffens's philosemitism relies upon a typological aesthetic that deems Jews different, and further, tenaciously unmodern—out of place, but also out of time. Scrutiny of the Jewish immigrant "hordes" in lower Manhattan was common in journalistic reportage. The *New York Tribune*, for example, spoke of the general nastiness of the Jewish quarter, describing it as "a place of embarrassing fecundity."[66] Jewish families were packed into tenement houses, lacking water, heat, light, even air, and with few or no regulations.[67] Nonetheless, they were still targeted in the popular press as contributing to their own poor living conditions. The unique anxiety provoked by the Jewish immigrant masses derived from their status as "uncanny" strangers on both cultural and religious levels, remnants of an inferior past since overcome by the progress of time, culture, religion, and history.[68] Because the massive growth of Jewish immigrant ghettos was attended by problems of poverty, overcrowding, and disease on an unprecedented scale, the religious resistance to immigrant Jews was just one of many xenophobic responses that attempted to locate cause in the religious, cultural, or moral characteristics of the immigrants themselves.

By contrast with these accounts, the comparatively socially conscious reportage of "muckrakers" like Riis, Steffens, Hapgood, and Richard Wheatly charted the "droves" of immigrants fleeing Eastern European persecution in the 1880s and 1890s, and responded more sympathetically to the widespread fears of both physical and moral contamination that characterize what Priscilla Wald has called "medical nativism."[69] Political Progressives sought to redress social problems of poverty and political corruption through the dramatic exposure of political and civic institutions, big business, finance, labor, and the penal system. By inciting public sympathy and outrage, they hoped to raise levels of readerly disgust and provoke institutional reform. Representing the Progressive political platform in their writing, they actually managed to "make things happen": "new laws and regulations, new electoral procedures, social legislation, conservation measures, improved food and drug standards, wage and hour reforms, and, in general, a movement toward a publicly accountable system of social and governmental controls."[70] Fueled by the success of his two articles published in *McClure's Magazine*, for example, Steffens published his pioneering exposé of American business, *The Shame of the Cities* (1904), which, along with Robert Hunter's *Poverty* (1904), John Spargo's *The Bitter Cry of the Children* (1906), and, most famously, Upton Sinclair's *The Jungle* (1905), constituted what Justin Kaplan calls a full-blown "literature of social concern."[71] Steeped in sociology and science and inspired by the moral forms and tones of evangelical Christianity, these works used "shame" to awaken the Christian consciences of their readers.[72]

Given the evangelical Christian influence on the "social gospel" movement, the typological aesthetic can be identified as a defining characteristic of the literature of progressive reform, perhaps nowhere more evident than in Jacob Riis's morally inflected indictment of Lower East Side slum housing, *How the Other Half Lives* (1890).[73] As Gregory S. Jackson has argued, Riis's public lectures were uniquely shaped by a Protestant homiletic tradition aimed at both moral and social improvement, in which representation functioned as a kind of "second sight." In effect, Jackson forces us to acknowledge, in addition to the "cosmopolitan embrace of scientific empiricism," the Protestant religious roots of both Progressive-era reform and realist aesthetics.[74] Considered the father of the American documentary, Riis combined photography and journalism to force the public to witness and respond to the social and health crises within New York's growing immigrant district. Riis condemned the slum and all of its institutional components for such horrible living conditions: the overcrowded tenements, overworked sweatshops, airless alleys, basement alehouses, filthy streets, and broken-down churches, schools, and shops all contributed to a world without light, literally and metaphorically speaking. He thus proposed myriad projects of institutional reform, from parks and fresh air funds to settlement houses and improved schools.

At the same time, Riis saw himself as an "older" model immigrant from Denmark, whose proper Protestant work ethic and sense of social and moral responsibility enabled him to become a good American citizen.[75] Riis contended that "every man's experience ought to be worth something to the community from which he drew it . . . so long as it was gleaned along the line of some decent, honest work."[76] Yet, unlike its sequel, *The Battle with the Slum* (1902), *How the Other Half Lives* falls prey to racial stereotypes of the period, wavering between a critique of institutions and moral condemnation of their victims, the immigrant poor. Riis criticized the slum dwellers themselves as lacking the requisite moral character to become fully Americanized, naming class and character types like the "tough," the "tramp," the "beggar," the "ragpicker," the "street Arab," the "ragamuffin," and the "dock rat" and racial and national types like the "Chinaman," the "Negro," the "Irishman," the "Italian," the "Greek," the "Bohemian," and—whether Russian or Polish—the "Jew." Anticipating ideas that Roosevelt would make explicit in "True Americanism" (mentioned earlier), Riis attached racial distinctions to each group of the Lower East Side according to street, location, trade, and degree of poverty, but also according to the moral values he derived from their individual appearance, dress, manner, and living habits.[77]

The 1890s may have witnessed the dawn of a "new philosemitism," as Handlin claimed, but Riis's account of "Jewtown" reveals rather allosemitic ambivalence, undergirded by the contradictions of typological thinking in the face of modern immigrant Jewish life. With Protestant reformist fervor, Riis painted a grim portrait of the neighborhood in which he lived and worked for twenty years in the Lower East Side of Manhattan, just where Mulberry Street takes a sharp curve south below Canal Street and toward Chatham Square. Riis covered this "beat," in the area known as "the Bend" (along with Chinatown and "Jewtown," as he dubs it), as police reporter from 1883 to 1895. Of "Jewtown," on one hand, Riis claimed that "thrift is the watchword," and he acknowledged "there is no worse paid class anywhere," thereby gesturing to the broader economic challenges of its denizens. But in the same breath he famously wrote, "money is their God. Life itself is of little value compared with even the leanest bank account."[78]

At once firmly located in Hester Street, yet displaced into biblical time and space, the Jews as he described them were completely situated in their modern materiality in terms of economic concerns, yet far removed from the contemporary material world when it came to upholding their religious beliefs. For example, in this anecdote of a Christian preacher trying to do the good work of converting local Jews in a nearby mission, the preacher recalls, "I felt justified in comparing myself to Paul preaching salvation to the Jews. They kept still until I spoke of Jesus Christ as the Son of God. Then they got up and fell to arguing among themselves and to threatening me, until it looked as if they meant to take me out in Hester Street and stone me" (82). Frustrated over Jewish resistance to Christian gospel, the preacher references atavistic Jewish barbarism, imagining them stoning him on Hester Street. Quoting this, Riis illustrates not just a Jewish prioritization of money but also a too-firm adhesion to the archaic moral traditions of the Hebrew Bible. The Jews have no moral sense, and yet it would seem, too much.

The two extremes finally collapse rhetorically in Riis's text, as the Lower East Side becomes a temporal palimpsest, a modern-day Calvary:

> . . . in all matters pertaining to their religious life that tinges all their customs, they stand, these East Side Jews, where the new day that dawned on Calvary left them standing, stubbornly refusing to see the light. A visit to a Jewish house of mourning is like bridging the gap of two thousand years. The inexpressibly sad and sorrowful wail for the dead, as it swells and rises in the hush of all sounds of life, comes back from the ages like a mournful echo of the voice of Rachel, "weeping for her children and refusing to be comforted, because they are not." (83)

Relying upon the hermeneutics of the Hebraic myth, Riis depicts an everyday experience of grief as the atavistic suffering of the biblical matriarch Rachel. His text thereby contributes to the long tradition of the typological aesthetic I have been tracing, in which an archaic Hebraism is understood as persistent anachronism. Time collapses, as if the Jewish immigrants stand in a several-thousand-year-old defiance of conversion, an eternal affront to Christian morality and faith. In "Jewtown," Riis noted the "Hebrew faces, Hebrew signs, and incessant chatter in the queer lingo that passes for Hebrew," which was really the everyday spoken Yiddish he failed to recognize (43). Limited to typological reading, Riis encountered forms of Jewishness either that his reporter's eye for types could not comprehend or that exceeded the Protestant homiletic framework for his realism.[79]

When Riis confronted a quintessentially religious Jew, a Talmudic schoolmaster, he tried to have it both ways. He claimed that on the surface, Jews' "religious life tinges all their customs," and yet a supposed "real Jew" lies hidden beneath each one, such as the schoolmaster, "stranded there [in the school], his native instinct for money-making having been smothered in the process that has made of him a learned man" (83). This rabbinic figure, in other words, appeared not religious at all. Simultaneously modern and unmodern, Riis's "Shylock" was yet one of many ancient "survivors," similar to those, we will see, featured in the poems of Emma Lazarus and Henry Wadsworth Longfellow. Traces of philosemitic wonder remain in Riis's attribution to Jews of such purportedly native values as industriousness, sobriety, and thrift. But this just made it easy for Protestant reformers like him to speak as much on behalf of the Jews as against their seemingly unregenerate ways. If Riis, like Steffens, exemplified what Irving Howe calls the "fashionable philo-semitism" at the century's end, they both relied upon Hebraic mythology.[80] Riis was a moralist, and Steffens a burgeoning local colorist, but despite these differences, their similar allosemitic stance belies a shared sense of antiquated, outmoded Jewish temporality characteristic of the typological aesthetic.

The Temporal Duality of Jewishness in New England Periodicals

Cahan's extensive training with Riis and Steffens as a "creative newspaperman" may have provided him the tools to craft subsequent fictions, but it was in the magazines of genteel New England literary culture that Cahan earned his name as a man of belles lettres. In that literary culture, editors, contributors, and readers also saw that strange region known as "the ghetto" tinged with what Howe describes as "traces of ancient glory": Jews may have been perceived as "mercenary, grasping, vulgar, and worse," but as we have seen, they were also jealously revered from Puritan discourse onward as "people of the Old Testament, the chosen, or at least the chosen who had strayed."[81] Two articles from the 1860s illustrate poignantly the temporal dichotomy associated with Jewishness, and the considerable popularity of Hebraic mythology in such high cultural, socially conscious literary periodicals as the *Atlantic Monthly, Century Magazine,* and *Harper's New Monthly Magazine.* With their nostalgia for a preimmigrant past of Old New York on one side, and fascination with the anachronistic Hebrew on the other, these articles suggest how the typological aesthetic shaped nonfictional as well as fictional renditions of the Jewish "ghetto."[82]

The image of the hoarding Jewish merchant dominates a travel piece in the *Atlantic Monthly* by Charles Dawson Shanly, "The Bowery at Night" (1867).[83] This early narrative of genteel "slumming" provided a middle-class readership possibly the only glimpse they might have into actual Lower East Side Jewish life, enjoyed at a safe literary distance. The Bowery referred to the vibrant, turbulent district bisected by that oldest thoroughfare in Manhattan, from East Fourth to just below Canal Streets, known for its lowbrow concert halls, brothels, beer gardens, flophouses, and pawnshops, and for a hotbed of street gang activity at its base in the "Five Corners."[84] Shanly creates this imaginative region for his readers, conjuring up its denizens as unnatural interlopers. He depicts the Jewish occupants in detail: they are objects of literary curiosity, but not so celebrated that we forget the Dutch settlement they have displaced.[85]

Beginning at the base of the Bowery at Worth Street and ending where it splits into Third and Fourth Avenues (what is now Cooper Square), Shanly's visual tour of this "great artery of New York trade and travel," is nostalgic for a time when it was not a seamy region of the city.[86] We are in "the Swamp," since the Bowery is built upon one, once a pastoral idyll: "over two hundred years ago, when Peter Stuyvesant pasteurized his flocks and herds hereabouts, the wayfarer would have been more likely to mark a solitary heron than a solitary policeman."[87] The figure of civilized restraint and order has replaced the bird, a symbol of freedom and nature, since now the Bowery after dark is home to night crawlers (602). Only the "gray rat of civilization" is visible (603). Anticipating James's "restless analyst" of *The American Scene* (1907), for readers titillated by literary slumming, Shanly figures himself an innocent "wayfarer" washed up upon "foreign" shores, privy to the secret underside of civilization, the shadowy nightlife of the urban ghetto.[88] Shanly's text has all the components of what, describing literature of later decades, Stephanie Foote calls "urban local color," the enumeration of colorful details and heterogeneous observations of immigrant others, fused together by nostalgia for a more pristine past, but without the reformist impulse she grants to writers like Riis.[89] Like many antebellum exposés of the Bowery, Shanly's text dislocates the ghetto denizens even as it articulates them. Walking from the Jewish quarter through Chatham Square, he describes "small, shrivelled [sic] Chinamen"; "packs of ragged little urchins"; "shop-girls . . . gossiping in groups of twos and threes"; a "negro girl with hot corn for sale"; a "large crowd of roughs"; and other colorful and exotic "striking effects" that make him pine for a preindustrial, preimmigrant past.[90]

In his rendition of the Polish Jewish section of the Bowery, where ready-made clothing shops spill their wares out into the street to be picked through, poked at, and haggled over, Shanly highlights three features: its cheapness (of quality and price), its backwardness, and its Jewishness: "Israel predominates here,—Israel, with its traditional stock in trade of cheap clothing, and bawbles that are made to wear, but not to wear long" (603). Since the early nineteenth century, the Bowery functioned as a border separating different manufacturing districts and ethnic immigrant enclaves, such that the "geographic partitioning of the economy was paralleled by an ethnic pattern of labor."[91] The garment industry, in particular, established in the 1840s and 1850s by German Jewish immigrants who opened clothing stores along Baxter and Chatham Streets, became a virtual economic gateway in the 1880s for Eastern European Jews, who came to dominate the industry by 1900.[92] Hence the Lower East Side, where immigrant Jews and cheap clothing came to be associated. While this industry provided mainly women with a variety of mass-produced fashions at affordable prices, democratizing the fashion industry, it also cheapened fashion, compromising the gentility, quality, and exclusivity that high fashion had promised the rich. The clothes manufactured in the Lower East Side were made to wear but not made to last. The proliferation of cheap clothing promised affordability at the cost of planned obsolescence, a shift in emphasis from quality to quantity that reinforced a centuries-long association between Jews and avarice.

If the Bowery and its resident Jews reflected all that was wrong with industrial modernity, even here present and distant past mingle, a past of both precapitalist primitivism and biblical anachronism. As businesses and homes, public and private spaces overlap, the temporalities of fluid leisure and measured market time both structure this world. One encounters "gaudy flannels and 'loud-patterned' cotton goods" so "closely crowded" together, indoors and out on the street, that the shops appear "like tents made of variegated dry-goods," not so much modern shops as nomadic abodes of an ancient wandering tribe.[93] One stall is "so confined that the occupant, rocking in his chair near the farther end of it, stretches slippered feet well out upon the threshold."[94] His shop becomes a place of both business and "leisure," just as tenement apartments doubling as sweatshops would be for the next generation of immigrants.[95] The clothes "waving overhead in the sluggish evening breeze" reflect for Shanly, moreover, the values and character of their dealers.[96] If the clothing is cheap, gaudy, and excessive, so are the people. The "short, thick-set clothier" is notable for his "curved nose, and spiral, oily hair," and the women are "stoutish and slatternly . . . with few clothes on, but plenty of frowsy hair" (603). Although Shanly does not deem such characteristics inherent, he does see them as inevitable: even these "little Hebrew maids will become stout and slatternly by and by, and have hooked noses like their mothers, and double chins" (603).

For all that Shanly couches well-worn stereotypes in the terms of a burgeoning genteel, journalistic realism, his portrait finally collapses into paradoxical impossibility: a dealer "sits out on the sidewalk and blows clouds from his meerschaum pipe," while his wife "lounges" nearby, perfect examples of "lazily industrious Jewry" (603). Just as the English colonists saw the Knickerbockers, the original Dutch settlers, as greedy materialists, slothful and drunken, the Jews are perceived as both hardworking and indolent at the same time. In this way, Jewishness becomes an elusive quality derived from disjunction, suspicion, and misrepresentation, much like the clothing for sale. When it comes to "Israel," things just are not what they seem to be.[97]

Shanly's nostalgia for Old New York reaches its apogee when he directs our attention "now again up the Bowery," past young men and girls unhooking their awnings with long poles and preparing to close up for the night, to find ourselves at the spot where once stood the gateway to the original "*Bouwerij*," Peter Stuyvesant's mansion, when New York was still Dutch Niew Amsterdam.[98] We are asked to recall the "traditional Stuyvesant pear-tree," brought from Holland and planted here by the governor himself, as now "nothing but the rusty old iron railing is left to show where it stood."[99] If the fruit-bearing, blossoming pear tree marks the past in all its pastoral fecundity and abundance, then the rusted iron railing is emblematic of 1867. Immigrant New York is a place of disease and decay, where memory and shadow alone mark a lost vitality, the price paid for industrial development and immigrant opportunity. The trade-off is clear: under Peter Stuyvesant's leadership, the small group of Jews in the Dutch colony were forbidden to run businesses, let alone own land or worship publicly.[100] Yet in Shanly's hands, those were ideal days, when resident New Yorkers lived in harmony with the Manhattan landscape. Now, by contrast, we are in a present state of decline, even if marked by the very features of the Bowery that make it worth writing about: its rich mercantile street life and, for better or worse, the array of ethnic figures that give it its "color."

If the merchant "Jew" represented the worst of modern urban life for Shanly, a stand-in for the most vulgar, excessive, and decadent aspects of the modern marketplace, religious Judaism offered other writers a dramatic alternative verging on mythical impossibility, as well as insight into that most important Jew, Christ himself. In 1868, Calvin Ellis Stowe contributed to the *Atlantic Monthly* an excellent example of Christian philosemitism. In "The Talmud," Stowe aimed to answer this question: "*Why should Christians feel interested in the Talmud?*"[101] A biblical scholar, professor of Greek and sacred literature, educational reformer, and theological seminarian, Stowe completed full-length studies of the Bible, most famously, *The Origin and History of the Books of the Bible* (1867). Stowe held myriad teaching posts at Dartmouth, Bowdoin, the Andover Theological Seminary, and the Lane Theological Seminary in Cincinnati, where Lyman Beecher was president and whose daughter, Harriet Beecher, Calvin married in 1836.[102] In response to the overwhelming popular success of Ernest Renan's classic 1863 study of the higher criticism *The Life of Jesus*, a stunning defense of Christian typology translated into English in 1864, Stowe aimed in "The

Talmud" to explain the apparent "interlacing of the human heartstrings with the name of Jesus."[103] In contrast with Renan's humanist account of Christ, Stowe wanted to emphasize the miraculous, namely the one "great miracle of all": how "*a Judaean [sic] peasant has revolutionized the religions of the world.*"[104] No matter how far Christ's teachings broke from Judaism, as Renan insisted they did, for Stowe, Jesus was a Jew first and foremost. We must therefore, he claimed, look to Jewish textual sources to find out just how Jesus accomplished this miraculous spiritual revolution. The Talmud would reveal the literature that "produced this wonderful and gifted son."[105]

If in Judaism the Talmud is a living text to be revisited, revised, and questioned, a process that projects into the endless future, for Stowe, by contrast, it is a fossil, a relic of the ancient past. According to modern religious scholars, the Talmud, or "oral Torah," is the "cornerstone" and "central pillar" of Judaism, "the most important book in Jewish culture, the backbone of creativity and of national life."[106] As its Hebrew name "Talmud" suggests, its central goal is the act of "study," "learning" itself, the fulfillment of a supreme religious duty.[107] To engage in ongoing debates of the Talmud is to partake in a temporal process: the oral "completion" of the Torah by which one inserts oneself into a holy discourse set in motion by God and participates in "passing it on," as the life of Torah continues to unfold in the human world.[108] Yet Stowe insists that in order to understand the unique workings of the Talmud, we must first "Orientalize our minds," that is, antiquate them.[109] Even in his most earnest, sympathetic attempts to grasp the Talmud through careful summatory accounts, Stowe's "philosemitism" relies upon the Hebraic myth, applying only to idealized Hebrews of the biblical past. If the sheer survival of the Talmud itself might strike readers as medieval and backward, Stowe suggests that for Jews, its oral tradition was the glue that held together a diasporic, persecuted people and sustained them through continuous suffering. He invokes the "learned Jews" of centuries-long persecution "beyond all endurance" as figures of great pathos. The Jews have endured "most hideous tortures," resulting in "overburdened souls" and minds that are "informed far beyond any contemporary standard" (674). Objects of great sympathy and praise, however, the Jews are nonetheless excessive. Their strong "pride of race" is so singular that it is "more justifiable than any other people ever have or can have," that is, warranted for the past, the future, *for all time* (675). Amidst this sense of the noble Jew of history, in other words, Stowe betrays an undertone of mistrust for actual, present-day Jews, who, by stark contrast, are deceptive: they appear in "guise," play the "mountebank," the trickster, whose ancient legends are "but the masks of unwelcome and dangerous sentiments" (675). His account thus warns of sympathizing too much with learned Jews, because the very source of their knowledge and ancient culture, the Talmud, can also be used as a disguise, a weapon of calculation and clever revenge.

The swings in Stowe's account between admiration and mistrust illustrate the fundamental paradox of typology, and the rhetorical bind of trying to honor a religious foundation that one must also, ultimately, reject. He thus lauds the Talmud as "the great repository of the mental products of a most vigorous and vivid race of thinkers, through long ages of degradation, persecution, oppression, and sorrow; and, as such, few human works are more worthy of, or will better repay, the student of human nature" (675). Yet he condemns "the Hebrews themselves" for having had "a most extravagant estimate of the value of their Talmud, even preferring the Talmud without the written law to the written law without the Talmud" (675). In other words, he critiques Jewish hubris in admiring their own articulations of law over God's, even as he proffers upon the Talmud lavish praise, comparing the miracle of its lasting tradition to God's miracle during the Jewish Exodus from Egypt: "There is something wild and romantic in the idea of this immense body of literature existing in the world from generation to generation in the aerial cloud-like form of tradition, like that pillar of cloud and fire which of old guided the wandering steps of the sacred nation" (676). Romanticizing the Jewish tradition is one way of distancing oneself from it. Stowe's seemingly philosemitic awe is therefore attributed only to mythical Hebrews, to ancient members of the "sacred nation."

In short, Stowe's piece is classic Christian philosemitism: the Talmud's key significance for modern-day Christians, he insists, is that it nurtured that most important Jew, Jesus Christ. The "biography of Jesus of Nazareth according to the Talmud" gives Christians what Renan's account lacks—evidence of His "stupendous miracles," recognizing "Jesus as a youth of great beauty, eloquence, and promise who, being educated at the

Jerusalem college of the rabbins, was led by ambition to set up opposing doctrines and to assert his authority in opposition to them" (684). Arguing for the superiority of the Talmud to other sacred books (excepting the Bible itself), Stowe's piece exemplifies the mixed responses to Jewishness that we have hitherto understood in affective terms, wavering between sympathy for the persecuted historical other and disdain for the modern ancestors of the mythical other. Yet, structurally speaking, the noble Hebrew is an anachronism that should have long been converted or otherwise superseded by Christianity.

For centuries, Jews were perceived in Europe as bearing the guilt of Crucifixion, and as symbolizing medieval close-mindedness. Stowe does little to contradict this centuries-old antisemitic ideology, one that regards living, breathing Jews as little more than their medieval, unenlightened descendants. Arguably in America, such views have not simply been passed down unreflectively. Rather, in the American context, argues Michael Dobkowski, "most people waiver between conflicting and often contradictory attitudes and seldom enjoy an undivided state of mind."[110] Yet as much as Jews were socially accepted in America, Stowe's ideas imply that Judaism has not always been universally well respected: typologically understood, the Jew is still a "rebel against God's purpose."[111] Within this prevalent Protestant American literary culture, Cahan's challenge to carve out a place in time for modern Jewishness meant mediating the temporal contradictions of Jews living in a predominantly Gentile world.

JEWISH PLACES, NOSTALGIC TIME: THE CYCLORAMA EFFECT

Writing at the height of the local color movement, Cahan fictionalized authentic East European "Old World" life for American readers, creating for them a sense of "commonality" located in specialized, ethnic enclaves at particular moments in history (like Sarah Orne Jewett's coastal Maine, Charles Chesnutt's former plantations, and Kate Chopin's New Orleans). We might call these places "*lieux de mémoire*," to use Pierre Nora's phrase, literally, "memory-places."[112] But if "*lieux de mémoire*" serve "to stop time, to block the work of forgetting, to establish a state of things, to immortalize death, to materialize the immaterial," in *The Imported Bridegroom*, the location of Asriel Stroon's nostalgia—the *shtetl*—fails on this count.[113] The story suggests that the *shtetl* Asriel revisits ought to redeem lost time, to encapsulate his unchanged past, just as memory-places reify moments suspended in time as they reinforce time's linearity. The *shtetl* fails as a memory-place, however, because, worn as much by time as he is, it bears little resemblance to the place he thinks he remembers. Unlike the tales of Jewett or Hamlin Garland, the plot of *The Imported Bridegroom* is grounded in various "Jewish" spaces, but each one is, in turn, revealed to be a place of inauthenticity. The story therefore laments not a threatened, cherished, pastoral scene but a lost condition, what Charles Taylor calls "fullness"—a "place (activity or condition) [when] life is fuller, richer, deeper, more worth while, more admirable, more what it should be. . . . We often experience this as deeply moving, as inspiring."[114]

The place of "place" in Cahan's writing has long been a subject in literary criticism of his work. Hana Wirth-Nesher is exceptional here, deeming Cahan a "realist" based on his use of dialect ("realism's central feature" and "democratizing poetic"); critics such as Jules Chametzky and Eric Sundquist have placed Cahan in the subgenres of local color and regionalism.[115] In his iconic Jewish American chronicle *The World of Our Fathers*, Howe characterized writing like Cahan's as a "regional literature" that "focuses on a contained locale, [and] displays curious or exotic local customs for the inspection of readers whose ways until recently have been assumed to constitute a norm."[116] Ronald Sanders deemed Cahan a nostalgic writer, with the dubious distinction of first "local colorist" of the Jewish immigrant quarter.[117] More recent definitions of the genre have complicated Cahan's easy place in it to some extent. Nina Baym likened local colorists to painters of genre scenes, and Josephine Donovan saw the "local color movement" as a self-conscious outgrowth of a New England women's literary tradition.[118] Richard Brodhead claimed for local color "a setting outside the world of modern development, a zone of backwardness where locally variant folkways still prevail"; but even this lens would render Cahan's Lower East Side a backward region, its denizens atavistic medieval throwbacks, rather than modern urbanites.[119] Amy Kaplan challenged the assumptions of pastoral nostalgia by redefining regional writing as a contested site of urban heterogeneity that offered "allegories of desire" for the "modern urban outsider," and Stephanie Foote went so far as to distinguish nostalgic "pastoral regionalism" from an "urban local color" about unadorned, present spaces.[120]

These reconfigurations of local color as a genre have led to multiple readings of Cahan that rely upon the language of landscape or space—a "cosmopolitan vista," a space of "containment," or one defined by the "local."[121] The emphasis on space of course makes sense, given that Hamlin Garland defined "local color" in 1894 as rooted in the very soil of America: "*Local color in a novel means that it has such quality of texture and back-ground that it could not have been written in any other place or by any one else than a native . . . a statement of life as indigenous as the plant-growth.*"[122] For Garland, nativist "veritism" was the aesthetic expression of true "Americanness": "the tourist," he insisted, "cannot write the local novel."[123] In perhaps the most interesting reading of Cahan, in light of Garland's formulation of the "local novel," Dalia Kandoyoti asks how a foreigner, an immigrant, can possibly write "local," indigenous literature, and how "the modes of regionalism and local color [can] be so easily collapsed with the genre of immigrant writing."[124] For her, Cahan's *Yekl* portrays the very outsiders against whose threatening presence local color appeared to be a nativist response. Her point is well taken, as is her conclusion that immigrant identity, especially Jewish identity at the turn of the century, is "recreated *through* space and spatial discourse."[125] For the nativist, the "ghetto" is, after all, the place of the immigrant, the "greenhorn," the "alien," the "new" American, the site of the very destructive modernity against which regional writing pits itself. But the discourse of contested space notwithstanding, Cahan, and also, as we have seen, Riis and other journalists, portray the Jewishness that constitutes the "local color" as exceeding the boundaries of this particular location in terms of time. And not the time of Stephanie Foote's "pastoral regionalism," either, which places folk ethnicity in a distant, idealized past, but that of a biblical past that is yet ever-present, continually revisited in rituals of memory, the ultimate redemption of which will be fulfilled in an indeterminate, anticipated future.[126]

What critics have not discussed, in other words, is the dimension of time, and how in the "ghetto" we find not continuity with a common past but a temporal disruption. Cahan's cyclorama metaphor shows the longing for past memory-places to be a fantasy about temporal stability itself. Just as actual cycloramas were meant to recollect and reify events of the American past, Asriel longs for a place to locate his personal past, yet fails because the memory enclosed in his cylindrical *shtetl*-fantasy is already false and cannot be made real: *lieux de mémoire*, Nora argues, "have no referent in reality . . . they are their own referent."[127] Memory-places occur rather between memory and history: they represent the precise moment when "real environments of memory"—or "*milieux de mémoire*"—disappear, when lived memory gets "torn" out of time and becomes a thing and no longer an experience, leaving only narrative history to smooth over the gap (7). If environments of memory exist in the present, then memory-places exist in nostalgic time. As Fred Davis notes, "nostalgia thrives on transition, on the subjective discontinuities that engender our yearning for continuity."[128] We can thus see why the turbulent late nineteenth century produced such a plethora of nostalgic memory-places.

As mass culture of the period shifted memory from lived, collective experience to collected and recollected moments for history, the experience of social belonging became increasingly mediated by a secularized culture of memorial objects, natural history collections, relics, and souvenirs, as memory became more nostalgic and less sacred.[129] "Memory installs remembrance with the sacred," Nora reminds us, but "history, always prosaic, releases it again."[130] Asriel's fixation on his birthplace thus produces this lonely experience of nostalgia. The more memory "attaches itself to sites," as Nora says it does, the greater the conundrum for the displaced, diasporic Jew struggling to locate a past place from which to orient his present and future.[131] Cahan's selection of the cyclorama, however, and the cyclorama's availability to an immigrant like Cahan as stand-in for the "remembered" sacred place of Jewish origin illustrates the modern triumph of history over memory.[132] Within historical time, nostalgia reaches back to grasp a sacred experience of memory alive in the present, that which history replaces, and thereby obliterates, with its exhaustive accounting and collecting for posterity. If we overlook the hermetic, self-contained gaze of Cahan's cyclorama, we fail to see how it challenges the nostalgic desire to locate Jewish immigrant experience in a fixed time and place.

Many Yiddish writers of Cahan's era knew that location mattered only as a backdrop for an already anticipated dislocation and dispersion.

Sholem Aleichem, with his arguably satirical fictional "Tevye the Dairy-man" stories, created a *shtetl* that, according to Dan Miron, "in richness of detail and liveliness of presentation . . . was second to no other locus, no other imaginary place, created by a modern Jewish writer."[133] As noted above, his stories also engaged current debates that Jews should secularize and modernize, particularly after renewed Russian pogroms in the Pale of Settlement in 1881. With no control over their rights, Jews in the Pale were excluded from local guilds, councils, and professions; were forced to pay humiliating taxes and go to Russianizing schools; and were subject to antisemitic laws, imprisonment, and forced expulsion. During the "black period" in Jewish history from 1881 to 1917, violent pogroms against *shtetls* were effectively condoned by the government, a primary "push fac-tor" for the estimated three million Jews who emigrated from this vulner-able region to the United States during this era.[134] In light of this, unlike the relentless determinism of Bernard Malamud's *The Fixer* (1966), a novel set in the context of Russian anti-Jewish violence within roughly the same period, Sholem Aleichem's "Tevye" stories are distinctive for their orality and giddy humor, though they chart a painful progression of Jewish dispersion and loss within the "historical panorama" of late-nineteenth-century Russia.[135] Miron thus reads the tales as mythic rather than novelis-tic in structure, transcending "sheer mimetic representation," even though they unfold in real time.[136] One by one, Tevye's daughters go their own way in spite of their father's efforts to marry them well: Tsaytl falls for Motl the poor tailor, Hodl for a socialist imprisoned in Siberia, Shprintze runs off with a rich dandy, and Beilke with a vulgar new-moneyed builder who whisks her off to America. In perhaps the most painful episode, Tevye's beloved Chava elopes with a Christian, at which point Tevye pronounces her dead to him, though he remains achingly haunted by this decision. His daughters dispersed like the Jewish people themselves, in the final story, "Lekh Lekho," Tevye, too, is expelled from his home and sent wander-ing. "Lekh Lekho," the biblical Hebrew injunction from God to Abraham to "take yourself and go" from his birthplace to a Canaan he will never enter, only underscores how Tevye's stubborn devotion to Jewish religious tradition—the very thing the assimilated Asriel mourns—accompanies permanent, bitter exile.[137]

Like the Tevye tales, *The Imported Bridegroom* reflects melancholy humor about the problem of place for Jewish immigrants within the historical panorama of late-nineteenth-century America. Thinking about Cahan's fiction in this context, it becomes clear how it, too, works to *de*-naturalize the relationship between region and identity, shifting our attention to deterritorialized, temporal formulations of experience. If American local color reacted to postbellum modernity with nostalgia, Cahan's fictions offer up modern forms of Jewishness that complicate nostalgia by dislocating the places they invoke. Like the trap of Lot's wife, nostalgia becomes the middle-class trap into which displaced immigrants fall—the frozen backward glance, the desire for home arrested in time and space. If we try to restore, or "re-place," that past, the lesson suggests, we, too, become frozen in time. As Cahan's readers and critics with our own persistent attachment to place, confined by secular, linear time, we, too, must consider how eschatology restructures the secular realist narrative and can reshape our understanding of the American realist novel.

Read within the context of Cahan's actual lived experience of diaspora, his *shtetl*-as-cyclorama anticipates this problem of nostalgic memorial culture and of whole disciplines devoted to recovering past places, by highlighting the un-place-ability of memory and the immateriality of remembering outside acts of sacred ritual. Asriel's old Aunt Sarah-Rachel, once "an exceedingly active and clever tradeswoman," is now a mere "bag of bones," and his friend, Shmulke, now a "somewhat decrepit" old man who "[struggles] to free himself from [Asriel's] unwelcome embrace."[138] Asriel feels his loss of the past hardest, however, at the Jewish cemetery, what Ezrahi would call a key "*lieu de memoire juive*," where the dead outnumber the living, an allusion to pogroms and the disappearance of actual *shtetls* and their denizens.[139] To his father's silent spirit he cries, "All is gone. . . . All, all, all is lost forever!"; the repetition suggesting different levels of loss—material, personal, familial, cultural, and also temporal, of an irreplaceable past from which a different present and future might otherwise have flowed.[140]

Asriel's failure of memory suggests to readers that past Jewish places like Pravly are gone for good and that there is no return home, outside memory, imagination, or art: Asriel "recalls not the place itself, but he can remember reminiscences of it" (100). He thinks how "his mind would conjure up something like the *effect* now before his eyes," like a picturesque "dream" (101). In other words, Asriel *remembers remembering* Pravly, but has apparently forgotten forgetting it, an inward displacement of memory that peaks as he faces the town's center. Just when the story should reveal the site of the really real of this Jewish place, Cahan aims his most pointed jab at local color:

> The same market place, the same church with the bailiff's office by its side! The sparse row of huts on the river bank, the raft bridge, the tannery—everything was the same as he had left it; and yet it all had an odd, mysterious, far-away air—like things seen in a cyclorama. . . . [I]t certainly was the same dear old Pravly, but added to it was something else, through which it now gazed at Asriel. Thirty-five years lay wrapped about the town. (103)

The image is poignant. Creating what we might call a "cyclorama effect," it inverts representation and reality as Pravly becomes a simulacrum, while the narrative voice, shifting between direct and free indirect discourse, disrupts the border between reality and illusion, insider and outsider. Real cycloramas compress hours, even days, of past events into a compacted visual experience, so that the featured place feels immediate. But here, Pravly is ever receding with an "odd, mysterious, far-away air." If cycloramas bring historical time into focus, time is external to Pravly, artificially "wrapped about" it like a circular cyclorama itself. Cahan's critique of nostalgia is deepest when, as Pravly "gazes" at Asriel, he becomes the spectacle, trapped in a cylindrical landscape reflecting only his own time-worn image.

A descendant of the panorama and a precursor to the motion picture, late-nineteenth-century cyclorama spectacles fed on popular, collective nostalgia for real places frozen in time. A larger-than-life mural on the walls of a cylindrical room, the cyclorama invited spectators to enjoy the illusion of occupying a historical moment or faraway landscape. Most common in the United States were Civil War cycloramas, attractions akin to post–Civil War memorial institutions like archives, cemeteries, monuments, and museums that proliferated in the 1880s and 1890s.[141]

Rendering decisive battleground scenes with historical fidelity and spatial accuracy, cycloramas invited one to enter them, experience a visceral hyperrealism, and enjoy a brief, vicarious encounter with the past. But even as they evoke moments from the linear past, within the encircling walls of any given cyclorama painting time unfolds in a circular, narrative loop. The visual technology promises the fantasy of time travel, but only by trapping one in the ever-repeating battle, a cyclical frozen past: what we might call *nostalgic time*.

In the closing decades of the nineteenth century, hundreds of cycloramas were built in the United States, from Boston to Omaha, Buffalo to Atlanta, attractions with an all-encompassing spatial scale **(figs. 1, 2)**. The "Battle of Atlanta Cyclorama," commissioned by General "Blackjack" Logan and first viewed in 1892, has been on display in the Atlanta Cyclorama and Civil War Museum in Atlanta's Grant Park since 1921. In February 2017 the "Battle of Atlanta" circular painting was moved to the new custom-built twenty-three-thousand-square-foot Lloyd and Mary Ann Whitaker Cyclorama Building at the Atlanta History Center, scheduled to open to the public in fall 2018.[142] The famous "Battle of Gettysburg Cyclorama," a 360-degree circular oil-on-canvas painting by Paul Philippoteaux, commemorated "Pickett's Charge," the climactic Confederate attack on the Union center on July 3, 1863 **(fig. 3)**.[143] This four-hundred-foot-long, fifty-foot-high, twenty-two-thousand-square-foot cyclorama—premiering in Chicago in 1883 and reproduced in Boston, Baltimore, and Philadelphia in 1884 and in New York's Union Square and Brooklyn's City Hall around 1888 and 1890—featured a three-dimensional earthen foreground littered with relics of battle, stone walls, shattered trees, and broken fences. Visitors, including veterans, were awed by the painting's spectacular realism.[144]

Primarily a spatial phenomenon, the cyclorama's temporal dimensions are easily overlooked. Surviving brochures of the Gettysburg Cyclorama emphasize the medium's spatial import. Some pamphlets include a large, circular, pullout map, labeled with a corresponding key, which might appear to reveal scrupulous mimetic accuracy of places. Its authenticating details of wounded bodies, however, represent, as in synecdoche, the whole battle. As one entry notes, "Sargeant Morris Killed . . . Gen Fairchild lost arm.

Figure 1. Cover, Brochure, Cyclorama of General Custer's Last Battle against Sioux Indians, or, The Battle of Little Big Horn, Boston, 1889. Courtesy of the Huntington Library, San Marino.

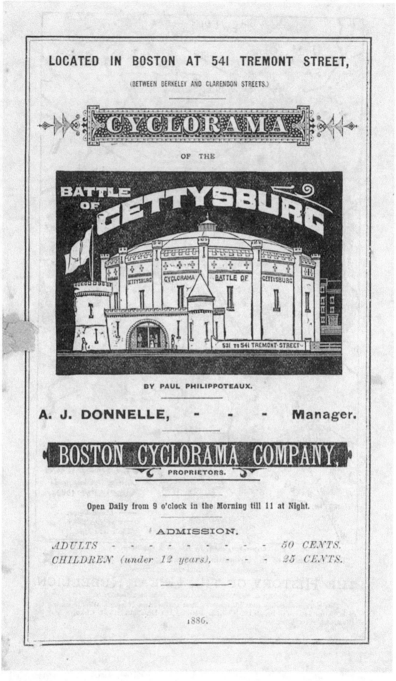

LOCATED IN BOSTON AT 541 TREMONT STREET,

(BETWEEN BERKELEY AND CLARENDON STREETS.)

CYCLORAMA

OF THE

BATTLE OF GETTYSBURG

BY PAUL PHILIPPOTEAUX.

A. J. DONNELLE, - - - Manager.

BOSTON CYCLORAMA COMPANY,

PROPRIETORS.

Open Daily from 9 o'clock in the Morning till 11 at Night.

ADMISSION.

ADULTS - - - - - - - - - 50 CENTS.
CHILDREN (under 12 years), - - - 25 CENTS.

1886.

Figure 2. Title page, Brochure, Gettysburg Cyclorama, Boston, Massachusetts, 1886. Courtesy of the Huntington Library, San Marino.

Figure 3. Cover, Brochure, Battle of Gettysburg Cyclorama, Baltimore, Maryland, ca. 1891. Courtesy of the Huntington Library, San Marino.

Gen. Paul lost both eyes. Gen. Dudley right leg" **(fig. 4)**. For ten cents, readers could study detailed maps of the battlefield and region, with a star marking the spot where the spectator stood **(fig. 5)**.[145] Such hyperrealism enacts a near obsession with place, harnessing nostalgia to patriotism to create an imagined community of spectators. Its appeal derived, art historian Angela Miller writes, from the sense of a "substitute reality" in which viewers could experience, "without the inconveniences of actual travel" (or time travel, in this case), the nation's memorialized past.[146]

Advertisements in cyclorama brochures evinced the nostalgic primitivism in these touring impulses. One such ad encouraged Battle of Vicksburg Cyclorama spectators in New York to take the elevated cars to South

Figure 4. Foldout circular map, Brochure, Gettysburg Cyclorama, Union Square, New York, ca. 1889. Courtesy of the Huntington Library, San Marino.

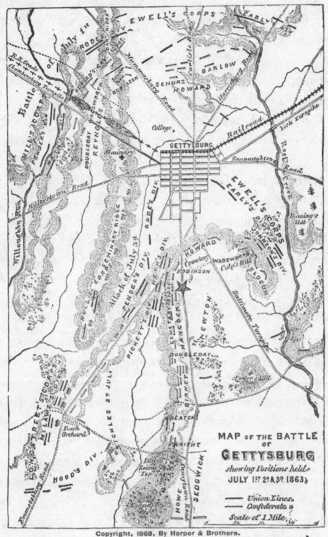

Figure 5. Map, Brochure, Gettysburg Cyclorama, Boston, Massachusetts, 1885. Courtesy of the Huntington Library, San Marino.

Ferry to see "The Latest and Greatest Attraction at Coney Island," "A Trip to Africa," and another in a Chicago brochure, a Japanese cultural exhibition (figs. 6 and 7). Mirroring the era's widespread epistemological craze, opened up by the tremendous flow of immigrants to the United States beginning in the 1880s, this tourism trend manifested the desire to experience and comprehend the foreign, strange, and exotic, as much as to map discursively the contours of urban poverty. Hence the Chicago World's Columbian Exposition of 1893 and its Midway Plaisance: epitomizing place-obsession and modern technology, it promised to bring the authentic sights, tastes, and sounds of Tunisia, Algeria, Egypt, France, Germany, Ireland, Japan, Java, Persia, and even Native America to twenty-seven million spectators, only two years after Riis published his exposé of urban immigrant destitution.[147] While Progressive reformers and genteel readers of Howellsian-sponsored local fictions thought themselves more sophisticated culture consumers than World's Fair crowds or cyclorama tourists, Cahan links them together through their shared nostalgia for pre-modern places, paradoxically harnessed through modern representational technologies.

The literary cyclorama effect thwarts both the imagined passage across space and time and the feelings of nostalgia that real cycloramas enabled. Cahan's metaphor instead exposes the desire for authentic places as itself a nostalgic fantasy, a *trompe l'oeil* mocking our search for located experience. If a cyclorama is a form of "simulated reality," in *The Imported Bridegroom*, the cyclorama as metaphor denies and displaces the referent for which "Pravly" stands.[148] The desire to recover place inheres in original conceptions of nostalgia—from *nostos* ("return home") and *algia* ("longing," or "sadness")—though now seen as an enduring condition in which time and space merge, a longing for a home that no longer exists or has never existed.[149] Svetlana Boym calls it a "romance with one's own fantasy," surviving only "in a long-distance relationship."[150] Asriel's quest clearly exemplifies what Boym calls "restorative nostalgia," which "stresses *nostos* and attempts a transhistorical reconstruction of the lost home" (xviii). Like the cyclorama, it tries to commemorate and freeze cherished moments and objects with "souvenirization," to repeat "the unrepeatable" and materialize "the immaterial" while erasing the fissures of time's passage (16, xviii).

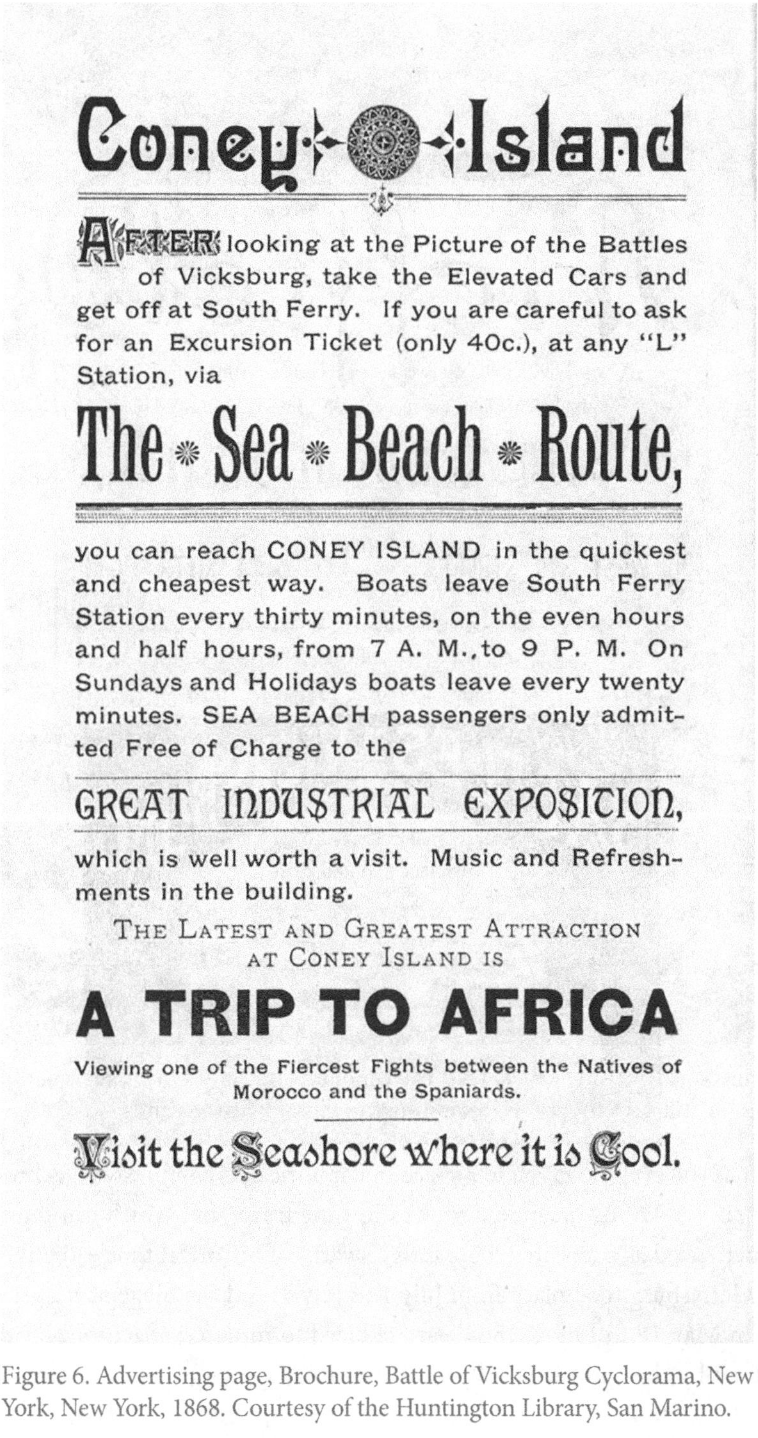

Coney ✦ ◉ ✦ Island

AFTER looking at the Picture of the Battles of Vicksburg, take the Elevated Cars and get off at South Ferry. If you are careful to ask for an Excursion Ticket (only 40c.), at any "L" Station, via

The ✻ Sea ✻ Beach ✻ Route,

you can reach CONEY ISLAND in the quickest and cheapest way. Boats leave South Ferry Station every thirty minutes, on the even hours and half hours, from 7 A. M., to 9 P. M. On Sundays and Holidays boats leave every twenty minutes. SEA BEACH passengers only admitted Free of Charge to the

GREAT INDUSTRIAL EXPOSITION,

which is well worth a visit. Music and Refreshments in the building.

THE LATEST AND GREATEST ATTRACTION
AT CONEY ISLAND IS

A TRIP TO AFRICA

Viewing one of the Fiercest Fights between the Natives of Morocco and the Spaniards.

_____

Visit the Seashore where it is Cool.

Figure 6. Advertising page, Brochure, Battle of Vicksburg Cyclorama, New York, New York, 1868. Courtesy of the Huntington Library, San Marino.

Figure 7. Advertising page, Brochure, Panorama of Gettysburg, Chicago, Illinois, ca. 1884. Courtesy of the Huntington Library, San Marino.

Just as the cyclorama renders space metaphorical, it compresses diachronic time: it makes us imagine ourselves in time travel, but which can only be experienced as a repeated loop. Large swaths of historical time—the Battle of Gettysburg took place from July 1 to July 3, and the Siege of Vicksburg from May 18 to July 4, 1863—are reduced to minutes, anachronisms disguised by the audacious realism of the visual spectacle. Yet, if cycloramas attempted to restore a seamless past, Cahan's tropic *shtetl*-as-cyclorama reveals the very inauthenticity of *shtetl* nostalgia, and its failure to reconstitute Jewish identity.

Trying repeatedly to author and enjoy his own fictions of the past, Asriel becomes trapped in nostalgic time, between memory and history. Through the structural irony of his failed restorative nostalgia, however, readers get to experience what Boym calls "reflective modern nostalgia," a meditation on the loss of time that "thrives in *algia*, the longing itself, and delays the homecoming"; "a form of deep mourning that performs a labor of grief both through pondering pain and through play that points to the future."[151] For actual immigrants, the Lower East Side may have "lent spatial dimensions to Jewish [collective] memory."[152] But Cahan's fictional New York is more a "place of forgetting" than a site of remembrance.[153]

In light of all this loss in the tale, the World-to-Come points to a sacred time here on earth, recuperating as it renders otherwise insignificant such places of forgetting, as sites of ongoing rituals of "remembrance" and even of anticipation. The cyclical remembrance of the collective Jewish past, through repeated religious prayer, ritual, and observance, transcends individual migrations, or memories of any single person's past, to address the problem of repeated, collective exile. To live according to this temporality renders historical places insignificant, deceptive. Boyarin thus reads political Zionism as the attempt to "put an end to exiles," the Jewish *Ur*-fantasy of place.[154] "When Walter Benjamin's angel of history stares backward in horror at a mounting heap of rubble," Boyarin argues, "what he perceives is certainly forgetting, not absence" (2). If political Zionism alleviates "absence," then, witness Asriel, it seems impossible, through recourse to place, to overcome the collective forgetting plaguing modern Jews. Cahan's disruption of the nostalgic temporality of local color is a formal echo of this thematic problem.

REALIST TIME AND THE WORLD-TO-COME

In *The Imported Bridegroom*, when Asriel speaks repeatedly of the "World-to-Come"—in Judaism, the future paradise on earth—he invokes for readers a different eschatological frame than the Protestant providential one: the end, or *telos*, of Jewish collective history with its own redemptive future.[155] Asriel's movements throughout the plot, from one purportedly "genuine" Jewish place in time to another, are contrasted with the fate of a secondary character in the novel, the prodigious Talmudic scholar and eponymous "imported bridegroom," Shaya Golub. When first introduced, appearing totally absorbed in ancient sacred ritual, Shaya seems the very embodiment of the noble Hebrew himself. Asriel beholds him standing among several hundred praying Orthodox Jewish men in the Pravly synagogue, "nodding or shaking their heads, or swaying their forms to and fro . . . in a convulsion of religious fervor," while he, "the prodigy," appears with "eyes shut, and his countenance stern with unfeigned rapture."[156] Asriel is completely taken with this vision of the "real thing," and thus "imports" him, first and foremost, as a sacred conduit to the "world to come" to secure his own place in it, and then, secondarily, as his daughter's arranged bridegroom. Once in America, however, things get complicated: Shaya is seduced by "New World" knowledge, and his ultimate apostasy and escape into the world of secular ideas upend Asriel's plan. Yet no matter how modern such ideas—Comtean positivism as opposed to Talmudic lore—Shaya still reproduces the formal experience of timeless, devotional ritual, but now with different content. At the novel's end, he seems more "worldly," modern, and temporally placed in the present for having embraced enlightened philosophy; yet he also forsakes his marriage and repeats the same Talmudic behavior he exhibited in Pravly when the reader first sees him. With no character successfully reconciling Jewish time in the American place, finally, the novella's ending marks Cahan's *maskilik* ambivalence about Jewish sacred time.

Preceding the waves of Eastern European Jewish immigrants to the United States, among whom Cahan arrived in 1882, what bound together religious denizens of the Jewish *shtetls* in Russia, Poland, and the Pale of Settlement were not only Yiddish culture and religious practice but also "Jewish collective memory."[157] Distinct from individual memories rooted in personal experience and recorded modern history, Jewish collective memory is maintained through shared religious traditions practiced according to the Bible, the record of God's "revealed history." Unlike secular historiography conveyed through narrative, sacred providential Jewish history flows through "ritual and recital," or "chronicle," and is believed to be redemptive for the entire "nation" of Israel, an eschatology that runs alongside, yet is largely indifferent to, historical time as we know it.[158] Marked by the destruction of the First Temple in Jerusalem in 586 BCE and subsequent launch of exile, redemption was (and for many still is) believed possible only by the Messiah's advent, at a future a time and place, the "World-to-Come," where the righteous dead will be resurrected to enjoy a Messianic Golden Age. In the Hebrew phrase "world to come," *olam ha-ba*, however, the ambiguous word *olam* can have a spatial *or* temporal reference: "'World to come' assumes the former," Rabbi Neil Gillman notes, while "'age to come' assumes the latter."[159] Accordingly, in this world, *olam ha-ze*, the age of history, constitutes mere "in-between time," a "realm of shifting sands" between a known biblical past and an assured messianic future.[160]

By the time Cahan began writing in the late nineteenth century, the seismic effects of the *Haskalah* were being felt in Eastern Europe. Significantly, the rise of political Zionism in response to modern and often nationalist antisemitism also provoked a crisis in an age-old messianic faith. This new uncertainty of the sacred, future bookend of time created a "break in the continuity of Jewish living and hence also an ever-growing decay of Jewish group memory."[161] These shifts paved the way for contemporary *Haskalah* writers to rebel against the religious "authorities" of the past and replace an insistence on providential Jewish history, with its disregard for the present (except as significant for that eschatology) and excess spirituality, with the nineteenth-century ideals of natural science, realism, and positivism. Turning their energies toward earthly problems of the present, and identifying with downtrodden Jewish masses, the radical *maskilim* sought to demystify the world in order to create a utopian enlightened future.[162] As they tried to reconcile the modern era with Jewish faith, they drew their positivist concepts indirectly from August Comte (1798–1857), who believed that "history was moving towards the positivist age," in which a scientific elite would examine and organize human life according to empirical, scientific laws.[163] This optimistic view of modernity became difficult to maintain in the 1870s and 1880s, however, amid virulent antisemitisim, eroding communities, and violent pogroms, a challenge that often manifested in literature as bitter, self-critical satire.[164]

Well before Russian and Eastern European Jewish immigration to the United States began in full force in the 1880s, then, upheavals in European Jewish religious culture were already underway, with the hope that the modern age would realize the religious tolerance and true equality that were already in jeopardy.[165] When persecuted *shtetl* Jews immigrated to the United States, their new lives shaped by poverty, poor labor conditions, and Christian culture, they faced new challenges to an already imperiled religious life. Emerging on the US literary scene in the midst of these upheavals, Cahan's work engaged intersecting issues and multiple audiences. In the midst of raging intellectual debates about modernity itself, Cahan superimposed *shtetl* Jewish "folkways" onto New York City, the heart of the "world of modern development," urging readers to consider how the New World, what happened there, and the promise it held as a new Jewish "home," figured in the providential view of Jewish history and the socialist utopian imaginary alike. Emerging Jewish fictions like Cahan's, hybrids of "Old" and "New World" culture, mediated these tensions between past and future, the worldly and the spiritual, the sacred and the secular, *already within* Jewish culture, helping new American Jews negotiate ongoing secular challenges to sacred beliefs as they tried to preserve an erstwhile-imperiled Jewish connection to sacred history.

Cahan's use of the cyclorama registers the complexity of these historical changes. If Mark Currie is right that all modern narrative has an "anticipatory" temporality, creating *itself* as a future past, "the object of a future memory," then as a nostalgic replica of the real *shtetl*, Cahan's cyclorama metaphor mirrors how the realist novel, a genre with fidelity to secular, historical time and place, can also be said to create nostalgia for the past it invents, as well as for the future past in which it participates as a cultural object of memory.[166] This proleptic function preserves what Mikhail Bakhtin calls the novel's chronotopes, its "organizing centers": the palpable "knots of narrative" that are "tied and untied" in order to "materialize time in space," and represent events or "scenes" now available for future experience within the bounds of any novel's covers, as it is read and reread.[167] Bakhtin even mentions the "special *creative* chronotope inside which this exchange between [literary] work and [real] life occurs, and which constitutes the distinctive life of the work."[168] Bridging these worlds, Cahan's novella participates in a shared experience of Jewish history and memory. Whereas the conventional version of realism's secular temporality becomes a cyclical, frozen past quite like that of the cyclorama, however, by contrast the sought-after "World-to-Come" driving the plot of *The Imported Bridegroom* invokes an order of sacred time that transcends realism's temporal loop and the nostalgia it generates. The cyclorama metaphor captures this limitation of realist time to reconstitute the past, as Cahan's novel instead looks toward an eschatological future it cannot, by definition, include in its plot, a perfect place to which the novel can only gesture, but not represent.

If Cahan's erstwhile realist tale illustrates temporal heterogeneity both thematically and through its formal enactments, it suggests that one problem is our assumption that realism's temporality is, in fact, linear and homogeneous. Jewish immigrant writing like Cahan's conforms to the narrative realism that Fredric Jameson describes, as we have seen, but the explicit tensions that Cahan's work navigates between the "past-present-future" of narrative, on one hand, and secular history and sacred Jewish time, on the other, exceed Jameson's expressly secular framework. Cahan's realism can perhaps more fruitfully be explained in Lloyd Pratt's terms as helping to "pluralize" the period's temporal repertoire by resituating the march of secular, historical time that guides individual characters' lives (and thus realist narrative) within the broader movements of sacred redemptive time.

From his first novel to his last, Cahan combined sacred and secular temporalities in texts that have been read through the critical framework of assimilation—that is, as narratives of unrewarding assimilation to Gentile, US culture. Read through the temporal lens, however, his otherwise "successfully" Americanized heroes illustrate how those who try to reconcile religious and secular life into a seamless Jewish past and present end up bitterly conflicted. In the final lines of *The Rise of David Levinsky*, Cahan's most famous novel and anticapitalist *bildungsroman*, for example, the wealthy but expressly disenchanted eponymous hero puts it this way: "I can never forget the days of my misery. I cannot escape from my old self. My past and present do not comport well. David, the poor lad swinging over a Talmud volume at the Preacher's synagogue, seems to have more in common with my inner identity than David Levinsky, the well-known cloak manufacturer."[169]

Levinsky's two simultaneous selves correspond almost identically with the doubled image of Jewishness this book charts—the modern Jew and noble but persistent, atavistic Hebrew—only here superimposed onto one fictional character. Poignantly, Levinsky describes his conflict of Jewish identity in terms of irreconcilable orders of time. Rather than a linear trajectory of irrecoverable loss, a lost past being the requisite cost of immigrant assimilation, Levinsky's journey from rags to riches comes full circle as he remains split in two, an enduring "old self"—specifically Jewish, religious, a mythical Hebrew of sorts, from which the present self cannot "escape"—and a "new one," the secular, worldly businessman. Levinsky's journey from religious to secular life through linear, homogeneous time, in other words, comes undone, as Cahan thwarts the plot of economic ascension and assimilation into Protestant America. It is not only hard to lose one's religion; apparently it is impossible. Here the religious self takes on a persistent, temporal existence all its own.

Levinsky's ultimate crisis suggests instead a heterogeneous Jewish relationship to time, how the Jewish past is never quite past but, rather, moving at its own pace, carries on alongside one and continues to beckon in the present. From a secular perspective, his final reflections sound like simple nostalgia for a past beyond recovery, or like the psychological and cultural perils of assimilation. Viewed through the lens of sacred Jewish history, however, this scene suggests that reentrance into the life of collective ritual and practice is always available to Levinsky, his religious "past" one with which he could reconnect at any time through renewed religious practice, to revivify the vision of his young self "swinging over a Talmud volume at the Preacher's synagogue." How, then, this chapter queries, can the realist novel—a genre traditionally defined in association with Enlightenment modernity, the rise of secularism, and homogeneous time—account for this alternate, fractured temporal experience?

If *David Levinsky* dramatizes the economic rise and concomitant spiritual fall of its eponymous hero, *The Imported Bridegroom* depicts Asriel Stroon as spiritually lost from the start. Asriel fails repeatedly to reconnect with his Jewishness precisely because he ignores the temporally structured rituals and practices of Jewish remembrance that David bemoans, not to mention the intellectual labor, commitment, and sacrifice that studying scripture demands. To presume the homogeneous time of the novel would be to miss how Cahan's fictional New York was an urban frontier of both historical progress and persistent religious practice simultaneously. A social schism may have divided assimilated, secularized, "modern" Jews from seemingly medieval, yet quaint, Talmudic scholars like those Steffens and Stowe admired—but by preserving the timeless rituals of Jewish devotion, the Ultra-Orthodox actually transformed the Lower East Side into a crossroads of different orders of time. Shaya's journey illustrates this temporally heterogeneous schism: he abandons Talmudic study, but his physical gestures bear traces of an authentic, prodigious "holy soul" engaged in devoted worship. Shaya embodies the intersecting temporalities of secular modernity and sacred redemptive history at once, registering the tensions surrounding those Jews who adapted their ancient rituals of reading and debate to a contemporary, Christian, typologically structured world more or less hostile to them.

CONCLUSION: THE DIASPORIC JEW AND "MILIEUX DE MÉMOIRE"

When Pravly fails to redeem Asriel's past, he turns toward his future, bringing the story to its ultimate, ironic conclusion. Through a fierce dowry-bidding war with the town's most respected elder, Asriel had all but purchased Shaya Golub, the town's Talmudic prodigy, as a "fifteen-thousand-dollar" imported bridegroom for his daughter and a son to "say *Kaddish* over [his] grave when he dies," bringing Asriel to his ultimate home.[170] Shaya at once becomes the latest "site" of hope in Asriel's search for place: approaching New York's shores once again, now with Shaya in tow, "[Asriel] was going home. He felt it more keenly, more thrillingly every day, every hour, every minute," so that "the deeper did Pravly sink into the golden mist of romance . . . the more real did the great American city grow in his mind" (119). As New York (metonymic for America) seems a new Zion, Asriel engages in what Susan Stewart calls the "narrative process of nostalgic reconstruction," as "the present is denied and the past takes on an authenticity of being," only here pointed toward the future.[171] Trapped in secular time, Asriel can only imagine redemption in the form of tangible memory-places. His dream of "genuine Judaism"—something he never observed himself—becomes embodied in the pious Shaya, imported to enchant and redeem the New World and Asriel's past and future simultaneously.

Upon their arrival, however, Asriel's plan comes undone: Shaya retains his Old World "sidelocks," those bodily "badges of divine learning and piety," but quickly discovers his new temple, the Astor Library. When Asriel catches his "Gift from God" smoking on the Sabbath, and later, to his great horror, eating in a *treyfe* restaurant, the greatest of blasphemies, Shaya transforms before his eyes into a figure of betrayal, an "*appikoros*," an apostate, a "secret, sneaking enemy."[172] Asriel pronounces Shaya dead to him, and utters the refrain, "All is lost!" Corrupted by "Gentile books," the "holy soul" becomes for Asriel a profane, "polluted, sacrilegious" body, the "precious stone" an "imported decoration," a mere *tzatzke*.[173] Likewise, Flora Stroon was hoping her father would bring back "diamonds, rubies, emeralds, sapphires, pearls" from Europe, not some medieval "greenhorn," "who could not say a word without performing some grotesque gesture or curling his horrid sidelocks" (119, 122, 123). She wants Shaya to be her "birdie boy" and go to college "together with nice, educated up-town fellows," a doctor who rides to work in a "buggy," not "an unkempt, long-skirted man who knew nothing of the world, took snuff, and made life a nuisance to himself and to others."[174] In short, she dreamed of a modern, educated, "worldly" sweetheart, not this "unworldly" prodigy of useless arcana (128, 139). The two do finally marry, but by the story's end, Shaya forsakes her, too, to join a ragtag group of philosopher-laborers, a secular minyan of Enlightened "insatiable debaters" who, like the Russian radical *maskilim*, meet weekly to discuss Comtean positivism (160). The novel thus concludes with bitter irony. Flora is estranged, and Asriel—betrayed, defeated, and disenchanted with Shaya, his daughter, and America too—seeks to begin life anew, departing at the story's end to live out his days in Palestine, "The Place" of all Jewish places.[175]

Like Pravly, Shaya fails to enact a memory-place of authentic Jewishness for Asriel, becoming instead, like the cyclorama, a site of subterfuge. The narrator laments, a "pang smote Asriel's heart. . . . It was as if he saw his temple, the embodiment of many years of labor, the object of his fondest cares, just completed and ready to be dedicated, suddenly enveloped in flames."[176] Even if a sacred Jewish site is destroyed in both cases, we can read this comparison between Shaya's apostasy and the destruction of the Temple—the most significant event in ancient Jewish history, ushering in a millennial condition of exile—only as showing the narrator's mockery of Asriel's feelings. Asriel's turn away from *treyfe* America and toward the future, to be "born again" and die a "righteous Jew" in the Holy Land of Palestine, would suggest that Zionism is a possible corrective for immigrant nostalgia, as for many perhaps it was (157, 158).

Asriel's concern with the World-to-Come, however, raises different issues of diaspora and Jewish eschatology that get at a fundamental tension about place in Jewish theology: "[I]s God revealed in time, in history, or in space, in 'the Land'"?[177] The destruction of the Second Temple in 70 CE ushered in the second, Babylonian exile, the expulsion of Jews from Jerusalem, and altered the Jewish relation to sacred space and time from thence forward. A once-centralized priestly liturgy, rooted in a sacred place, was thus made portable through devotional textual interpretation, strict adherence to biblical law, observance of the Hebrew calendar, and the carving out of new spaces, made sacred by observances of sacred time like the Sabbath.[178] The meaning of postbiblical Jewish "history" also changed: life was now seen as divided into "two endless days," the "Biblical yesterday" and the "exile of today," so that history became less a vertical movement through time than a "horizontal simultaneity."[179] Late-nineteenth-century Zionism brought these ongoing theological tensions to the fore.[180] Where Zionists saw national settlement as an active step toward collective redemption, their opponents saw Zionism as a secular, false solution to exile; redemption was in God's hands only.[181]

Asriel's final Zionist turn is thus compatible with restorative nostalgia, as a fantasy not of the irretrievable past but of a salvageable future. After all, what was political Zionism, if not a future nostalgia for a lost past, a fantasy that modern Palestine would redeem the preexilic Jewish state, or even prelapsarian Eden?[182] Asriel's naive longings thus represent the aim to literalize place as "The Place" and realize the bookends of exilic history.[183] But with his failed attempts to locate "authentic Judaism," his turn to Palestine seems doomed to repeat this failure. Asriel is trapped in a debased present, in Benjamin's empty, homogeneous time—a cyclorama of sorts for the spectator who takes the illusion for reality. He remains caught in a cycle of doubt and despair, his piety a zero-sum game, as if, with sound investment, he could speculate on his future. Unable to reenchant his worldly places, his World-to-Come, we can conclude, may never arrive.

Shaya, however, presents a diasporic alternative to both immigrant nostalgia and nationalist Zionism. He longs for neither past nor future homeland; rather, he embodies Boyarin's diasporic, enlightened Jew. Shaya's turn to positivist philosophy seems an obvious reference to the radical *maskilim* discussed above, Cahan's contemporaries, for whom Shaya's transformation from pious greenhorn to secular intellectual would be worthy of celebration. But the narrator's ambiguous position challenges an easy reading of the story's conclusion. On one hand, Shaya forsakes the Talmud, albeit depicted as a competitive practice of memorization, static recitation, and performance in Pravly. The narrator even emphasizes Shaya's unenlightened "savagery" when he was engaged in prayer: "his eyes shut . . . his countenance stern with unfeigned rapture . . . violently working his lips," and later, in a scene of masterful Talmudic debate, "thrusting his curly head in his opponent's face, and savagely gesticulating. . . . His blue eyes flashed fire, his whole countenance gleamed, his singsong rang with tuneful ferocity."[184] Yet in the novel's final scene, Shaya retains the same outward form when engaged in ecstatic philosophical debate: "engrossed in the reading; and only half-conscious of Flora's presence, he sat leaning forward, his mouth wide open, his face rapt, and his fingers quietly reproducing the mental gymnastics of Comte's system in the air" (160). Devoid of religious content, Shaya's secular conversion retains the ecstatic gestures formerly of prayer—the Talmudic twirl of a finger, the snapping.[185] Cahan's story thus ends with a new temporality made sacred by ritual, the collective reading practice of the scholarly group. Concluding with a degree of utopian hope, the story does end with a redemptive environment of memory, of sorts.[186]

"You don't know me yet," Shaya tells Flora at the story's conclusion. "I tell you you don't begin to know me."[187] For Philip Joseph, this moment "gives expression to Cahan's unfinished deliberation over the possible outcomes of Jewish relocation in America."[188] What if, instead, Shaya's reading group exemplifies not relocation but dislocation? Read this way, the scene dramatizes the bridging of multiple temporalities through devotion to the modern philosophical text, formally analogous to the reading rituals of collective memory that mediate the biblical Hebraic past and the redemptive future. With Shaya Golub—a modernized, noble Hebrew—at its vanguard, Cahan's fictional New York thus presents readers with an urban frontier of modern, historical progress and ancient religious forms simultaneously. Its actual Jewish community may have been rent by a schism dividing secularized "modern" Jewish men from a persistent core of "backward" religious devotees—bearded, bespectacled, black-clad, praying in small storefront *shuls* across the Lower East Side.[189] But Cahan's story suggests how this reenactment of Jewish rituals also created new environments of memory that transformed the Lower East Side into a temporal crossroads.

The ambiguous conclusion to *The Imported Bridegroom*, marked by Asriel's Zionist emigration, Shaya and Flora Golub's forsaken nuptial intimacy, and Shaya's turn from a unified past toward an uncertain future, allegorizes conditions of Jewish diaspora, leaving these tensions of Jewish time unresolved. This is quite different from the message of US cycloramas that, at this same moment, invited visitors nostalgically to mourn historical Civil War battles that engendered a romance of national reunification and, assimilating past into present, homogenized time. At the May 1886 New York opening of the Battle of Vicksburg Cyclorama, for example, General George A. Sheridan's impassioned address recounted the painting's purpose: "[w]e want those who come after us to be true to the land we saved them, and I know no better way of teaching the children of a nation loyalty than by letting them see, as they come here, the fierce fight their fathers waged for the unity of the Republic."[190] Sheridan infused the popular spectacle with patriotic sentiment for the since-healed nation, even as the speech's timing reminds us that by 1886, anti-immigrant backlash also reached new heights. For many, the United States was under siege again, this time from foreigners.[191] If we read *The Imported Bridegroom* in the context of the nativist nationalism underlying these cycloramas, then Asriel's longing for a homeland resembles the patriotism of many Americans who, ironically, wanted to exclude immigrants like him from the nation. In this light, Cahan's cyclorama effect functions as a challenge to immigrant and nationalist restorative nostalgia simultaneously, illustrating the problem of trying to relocate "authentic Judaism" for the local color writer and the displaced immigrant alike.

If Asriel Stroon represents absence and burgeoning American Zionism, and Flora Stroon represents forgetting and Americanization, Shaya Golub forces us to remember. Shaya's reading group may be the exclusive purview of men, but it gestures toward both the Kantian cosmopolitan ideal, with its millennial utopia of the enlightened, and the messianic one, with its sacred, ever-anticipated "world-to-come."[192] With an open-endedness resolved only by the bounds of Cahan's book itself, the conclusion of *The Imported Bridegroom* also allegorizes the problem of writing modern Jewishness. At a time of historical crisis for both "Old World" and "New World" Jews—the binary itself a nostalgic fiction—the story illustrates the representational challenges modern Jewish life poses to literary realism: the uncertainty of places (Europe, America, Palestine) for rooting Jewish experience, and the need for portable, temporal, Jewish rituals. Just when so many East European Jews sought to redress their rootlessness by immigrating to America, *Die Goldene Medine* ("the Golden Land"), the cyclorama phenomenon flourished, designed above all to transport its guests to a prior time and place in America that preceded their very arrival. Registering this irony, Cahan's text becomes a portable repository of Jewish experience—yes, a future past about which one might be nostalgic—but also an occasion for the devotional, repetitive ritual of reading and rereading that literature demands. It concludes by depicting a *milieu de memoire* centered on collective reading, and enacts the living practice of just such a milieu, a ritual even now mediating past and future, individual and collective experience, adding yet another temporal dimension to American realism.

The scholar-apostate Shaya Golub illustrates for Cahan's readers that one way forward is to mediate the biblical Hebraic past and modern Gentile present by adapting sacred formal rituals of Jewish collective memory to secular content. Cahan may have felt beholden to reproducing Jewish "types" for a Gentile readership, but his fictions also modernize the Hebraic myth and its neat temporal associations with the past. Whereas Shaya's story is one of Jewish religious life turned secular, in Henry James we begin with the secular life—that of the professional literary realist—turned sacred. With James, we plunge into the fictional Gentile world, but also into a highly theorized realism that raises literary production, and the creation of literary "values," to the level of religious ritual. For James, the professional writer forced to sell his wares, materiality is made spiritually valuable, made sacred even, in that most unexpected of commercial locations, the pawnshop. There, materiality and spirituality, commerce and friendship, past and present, are all mediated by none other than the figure of "the Jew."

2

The Curiosity Shop of Time

Henry James, Cosmopolitanism, and "The Jew"

> Souls are mixed with things; things with souls. Lives are
> mingled together, and this is how, among persons and things so
> intermingled, each emerges from their own sphere and mixes
> together. This is precisely what contract and exchange are.
>
> —Marcel Mauss, *The Gift*

IN THE LAST, "MAJOR" phase of his writing career, upon "re-perusal" in 1908 of his famed novel *The Portrait of a Lady* (1881), Henry James composed for it a new preface, part of a last-ditch gesture of market mastery and sovereign expenditure.[1] From 1907 to 1909, he reissued a majority of his *oeuvre* as the *New York Edition*, complete with new prefaces and illustrations, revised, repackaged, and reprinted as a modern grand collector's set. On the heels of the devastating theatrical failure of *Guy Domville* in 1895, the release of the *New York Edition* crowned James's late phase as a realist, his protomodernist style, and promised him a second chance for commercial success. Yet, though James may have produced what Leon Edel called a "literary monument," in terms of sales, it flopped.[2] James could only have been keenly aware of his dual role as artist and aesthetic broker, as a cultural and economic middleman of sorts, perhaps explaining why critical attention in recent decades has focused on his representations of another "minority in the middle," the figure of the Jew.[3]

In his retrospective *Portrait* preface, James conveys how he conceived the figure of Isabel Archer with an elaborate, extended metaphor of petty commerce and value speculation. Conceiving his work this way, he indirectly connects himself with the unlikely, marginal figure of the Jew by employing the same language used to describe the domain of the Jewish Bloomsbury "shopman" of *The Golden Bowl* (1904). More specifically, revising his role as well as his work, he links himself, a writer at odds with the literary market upon which he depends, to the debased figure of the pawnbroker, a stock literary Jewish type:

> The figure [Isabel] has to that extent, as you see, *been* placed—placed in the imagination that detains it, preserves, protects, enjoys it, conscious of its presence in the dusky, crowded, heterogeneous back-shop of the mind very much as a wary dealer in precious odds and ends, competent to make an "advance" on rare objects confided to him, is conscious of the rare little "piece" left in deposit by the reduced, mysterious lady of title or the speculative amateur, and which is already there to disclose its merit afresh as soon as a key shall have clicked in a cupboard-door.
>
> That may be, I recognize, a somewhat superfine analogy for the particular "value" I here speak of, the image of the young feminine nature that I had had for so considerable a time all curiously at my disposal; but it appears to fond memory quite to fit the fact—with the recall, in addition, of my pious desire but to place my treasure right. I quite remind myself thus of the dealer resigned not to "realize," resigned to keeping the precious object locked up indefinitely rather than commit it, at no matter what price, to vulgar hands. For there *are* dealers in these forms and figures and treasures capable of that refinement.[4]

In the "dusky, crowded, heterogeneous back-shop of the mind," James is the reluctant dealer, only the "rare object" of curiosity left "in deposit" is the character, Isabel. Her "figure" has been "placed" in James's imagination, as if by an unknown "reduced" noblewoman or a "speculative amateur." Isabel possesses no inherent value; she is a discovery, a rare find, with a past, whose value thus derives from the misfortune and loss of whomever let her go. James finds himself in an ethical double bind: to sell Isabel for profit would be to exploit that loss, to become a stereotypical pawnbroker. He would prefer not to "realize" her, not to make real, where making real means "commit[ting]" his treasure, at some price, to "vulgar hands." Yet to keep Isabel (or Maggie, Charlotte, or any of his treasured creations) "locked up indefinitely" would be to exact her social death, like that of Claire de Cintré at the conclusion of *The American* (1877). Not to sell Isabel would mean hoarding her value, nullifying it, and pulling her out of time.[5] By the time James reissues his novels for the *New York Edition*, however, his preface suggests the emergence of a fully modern sensibility, according to which art and money, creation and exchange, are fully intertwined. Formal circulation is therefore essential, and James assumes the risk of "realiz[ing]" Isabel's value under the condition that he "place his treasure right." For James the question becomes not whether to sell but rather to whom: by *embracing* the market, James transformed his commodities into the gifts of a true sovereign, to be used, to be changed, to be interpreted, passing to readers an ethical responsibility to receive his treasure, not with "vulgar hands" but "right."

One hallmark of the modern realist novel is its depth of economic logic and expression. For Leon Edel, who argued that James's foray into commercial theater was a mere anomaly, James must have seemed a familiar romantic anticapitalist, or just a snob, who equated publishing with selling (out), the printed word with the dollar, and thus professional authorship with vulgarity.[6] Like Michael Anesko and others, however, I would disagree: James's metaphor of the writer-as-pawnbroker forces us to see not only how James's professional authorship was shaped by what Anesko calls his "friction with the market" but also something far less obvious: that producing fiction is neither a business of buying cheap and selling dear nor of creation *ex nihilo*, once and for all.[7] Rather, it is an ongoing process of value production, just as the ritual exchange, placement, and recontextualization of objects renders them, with all of their *pastness*, socially valuable. As Georg Simmel argued in 1900, objective value is rooted in our subjective desires. Therefore, when we trade objects with others to satisfy those desires, they obtain economic value through exchange.[8] The true heart of economic value is thus relative, dynamic, and temporal, but when standardized it becomes reified in the form of "abstract value," namely, money.[9] Money becomes the highest "expression or symbol" of value when "qualitative determinations" are subordinate to "quantitative ones"; but even so, latent in the reified form of money is the contradiction created between "life's eternal flux and the objective validity and authenticity of the forms through which it proceeds."[10] This "eternal flux," this movement through historical time, is glimpsed in the dynamics of material exchange and contained by exchanged forms themselves. Hence the notion of "goods": "economic exchange creates value," writes Arjun Appadurai, and "value is embodied in commodities that are exchanged."[11]

As we exchange goods, an ongoing process that takes place in time, we become bound together in ways Marcel Mauss attributes to forms of gift exchange within so-called primitive economies. An institution of "total services," gift giving involves several temporal dimensions: for Mauss, it entails the obligation to receive and to reciprocate, a dialectical, open-ended relationship that unfolds in time.[12] As best elaborated in his 1950 study *The Gift*, which Mary Douglas calls "a plank in the platform against utilitarianism," the intermingling of obligation and liberty inherent in noble gift giving also persists as the atavistic moral residue underlying utilitarian thinking.[13] In true dialectical fashion, Mauss sees the gift economy not as overcome by the capitalist economy but rather as constituting its very basis in a way that collapses the "pre" in "precapitalist." For Mauss, consequently, "material and moral life, and exchange, function within [the system of the gift] in a form that is both disinterested and obligatory."[14] Gift giving erodes the romantic distinction between calculation and sacrifice. In James's metaphor of the writer-as-pawnbroker, he, too, reminds us of the residual excesses of noble sacrifice a writer makes in surrendering his goods to his reader, those stories previously given to him, and which can never be fully recuperated for profit. James wants us to recognize his "precious object"—in this case the human "value" his literary character is meant to evoke—as a relic of sorts, a gift whose seemingly untranslatable value, gathered over time, must still be translated, negotiated, and repeatedly exchanged to be recognized as a value in the first place. If, as James suggests, "there are dealers in these forms and figures and treasures capable of that refinement," and he is one of them, he aligns himself, consciously or not, with that other more stereotypical pawn-broker, the Jew.

The relationship between James and the figure of the Jew has been duly noted, part of a shift in James studies over the last several decades that effectively produced a new Henry James.[15] Some critics have read the "Jew" in James as performing a compensatory function, for Ross Posnock, a "poli-tics of non-identity," for Greg Zacharias, "the ideal cosmopolitanism James sought for himself," while Jonathan Freedman has read the "abject" Jew as the symptomatic self-projection of James's insecurity as a "degenerate" art-ist.[16] In these and other renderings, James, the estranged, displaced nativist, remains the literary master, who self-consciously undermines his own mas-tery as a form of "second-order mastery," an arbiter of high cultural taste who is fully engaged in the literary market.[17] In this newly celebrated, radically ambivalent Henry James, contemporary critics get to have it all—high cul-tural capital and transformative political self-consciousness—particularly when it comes to James's attitudes toward the Jew.

Clearly James was ambivalent, but what then? By raising broader ques-tions concerning the production, circulation, and reception of value, we can examine the temporal dimensions of James's portrayals of the Jew that debates about affect and identity neglect to address. If Barbara Herrnstein Smith is correct in asserting that all value is radically contingent, then in James this is nowhere more the case than in the pawnshop, a liminal space where value and time are suspended and negotiated.[18] Placing James, along with two of his recurring creations—the cosmopolitan and the Jew—in a discursive shop of curiosities allows us to see how aesthetic, moral, eco-nomic, and even transcendental value is produced as flawed objects of dif-ferent "pasts" change hands. Such valuable pasts also accrue for people in circulation: Madame Merle, the key cosmopolitan of *The Portrait of a Lady*, claims to "belong to the old, old world," just as the precious, eponymous golden bowl, the Jewish shopman informs Charlotte, has been crafted by "some very fine old worker and by some beautiful old process," like the noble Hebraic myth, a relic of "a lost art."[19]

These complex negotiations of value find their most extended medita-tion in *The Golden Bowl* in the figure of the Jewish Bloomsbury shopman, no longer a Jewish stereotype but an arbiter of value who, like his author, bridges multiple economies and mediates their temporal registers. James's choice of the pawnshop for the locus of the literary in modernity, one that places the key metaphor for the art of the novel in Jewish hands, may itself seem anachronistic. James's pawnbroker is no sentimental figure, however; rather, here he is omniscient (key questions are raised in the pawnshop—of plot, morality, epistemology), he is ethical, and he becomes a noble Hebrew by the novel's end. Neither is he a mere throwback to the biblical past. Rather, this figure mediates and collapses distinct, yet overlapping orders of time (past and future, secular and sacred) structuring the novel's plot. Just when Eastern European Jewish immigration to the United States, amid fervid antisemitism, approached its all-time peak, the old-moneyed Protestant writer revised the common stereotype of the money-worshipping, hoarding "Jew." Simultaneously, James modernizes the "noble Hebrew" of the Hebraic myth, transforming him from exotic "curio" to premodern, noble *kurios*, a dynamic figure who enables the reconciliation, and hence future, of the novel's central married couple and brings the novel's plot to its resolution.

The comparison between James and the Jewish shopman allows us to examine what the two share—cosmopolitanism, authority on taste and value, marginal status—and what they do not—namely, Jewishness. Yet, with the shopman mediating between the "golden bowl" and the novel's protagonists, James endows the merchant Jew with a noble humanistic purpose, making him a seller of value(s) who, like the professional literary writer, cares deeply for his wares and their ultimate placement. The stateless Jew, like the late-nineteenth-century cosmopolitan and expatriated writer, stands at once outside and at the center of the modern industrial state and all its institutional protection, thus registering the antinomies of pre-capitalist ethics and bourgeois morality, of noble generosity and economic rationalism. Having himself migrated from the Old World to the New, from Paris to New York, during the time of this novel's composition, James emerged, as William Spengemann suggests, "neither an American nor a European . . . [a] sojourner in both places, but at home in neither."[20] Being at home both everywhere and nowhere epitomizes the marginal status of the cosmopolitan, as well as the diasporic, nineteenth-century immigrant Jew. Because late-nineteenth-century cosmopolitanism was ideologically bound up with the dispersed status of "international" Jews worldwide, understood in tension with the nationalist politics of emerging Zionism, I set James's late writing against these historical formations. Doing so illustrates how liminal cosmopolitan and Jewish figures in James betray fantasies of essential "value"—commonly taken as an objective quality or static determination of worth—and reveal value to be something mediated, fluid, negotiable, and, most importantly, temporal. In James's work, value, like ethical behavior, bridges past and future by marginal figures who mediate the universal and particular, sacred and profane, realms.[21]

Throughout his work, James produced an array of cosmopolitan characters, most of whom are not explicitly Jewish but share with his Jewish characters signs of the "wandering Jew," albeit with privilege. Set in the context of his meditations on Old- and New-World values dramatized in *The American*, and of cosmopolitan figures in his story "The Pupil" (1891), James's literary figurations of the Jew, particularly in such major phase works as *The Golden Bowl* and *The American Scene* (1907), complicate the affective philosemitic/antisemitic dichotomy that has long characterized critical discussions of Jewishness in James, and that this book aims to reframe.[22] James compares himself to the Jew but not, I argue, in terms of identity. Rather, he links himself to the Jewish pawnbroker through their common function as negotiators of worth and mediators of time, so as to explore the writer's role in the production of value. In spite of its persistent associations with avarice and usury, James's revised figure of the Jewish pawnbroker shows how value is socially negotiated in and through time, and best captures for him the position of the modern cosmopolitan writer. An unlikely pair, but both figures are uprooted, transnational peddlers of sorts, forced to prove the value of their wares. Both occupy the shifting terrains of temporality and value production—positions of power and responsibility—at the nexus of capitalist exchange and the gift economy.

"THE INTENSITY OF THE JEWISH ASPECT": *THE AMERICAN SCENE*

James was hardly immune from the pitfalls of antisemitic representation. From the requisite Jewish merchants, petty shopkeepers, and demonic lovers sprinkled throughout his early novels, short stories, and literary reviews to his extended meditation on the "swarming" Jewish immigrants of New York's Lower East Side in *The American Scene*, James makes charges of patrician racism and nativist antisemitism only too easy for critics to level.[23] Yet simplified claims of vulgar antisemitism disable meaningful literary interpretation, through which we might otherwise gain insight into the challenges that Jewishness poses for realist representation. Whether immigrant, cosmopolitan, or Zionist, the Jew has long been understood as a figure at the nexus of religion, race, and culture, bearing a conflicted relationship with Protestant American national identity. It is hardly a wonder that as Jewish migration to the United States reached its peak at the turn of the twentieth century, literary representations of Jewishness, realist in particular, brought these conflicts to the fore.[24] As scores of East European Jewish refugees poured onto eastern U.S. shores, the Jew emerged on the American literary scene as a function of revived, mutually exclusive metaphors: both philosemitic (the noble, biblical "Hebrew" of the ancient past) and increasingly antisemitic (the threatening, money-worshipping, racialized "Jew" in one's midst). How, then, to resolve this bifurcated vision of Jewishness, this "dual image"?

Jewishness posed significant challenges to realist representation for Jewish and non-Jewish writers alike. As Jewish immigrants became increasingly Americanized—culturally assimilated, economically mobile, secular, white—representing Jewishness realistically required penetrating the surfaces of both racial and religious typologies and moving beyond colorful sketches of outmoded religious ritual. If one rejected the popular image of the hook-nosed, avaricious pawnbroker, one likewise could not typify Jews as anachronistic East Side Talmudists in prayer shawls gesticulating over tomes of inscrutable text. Representing the social and psychological complexity of real, modern Jews demanded the construction of individuated interiority with a clearly identifiable set of Jewish values. James took the challenge and responsibility of artistic realism seriously; he regarded fiction writing, after all, as a "sacred office."[25] If, for James, the sacred value of literature consisted not in its didactic morality but in the successful rendering of "a personal, a direct impression of life" in all its intensity, then James needed to search for viable impressions of Jewishness.[26]

If one key task of *The American Scene* was to find such impressions, James nonetheless reproduced there, as we have seen, the typological aesthetic this book has been tracing. He portrayed the immigrant Jew, on one hand, as the epitome of modern industrial, capitalist culture in the United States: their homes doubling as sweatshop factories, their lives circumscribed by monetary concern, their aspirations to be the kind of American capitalists James might have become had he remained on "The Jolly Corner" rather than expatriating himself to Europe twenty-one years earlier. Upon revisiting New York, he felt displaced, alienated by these new "aliens," dispossessed by crowds of immigrant Jews with "their note of settled possession . . . so that *un*settled possession is what we, on our side, seem reduced to."[27] On the other hand, as we have seen, he also imagined that each individual Jew magically retains the entirety of her or his "race-quality," some unquantifiable, inassimilable, portable otherness, so that each retains, like a "splinter" or "fine glass particle," his or her individual share of the whole hard glitter of Israel" (100). In Beverly Haviland's view, such remarks exemplify James's uncomplicated, yet inexplicable celebration of the Jew's successful continuity with the past.[28] As the previous chapter has shown, however, such continuity with the past exists not inherently, or "racially," as James's language suggests, but only through practice, through cyclical ritual. What we are seeing, then, is another example of the Hebraic myth, such that for James, each individual Jew becomes synechdochic for the whole "race" and bears the weight of a retrograde biblical history.

James was astonished by the "intensity of the Jewish aspect" in New York's Lower East Side of 1904, wondering what "makes the individual Jew more of a *concentrated person*, savingly possessed of everything that is in him, than any other human, noted at random."[29] He was keenly aware that the immigrants' Jewishness—their distinguishing element—also posed the highest challenge to literary representation. Three decades earlier, James had staged a discussion among three hypothetical readers about the most elaborate realist literary portrait of a Jew to date, George Eliot's *Daniel Deronda* (1876). In his essay "Daniel Deronda" (1876), Constantius, the moderate reader, claims, "All the Jewish part is at bottom cold. . . . It is admirably studied, it is imagined, it is understood, but it is not embodied."[30] Constantius voices the realist challenge to "embody" the Jew without reinscribing what Sander Gilman calls the Jewish Body—without reducing him, as Pulcheria does, to the "solemn, sapient young man" with the awful Jewish nose.[31] To "embody" the "Jewish part" meant to bring to life and to give form to something at once material and immaterial, a "value" or quality identifiable neither by birthplace nor by biology alone. In "The Art of Fiction" (1884), James insisted that "the novelist must write from his experience," which is "never limited . . . never complete," never fixed once and for all; rather, "it is an immense sensibility . . . a kind of huge spider-web of the finest silken threads suspended in the chamber of the conscious-ness," built upon collected impressions and "the power to guess the unseen from the seen."[32] Yet when he, himself, faced the "portent" of "too many" Jews, James clearly had difficulty countering Eliot's idealization without resorting to hardened, inherited types.[33] In his own attempt to "guess the unseen from the seen," then, to articulate the "Jewish part"—the stuff that Hutchins Hapgood called "the Spirit of the Ghetto"—James turned to the language of typology, of Hebraic mythology, in which the Lower East side became, however ironically, "the new Jerusalem on earth."[34] If the immi-grant Jews—metonymic embodiments of the whole of ancient Israel from the biblical era to now—had, in a collapse of historical time, at last found a resting place in New York, then James, upon his return to a home no lon-ger familiar, became a metaphorical "wandering Jew" in "foreign" territory, unable to enter "the Promised Land."

Within and among a constellation of inherited stereotypes, Jewish val-ues were often associated on one side with Levitical severity, rational jus-tice, intellectual debate, yet biblical nobility (Arnoldian Hebraism) and on the other side with capitalism, calculation, and usury (modern antisem-itism).[35] Jacob Riis, as we have seen, could not reconcile the dual image of the petty pushcart merchants and tenement sweatshop laborers crowding Hester Street and the bearded rabbis chanting in their solemn black hats and prayer shawls, like patriarchs resurrected from the biblical era. At both extremes—sacred and secular—supposed "Jewish" values revealed the best and worst of postbellum American values, whether the "spirit of capital-ism" that Max Weber identified with the industrious Protestant ethic, or the "incredible rottenness" of Mark Twain's eponymous Gilded Age.[36] To articulate his impression of Jewishness as a value in itself, then, James had to negotiate these paradoxical stereotypes of Jewish values: their apparent worship of both an "Old Testament" God and money at once.

For their supposed love of commerce, Jews were unfairly scapegoated, to be sure—for what realist writer in this period could escape the exigencies of money? James once said of Honoré de Balzac, the great French realist, "the general money question so loads him up and weighs him down that he moves through the human comedy, from beginning to end, very much in the fashion of a camel, the ship of the desert, surmounted with a cargo. . . . [H]is universe goes on expressing itself for him, to its furthest reaches, on its finest sides, in the terms of the market."[37] In 1893, William Dean Howells concluded the "man of letters" to be a terrible "man of business," but James insists that when we read Balzac, we "feel ourselves thinking of him as a man of business doubled with an artist."[38] The realist novel is considered the literary form most closely linked to economic life.[39] So how does one produce realist articulations of Jewishness, and of Jewish life as a constellation of social and economic conditions, without scapegoating Jews and reinforcing the stereotypical link between Jews and money? Conversely, how does one represent the transcendent value of religious Jewishness without reifying the Jew as atavistic and inassimilable, or lapsing into repetition of an idealized Hebraic myth of the ancient past, from which remain only quaint Talmudists, picturesque creatures, and nostalgic relics to be fetishized?

Without disregarding James's language of race, I still insist we rethink James's insistence on Jewish "race-quality" as a label neither altogether pejorative nor altogether about race as it is now understood.[40] Although Jonathan Freedman finds James's "note" of "race essentialism" to be "ominous," it also seems that James uses the term "race-quality" when and wherever anxieties about essential value arise and distinctions threaten to be leveled.[41] James clearly employs a contemporary language of race essentialism, but essential value also derives for James from something like "age," the direct (or even associated) history and experience of a person or thing, its "Old World" quality. As an equally salient "value," then, the age of a thing—its temporal quality—is a mark of distinction and worth. The Jew and the cosmopolitan in James are racialized but also share the status of "worldliness," not in the sense of being *of the world*, signifying base materialism, but in the sense of having *been in the world*, that is, over time, implying experiential authenticity, wisdom, maturity, agedness, and, hence, a rare value.

In the Protestant New World, the immigrant Jew was thought to provide access to this "Old World" European value and the even older, biblical value of "the Chosen." Though immigrant Jews as a group offended James's genteel sensibilities, the "individual Jew" for him was "more of a concentrated person," each carrying the weight of his entire race.[42] In an increasingly democratized, commercialized, standardized, colorless, and formless world, he still expected the Jew, though modern merchant, to bear the weight of historical and religious authenticity. Like so many other nineteenth-century American writers, James singles out "The Jew" precisely as the biblical Hebraic bearer of the Ancient past—the recovered authentic kernel of American Protestantism, the return of its typologically repressed. Reminiscent of George Eliot's two versions of Ezra Cohen—the one a shiny, fattened shopkeeper, the other whose noble mission of Jewish redemption is fated to be carried out by Daniel Deronda—James contrasts the refined Bloomsbury shopman with Gutterman-Seuss, the "smart and shining" head of his "tribe," comprised of "fat ear-ringed aunts" and "glossy cockneyfied, familiar uncles."[43] "The Jew" for James is thus both in and out of time, *the* figure of the market, presumed to convert all nonreified values into the least common economic denominator and to transform all values into profit-yielding opportunities. Yet, simultaneously, he embodies the vestigial value of noble, "old" authentic culture that somehow rises above the moral and temporal exigencies of the market.

If, for James, Jewish immigrants lacking a nation or otherwise significant attachment to place become bearers of time, in this way they illuminate what Daniel and Jonathan Boyarin consider the cultural and political advantages of Jewish diasporic culture. "Diaspora," they assert, disrupts categories of identity founded on either genealogy or geography, and may therefore be "the most important contribution that Judaism has to make to the world."[44] The model of diaspora enables imagining collective identity without territorial nationhood, and thus realizes the Pauline ideal that permits a "stubborn hanging-on to ethnic, cultural specificity but in a context of deeply felt and embraced human solidarity."[45] James recognized the potential for

Jews to maintain their distinctive culture amid international geographic change, like himself and his many globetrotting characters. As he struggled in his late literary works to articulate the dialectical potential and pitfalls of multiple cultural and religious affiliations, he came into curious contact with those "other Others," yet lacked the term "diaspora" with which to name their compelling condition.[46] Given the Boyarins' formulation, however, we see how the Jew in James performs the ethical role of bridging the purported divide not just between precapitalist ethics and bourgeois morality but between sacred and secular "nations," as well as perceived links among past, present, and future.

Put simply, if we read James's representations of Jews and Jewishness as expressions of his attitude toward or feeling about Jewish people—which the categories "antisemitic" and "philosemitic" suggest—then we risk reinforcing the stereotypes these categories organize. If we instead read these complex images as signs of an ongoing struggle to give aesthetic form to changing, socially contingent values and to give new value to changing, socially constructed forms, we see how cosmopolitan circulation and marginal social status make ethical evaluation possible. Following the model of James's Bloomsbury shopman and his golden bowl of a "lost art" and indeterminate value, we stand to profit if we bring these literary forms to the fore, uncongeal them, so to speak, and reveal the complex convergence of religious, aesthetic, and economic values of which they are composed. If the Bloomsbury shopman is a keeper of "old" values, he shares this quality of access to a valuable past, to what is well worn over time, with such Jamesian cosmopolitan figures as Madame Merle and, in *The Golden Bowl*, Charlotte Stant and Prince Amerigo. It is therefore helpful to clarify how understandings of cosmopolitanism have changed since James's day.

"ULTRAMOREEN": COSMOPOLITANISM AND "THE PUPIL"

In recent reconsiderations of abstract universalism, "cosmopolitanism" has been redefined to describe transnational experiences, affiliations, and cultural formations in the wake of global capitalism. This "new cosmopolitanism," according to Amanda Anderson, is characterized by a "cultivated detachment from restrictive forms of identity" that allows for "reflective distance" from the parochialisms of extreme alliances to nation, race, and ethnos.[47] In other words, contemporary scholars have managed to rescue "cosmopolitanism" from its privileged elitism—perhaps best associated with the likes of Henry James and his fictional heiresses abroad—while yet retaining the political potential of its Kantian utopianism for such projects as postcolonial cultural criticism, cultural anthropology, or even the political viability of academic intellectualism.[48] The cosmopolitans of today are no longer the privileged expatriates of the leisured class. Instead, they are either secular critics struggling against institutional constraints, or those forced out of their homes: refugees, people of the diaspora, migrants, and exiles.

Although it began as an Enlightenment ideal, in the late nineteenth century, "cosmopolitanism" was equally complicated, holding strong associations with the privileged, leisure class and stateless Jews alike. According to Kant, the cosmopolitan ideal involved "the achievement of a universal civic society which administers law among men," a society that, given competing desires and inevitable conflict, would "maintain the perfect balance between freedom and limitation" to ensure the greater good for all.[49] Kant's notion of an international moral utopia predicated on natural human discord, or "unsociableness," however, was first used in English as an adjective ("cosmopolitan") to describe conditions of political economy. John Stuart Mill wrote in 1848, "capital is becoming more and more cosmopolitan," thus linking cosmopolitanism to capitalism and to international finance, which would eventually be (negatively) associated with such famous international, Jewish banking families as the Rothschilds, and, to a lesser extent, the Seligmans.[50]

At the turn of the century, cosmopolitanism was widely debated in and about Jewish circles, too, primarily in response to urgent questions of nationalism and national identity. In contrast with an emerging Zionism, cosmopolitanism became an alternative ideal for many secular Jewish thinkers of the *Haskalah*, the nineteenth-century Jewish romantic enlightenment. The liberal, largely Western and Central European *maskilim* tended to embrace a nationalist cosmopolitanism: secular Jews belonged first and foremost to their home nations and national cultures. These *maskilim* were considered "assimilated Jews" by more Orthodox, East European, traditionalist Jews, who in turn understood themselves as a separate Jewish people united by religion. For their part, the *maskilim* (like writers Sholem Aleichem and Mendele Moykher-Sforim, discussed earlier) condemned their Orthodox coreligionists as self-ghettoizing and as jeopardizing Jewish political and economic emancipation.

Malachi Haim Hacohen points out that with the rise of late-nineteenth-century "ethnonationalism" in Western and Central Europe—which eventually developed into full-blown theories of race-nations—cosmopolitan nationalism reached a crisis.[51] So long as German nationality, for example, was defined culturally, Jews could have access to it; however, once German-ness became defined racially, Jews were barred from national membership. By the century's end, some Jews followed Theodore Herzl's lead and became political Zionists, declaring Jews not just coreligionists but an exiled political "nation" in need of a homeland. Whereas "diaspora-nationalists" wanted Jewish cultural autonomy within European society, Zionists wanted their own national territory, Palestine (119–20). Other Jewish intellectuals continued to fight for a utopian cosmopolitanism: they renounced both German and Jewish identity, nationalism and religious particularism, in favor of a universal humanism, an "Open Society." Although the choice to give up "tribal religion to join humanity" was common, many Jewish intellectuals really just confused cosmopolitanism with assimilation (146).

David Hollinger considers immigrant Jews in America to have been ethnically suited to achieve the Kantian cosmopolitan ideal as they tried to assimilate, yet maintain their cultural heritage, Yiddish language and customs, and an intellectual tradition that encompassed the coexistence of these universal and particular ways of life. Yet, like Hacohen, Hollinger argues that this understanding of cosmopolitanism tended to become confused with notions of "assimilation" (of immigrants) and "alienation" (of expatriates), both terms that obscure the fundamental antiparochialism of cosmopolitanism.[52] To late-nineteenth-century nativists and nationalists alike, the cosmopolitan posed a grave threat to both national identity and national values. Lacking a nation, so-called cosmopolitan Jews were feared worldwide as infiltrators, impostors, economic vampires, and international conspirators, culminating with the 1905 publication in Russia, throughout Europe, and in the United States of the insidious fabrication *The Protocols of the Elders of Zion*.[53]

In late-nineteenth-century America, proponents of "assimilation" were focused less on the privileged cosmopolitans than on the impoverished immigrants flooding Ellis Island and elsewhere; yet both groups were held to the same ideological standards of citizenship. The American controversy over national identity and the notion of Americanness dated back to J. Hecter St. John de Crèvecoeur's fundamental question, "What is an American?"[54] Echoing Crèvecoeur's agrarian ideal, Theodore Roosevelt bemoaned the cosmopolitan as one who becomes "Europeanized," who "loses his love for his native land," becomes "overcivilized, oversensitive, overrefined," and therefore "ceases being an American, and becomes nothing."[55] Far worse than the immigrant struggling to become part of the New World was the American citizen who *chose* to go back to the Old. Whereas James portrayed the cosmopolitan as a refined "citizen of the world," a person of culture and leisure like himself and so many of his beloved protagonists, he also knew that globe-trotters at home everywhere might find themselves at home nowhere, that being cosmopolitan risked charges of being "un-American." In James's 1898 essay "Democracy and Theodore Roosevelt," he rebuked Roosevelt's nationalist claims:

> Mr. Roosevelt makes very free with the "American" name, but it is after all not a symbol revealed once for all in some book of Mormon dug up under a tree. Just as it is not criticism that makes critics, but critics who make criticism, so the national type is the result, not of what we take from it, but of what we give to it, not of our impoverishment, but of our enrichment of it. We are all making it, in truth, as hard as we can, and few of us will subscribe to any invitation to forego the privilege. . . .[56]

A cosmopolitan abroad himself, James had apparently been "invited to forego the privilege" of "making" the "'American' name," and, as late as 1898, he rejected that invitation. James resisted the notion that, as an American, the cosmopolitan was "nothing"; quite to the contrary, the cosmopolitan could make valuable contributions to an Americanness he saw as dynamic and inclusive. James's choice to publish "The Figure in the Carpet" in the newly founded journal *Cosmopolis* (1896) and to create so many cosmopolitan protagonists in his late work suggests he was exploring forms of cosmopolitanism that reached beyond the privileged classes. This culminates in his late novel, *The Golden Bowl*, where he places cosmopolitan figures like Charlotte Stant and Prince Amerigo in connection with the Jewish Bloomsbury shopman, all characterized by their social marginality; their transportability and adaptability; their international or multiregional allegiance; their polyglot linguistic capabilities; and, above all, their aesthetic taste, conversation, and social grace. I thus use the term "cosmopolitan" to register this tension between the "citizen of the world" and the "citizen of nowhere," as James did, but also as it was understood historically, carrying associations with immigrant, diasporic Jews.

Cosmopolitanism in James is typically associated with the privilege of a Lambert Strether or James himself, yet "homelessness" and displacement are common to both the "restored absentee" and the "wandering" immigrant Jew. Both "types" unmistakably transcend national boundaries, though a key distinction between them remains their degree of financial comfort, and whether such wandering is the result of persecution or self-imposed exile, a running to or a running from. The problem for interpretation is when the one is disguised as the other, when necessary flight, smacking of desperation, is masked as disinterested leisure. James dramatized the struggle over this distinction in his short story "The Pupil" (1891), in which the protagonist, a tutor named Pemberton, is hired by an American family living in Europe to tutor their physically frail but precocious child progeny, Morgan Moreen. The central drama of the tale revolves around how Morgan's family essentially manipulates Pemberton to tutor Morgan for free, by virtue of his growing affection for the boy and their convenient neglect in paying him. Whenever Pemberton manages to broach the awkward subject of salary, Mrs. Moreen, with her "fat, jeweled hand" and "intermittent" elegance, insists that he dwells too much on minor details.[57] Yet Pemberton is virtually broke, and the Moreens' source of family income—which will finance his—is obscure, unreliable, and finally runs dry. Little Morgan, keenly aware at his young age of his parents' shabby pretensions to bourgeois respectability, lives in constant shame and romantically dreams of Pemberton taking him away. When that opportunity finally arrives, however, Morgan's weak heart cannot stand the shock and he suddenly dies, leaving his parents bereft and blaming Pemberton for exciting him so, although his father is said to take "his bereavement like a man of the world" (460). What does it mean here to be a "man of the world"?

Pemberton first deems the Moreens "cosmopolite," an idea that later "seemed feeble and colourless enough—confessedly, helplessly provisional" (415). Sent to live with them first in Nice, then in Florence, and eventually in Paris, Pemberton remarks on his difficulty deciphering the source of the Moreens' "queerness": the "whole mystic volume in which the boy had been bound demanded some practice in translation."[58] The "queerness" of the Moreens may have something to do with a kind of crypto-Jewishness. Their strange quality of "otherness," an unnamable difference related to their language, their thrift, and their elusive cosmopolitan status, makes them "queer," just as the Jews at Ellis Island and in the Lower East Side struck James as "phantasmagoric" and uncanny.[59] The family is figured as not only a multilingual text but an untranslatable one at that, a "mystic volume," like the Talmud or the Kabbalah. They *appear* cultured, but betray signs of first-rate imitation, in Pemberton's recollections, more like a "band of gypsies [*sic*]" (415):

> Their sociable strangeness was an intimation of that— their chatter of tongues, their gaiety and good humour, their infinite dawdling . . . their French, their Italian and, in the spiced fluency, their cold, tough slices of American. They lived on macaroni and coffee (they had these articles prepared in perfection), but they knew recipes for a hundred other dishes. They overflowed with music and song, were always humming and catching each other up, and had a kind of professional acquaintance with continental cities. They talked of "good places" as if they had been strolling players. They had at Nice a villa, a carriage, a piano and a banjo, and they went to official parties. They were a perfect calendar of the "days" of their friends. . . . Their romantic initiations gave their new inmate at first an almost dazzling sense of culture. . . . They could imitate Venetian and sing

Neapolitan, and when they wanted to say something very particular they communicated with each other in an ingenious dialect of their own. . . . (415–16)

From this rich passage, many "cosmopolitan" characteristics emerge: multilingualism *and* a metropolitan sense of culture and society, of who's who and where's where. One cannot, however, overlook Pemberton's suspicion of their "professional acquaintance of continental cities"; their seeming calculation, even routinization, of such knowledge betrays the economic grasping beneath such signs of purportedly bourgeois leisure. The Moreens successfully imitate numerous national and cultural practices, but seem merely a conglomeration of these imitations, adding up to no one complete identity in particular: Mrs. Moreen's "parts didn't always match" (414). With "an *almost* dazzling sense of culture," then, the Moreens are best understood as mimics, as *inauthentic cosmopolitans.*

Pemberton's revised portrait confirms his initial suspicions: "The Moreens were adventurers not merely because they didn't pay their debts, nor because they lived on society, but because their whole view of life, dim and confused and instinctive, like that of clever colour-blind animals, was speculative and rapacious and mean. Oh! They were 'respectable,' and that only made them more *immondes*" (426). The "law of their being," he goes on, was that they were "adventurers because they were abject snobs" (426). The Moreens' false respectability makes them not *mondains*—that is, *of the world or worldly*—but "*immondes*," filthy, low, nasty, and vulgar, literally *out of this world*. Only by defining himself against these "abject snobs" can Pemberton distinguish himself as the "aesthete," the moral social critic James and his "cosmopolitan" ilk represent. Even precocious Morgan, their own son, knows not what to make of his parents:

> "I don't know what they live on, or how they live, or *why* they live! What have they got and how did they get it? Are they rich, are they poor, or have they a *modeste aisance?* Why are they always chiveying about—living one year like ambassadors and the next like paupers? Who are they, any way, and what are they? I've thought of all that—I've thought

of a lot of things. They're so beastly worldly. That's what I hate most—oh, I've *seen* it! All they care about is to make an appearance and to pass for something or other. What do they want to pass for? What *do* they, Mr. Pemberton?" (438)

Morgan's problem with his parents is their hopeless social climbing, their pretense, and their lack of stable character. At once "ambassadors" and "paupers," two extremes thought to meet in the immigrant Jew, the Moreens seem to lack authenticity, or essential value, because neither their actions nor their "law of being" exists for its own sake. Rather, all seems calculated toward some other end: social acceptance, prestige, what Morgan describes as "that fifth-rate social ideal, the fixed idea of making smart acquaintances and getting into the *monde chic*" (442). For Morgan, to be "worldly" like his parents is to be *inauthentic*, "beastly," and materialistic. It is to falsely represent oneself to the world, to violate the moral dimension of what Erving Goffman calls the "presentation of self in everyday life."[60] In James's story, then, to be "worldly" is to try to *pass off* a certain class status. As James thus works to separate the Madame Merles from the Moreens, the "taste of freedom" from the "taste of necessity," in Pierre Bourdieu's terms, we see the anxiety of class consciousness and eroding social distinction sneak in through the back door of individual moral judgments of taste.[61]

One thing does, however, set the Moreens apart from the comforting and familiar categories of race and national identity: their unique, secret, "ingenious dialect." Morgan calls it "the family language—Ultramoreen."[62] Whereas most languages reflect a distinct *national* membership, this secret language, later called the "family Volapuk" (449), is clan-based and thus accessible only by blood. It marks, on the one hand, a sphere of knowledge to which Pemberton will never gain access, and, on the other, the Moreens' absolute otherness, preventing them from fully "passing" in high society. This "migratory tribe," "a houseful of Bohemians who wanted tremendously to be Philistines," can only aspire to that middle-class status that Matthew Arnold disparaged as marked by "fanaticism, business and money-making."[63] Granted, the Moreens are neither named Jewish nor is their particular dialect necessarily Yiddish; however, the narrator (indicating Morgan's perspective) explicitly compares them to Jews, calling them "good-natured, yes—good-natured as Jews in the doors of clothing-shops! But was that the model one wanted one's family to follow?"[64] The narrator goes on:

> Morgan had dim memories of an old grandfather, the maternal, in New York, whom he had been taken across the ocean to see, at the age of five: a gentleman with a high neckcloth and a good deal of pronunciation, who wore a dress-coat in the morning, which made one wonder what he wore in the evening, and had, or was supposed to have, "property" and something to do with Bible Society. It couldn't have been but that *he* was a good type. (442)

This family has apparently fallen from grace. Their "migratory" status, combined with a tendency to assimilate various languages, yet to maintain one "family language" for particular ideas, makes them comparable to popular views of Yiddish-speaking immigrant Jews in multiple ways, at best clannish and struggling to achieve middle-class respectability, at worst conspiratorial, instrumental, or just plain vulgar. If the Moreens are like partly assimilated Jews, descendants of Ellis Island immigrants, pious and somewhat successful economically, what makes them less "good types"—"type" being a particular concern for the realist writer—is their having abandoned an authentic "type," their having become more "worldly" in appearance, yet all the while maintaining tribal allegiance. What ultimately separates Morgan out from his family is his ability to make this distinction at all: to make the final ethical leap, he distinguishes himself through his awareness of their lack of consistent form, their cultural malleability, and thereby re-forms himself by *conforming* to more stable structures of aesthetic taste and disinterested judgment. By denouncing his family and renouncing clan membership, through this sacrifice he becomes an "authentic" cosmopolitan, a Bourdieuvian "cultural noble," a *mondain*, or true citizen of the world.

Morgan cannot, however, ultimately sustain this status. He dies a "pale, lean, acute, undeveloped little cosmopolite" who might have been thought of at school "rather a polyglot beast," finally too frail to escape the clutches of his clan (418–19). If James managed to punish the Moreen family for their worldly attempts to "pass" as genteel people with taste by taking their precious son's life, it is as if James's imaginary repressed return with a vengeance in Central Park fourteen years later to haunt him, as recorded in *The American Scene*, with their incessant multilingual chatter. We might recall the "polyglot Hebraic crowd of pedestrians" James encounters in Central Park, who have "none but the mildest action on the nerves," if only because their voices compete with the "condensed geographical range, the number of kinds of scenery" of the New York summer in bloom.[65] The "hordes" of Jewish immigrants at Ellis Island produce a similar effect on James to that the Moreens produce on Pemberton. Upon a first encounter with the "inconceivable alien," James insists one feels one has witnessed "an apparition . . . a ghost in his supposedly safe old house" (83). Pemberton likewise reflects that "after a considerable interval, there is something phantasmagoric, like a prismatic reflection or a serial novel, in Pemberton's memory of the queerness of the Moreens," the "queerest thing about them" being "their success."[66] Unable to explain either the "queerness" of the Moreens, their success won through self-presentation, or their partial assimilation masked as cosmopolitanism, James resorts to the phantasmagoric. Whereas in *The American Scene* the haunting was the return of the typological past, here this "phantasmagoria" results from the encounter with one's inauthentic double, a foreign replica of a familiar self whose uncanny menace derives from its success—its potential, as your shadow, to *replace* you altogether.[67] The haunting underside of a cosmopolitan world, in which manners and "things" substitute for more traditional markers of race, class, and nationality, is that such a world is open to anyone who can acquire them.

OLD MONEY, NEW MONEY: A CRISIS IN VALUE IN *THE AMERICAN*

Although James's concerns about value, authenticity, and evaluation are revealed throughout his work, before examining in detail the particular case of the noble Jewish "type"—the Bloomsbury shopkeeper in *The Golden Bowl*—it is helpful to map out James's changing view of American cultural value and value production, already undergoing a crisis to which the immense influx of Jewish immigrants only contributed. By his major phase, the mature realist depicts an aesthetic (as well as social and sacred) realm fully interpenetrated by economic logic and language. Yet, if in his later novel James employs Jewishness to reconcile the value of the "old" with that of the "new," the timeless and the timely, past and future, in his early novel *The American* (1871) he distinguishes the realms of eternal art and finance absolutely. He does this with the novel's protagonist, Christopher Newman, who, though only ten years younger than Adam Verver, the antagonist of James's last published novel, *The Golden Bowl*, represents an earlier moment in James's thinking about value. Newman, thirty-six years old, Wall Street millionaire, has just arrived in one of Europe's great cultural capitals, Paris, while Verver, forty-seven, American billionaire, has lived in Paris, and now London, for decades. Both entrepreneurs, though in different life stages, have a distinct relationship to art, to time, and its value. They both have the financial capacity to explore the world as well as to invent and reinvent it, inherently determining what is valuable in and for it. This position of great power is not unlike that of the author, but for James such power entails great ethical responsibility. Newman and Verver, created as they are at opposite ends of James's career, reside at opposite ends of the spectrum of value production in James. Both figures embody the crucial intersection of aesthetic evaluation on one side and the capitalist cash nexus on the other, a liminal point of conflicting moral values that, as we will see in the next chapter, was frequently associated with successful Jews in banking and finance.

The question of moral responsibility emerges logically from Newman's flaws: his "sole aim in life had been to make money," but having secured his winnings, he doesn't quite know what "to do with them."[68] Upon arrival in Paris, a fledgling cosmopolitan, Newman confronts Old World culture with New Money naiveté. A novice of a collector "rather baffled on the aesthetic question," he settles upon purchasing not artistic originals but copies; after obtaining his first one, he suddenly "became conscious of the germ of the mania of the 'collector'" (45). Adam Verver, by contrast, a true "connoisseur," is known far and wide for his expertise as an art collector. A modern-day Alexander the Great, Verver has plundered the corners of the world for spoils, eventually to be preserved in his own museum, American City, a monument to the religion of eternal "perfection at any price."[69]

Such pursuits, however, are not *just* about art. Like Verver, Newman seeks a wife, "the best article in the market."[70] Yet at James's hand, Newman cannot acquire the "beautiful" woman, Claire de Cintré, if he is to acquire a sense of the "beautiful." To achieve the Arnoldian ideal, he must first shed his Philistine values. From his commercial *interest*, in other words, he must learn to be *disinterested*.[71] To preserve his "good nature," Newman's financial prowess is thwarted; to preserve a sense of value beyond money, to learn both aesthetic and ethical human value, the capitalist is forced into a conversion. Verver, however, is exceedingly cultured yet willingly collects people. By that novel's end, he has successfully acquired what he sees as two valuable "*morceaux de musée*": Prince Amerigo, a husband for his daughter Maggie, valued like an "old embossed coin, of a purity of gold no longer used"; and Charlotte Verver, a wife for himself.[72] Through Newman we learn that human value, like aesthetic value, is timeless and irreducible to the dollar; the ethos of the novel, and the novelist, is set against that of the capitalist. Through Verver, by contrast, we learn that in time, everything, indeed everyone, has their price; the realist novelist by this point in his career has confronted and embraced a modern crisis in value.

Christopher Newman's story is a kind of *bildungsroman*, in that culture and education is certainly what he seeks. But, James asks, will aesthetic education inevitably engender the expected fruits of spiritual and ethical improvement, needed to counteract the decadent "commercial spirit" that the American "new man" epitomizes? Martha Banta has aptly summed up Newman as "not the man of the past who possesses history—that is, the manners and memories out of which culture is made." This American is, in her words, "the modern man with *culture* quite left out."[73] What Newman lacks—a sense of history, of value for the past for its own sake—Adam Verver possesses; Verver is the modern man with *culture quite put back in*. This begs the question: if Newman is a nascent American man of culture and Verver is a cultured Christopher Newman, what, then, is the value of "being cultured" in James?

In Newman, we first meet a tourist, complete with Baedeker in hand. Yet he is exceptionally self-possessed, "reclining at his ease on the great circular divan" at the center of the Salon Carré in the Museum of the Louvre.[74]

Sitting literally in the middle of one of the world's finest collections of original artistic masterpieces, this man of youthful "vigor" is completely at ease, as if not in public but his own living room, "his head thrown back and his legs outstretched," resting after a long day of cultural consumption (33). Newman is a naturally "muscular Christian," a "powerful specimen of an American"; but, our narrator also wants us to know, he is bereft of cultural faculties. After just one day spent in the Louvre, he suffers from "an aesthetic headache" (33). Before his European departure, Newman began to undergo what is depicted as a conversion, one, we might say, of value. Back in New York City, sitting in an "immortal, historical hack" and contemplating a "very mean trick" on a fellow Wall Street broker to avoid the loss of $60,000, a mystical epiphany comes upon him with a snap of the fingers "like *that*" (56). Newman there renounces his "commercial spirit" in search of salvation. Henceforth he will try to be a man of leisure, of artistic appreciation, in short, of noninstrumental value. He suddenly "seemed to feel a new man inside [his] old skin, and [he] longed for a new world" (57). Undoing the East European Jewish immigrant trajectory, in a kind of "reverse immigrant narrative," as Donald Weber argues, Old World Paris promises to be Newman's place of rebirth and redemption.[75]

Though seemingly innocent, however, Newman poses a threat to the world of art. Newman's plan, he claims, is "to rest awhile, to forget the confounded [pile of money I have made], to look about me, to see the world, to have a good time, to improve my mind, and, if the fancy takes me, to marry a wife."[76] In the Salon Carré of the Louvre, however, Newman observes "innumerable young women" devoting themselves to "the propagation of masterpieces," but the narrator confesses, "if the truth must be told, he had often admired the copy much more than the original" (34). Here is a man who not only intends to shop in a museum but, worse, who can afford any original and yet prefers copies. Indeed, when Tom Tristram asks him if he's sure that the paintings on the wall are, in fact, originals, Newman cries, "I hope so . . . I don't want a copy of a copy" (48). Comedy aside, Newman's aesthetic ignorance is not perfectly benign, for the power of his money, like a "huge democratic broom," threatens to sweep away all such distinctions.[77] As Carolyn Porter puts it, "a copy that imitates the original so successfully as to displace it on the market threatens to dilute its value as the original. If the original is to retain its inherent primary value, the distinction between it and all copies must be preserved."[78] *The American* thus poses the problem: How will the sanctity of Old World European originals remain intact if New World American money begins to dissolve the difference between original and copy? If both things and people can be purchased, the fate of all historical distinctions and determinations of value lies in the hands of the purchaser: the new man. What will *be* this new man's standard of evaluation?

From one perspective, buying and selling things amounts to killing their vital essence, as Simmel would see it, to destroying their Benjaminian aura. Newman certainly has the power and wealth to reduce all values to the quantitative. In *The American*, then, James presents us with two mutually exclusive realms of value, in the form of Newman's two potential marital choices. The commercial and the aesthetic are embodied, respectively, in the inauthentic "*franche coquette*" Noemie Nioche and the authentic French noblewoman Claire de Cintré.[79] In Georges Bataille's terms, Newman learns the difference between the "restricted economy," characterized by profit-seeking, calculation, and recuperation of surplus value, and the "general economy," in which sovereignty is gained through disinterestedness, waste, sacrifice, or expenditure without expectation of return.[80] Yet the cost of forcing these two realms into exclusivity results for James in a highly problematic outcome. Newman's ultimate decision to renounce both Claire and his plans to avenge her family preserves his "good nature." He emerges a moral aristocrat, but the price to pay for moral sovereignty is much more than $60,000. It is Claire's social death: in the novel's conclusion, she is shut up for life in a French convent, out of circulation permanently. Her "value" becomes not just reified but mortified in this metaphorical tomb.

Newman's standard for evaluating Claire is a carefully cultivated one for which Mrs. Tristram prepares him: "[Claire] is not a beauty, but she is beautiful, two very different things. A beauty has no faults in her face; the face of a beautiful woman may have faults that only deepen its charm. . . . She is *perfect!* I won't say more than that."[81] Like the cracked golden bowl, as we will see, whose flaw is it supreme virtue, Claire's perfection lies in her imperfection. As Newman reflects upon Mrs. Tristram's words, he comes to appreciate Claire's unique beauty in a mediated way, a "kind of beauty you must be intellectual to understand" (76). Her ultimate retreat into the convent may enhance the sacred aura around Claire as a scarce commodity. Yet only when she is extracted from the economy, made altogether unsellable, and removed from time can Newman understand her mother's attempt to exploit her for profit as an extreme moral affront. Newman must learn the limits of exchange value in order to grasp that aesthetic value, like moral value, to use Porter's phrase, is "designated by the sign 'not for sale.'"[82]

In this zero-sum game, Newman's sense of eternal, noneconomic value is won only at the cost of Claire's freedom. As William Spengemann suggests, the novel "cannot admit what it discovers," that if Newman took revenge on the Bellegardes, "there would be no moral forms at all, neither Old World traditions nor New World conscience, just selfish expediency on one side of the Atlantic and rapacious appetite on the other."[83] Just as Simon Rosedale's wealth could save Lily Bart in *The House of Mirth*, if Wharton would marry her to a "Jew," as we will see in chapter 3, Newman's money could, in other words, rescue Claire's "cultural value," but, for James, that would amount to conceding all value determinations to that of the dollar. In order simultaneously to preserve the theme of Newman's superior conscience and the possibility of some eternal value putatively beyond time, beyond exchange, and therefore beyond the cash nexus, James distorts the realist novel, creating what he himself considered to be an untrue and therefore inartistic ending, what Porter has called an "imperfectly executed Romance."[84] James had to produce an essentially unrealistic novel, then, in order to maintain an aesthetic realm bordering on the timeless and utopian. Newman is on his way to becoming a true cosmopolitan, if only because he risks abandoning his comfortable status as a "good fellow," as a comfortably wealthy American, and instead approaches a status where his money cannot shield him from "minding." Yet Newman abandons his European adventure and returns to his home, America, where he will enjoy a freedom and safety quite apart from the gritty, more "realistic" experience of the immigrant Jew.

Merchants of Realism

James is hardly unique in his repeated return to the theme of changing values between ancient and modern eras, but unlike in *The American*, his later work reveals less separation than interpenetration of values old and new, sacred and profane. American literary realism has long been defined by the economic values of the postbellum era. Scholars such as Alan Tractenberg, Amy Kaplan, Richard Brodhead, and others have demonstrated how industrialization, consumer culture, and speculative capitalism marked the transition from a slavocracy to economic modernity.[85] Consequently, Gilded Age culture was obsessively concerned with issues of money and class. From the scintillating rise of the new millionaire to full-scale economic depression, widespread poverty, and corporate scandal, money was a fundamental realist concern, for Twain, for Howells, and even for James. It was "the age of the *romance of money*," writes Eric Sundquist, "money not in any simple sense but in the complex alterations of human value that it brings into being by its own capacities for reproduction."[86] The ability of money to reproduce itself within a growing credit economy made the practices of speculation and gambling particularly taboo. For evangelical reformers like Henry Ward Beecher and populist farmers alike, as we will see in chapter 3, speculation, often linked to Jews, was deemed morally and politically objectionable.[87] Implicit in these critiques is the threat posed by money itself: its magical ability to recreate itself as a value *ex nihilo*, to replace honest labor on one side and God on the other.

The realist novel was also institutionalized in American culture at precisely the same time as the social scientific disciplines of sociology and anthropology. "The most vivid link between social and novelistic writings of the period," Susan Mizruchi writes, "is their shared interest in the language of social types."[88] They also share, I would add, an interest in the social origins of sacred ritual, feeling, and meaning. When Georg Simmel launched his critique of the "modern quantitative tendency" of his day, the reification of value and desire in the form of money, he extended his analysis to cultural and religious forms.[89] Having absorbed the Counter-Enlightenment belief that the infinite can only be known in its finite manifestations, the universal in the particular, Simmel saw all forms—from religious doctrines and cultural traditions to types of currency—as imperfect but necessary, functional media that channel life forces. Similar to Weber's "ideal types," however, they result in the death of the vitalist impulse, or flux of life they are meant to express. To ward off reification, for Simmel, such forms must be continually destroyed and remade: casting off narrow and rigid religious practices, for example, would allow the "tendency for forms of religious *belief* to dissolve into modes of religious *life*" (23). Like James, Simmel knew that a world without forms was impossible, though he rejected *a priori* forms of truth, belief, and cognition. He thus espoused a de-reified "religiosity," preserving it as an abstract experience without an object: "Religion can be robbed only of its clothing but not its life" (24). In this way, Simmel freed inspiration from religious forms, life from cultural forms, and value from economic forms.

Like Simmel, as well as Weber, Émile Durkheim, and other contemporary sociologists, James provides a vocabulary of value, demonstrating the affinity between metaphors of money and morality, credit and credibility. Art, according to James, may be "mysteriously" opposed to morality in some didactic way.[90] However, engaging with the novel—a living medium for the social exchange of aesthetic values—becomes a moral and ethical practice, requiring the same kind of trust as in a ruthless, speculative economy. Literature puts into words, into explicit coined phrases, the implicit social value generated by the commitment to the exchange of meaning—and the meaning of exchange—between author and reader.[91] The author qualifies what money quantifies, just as the pawnbroker quantifies what his wares qualify.

While the notion of pawning reconfigures our sense of the business of literary production, the business of pawning, viewed through the lens of professional writing, also gains new significance: no longer reprehensible, it can be performed with care, turning objects of little value into valuable ones when placed with the right people. Typically, the figure of the pawnbroker absorbs the excesses of shame and vulgarity attached to others' losses, profiting as he does by their misfortunes. In much of nineteenth-century American literature, the Jewish pawnbroker (like the speculator) is ill-reputed as profiting from stolen goods or abusing those in need. This figure appears as a scavenger, suspiciously multilingual, crafty, and exceedingly calculating. Images of cruel pawnbrokers were abundantly available to James, from as early as Herman Melville's *Redburn* (1849) and E. D. E. N. Southworth's *The Bridal Eve* (1864) to Albert Aiken's dime novels and, later, Thomas Nash's cartoons. Aiken's *The Genteel Spotter* (1884), for example, features Sheeny Lew, a Five-Points thug "with a foxy face and a shambling way . . . a most unworthy representative indeed of the Hebrew Line."[92] We also meet a "Jew pawnbroker" named "Slippery Moses" Cohenson, a "smooth-spoken, oily sort of chap, with a squeaky voice and a sneaky manner," his refrain, "Yesh, yesh . . . mine fr'end" accompanied by vigorous hand washing in invisible soap and water (11). The pawnbroker is a benefactor we pay, a confidante we cannot trust, a double agent, a spy. He possesses superior knowledge: the crime of the thief, the shame of the poor, and the sorrow of the widow. Although attributed to his Jewishness, the pawnbroker's crime consists in how, from the margin and center simultaneously, he collapses values that accrue over time, translating them into the common denominator of money for profit. He threatens one's ability to distinguish interested behavior from disinterestedness, and this duplicity is the source of his power. Walking a fine line between business and friendship, between contract and exchange, the figure of the pawnbroker challenges inherited notions of value; freeing it, as such, from encrusted traditional forms and redefining it. The danger of haggling with the pawnbroker, under conditions of high stakes, is therefore akin to gambling: both entail the charismatic enchantment of otherwise contractualized economic transactions.

The difference between gambling and haggling, however, is the difference between chance and ethics: the pawnbroker has control. Whereas gamblers vie against odds for the most reified form of value, money, the pawnbroker himself confers value upon questionable objects. The world of the pawnbroker contains ambiguous signs, valuable relics of dubious authenticity, where the evaluation of precious old, used things—deposited, sold, bought, and stripped of their context—depends upon acts of interpretation. The negotiation of price—a practice at least as old as the Medicis (whose coat of arms, with its balls on a gold shield, recurs as a visual symbol of the pawnshop and the pawnbroker's usurious ways)—becomes a battle of competing desires, with value exposed as unstable and arbitrary.[93] Often distorted to demonic proportions and rendered Jewish, this figure is forced to absorb the fears unleashed by his role, revealing how authentic value—like any guiding ideal—is socially constructed, flexible, and easily manipulated. A belief in reified use value—in an inherent, objective property of an object to which we can defer—shields us from the discomfort of identification and distinction involved in negotiating exchange value. The pawnbroker disrupts this belief.

Perhaps James found a rootless Jewish shopman the likely realist type to fulfill his purpose: an excellent figure for illustrating the debased morality of the pawnshop—the usurious, calculating underside of capitalist social relations. But James's Bloomsbury shopman seems to exceed the Shylockian stereotype. After all, he is neither stock type, nor does he demand a pound of flesh. We might, therefore, consider how the pawnbroker can be read as a nostalgic holdover of the preindustrial capitalist past, capable of work that, as Vincent Pecora argues, "declined, at least in the eyes of the old elite and their sympathizers, in proportion to the rise of socially defined labor, efficient production, utilitarian morality, and professional expertise."[94] In this sense, it becomes more accurate to consider James's Jewish shopman a sophisticated pawnbroker.[95] In James's literary figurations, the Jew, the cosmopolitan, and the writer are all creators, distributors, and arbiters of value who perform the noble work of the precapitalist feudal household by exposing the ethical cracks in impersonal, impenetrable, and otherwise mechanical forms of commodity exchange. James's figure of the Jewish shopman reveals the implicit ethical contract within corporate capitalism—the human value that adheres to things—and the necessary stigma attached to those liminal figures who uphold it, straddling as they do the divide between interest and disinterest, placement and displacement. In this key figure, who mediates between the golden bowl and the novel's protagonists, James endows the Jew with a noble humanistic purpose, making him a seller of value(s) who, like the professional literary writer, cares deeply for his wares and their ultimate placement.

"Age-Value," Friendship, and the Jewish Shopman

The Bloomsbury shopman of *The Golden Bowl* resides at the center of international market relations yet, like the wary dealer in James's "backshop of the mind," is equally concerned to "place his treasures right."[96] This marginal character runs the bric-a-brac curiosity shop in Bloomsbury that houses the eponymous golden bowl. A perfect gilt crystal, the bowl is the perfect wedding gift from Charlotte Stant to her friend Maggie Verver upon her marriage to Prince Amerigo, except, that is, for its invisible flaw, a possible crack marring its value. As Charlotte negotiates its price with its seller, her shopping companion and former lover, the Prince—Maggie's betrothed—is superstitious ("A crack's a crack—and an omen's an omen"), and, loath to engage in crude haggling with the little Jewish "rascal," he impatiently exits the shop.[97] Finally, deciding that the shopman's price is altogether too much, Charlotte, too, exits without making a purchase.

The tension of this complex scene derives from the penetration of sacred social relations by the profanations of the economic, embodied in the figure of the impertinent Jewish shopman, as well as a subsequent reversal of moral expectations. As the scene unfolds, we quickly learn that the errand to purchase a wedding gift provides an alibi for the two former lovers—the last possible opportunity to set the terms of a relationship about to change permanently due to the marriage of one. The journey into Bloomsbury thus doubles as a tryst Charlotte requests with the Prince, the essence of which is its "absolute secrecy," on the very eve, moreover, of his wedding to Maggie (105). They communicate in Italian, privately, or so they think, as Charlotte offers her love, with no expectation of return, to the betrothed Prince. But their privacy is disrupted by the Jewish shopman, who, it turns out, is fluent in Italian and fully comprehends their exchange. From the perspective of gentility, the shopman has rudely violated the privacy of his clientele, as well as his place in the social structure. Hence the Prince's anxious and abrupt departure from the curiosity shop. The subtextual significance of this scene thus rests in the couple's imagined privacy—a gamble, to be sure—of a conversation conducted in public. When the shopman speaks Italian to them, he reveals his power and seems a figure of deception, an audacious polyglot who reverses social decorum. But he also exposes a lie. If the pair came to the obscure shop with the intention of evaluating the dealer's wares, they ultimately find themselves evaluated, their secret left with him on deposit.

In this scene, then, the shopman acquires something precious, though he does not yet know its value; the fate of four characters now lies in his hands. Like the "dusky, crowded, heterogeneous back-shop of the mind" of James's preface discussed above, this shop is also "dusky," a "rather low-browed place, despite its glass doors," its contents "heterogeneous and not at all imposing" (113, 114). Like all pawnshops, the Bloomsbury shop houses objects of questionable worth, obscured by the dust of time; it is a veritable graveyard of forsaken "valuables" from past eras:

> old gold, old silver, old bronze, of old chased and jeweled artistry . . . small florid ancientries, ornaments, pendants, lockets, brooches, buckles, pretexts for dim brilliants, blood-less rubies, pearls either too large or too opaque for value; miniatures mounted with diamonds that had ceased to daz-zle; snuff-boxes presented to—or by—the too-questionable great; cups, trays, taper-stands, suggestive of pawn tickets, archaic and brown, that would themselves, if preserved, have been prized curiosities. (115)

Unlike the portraits hanging, say, in the Louvre, whose placement on those walls attests to their undeniable (if reified) aesthetic value, the value of these once "prized curiosities," extracted from their historical contexts, their owners and patrons, and placed precariously in a shop to be nego-tiated and reevaluated, remains potential, not yet "realized." Their final destiny—where they will be placed, and at what price—is very much in the hands of the shopman.

These objects of old retain traces of authenticity, of history, of their Ben-jaminian aura; much like Prince Amerigo himself, whose royal genealogy, or "age-value," is otherwise unattainable to those of new wealth.[98] How-ever, "too large" and "too opaque," these former possessions of the "too-questionable great" possess a past too excessive to be adequately translated into exchange value or rational categories of knowledge.[99] Charlotte, too, is described in terms of excess, her face "too narrow and too long" (72). A misplaced cosmopolitan, she, too, is collectible, an original, at least for the Prince, who views her beloved traits as "a cluster of possessions of his own . . . as if . . . they had been 'stored'—wrapped up, numbered, put away in a cabinet" (72). Just as Charlotte will eventually be placed in marriage to Maggie's father—the Hurst-like art mogul Adam Verver—her value fixed once and for all, the shopkeeper cares for how placement will affect the value of his precious objects. He will negotiate price, but refuses to sell out each object's worth, specifically that of his golden bowl. For this reason, it attains a certain preciousness, so that when he uttered the words "My Golden Bowl," it "sounded on his lips as if it said everything" (118).

The shopkeeper never explicitly claims the bowl to have a fixed value, but merely allows Charlotte to draw her own conclusions—to invest it with whatever value she deems appropriate. When she asks if it is "really gold," he tells her, "Look a little, and perhaps you'll make out" (119). He claims that, like the Prince in Verver's estimation, we later learn, the bowl is a "perfect crystal," and that he "can part with it for less than its value," but he never states what that value is (119).[100] Charlotte pushes him until he concedes that he thinks he can promise that it possesses no flaws, even if she were "to scrape off the gold" (119). Ultimately, the shopman's final price of "fifteen pounds" is, for Charlotte, "altogether too much" (120). The price may be arbitrary, but he insists he has asked "too little . . . almost nothing" (120). Since he has already "had [the bowl] a long time without selling it," he will hold it for Charlotte, rather than sell it to her at a lower price (120). He is in no rush; like James, he is unable to commit it to potentially vulgar hands. Whereas the Prince regards the bowl's crack as an omen, rather than the affair it symbolizes, the shopman believes that "if one knows of" a flaw, "one has only to mention it. The good faith . . . is always there" (121). Charlotte takes a similar view: "thank goodness then that if there *be* a crack we know it! But if we may perish by cracks in things that we don't know—! . . . We can never then give each other anything" (123).

For Charlotte, knowing the flaws in gifts allows one to negotiate their value. She believes that no gift can be perfect, and that with no possible guarantee, one is better off knowing in advance what one will purchase. Her attitude suggests a greater value for giving, for the act of exchange, than for the gift, unlike for Maggie Verver, who, protected by her father's faith in the perfection of his collectibles, wishes to see her betrothed Prince as perfect. Aware of this, the Prince knows he must hide his flaws, protect his symbolic value, if he is to remain an object of any worth to the Ververs and remain afloat in Adam's billion-dollar "boat" (228). The Ververs finally take Charlotte on board to be of use, to balance out the familial equation in her marriage to Adam, but reviving her relations with the Prince, she ends up being used "ever so differently and separately—not at all in the same way or degree" by each of them (377). The result, Maggie realizes, is an incalculable remainder, a surplus. The "wonderful act" of marriage "had tipped the house down and made the sum wrong" (380). Because Maggie ultimately protects Adam from ever knowing the extent of the imbalance amongst them (her husband's affair with her father's wife), she alone learns the moral lesson of trying to add and subtract, to buy and sell, human beings like so many collected treasures.

Monetary value—such as the price of a bowl over which people haggle—is thus really an arbitrary, reified, and yet authentic form of dynamic individual desire: hence the personal nature of haggling and the Prince's discomfort with it. For Simmel, forms are necessary, but to ward off their reification they must be continually destroyed and remade. James confronts a similar problem: how to preserve certain aesthetic, cultural, and historical values from the "main American formula": "[t]o make so much money that you won't, that you don't 'mind,' don't mind anything."[101] James's cracked golden bowl—infused with the value of the social relations of its exchange—cracks open contractual social forms, such as marriage, decorum, and even mimetic realism, to reveal instead "life's eternal flux."[102] The bowl allows him to construct an allegorical meditation on the ethical value inherent in social forms and their revision.

Whereas Charlotte rejects the flawed bowl as an unfit gift for Maggie, tinged as it is with the guilt of exposed infidelity, the bowl takes on what Appadurai would call a "social life" of its own, set in motion by the shopman.[103] In the novel's second book, Maggie, in search of a gift for her father, comes across the same "funny little fascinating" place she recalls Charlotte having mentioned.[104] There she meets the "small antiquarian, a queer little foreign man," who sells her the very same golden bowl (433). Now the receptacle of a secret truth, the bowl comes into Maggie's hands as a mystical "*ricordo*"—a souvenir, or token of remembrance—of her husband's extramarital affair (116). It retains the relations of its social exchange and becomes, in effect, priceless: a "*ricordo*" of a past Maggie was never meant to know, much less revisit, much less bring home. The shopman's initial refusal to reduce his price for Charlotte prompts a chain reaction that recuperates the object's noneconomic higher value for Maggie, in an uncanny coincidence upon which the entire plot turns. Granted, Maggie is no saint; she views his act as "remarkable to his own commercial mind" and "almost unprecedented in the thrifty children of Israel" (479). But she also recognizes a gesture of good faith when she sees it: he could not allow her to give a flawed bowl, a "thing of sinister meaning and evil effect," to a "loved parent," and seeks her out to return the profit he would turn on an otherwise "most advantageous bargain" (479). The exceptional nature of this gesture makes the shopman all the more ethically heroic, traversing the boundary, as he does, between business and friendship. Maggie refuses the money, but inside her home the shopman recognizes photos of Amerigo and Charlotte and mistakenly identifies the erstwhile lovers as a married couple. He thus reveals the secret narrative of the bowl, disabusing Maggie of her ignorance and innocence, now bestowing a gift she "wouldn't have missed . . . for the world" (433). At once, this minor figure becomes a major one, as Maggie realizes the life her husband and her friend share, witnessed in a moment of stolen intimacy. The bowl, a telling souvenir, becomes a vessel of truth, a "reportable" repository of historical narrative in Susan Stewart's terms, and, with its foreboding crack, a metaphor for Maggie's now broken marriage.[105]

However accidental, the shopman mediates the exchange of the novel's most meaningful object, and his cosmopolitan multilingualism grants him the information that resolves the plot. As a middleman, he enjoys the vantage point of "cultivated detachment," which Amanda Anderson attributes to the cosmopolitan.[106] The shopman—of whom the bowl becomes an extension—emerges as the essential repository of past knowledge and mediator of value, at once central to, yet outside, the social sphere of the Verver clan. He thereby provides James, and his readers, a unique locus of consciousness from which to critique the dominant value systems of the novel. He is object of evaluation (the "Jew") turned subject who evaluates: by a twist of fortune a marginal outsider turned central insider. His simultaneous subject/object, insider/outsider status offers James a position from which to explore the transferability of meaning between past and future and of value between people and things, and the ethical economy that undergirds acts of material exchange and the production of exchange value.

The shopman's uncalculated gift to Maggie of the bowl's knowledge, as it were, is inextricable from its sale. In this instance, buying and selling does not kill the vitalist impulse of exchange but creates a new one. The cracked bowl cracks open the dead forms of Maggie's purportedly perfect marriage, and of the novel itself. Though the bowl is exchanged within the "restricted economy," the crack provides a glimpse into the "general economy," revealing a value that no longer resides in the actual bowl, but rather in the ethical and psychic resonances it carries.[107] The cracked crystal is infused with past social relations, for back in the Bloomsbury shop, as we know, Charlotte and the Prince had negotiated far more than the worth of a small gilt bowl. Maggie recognizes this dynamic social value:

> I inspired [the shopman] with sympathy—there you are! But the miracle is that he should have a sympathy to offer that could be *of use to me*. . . . I can only think of him as kind, for *he had nothing to gain. He had in fact only to lose.* It was what he came to tell me—that he had asked me too high a price, more than the object was really worth. There was a particular reason which he hadn't mentioned and which made him consider and *repent*. He wrote for leave to see me again—wrote in such terms that I saw him here this afternoon.[108]

The shopman gives Maggie, however inadvertently, something "of use to her," rather than of value to himself. The value of the greater truth he reveals far exceeds the small confession he intended, a disinterested sacrifice for which Maggie can only account as motivated by "sympathy." She may go too far in reading his act as a form of Christian repentance, since, properly speaking, Jews tend to atone rather than repent for their moral sins, as on Yom Kippur, the Day of Atonement. The difference has everything to do with the logic of reciprocity.[109] In both cases—Christian and Jewish—repentance is only one side of atonement, the human side, requiring God's mercy to be realized. But if atonement closes the economy, or cycle of sin and redemption, Maggie's description of the shopman's act as repentant means it demands her mercy, reinscribing the act into a dialectic of reciprocity, rather than of profit, one that remains temporally open-ended. His act, together with her mercy, reconciles the rift between precapitalist ethics and bourgeois morality, and between noble culture and base materialism.

Having experienced a *felix culpa*, Maggie can now put her marriage back together, but at a higher level, with the knowledge of having faced the ultimate risk, the fissure in her relationship. For this gift, she thanks the "little man in the shop." As she tells the Prince, "he did for me more than he knew—I owe it to him. He took an interest in me."[110] This "interest" dances between the economic and the ethical. Unlike Adam Verver, interested only in profit, power, and prestige gained through acquiring collectibles, the Jewish shopman trades things of the past for future interest. But he also earns moral prestige by his interest in the greater good of others, by not allowing "moral value" to be consumed by "cash value" at every turn.[111] The Prince can only remember him as "a horrid little beast," a deceptive polyglot who spies on the intimate pair. But the Prince knows all along that he himself is the deceiver, who falsely sold himself to Adam Verver as a "perfect crystal." This anxiety emerges in his negotiations over the golden bowl, when he scapegoats its seller venomously as "the little swindling Jew."[112] Yet it is the cosmopolitan Jew, the pawnbroker, who performs the act of supreme honesty in a situation with deception at its base. His gesture of uncalculated generosity places him at the center of both the cash nexus and the moral order. This typically debased figure unveils "the horror of finding evil seated all at its ease where she had only dreamed of good; the horror of the thing hideously *behind*, behind so much trusted, so much pretended, nobleness, cleverness, tenderness" (489). The shopkeeper teaches Maggie the fact of duplicity, of which he, an arbiter of uncertain values, may be master, but he treats this mastery with the utmost responsibility.

The archetypical Jewish profit-seeker thereby undergoes, at least to Maggie's mind, a conversion of sorts: he "repents" over his profit motive and abandons it in favor of the gift. The exchange of this gift produces a kind of Durkheimian "social solidarity" between the shopkeeper and Maggie.[113] His economic loss, or sacrifice, reveals the arbitrary and even violent nature of economic evaluation and asks us (through Maggie) to forgo the economic reduction to dollars and cents in order to expose the hidden moral truth of modern economic exchange: the intermingling of past and present, of souls and things. Maggie defers to the bowl as proof of the Prince's intimacy with Charlotte. "That cup there has turned witness," she remarks, "by the most wonderful of chances."[114] Like Benjamin's authentic object of historic cult value, the bowl becomes both witness to and document of the past crime. Even when the bowl is later smashed to pieces, its value, and its history, have already been conferred onto Maggie. She has gained its knowledge; as a material object it becomes useless. Having witnessed the balanced structure of her life dashed to pieces, Maggie must now reconstruct it on a firmer foundation. By rethinking the economic value of the cracked golden bowl and placing it in the right hands at the right price, the Bloomsbury shopman enables Maggie to transcend the flaw in its "artistic value" in favor of its "other value," what lies "behind," the truth of the past it reveals to her (455). The shopman allows James to redeem the curiosity shop as a site of contested values (aesthetic, ethical, and economic) and temporal registers (past, present, and future) and, moreover, to locate such negotiation in the figure of the Jewish pawnbroker.

Negotiating these categories and determining value, in turn, requires a certain interpretive skill. Here the shopman excels; his real gift is his ability to read his clients. When Charlotte and Amerigo entered the dealer's shop in Bloomsbury, he fixed "on his visitors an extraordinary pair of eyes and looked from one to the other while they considered the object with which he appeared mainly to hope to tempt them" (113). The narrator informs us, "he was clearly the master and devoted to his business"; his mastery "might precisely have been this particular secret that he possessed for worrying the customer so little that it fairly threw over their relation a sort of solemnity" (113). This "particular secret" for creating such "solemnity" can be read in at least two ways: either he casts the charismatic magic spell of the fraudulent miracle-maker, an inauthentic Moses, or he genuinely transforms a quotidian business transaction into a sacred ritual, a "*living* affair" much like that involved in our reading of *The Golden Bowl*.[115] The shopman is both shaman and charlatan at once: he raises the same tension created by the realist writer, who enacts the dream of transparency and the anxiety of mimicry. Charlotte believes him well intentioned, and she is ultimately proven right. She is impressed by the *antiquario*'s care concerning the kinds of sales he makes, what and to whom, in language that bears remarkable resemblance to James's description of himself as the dealer in the Preface to *The Portrait of a Lady*.

For our part in the interpretation of value, we can read the shopkeeper's various objects, in particular the golden bowl, as capable of transmitting their history to whoever touches them. The buying and selling of such circulated objects produces a kind of social effervescence by means of what Durkheim calls "contagion": "the idea of a thing and the idea of its symbol are closely linked in our minds; the result is that the emotions provoked by the one extend contagiously to the other."[116] Like the Jew with his certain "race-quality," both the shopkeeper and his objects are curiosities whose value derives from their placement and displacement, and their ability to carry a whole distinct history in each fragment.[117] As in the gift economy, the shopman's actions entail obligations both to receive and to reciprocate, therefore setting in motion an ongoing, dialectical, social dynamic.[118] With the knowledge gained from the shopkeeper, Maggie unexpectedly extracts herself from an economy of revenge and, following his example of power and generosity, nobly gives away her knowledge to the Prince, then sits back and waits. She even comes to feel compassion for her adversary, Charlotte, who ends up horrifically placed, tragically kept as Adam's despised and lonely wife, the future queen of his imperial museum of spoils and collectibles, "American City."

James is unflinching in his critique of Verver's museum mentality, how he removes precious objects (and people) from their sphere of social circulation and thus from time. Yet, by this point in his career, James is no anticapitalist. Much as he would like to remain above and beyond the vulgar marketplace, he knows it is impossible and undesirable: to keep Isabel Archer, Maggie Verver, Charlotte Stant, or any of his treasured creations "locked up indefinitely" would be to exact their social death. Rather, James must cash in on his heroines' value in order "to disclose [their] merit afresh."[119] Not only did he have to circulate his aesthetic creations in time in order for them to be valued by others, but he embraced the market, cleverly transforming his commodities into the gifts of a true sovereign, to be used, exchanged, and interpreted. James may be a fraud, a purveyor of cracked wares who knowingly peddles literary golden bowls, open-ended and imperfect. But by revealing aesthetic value to be not absolute but negotiable he engages his readers in a dialectic of value, through which we also participate in temporal acts of value production and preservation.

Time and the Production of Value

For an old-moneyed Protestant writer like James to revalue the stereotype of the money-worshipping Jew as a premodern, noble *kurios* had especial importance in a period of mounting antisemitism in the United States. Michael Dobkowski dates the major acceleration of American antisemitic ideology to the most publicized antisemitic event in the United States prior to 1900, when, on June 13, 1877, as we have seen and will explore more fully in the next chapter, the Grand Union Hotel in Saratoga Springs, New York, under the control of Judge Henry Hilton, refused the patronage of the genteel, German Jewish banker Joseph Seligman and his family.[120] By 1904, increasing social and economic instability, class conflict, spreading nativist ideology, and hostility to plutocrats all contributed to antisemitic and anti-immigrant sentiments among agrarian populists, patrician intellectuals like Henry Adams, and the poorest classes in urban centers.[121] Antisemitism during this period, in comparison to, say, the pogroms in Russia or Jim Crow violence in the United States, was minimal. Still, it was increasingly common for Jews to be excluded from elite social clubs, universities, and real estate transactions. The most egregious act of American antisemitism involved the 1915 lynching of Leo Frank, a northern Jewish businessman who, in 1913, received a life sentence, commuted from the death penalty, for the alleged murder of a thirteen-year-old girl in 1913 and was subsequently lynched by a mob in Atlanta, Georgia.[122] By 1920, Henry Ford launched the most sustained antisemitic campaign against the "international Jew" in the United States yet.[123]

So what can we conclude about the Jew in James? If a newly successful class of wealthy German Jews frequently did, as we will see, act as middlemen in different levels of banking and finance, as James developed his expression of the relationships between people and things, he was at least able to demonstrate that even in the most calculated and material forms of temporal exchange, the production of timeless, sacred value is possible. We can best discover this phenomenon in James's work by examining those figures engaged in significant modes of commercial, aesthetic, and cultural exchange: not the collectors but the pawnbrokers and cosmopolitans of his late phase. Because these latter figures bring a worldly perspective to the evaluation of things, they command authoritative posts at the door of value determination, bridging the past and future. Whether cosmopolitan or disaporic, each of these figures is objective for being displaced, as well as central to modes of exchange that transcend local boundaries. Standing just beyond the constraints of American social life and its institutional formations, these marginal figures challenge tradition and institution by virtue of their dislocated positions. Collectively, these liminal figures reveal the suppressed ethical contract underlying capitalist forms and illuminate that fluid, atemporal space between the potential of qualitative value and the limits of quantitative determinations.

For James, history, the past itself, has a particular value. The passage with which we opened is not the first "dusky back-shop" of curiosities we find in James. In *The American Scene*, describing his visit to Concord, Massachusetts, James ponders the "operative elements of the past": "Emerson and Hawthorne and Thoreau," but also the "little old Concord Fight."[124] Meditating on the historical value of the Battle of Lexington and Concord and its commemorative site, James considers the disproportionate sense of the gift the revolutionary soldiers who died there have given us. Each of them completed a "short, simple act, intense and unconscious," but the value of that act compounds over time, resulting, for example, in the ongoing freedom we since have taken for granted. The passage of time gives us the advantage of recognizing their ability "to determine the future in the way we call immortally" (194). We know the "sense that was theirs and that moved them," these "fallen defenders," but with hindsight we also know much more, and this forms "our luxurious heritage" (194): luxurious because we gain so immensely, perhaps undeservedly, by our inheritance of their laborious sacrifice. Thus, we who retell these stories become like pawnbrokers of history:

> Was it delicate, was it decent—that is *would* it have been—to
> ask the embattled farmers, simple-minded, unwitting fold,
> to make us so inordinate a present with so little of the con-
> scious credit of it? Which all comes indeed, perhaps, simply
> to the most poignant of all those effects of disinterested sac-
> rifice that the toil and trouble of our forefathers produce for
> us. The minutemen at the bridge were of course interested

intensely, as they believed—but such, too, was the artful manner in which we see *our* latent, lurking, waiting interest like, a Jew in a dusky back-shop, providentially bait the trap. (194–95)

Like the pawnbroker to his pawns, we derive a great profit from history—the meaning, or value, we seek from the past and produce from morsels of truth we trap and discover. Because we prey on the past and the unconscious gifts our "unwitting" forefathers continue to "produce for us," our intense "interest" makes us little more than "back-shop" Jewish pawnbrokers. For Gert Buelens, this passage suggests that the historical "gulf" between James and his American ancestors is so great that he "ends up likening himself to a member of that class of immigrants that will strike him elsewhere on the American scene as so utterly 'alien.'"[125] Accordingly, the simile suggests a relation of identity between James and the Jew: a likeness based on the shared experience of alienation. What I have been suggesting, however, is a different dynamic: a likeness based on their analogous function of temporal mediation, rather than condition. The relationship of the writer to his material is like that of the pawnbroker to his treasures: both agents bear the responsibility of evaluating their wares according to a sense of the social relations, and value accrued over time, that they embody in reified form.

Shot through with economic language, the passage claims the historical soldiers (and all figures of history) made a "huge bargain for us," which amounts to "the gift of the little all they had."[126] Whereas the "homely rural facts grouped [in Concord] together have appeared to go on testifying" to the "modesty" of this gift, James reminds us that this gift is not modest at all; their "disinterested sacrifice" of human "toil and trouble" becomes a veritable potlatch of ongoing freedom (194). As if the economic scales weren't tipped enough, the "embattled farmers" gave but once, while we continue to enjoy the "brilliant advantage" of time, "unfairly" and "at their cost," since these events only continue to accrue value, not as ossified objects but as an ongoing, living legacy (194). James bridges the "gulf" of time by reconceiving our relationship to historical Americans as one of obligation, just as a pawnbroker is (or ought to be) indebted to his clients. We prey upon our "forefathers" for knowledge—for the legacy of American collective memory and renewed meaning—the way a pawnbroker profits on the misfortunes of those who sell him their treasures cheap. Consequently, to produce goods—historical, literary, or luxury—we have no choice but to keep exploiting our unwitting sources. The recognition of our obligation to them can, however, foster an ethical call, in turn, for us to continue, in an ongoing gift exchange of memory, to "place our treasures right."

In James's late fictional social world, the figure of the Jew is actually redeemed. Like the immigrant and the cosmopolitan author, the diasporic Jew crosses and connects overlapping social, sacred, and aesthetic economies. Embodiments of universal and particular affiliations, mediators of universal and particular values, and reminders of different orders of time, these figures share the ability to disrupt facile categorization, to complicate the epistemology of appearances, and to mediate an ongoing dialectic between sacred and profane realms. All three types reside along that ever-shifting boundary between calculation and sacrifice, materiality and transcendence, thus serving to reenchant with ethical value otherwise disenchanted, rationalized literary forms. By what has come to be called his major phase, James—caught in a tangled web of competing value systems—negotiated an explicit position for himself from within the commercial world, one in which the production of aesthetic value could yet become, as noted, "a sacred office."[127] If, early in his career, James could not find a compromise between the commercial and the aesthetic realms, between economic and noneconomic value, he ultimately found that it was only through compromise that he could continue to produce art. He had to engage the market ethically, and this possibility inheres best in his reimagined figure of the ethical pawnbroker. A figure at once central and marginal, local and cosmopolitan, of Old-World culture and New-World business, the Jewish shopman—in diaspora—dialectically resolves James's conflict of value, as a metaphor for the displaced, cosmopolitan writer himself.

If, as James suggests in the preface to *The Portrait of a Lady*, the shopkeeper is the realist writer himself, this moral capitalist par excellence expresses ethical and aesthetic values through carefully wrought, self-conscious objects, created precisely to transmit the past in an ongoing exchange, a living legacy. For Simmel, to represent is to evaluate, and thereby to reduce vitality to concrete form; but James raises representation to the level of the "living thing."[128] As the novelist fulfills the economic, moral, and spiritual demands of his "sacred office," the novel with its central crack becomes a dynamic, continuous engagement with past and future alike: it demands constant reevaluation and ongoing moral action that resists reification at every turn. Placing his treasures in our hands, James asks us to recognize with solemnity and to share, repeatedly over time, their higher moral, non-rational value. Perhaps, then, to create value in James is not to opt out of the economy but to participate more fully in it: to circulate flawed cultural objects in time, to meet the challenges they engender, and to find social and ethical value in the economic activities that constitute the Jamesian "religion of doing."[129]

Publishing alongside the many writers rehearsed so far, for whom the noble Hebrew and avaricious "Jew" were staple Jewish "types," James yet revised and reconceived this duality into a more complex realist portrait of the ethical Jewish man of business. In the Bloomsbury shopman, James presents an omniscient, modern, noble Hebrew whose mediation of business and friendship, and reconciliation between past and present in the novel's plot, heals the novel's central "crack," paving the way for the future intimacy of its two protagonists. As this figure moves from Jamesian realism into naturalism, we see the limits of the noble Hebrew's modern ethical potential in a realm James didn't dare to address: intimacy with "the Jew." The next two chapters turn to literary engagements with the "Jewish Problem" as it plays out on the domestic, intimate plane of intermarriage, and reframe arguments about Jewish assimilation, modernization, and cultural adaptation in terms of time. It was one thing for Jews to enjoy political, economic, or cultural acceptance, or even to handle financial investments for non-Jews; it was another for one's Gentile daughter to marry one.

3

Borrowed Time
Edith Wharton and Fictions of Decline

"Why are the American greenbacks like the Jews?"
"Because they are the issue of Abraham (Lincoln) and know
not when the redeemer cometh."

—Leaves from the Diary of Henry Greville:
1861–72, March 1, 1863

As we saw in the introduction, the Seligman-Hilton affair of 1877
was a lightning rod for public tensions about race, class, and also religious
differences. Joseph Seligman was by most accounts an American myth
himself, an embodiment of Algeresque success, rising from "immigrant
foot peddler to a financial adviser to the President of the United States" in
just over twenty years.[1] During the Civil War, according to Stephen Birmingham, Seligman won over Washington by selling more than $50 mil-
lion in Union bonds on the Frankfurt Stock Exchange.[2] By the war's end,
J. & W. Seligman and Company, World Bankers, was established in New
York, London, and Frankfurt, and, in 1869, Seligman was offered the position of secretary of treasury by President Grant, though he turned it down.[3]
In 1874, however, Seligman made a successful bid to Grant's new secretary
of the treasury, Benjamin Bristow, to handle the sale of $25 million in US
bonds. He managed to form a partnership with the famous British bankers
the Rothschilds, and created the most powerful alliance in banking history, selling bonds worth $55 million to English and German investors.[4]
By 1877 he had attained national prominence both in Wall Street and in
Washington. Shortly before Seligman headed for vacation in Saratoga that
year, President Hayes's secretary of treasury, John Sherman, accepted his

plan for further untangling the nation's post–Civil War economy and refinancing the balance of the US government war debt.[5] It turned out to be a golden plan, effectively bringing the dollar up to par.[6]

In spite of these and many other impressive accomplishments—serving as presidential financial advisor, as president of the prominent reform synagogue Temple Emanu-El in New York, as founder of the Hebrew Benevolent and Orphan Asylum Society, as vice president of the prestigious Union League Club (into which Hilton vainly sought entry)—Seligman's financial achievements cut both ways.[7] His efforts helped move the US Reconstruction-era economy into the future—into a new corporate economy built on systems of credit.[8] But in doing so, especially together with the Rothschilds, the prominent Jewish banker also fueled fears of an international Jewish conspiracy to take over the world's finances, best captured in the infamous antisemitic forgery the *Protocols of the Elders of Zion*.[9] In the Seligman-Hilton affair, in short, the Money Question and the Jewish Question came together. The former asked: What does money even represent? What is the source of its value? And the latter: Who are the Jews, can they be considered "true" loyal Americans, and what does it mean that they hold the keys to our financial future? Strangest of all, even "Jews" like Seligman were vilified as vulgar upstarts, whose connections to modern banking, speculation, and finance only made them more suspect, déclassé. Yet even while hurling antisemitic slurs, Hilton and his supporters bizarrely clung to the "philosemitic" notion of the noble, religious "Hebrew." To be a good Christian, it seemed, no matter how much you disliked the Jews, you had to respect the Hebrews, whoever they were, and you certainly had to know the difference.

This difference, it turns out, made all the difference for Hilton, forming the basis for his entire argument against the likes of Seligman. A total cause célèbre, the affair enjoyed press coverage that went on for months, beginning with this *New York Times* headline:

> A SENSATION AT SARATOGA. NEW RULES FOR THE GRAND UNION. NO JEWS TO BE ADMITTED. MR. SELIGMAN, THE BANKER, AND HIS FAMILY SENT AWAY. HIS LETTER TO MR. HILTON. GATHERING OF MR. SELIGMAN'S FRIENDS. AN INDIGNATION MEETING TO BE HELD.[10]

Seligman published a scathing letter to Hilton in the *Times*, Hilton published an equally defaming retort, followed by numerous letters and editorials in both Jewish and Gentile papers, pro and con; even cartoons in *Puck* magazine caricatured the scandal.[11] Why such a public uproar? Yes, both men were wealthy and famous, and perhaps people were genuinely surprised to learn that such hatred existed against the Jews as a group, or that such a thing could happen to one of Seligman's stature.[12] Yet Hilton's pointed distinction between "true Hebrews" and "Seligman 'Jews,'" readily picked up in the press, made one thing clear: Hilton had crossed a line in his public denigration of Jews—like a latter-day Donald Trump, he gave license to public hate speech. But at that time religion was still off-limits, and the Hebraic myth provided a cover of respectability behind which Hilton could pronounce distinctions of class, taste, and what amounted to base racism. Veneration for the more antiquated, traditional aspects of Jewish culture was thus mobilized to justify racial resistance to modern Jewry.

The day after the story broke, the *New York Times* published a letter from Seligman to Hilton in which he declared that the "civilized world is beginning to be more tolerant in matters of faith or creed or birth than you believe or would have them," that they "will not patronize a man who seeks to make money by pandering to the prejudices of the vulgar."[13] Given that the Grand Union was owned by A. T. Stewart & Co., over whose estate Hilton had recently been granted control, Seligman tried to pin vulgar, mercenary motives upon Hilton and defend himself on the sacrosanct basis of "faith or creed." As Seligman's attorney, Mr. Edward Lauterbach, quipped, "What the difference is between a Hebrew and a Seligman Jew I am not advised; but I do presume the Judge Hilton's etymological education is on a par with his aesthenial culture, . . . Judge Hilton always was a bigot."[14] In his subsequent public response to Seligman, Hilton more deeply defended the distinction between a "Jew" and a "Hebrew"; he argued that Seligman was full of "Shylockian meanness," that he was not an "orthodox Hebrew," that any assertions to the contrary were concocted by his lawyer, and that he was dismissed from the Grand Union not "because he is a Hebrew, but because he is not wanted."[15] Hilton then offered an extended portrait of what he coined as "the Seligman 'Jew,'" which I quote at length, because it so clearly illustrates what this book has been tracing: the dependence of modern antisemitic logic upon the "philosemitic" Hebraic myth:

> ...he is the "Sheeny." He has made his money; he must adver-
> tise it in his person. He is of low origin, and his instincts are
> all of the gutter—his principles smell—they smell of decayed
> goods, or of decayed principle. . . . He is too obtuse or too
> mean to see his vulgarity, or to go where it may not be on pub-
> lic exhibition. He is shoddy—false—squeezing—unmanly;
> but financially he is successful, and that is the only token he
> has to push himself upon the polite . . . he is as vain as he is
> devoid of merit; and he is puffed out with as much impor-
> tance as he is poor of any value. He comes to the Grand
> Union big with himself and little with everybody else in
> the decent world; planks down his cash with his royal order,
> and having never seen respectable food, he can't get enough
> to eat unless he gorges down his unpracticed throat six
> meals a day, and then for fear folks will not know that he
> is an old epicure, he protrudes his ill-shaped pod into the
> gaze of every unfortunate person in his path who has open
> eyes, and then goes to his room and prepares himself for
> next day's gluttony by ridding himself of his torturing load
> all over the furniture, with groans at its loss that disturb
> every decent person within 10 rooms on every side of him.
> They have deserved the common contempt they get—and
> they have brought the injurious reflection of their vulgarity
> upon the true Hebrews. It is no wonder that Americans are
> down on the Seligman "Jew."[16]

The "Seligman 'Jew'" is sensuous, monstrous, and bodily, all gluttony and girth, deception and decadence, while the "Hebrew" is its antithesis—"true," pristine, ideal. As with the typological aesthetic in Longfellow's and Holmes's poems discussed above, abstract "Hebrews" are noble—virtual models of class and superior breeding with which to contrast and shame their real, modern, Jewish counterparts.

Even contemporary readers saw the contradictions in Hilton's rhetoric. *Times* reporters interviewed Jewish clothing traders who were calling for an immediate industry boycott of A. T. Stewart & Co., the owners of the Grand Union hotel, and one firm owner, Mr. Hoffman, called Hilton out for his attempt to mask racism behind specious theological arguments:

> . . . it is idle for Judge Hilton to try to split the hair by an attempted discrimination between the Jew and the Hebrew on the score of religion. Jews in this country do not consider the orthodox question—it I [*sic*] exist. They have as many and as wide differences of theological opinion as Protestant Christians have; they are not at all united on religious opinion, but they are all Jews as a race, and as a race they are united against the outrage upon one of their fellows.[17]

Although galvanizing the category of "race" for his polemical advantage, Hoffman's comments lay bare the Hebraic myth for what it is, an invention that often served anti-Jewish arguments. Calling Hilton's bluff, Hoffman denies the religious distinction any credibility, calling it merely a polemical imposition from without. Hoffman defends Seligman as "a splendid American citizen," who "has done more for the foreign credit of this country than any other man in it," regardless of his level or denomination of religious observance.[18]

As the Seligman-Hilton affair came to a head, Henry Ward Beecher, social reformer and pastor of Plymouth Church in Brooklyn, also weighed in, in a sermon that made the religious question explicit, invoking Christian typology and Hebraic myth alike.[19] Beecher praised the Seligman family with whom he "summered" for many years as behaving "in a manner that ought to put to shame many Christian ladies and gentlemen" (52). He was shocked—"no other person could have been singled out more sensibly" than Seligman for this "unnecessary offense" (52). He then praised all Jews for their strength before centuries of "hatred and contempt and persecution," and for giving the world an "ethical religion" that developed the "character of men" (53, 60–61). To this "heroic people," he praised, we owe our familial and public institutions, our sense of morality, justice, and the "seedcorn" of our existence and civilization, as we are all "descendents of Abraham" (54). Beecher's praise of the Seligman family was surely genuine, but also exemplary for being framed in clear typological terms: the Jews, he emphasized, gave us the greatest gift of all, "our Lord and Saviour Jesus Christ"—the "ideal man of the ages" and "grandest interpreter of the Old Testament Scripture" (64). Such a "virtuous people," he concluded, should ignore these "petty slights"; "A hero may be annoyed by a mosquitto [sic]," but to "put on his whole armor" and make "war on an insect would be beneath his dignity" (74). To be sure, Beecher wished to dismiss the "petty slights" of Hilton's antisemitic slurs. By invoking a noble Jewish warrior of biblical myth to do so, however, one whose greatest achievement is originary and ancestral, Beecher's praise illustrates the temporal structure of the Protestant imaginary, and of Christian philosemitism, which offers a "love" only of Jews who are antecedents, metaphors, who are noble in all of their rich "pastness."

It is no surprise that for her character Simon Rosedale, German-Jewish stockbroker and investment banker in *The House of Mirth* (1905), Edith Wharton likely used Joseph Seligman as a model.[20] It is true that by the time she was writing the novel, there were three "communities" of Jews in New York, including the well-established Sephardic Jews of Lazarus's ilk and the most recent arrivals, the poorer classes of Eastern European Jews.[21] But, among them, it was the German Jews like the Seligmans, the newly powerful Wall Street investment bankers, who rankled high society most. Their social presence, necessitated by their "strong patriotism and financial support of government activities," was invasive, and the fact that, like Rosedale, they were in positions to provide the wealthiest classes with financial "tips" to preserve and expand the latter's estates only led to greater resentment.[22]

In *The House of Mirth*, Rosedale may seem a minor character, perhaps no more than a stereotype. When critics discuss him at all, they deem Rosedale emblematic of Wharton's patrician antisemitism toward the German-Jewish immigrants of her era who made their fortunes in banking and retail—the Seligmans, Altmans, Bloomingdales, Lehmans, Goldmans, Kuhns, Loebs, and others—memorialized in Stephen Birmingham's definitive collective biography, *Our Crowd* (1967).[23] As noted above, this was partly because, for wealthy WASPs like Hilton and possibly also Wharton, this powerful class of German Jews threatened the very American future. They were not just rubbing elbows with Gentile society; they controlled their finances and were marrying their daughters. As Beecher warned, the "Israelites," for better or worse, *are* the American future: whereas for two thousand years they had invested only in movable property, he notes, here in America they were "now buying land," and their (racial) "stock" would eventually "merge with the American stock."[24] Fears of intermarriage may have been expressed as racial, but, as Hilton made clear, the prominence of the "Seligman Jew" stood to erode all "principles," traditions, and standards of "value." Where the Money Question met the Jewish Question, the fear was that all standards would be reduced to that of the dollar, whose value itself, as we have seen, was dubious in the first place.

In Wharton's novel, these questions and problems meet in the potential marriage plot between heroine Lily Bart and parvenu Simon Rosedale. As Lily suffers a fateful financial decline, Rosedale's millions promise a way out, providing moments of hope and suspense that punctuate the plotline. Over and over, readers must ask: Will she actually marry Rosedale? Will he save Lily Bart? Given this possibility, Wharton's choice to have Lily die rather than marry "the Jew" creates a temporal disjunction, placing Rosedale's Jewish otherness at the nexus of two competing systems of value and corresponding orders of time: the inexorable linearity of naturalist decline, and the unpredictability of chance that disrupts it.

Like Seligman's economic rise, Rosedale's rise is concomitant with the emergence of a modern credit system, speculative capitalism, and the professional manipulation of future values, linked in the novel to anxieties about value and time. Seligman's story illustrates this time-value linkage: as early as the 1850s, he and his brothers had established practices of selling on credit, loaning money, buying and selling IOUs, and generally staying liquid in their business dealings. As Birmingham describes, Joseph made an "important discovery" about the power of money in relation to time:

> There was a considerable difference between buying and selling undershirts and buying and selling funds and credit. Undershirts could earn profits for the merchant only during

the hours his store was open; otherwise it stood idle, a liability. But *money stayed active around the clock*. Credits were not subject to opening hours. When money was put to work, it worked twenty-four hours a day, seven days a week, three hundred and sixty-five days a year, and stopped for no holidays, Jewish or gentile.[25]

For reproducing wealth, the credit economy absorbed the entire time frame of work by transforming leisure hours into business hours. The buying and selling of "funds and credit" also meant creating future value out of nothing, based on contracts of trust and promise. In anticipating a lucrative future, speculation dematerialized value, detaching it not just from objects but also from the temporal cycles of past and present labor. Wharton dramatizes the social effects of the dependence of the upper classes on stock market speculation and finance. For Lily Bart, herself a gambler, it means that all time becomes business time, and all social interactions become gambles with real, financial stakes. Wharton thus creates a world in which significant units of modern time—leisure, ritual, social, and durational time, or life span, particularly for aging women—are subject to monetary measurement, purportedly in the hands of one like Simon Rosedale, the novel's closest likeness to the "Seligman 'Jew.'"

REPLOTTING NATURALISM: ALTERNATIVE FUTURES

From the novel's outset, Lily Bart is running "out of time."[26] The ill-fated heroine struggles against the exigencies of an elaborate social machine in which security, for women, derives from a combination of great wealth and respectable marriage. Lily has neither; as she confesses to Lawrence Selden, she is "horribly poor—and very expensive" and so "must have a great deal of money."[27] Orphaned and supported by her frugal Aunt Peniston, Lily needs to marry well, and soon, for her greatest assets, her youth, beauty, and income, are dwindling. Time is not on Lily's side, but marriage for money would create a different temporal trap. It would free her from daily financial concern, but only to enclose her in a "great gilt cage" of social rules, obligations, and conventions—a world of tightly ordered, well-scheduled leisure (45).

When the novel opens, Lawrence Selden finds Lily outside the social routine altogether, poised in the midst of the "afternoon rush of the Grand Central Station," standing "apart from the crowd, letting it drift by her to the platform or the street" (5). One couldn't find a place more structured by time than the busiest train station in Manhattan at its busiest time of day. That Lily stands there, at its center, indifferent, in limbo, with a perplexing "desultory air" highlights her precarious state (5). She has apparently missed her train. The time is also specific: "a Monday in early September," between three thirty and five thirty in the afternoon, between trains, meals, and seasons, placing Lily out of sync with the social calendar, "in the act of transition between one and another of the country-houses which disputed her presence" (5). Teetering between houses, trains, decisions, between her definitive past and a still open future, Lily stands, momentarily, outside of time itself. She cannot remain there, of course, since time, Johannes Fabian reminds us, is a constitutive dimension of social reality; once Lily turns the chance encounter into a tea at Selden's nearby apartment, she reenters the social grind, back on the clock, marking the first of many risks Lily will take, and lose, in her ongoing gamble against time.[28]

Between the ticking of social and biological clocks in *The House of Mirth*, time shapes female experience. To maintain her reputation, a woman like Lily must constantly negotiate time: not only her age but also temporal rules of social propriety—when, as well as where and with whom, she may be seen. Any acts of defiance are figured as acts of gambling, as in her meeting with Selden, described in terms of chance: "Mr. Selden—what good luck!" Lily twice exclaims before venturing out of the station to accept his invitation to take tea (5). "Why not? It's too tempting—I'll take the risk"—and although he reassures her that he is "not dangerous," the "links of her bracelet," "like manacles chaining her to her fate" remind us of more powerful social forces at work (7, 8). By nineteenth-century conventions, thirty was the established threshold of "girlhood" and marriageability for women.[29] Verging thus on the outer edge of "youth" at twenty-nine, Lily veers between various "practical" marriages and her freedom. To maintain the latter, she resorts to gambling, wagering her most valuable asset, her beauty. Though Selden sees her beauty as timeless, reflecting "eternal harmony," we see it subject to the early stages of aging, precarious and in limited supply.[30]

Both timeless ideal and commodity with a shelf life, Lily's beauty is synechdochic for her unstable position at the nexus of the economies of marriage, art, and finance. Evaluated by turns as a suitable (or unsuitable) wife; a rare, collectible *objet d'art*; a timeless ideal; and, at worst, a common sexual object, Lily's credit is quickly placed into the hands of the key financial speculator in the novel, Rosedale. Like James's shopkeeper, Rosedale mediates tensions between leisure time and business time, between friendship and business, trust and risk, capitalist exchange and the precapitalist gift, for which the character Lawrence Selden serves as nostalgic reminder. For this, of course, Rosedale pays a price: the antisemitic judgments of others. Initially, Lily dismisses Rosedale as a suitor, one whom others in her set regard as "fat and shiny" with a "shoppy manner," as Gus Trenor puts it (65). But Trenor also notes, "the people who are clever enough to be civil to him now will make a mighty good thing of it. A few years from now he'll be in it whether we want him or not, and then he won't be giving away a half-a-million tip for a dinner" (65). In spite of Rosedale's seeming vulgarity, he yet emerges as a figure of future financial security and magical good fortune. As the plot unfolds, we will see, his ultimate decency—in contrast with Trenor's loathsome brutality—highlights the hypocrisy of the debased social position accorded him by those who also depend upon him.

The novel's opening scene of risk, the suspense it generates, and the temporal complexity it opens up capture the point of this chapter: what begins as an instance of "luck" devolves into that of "fate," as the spontaneous morphs into the determined. Lacking financial capital, Lily Bart will gamble on her symbolic capital, but her reputation is an unstable commodity (based as it is on beauty and respectability), so each risk results in ever steeper drops in her value.[31] Lily's initial moment of "chance," of sheer spontaneity, out of which anything might happen, reads retrospectively through her death at the novel's conclusion as an act of peril, precipitating her inevitable social decline. For Wharton, this structure of decline *was* inevitable, in a world in which unmarried women enjoyed only relative freedom. As she wrote in *A Backward Glance*, "a frivolous society can acquire dramatic significance only through what its frivolity destroys. . . .

What [the novel's] climax was to be I had known before I began. My last page is always latent in my first."[32] For Joan Lidoff, Wharton sacrifices Lily to critique the misogynist cruelty by which women who seek economic agency are punished, even fatally.[33] Perhaps so, but this does not explain Rosedale's complicated role. Knowing that Lily Bart would be destroyed, Wharton's question must have been, "How?" How will Lily's debt be paid, who will collect, who will forgive? The novel repeatedly flirts with Rosedale in this role: at his first proposal, Lily puts him off, then once ostracized by Bertha Dorset, she comes around, but too late, and he refuses her. Yet, overall, her fate seems tied to his character, so that their crossings mediate the two orders of time structuring the narrative: the inexorable linearity of naturalist decline and the unpredictable futurity of chance, hope, and suspense that disrupts it.

As they say in the casino, "the house always wins." If the opening scene dramatizes a gamble, with Selden's apartment as the casino, then Rosedale literally owns the house. Rosedale embodies the broader systemic forces of the social class he has striven to enter and which effectively stack the deck against Lily. He catches her not only in the act of visiting a gentleman's abode alone but also in lying about it, so that the scene veers between forces of randomness and destiny—between *Chronos*, the personification of sequential time, and *Kairos*, or opportune time, the supreme, sacred time in which one's fate is decided.[34] For Lily's risk, exposure to Rosedale, the "Jew," is the price she pays, evident in the narrator's description of him as "a small glossy-looking man with a gardenia in his coat, who raised his hat with a surprised exclamation. 'Miss Bart? Well—of all people! This *is* luck.'"[35] The "twinkle of amused curiosity" in his eyes suggests his opportunism and confidence, in contrast with Lily's "irrepressible annoyance" with the "sudden intimacy of his smile" (13).

> "Been up to town for a little shopping, I suppose?" he said, in a tone which had the familiarity of a touch.
>
> Miss Bart shrank from it slightly, and then flung herself into precipitate explanation.
>
> "Yes—I came up to see my dress-maker. I am just on my way to catch the train to the Trenors."

"Ah—your dress-maker; just so," he said blandly. "I didn't know there were any dress-makers in the Benedick."

"The Benedick?" She looked gently puzzled. "Is that the name of this building?"

"Yes, that's the name: I believe it's an old word for bachelor, isn't it? *I happen to own the building*—that's the way I know." (13–15; emphasis mine)

Rosedale's interest repels Lily, and the narrator, who can only read it in pecuniary terms: "He had his race's accuracy in the appraisal of values, and to be seen walking down the platform at the crowded afternoon hour in the company of Miss Lily Bart would have been money in his pocket, as he might himself have phrased it" (15). Lily's social superior, Judy Trenor, later recalls him as the "little Jew who had been served up and rejected at the social board a dozen times within her memory" (16). Rosedale's extraordinary wealth, in short, cannot undo the stigma of "Seligman 'Jewishness,'" what with his "screwed-up lids," too-familiar smile, and "small sidelong eyes which gave him the air of appraising people as if they were bric-a-brac" (13). Clearly this *is* punishment: "Why," the narrator bemoans, "must a girl pay so dearly for her least escape from routine?" (15).

If Lily's trajectory is marked by temporal tensions and conflicts, they are thematically and structurally mediated by the figure of the Jew. Moments of risk, of stolen freedom from social rules—at Bellomont, on board the Dorset's yacht at Monte Carlo, with Norma Hatch—create suspense, because in each, Lily falls out of the narrative temporal order into a liminal time-space before consequence strikes. Such scenes form a pattern in the novel: they precipitate Lily's decline, but are articulated in the language of spontaneity, impulse, chance, or luck, signaling this crossroads of *Chronos* and *Kairos*, of competing temporal orders. Whenever Lily is absorbed back into social time, moreover, Rosedale appears. Safely inside a cab after her initial encounter with him, for example, Lily regrets having rejected his offer to drive her back to the station, and how for "the luxury of an impulse" she is now indebted to him (15). She might have "purchased his silence"; now her mistake was "going to cost her rather more than she could afford," since "within twenty-four hours the story of her visiting her dress-maker at the Benedick would be in active circulation among Mr. Rosedale's acquaintances" (15–16). Lily's impulsiveness, haste, and embrace of risk contrast sharply with her fears of Rosedale's cunning calculations, motivated by self-interest and profit, even if "her own course was guided by as nice calculations" (16).

Rosedale's appearance so early in the novel, just after Lily's taboo tea with Selden, establishes the two male characters as foils who cipher competing value systems in the novel—rational, calculated self-interest and disinterested friendship—each with different relations to time. Selden, after all, introduces her to his "republic of the spirit," an imagined realm of freedom "from money, from poverty, from ease and anxiety, from all the material accidents" (55). Like their tea, it promises a spontaneous escape from society's temporal contingencies and strategic calculations. Rosedale, by contrast, stands for keeping time, drawing Lily back into the measured time of society, commerce, exchange, and self-interest. Bringing her initial escapade to an end, Rosedale's knowledge of the secret visit also charges their relationship with debt and obligation: Lily's few moments of borrowed time with Selden seem, in this sense, borrowed from Rosedale.

If Selden promises timelessness and disinterested appreciation of beauty, Rosedale initially appears to represent the quantified time of usury and discipline. By the novel's conclusion, however, Rosedale's marital promise suggests he would, if allowed, actually arbitrate these binaries of time: business and friendship, commerce and art, social time and spontaneous freedom. That Wharton gets so close but finally refuses to marry him to Lily, however, signals an inability of romantic strains of naturalism to accommodate new, modern forms of Jewishness outside the well-worn dichotomy this book has been tracing. Lily's deceased body instead marks the terrain, and casualty, of a battle between disinterested leisure and the interests of business, between the values of a precapitalist past and those of a commercially driven future marked as Jewish. Lily's conflict between these social values is framed, as I will show, temporally—the ritual time of leisure she cannot afford, the timelessness of the republic of the spirit she cannot enter, the mechanized time of labor for which she is ill-equipped, and the relentless linear time that ages her. Yet, for all this, readers are led to see Rosedale, the figure of the Jew, as holding out the best promise for reconciling these temporal conflicts, a promise that, because it remains unfulfilled, posits an alternate future that the novel fails to realize. Whether or not Wharton shared her characters' prejudices, she eschews the marriage plot with ruthless determinism, so that the story of Jewish-Gentile intermarriage that Rosedale might otherwise tell does not hew to the logic of naturalism.

In terms of time, Wharton lets readers have it both ways: the plot of *The House of Mirth* is determined yet open-ended; nostalgic yet progressive, placing the uncertain economic tides of modernity in the power of those who, like Rosedale, have their hands on the ropes at the helm.[36] If for Christian philosemites the Jew *was* the future, in *The House of Mirth* that future is unredemptive. In Rosedale the pasts of gambling, pawning, and usury resurface in the modern figure of the speculative finance capitalist as its atavistic residue, "the Jew" bearing realism's haunted past. Yet, in this same character "the Jew" also opens up what Anthony Giddens calls the "disembedding" processes of modernity to "expert systems," like the stock market, that shape the future.[37] In proposing marriage, Rosedale offers Lily a voluntary, even exchange: she commits blackmail against Bertha Dorset to clear her reputation, and, in return, he will free Lily from financial contingency and commercial concern altogether: "you know it's the showy things that are cheap. Well, I should want my wife to be able to take the earth for granted if she wanted to. I know there's one thing vulgar about money, and that's the thinking about it; and my wife would never have to demean herself in that way."[38] It is a great deal, but to the wealthy who freely squander their time, Rosedale's seeming defiance of "time-discipline," of time's rationalization in the form of work so soon in his social ascent, seems like his greatest offense.

Irene Goldman-Price argues that, just as Hilton claimed of Seligman, Rosedale is not a "Hebrew" but a "Jew," more Shylock than Abraham.[39] Yet the real surprise of the novel is that he never does collect his pound of flesh. Rosedale's uncouth money talk merely lays bare the economic underpinnings of all of the novel's social, marital, and even sexual relations, as one or more exchanges of symbolic for financial capital.[40] As Carry Fisher says to Lily, "Mr. Rosedale wants a wife who can establish him in the bosom of the Van Osburghs and Trenors. . . . And so *you* could—with his money! Don't you see how beautifully it would work out for you both?"[41] When finally scandalized and disinherited, Lily lingers over this mutually beneficial arrangement. She comes close, in other words, but for the inescapable sexual component: "Yes, he would be kind . . . kind in his gross, unscrupulous, rapacious way, the way of the predatory creature with his mate," but kind, nonetheless (195). For Goldman-Price, Lily fears that to bear Rosedale's children "would be to alter the purity of [her] lineage."[42] Perhaps this fear extends to Wharton. Rosedale's "friends" depend on him immensely to reproduce their wealth. But when Rosedale presents Lily with a different kind of reproduction, we see how Jewish-Gentile relations, for Wharton, reached their limits.

Rosedale's promise to resolve Lily's debt and her experience of fractured time would mean not the separation of business and leisure but their more complete interpenetration. In this imagined alternate future, as an equal business partner of sorts, a Lily Rosedale could safely reenter society on her own terms. But such a future is only posited. Lily instead dies tragic and noble, holding out for a free, ideal, contingent-free love with Lawrence Selden that he is too cowardly and hypocritical to make reality. If Lily could only have joined Rosedale as a commercial agent, the novel implies, Rosedale would have gotten her back on track, back in time. Marrying Rosedale would have meant catching the train.

Trust, Gambling, and Speculation

I have already argued that authors like Abraham Cahan and Henry James manage to preserve within the ostensibly secular realist novel transcendent forces that disrupt its form, offering glimpses of sacred value and time. The revived figure of the noble Hebrew, a modernized Hebraic myth, is at the center of these temporal negotiations. As the character of Simon Rosedale also disrupts inherited dualities of Jewishness in *The House of Mirth*, he does so by replotting time, if only potentially, into an integrated, viable future that can be imagined, if not realized. The thematic and structural mechanism for this disruption is economic risk and the suspense it generates. In order to set the stage for a more detailed reading of risk in the novel, however, it is worth a brief look at the literary, economic, and historical background against which it appears.

That literary writing and economic logic have been imbricated since at least the eighteenth century is hardly news, particularly as literature registered responses to the rise of national banking, to new speculative currencies, and to the public debts they created, on both sides of the Atlantic. Examining the culture of debt and speculation in early America, Jennifer Baker contends that writers of the revolutionary period saw the instability of paper currency as its "greatest asset": they imagined "new modes of financial speculation and indebtedness as a means to build American communities and foster social cohesion."[43] Baker argues that well-managed national debt created greater public credit, or faith, in the government and community at large, so that the risk created by the advent of paper money was not aesthetic but pragmatic, requiring a real belief in government-backed paper money.[44] The paper money debate that dominated political discourse from 1825 to 1875, as Marc Shell notes, however, was primarily "concerned with symbolization in general, and hence not only with money but also with aesthetics," that is, with representation itself.[45]

Of course this wasn't new—in the British context, as Mary Poovey has shown, the credit economy created tremendous anxiety about the stability, or instability, of monetary representation.[46] This anxiety often played out in literature. Sandra Sherman and Patrick Brantlinger both read the interlacing of British moral and economic discourses as intrinsic to the rise of the novel form and the corresponding development of a credit economy.[47] Credit was so upending that, as Terry Mulcaire argues, it became allegorized in eighteenth-century writings as the "inconstant female figure" of both fecundity and instability, Lady Credit, as Daniel Defoe dubbed her.[48] The rise of literary realism coincides with the period in which economic credit came to be accepted "as a basic, unavoidable aspect of modern money and modern economic processes," so much so, for Brantlinger, that the two systems—money and fiction, both relying on credit—seem interchangeable: "money as the fiction of gold or of absolute value; fiction as a commodity, exchangeable for money."[49] The realist novel arose as a commodity that "begged to be 'credited'" with truth (150).

In the United States, with the shift from an eighteenth-century emphasis on public credit and an indebted nation to a nineteenth-century emphasis on the credit-worthy and trustworthy individual, the "confidence man" arose as a deceptive figure in US urban culture.[50] According to Karen Halttunen, the "confidence man" is the literary embodiment of an anxious response to rapid social change.[51] By the early nineteenth century, mercantile capitalism began to break down the institutions of apprenticeship, craft and artisan studios in the home, and the economic structures that maintained the patriarchal family as the primary social unit. With developments in agricultural technology, Halttunen notes, young men flocked from rural towns to urban centers, creating a massive expansion of "the urban world of strangers" (193). The absence of familiarity, known genealogy, or social recommendations for urban strangers meant relying upon appearances as markers of individual character. Yet these could be deceptive and, worse still, manipulated for profitable ends. In moral advice manuals, mid-nineteenth-century evangelical reformers like Beecher warned of the "confidence man," reflecting concerns of duplicity and hypocrisy in the modern urban world, which then hardened into late-nineteenth-century facts.[52]

Threats of urban duplicity revived older Puritan concerns about the false "appearance" of salvation or the deportment of the saved, but also reflected fears of nineteenth-century economic shifts from systems of local exchange and subsistence to those of anonymous capitalist speculation. The expanding market economy was feared to be hazardous, as was the bank, that great "money power" accused of constructing a "mysterious, swaying web of speculative credit" by Jacksonian Democrats, who waged war against it.[53] Within an emerging speculative economy, credit was thought to have what Mulcaire describes as "quasi-magical value-making power."[54] Like "confidence men," speculators were noted for their demagoguery and charisma, and were portrayed as predatorial tricksters who, Halttunen notes, pretended to be sincere in order to lure young innocents into a world of vice. Beecher thus asserted that, morally speaking, gambling was directly linked to speculation; they were "one vocation, only with different instruments," and both were "groundless, hazardous, overcommitted and undercontrolled."[55]

Beecher opposed gambling and speculation alike, since such practices encouraged aversion to the Protestant ethic of industry, led to cheating, and undermined the "principle of mutual confidence" upon which commerce rested.[56] Whereas commerce could be thought of as created by God to bring out the "noble heart" between people, speculation was understood as the "cool, calculative, essential spirit of concentrated avaricious selfishness." By unraveling these structures of mutual confidence, the "confidence man" posed a dual threat to one's purse and one's moral "character," which, in turn, through contagious forms of "influence," became threatening to others.[57] If gambling and speculation exposed the irrational, potentially sacred underside of rational capitalism, then the gambler and the speculator became like one, merged in the public mind in the image of the newly powerful German Jewish bankers, particularly those underwriting the nation's debts, as capitalism's atavistic magicians. Jews in these roles, and the anxieties they provoked, exposed what Émile Durkheim described as the "contagious" eruptions of atavistic religious life that attended routinized capitalist calculation.[58]

The positive mirror image of the "confidence man" was the "self-made man," the liminal man on his way up the capitalist ladder. The ideal figure for all Americans, the self-made man reflected cherished notions of American individualism, freedom, economic opportunity, entrepreneurialism, and industrial capitalist heroism—the "pluck" of rags-to-riches figures like Ragged Dick, if not a Joseph Seligman.[59] Yet this ideal was always haunted by its shadowy underside, by the possibility that the unfixed, liminal, Western "backwoodsman," Mississippi boatman, or Crockett-like frontier hunter was *already* the confidence man.[60] Writers of advice manuals who extolled sentimental virtues of sincerity and transparency were thus forced to warn young men of being too sincere and too easy targets. One must *appear sincere*, but remain wary.[61] In effect, perhaps inadvertently, they taught them to behave hypocritically, to imitate confidence men in order to protect themselves from them.

The House of Mirth is set squarely at the center of a full-fledged "speculative economy," the abstract "expert system" of the stock market, whose moral foundation of credit and trust was dependent on confidence in rising experts like Rosedale. That Rosedale is marked Jewish alludes to the larger historical problem of faith in the Jewish bankers who underwrote the postbellum US government debt.[62] But it also points to fears of Jewish confidence men, how the credit economy was susceptible to manipulation, its potential for duplicity its greatest advantage and greatest danger in both a modern metropolis like Wharton's New York and the networks of international banking. *The House of Mirth* illustrates this anxiety as a deterioration of trust within the concentric circles of family and local community as specifically Jewish outsiders penetrate them. This reflects, on the one hand, the context of social, racial, and ethnic heterogeneity created by immigration and international capitalism; on the other, it reflects how "trust" itself became commercial in the early 1880s, associated with business and speculation in stock.[63] These corporate structures acquired their name because of reliance upon the trust of their stockholders, whose faith in the other members and willingness to entrust their economic assets to others' hands constituted their foundation. As with the idea of "credit," both economic and ethical forces converge in the historical concept of "trust."[64]

The novel also registers anxieties about the risks of gambling, a practice whose prohibition from the early eighteenth century through its illegalization in the 1890s had its basis in a morality that adapted to shifts in political economy. Ann Fabian has shown how early-nineteenth-century reformers condemned gambling as dishonest, unproductive, irrational, and unpredictable, "a menace to the very structures of trust and credit on which an expanding economy, and ultimately the republic, depended."[65] If gambling provided the "essential ingredients" of risk and rapid gain central to "rational capitalist speculation," Fabian notes, speculators were "the 'new' gamblers" (3). Presenting themselves as virtuous, rational citizens, as compared to "old," evil gamblers, they profited from an "ever more rapid transfer of property" on the stock exchange, and the seemingly "magical fertility of speculative markets" (3). As speculative capitalism became the dominant economic form in the United States, its practitioners tried to repress its foundations in the older practice of petty gambling as play, given the associations with gambling and vice, uncontrollability, and irrationality.[66] But speculators ultimately found it difficult "to assert a vast moral difference between stock markets and gambling casinos," since Wall Street earnings often resulted from "lucky gambles."[67] The associations among speculation, finance, and the prominent Jewish world bankers described above only helped to keep that atavistic fear alive.

It is hard not to see a connection between anti-Jewish xenophobia and the distrust of speculative capitalism peaking in the 1890s as related phenomena that made their way into literature. This distrust was especially evident among agrarians, according to Fabian, the angry farmers who protested the commodities exchange, deeming agricultural speculators direct descendents of "evil gamblers."[68] If the producing classes were the "industrious makers of things," the majority who, in Andrews Jackson's words, comprised "'the bone and sinew of the country,'" then speculators were "the parasitic makers of money," an "idle, conspiratorial few."[69] In Frank Norris's *The Octopus* (1900), such parasitic figures take several forms, from the fictional Pacific and Southwest Railroad itself, when it murders an entire flock of sheep, to its ruthless head, S. Behrman.[70] Although Behrman is not named Jewish in the novel, with his German Jewish name he bears all of the signs of the stereotypical Shylock, calling to mind the real German Jewish bankers who invested in US railroad stock—Seligman, but also Jay Gould, Jacob Schiff, Abraham Kuhn, Solomon Loeb, and others.[71] Donald Pizer, a renowned authority on American naturalism who has given the subject of literary antisemitism book-length attention, has made an excellent case for linking Berhman as the "octopus" figure with populist antisemitism.[72] After all, Behrman is a fat, avaricious, exploitative, giant parasitic bloodsucker, metonymic for the "octopus" for which the railroad is named, itself a key stereotype of nonproductive occupations.

Hamlin Garland, an avid populist raised on farms in Wisconsin, Iowa, and the Dakota Territory before eventually moving to Boston in 1884, also advocated for Midwest farm improvements. He pressed for the single tax, which sought to do away with profits earned by an increase in value of land favoring property owners over farmers.[73] While populism picked up the single tax movement's critique of private ownership of land, Garland's notion of literary "veritism" shaped his ideas of "local color" writing, as we saw in chapter 1, but he also held nativist ideas of Jewish racial inferiority. Pizer enumerates how, in his diaries, for instance, Garland addressed the "Jewish Problem" explicitly, arguing that Jews were foreign, were inassimilable, and would change what it means to be "American."[74] Pizer shows how Garland critiqued the negative Jewish influence on American culture, argued for immigration restriction, and at one point even referred to "Jew York" (8–11, 13). In Garland's most sustained populist novel of farmers' revolt, *A Spoil of Office* (1892), Pizer notes, the model for his heroine Ida

Wilbur was Mary Elizabeth Lease, a grange speaker and alliance activist who in her book *The Problem of Civilization Solved* (1895) engaged explicitly in antisemitic rhetoric (6–7).

Pizer therefore regards Garland as a "passive anti-semite," one who represents "all the major trends in the makeup of late nineteenth- and early twentieth-century American anti-Semitism" (1). Also significant is how the agrarianism he espoused provided a ready discourse for emerging ideological antisemitisms, warranted by intense Jewish immigration and rumors of an international Jewish conspiracy, linked, as noted, to distrust of famous Jewish banking families like the Seligmans and Rothschilds. As John Higham makes clear, populist farmers at the center of the "agrarian" tradition attacked speculators and dealers in paper credits for corrupting republican virtues, "a reaction against the whole system of centralized patronage, power, and corruption associated with the growth of banks and public credit."[75] Higham reminds us how, from Jefferson through Jackson to Veblen, this tradition shaped the nativist American criticism of capitalism. But beneath these arguments lay equations between Jews and unproductive labor that "tapped an authentic vein of indigenous social criticism" that already had targeted a "class of idle rich in their midst" (160).

The populist critique of unproductive labor dovetails with Protestant concerns about "wasting time" rehearsed earlier. As I suggest in the introduction, usury was always defined in terms of time: it was prohibited by medieval Christians not because it amounted to profiting off the work of others—the parasitical model that came to be associated with diasporic Jews in the nineteenth-century ethno-national context—but because "their profit implied a mortgage on time, which was supposed to belong to God alone"; if the usurer is "*selling what does not belong to him*," he is, in effect, selling borrowed time.[76] In seventeenth-century Puritanism, too, according to E. P. Thompson, time was revered as a "sacred ware" "which converted men to new valuations of time; which taught children even in their infancy to improve each shining hour; and which saturated men's minds with the equation, time is money."[77] For Puritans like Richard Baxter, Thompson argues, the metaphor of the clock was thus used to measure one's inner morality, as in the theme of "Redeeming the Time"—"'use every minute of it as a most precious thing, and spend it wholly in the way of duty.'"[78] These notions gave way to an eighteenth-century sense of time as a worldly commodity, creating a new sense of morally inflected "time-discipline": "the division of labour; the supervision of labour; fines; bells and clocks; money incentives; preachings and schoolings; the suppression of fairs and sports," part of an ongoing "propaganda of time-thrift" aimed at working people.[79]

Naturalist fictions suggest that by the late nineteenth century, "work time" became the counterpart to structured leisure, so that even social relations were vulnerable to calculation and usury. Like Rosedale in *The House of Mirth*, the figure of unproductive labor bears all these immoral associations with money, and cannot by definition enjoy the dignity of time honestly spent on work according to Weber's Protestant work ethic.[80] But even as the economics of time were blamed on Jews, the noble Hebrew persisted. Versions of the Hebraic myth appear in numerous works by Theodore Dreiser, such *The Titan* (1914) and *An American Tragedy* (1925), featuring both Jewish "brute others" and noble Hebrews.[81] Dreiser's rarely discussed play, *The Hand of the Potter* (1916), features a cast of immigrant Jews living in New York's Lower East Side and unfolds a plot about rape and mental illness centered on a perpetrator, Isadore Berchansky, his victim an innocent eleven-year-old girl.[82] Isadore's father is a noble, anachronistic patriarch, even if his naïve goodness only contributes to his son's demise. The only Jewish male alternatives to Isadore are thus a noble but nostalgic and incompetent Jewish father and a vicious, parasitic landlord, human but Shylockian—for Abraham Cahan, who still reviewed the play favorably, evidence that Dreiser knew no actual Jews.[83] The Jewish female characters fare only slightly better: Isadore's overbearing mother and vulgar sister, Rae, both lie for him during his trial, and his other sister, Masha, is physically lame. The noble father confesses the family's lies, landing his only son in jail, so that, helpless before forces greater than he, the only way forward is down.

The House of Mirth is also a naturalist narrative of decline, yet this trajectory is complicated by Rosedale's ascent. Unlike the traditional "confidence man" who would marry a wealthy heiress only to take her money and run, Rosedale already possesses all the money he needs, ultimately rejects the disinherited would-be heiress (Lily), and turns out to be the most honest character in the novel. If modern "society," the "other, luxurious, world" for which Lily yearns, is one whose "machinery is so carefully concealed that one scene flows in to another without perceptible agency," conducted like a seamless performance whose success derives from its apparent spontaneity, this only confers credit upon its most skillful director.[84] In Lily Bart's world, this director is Rosedale: his magical stock market "tips" allow others to pull off successful speculations. Wharton's plot points to how the trust and confidence that once attended face-to-face economic interactions became replaced by the mystified "invisible hand" of capitalism. In a world of confidence men characterized by "fluid self-aggrandizement," one could literally rise from nowhere, as many immigrants did, and just as easily fall, like Lily Bart, into complete obscurity.[85] Lily seems easy prey for the suspected "confidence man" in Rosedale. Yet if the early-nineteenth-century confidence man was an actual man, a clever trickster who embodied the dangers of speculative capitalism, the early-twentieth-century confidence man is no longer a "man" at all, but a mysterious amalgamation of invisible forces, a magical, disembodied diffusion of the stock market itself.

The ongoing speculations of an old guard member like Trenor suggest the dependence of a dying aristocratic class on just such stock market forces, although it is Rosedale who bears their social and moral brunt. The novel maps the atavistic moral residue of rustic gambling onto the modern stock market, and collapses, through allegory, the temporal distinction between the two economic phenomena. Scenes of actual gambling thus serve as haunting reminders of the moral stakes in a speculative economy that operates on equal parts reason, faith, and trust. The novel's thematic tensions about business and leisure, marriage and freedom, open up conflicting temporal registers: how the suspended *telos* implied by chance—the deferral of profit or loss inherent to risk—is articulated within an otherwise linear, deterministic naturalist literary mode. Lily Bart's speculations in the marriage market open up multiple possibilities for an unknown future, disrupting a plot destined to culminate in her failure. Lily's downward spiral proceeds in one direction, even as it gestures toward a future promised in the figure of "the Jew."

"YOU'LL GET IT ALL BACK . . . WITH YOUR FACE": CLOCKS AND SOCIAL TIME

The social world that Rosedale underwrites and in which Lily seeks secure placement is structured by seasonal activities, day and evening rituals, arranged according to a strictly-adhered-to social calendar of punctual dinners, luncheons, teatimes, and scheduled house visits. Though she is twenty-nine when the plot begins, her story is marked by the bookends of her birth as a beautiful girl—raised and groomed to secure in marriage the proper man of the proper class—and her untimely death. In between, along the way, she confronts rules of temporal propriety—not just *where* an unchaperoned young woman may publicly or privately appear, and *with whom*, but also *when*, rules with whose enforcement ubiquitous Time itself seems complicit, punctuated by glances at clocks and watches, train timetables and church bells, most notably in the moments when Lily deviates from them. And she does deviate—willingly, inadvertently—suffering fresh punishments each time, foreclosing her future a little more.

Lily's race against time—to marry before either age or social decline prevents it—is accelerated and disrupted by moments of coincidence, missed opportunity, lateness, and spontaneity, which, in turn, are brought to abrupt conclusions by reminders of clock time. In the first scene at Selden's, just when they "both laughed for pure pleasure in their sudden intimacy," Lily "glanced at the clock": "Dear me! I must be off. It's after five," she declares.[86] On her way out the door, pausing at her reflection in the mantelpiece, she beholds "a kind of wild-wood grace to her outline—as though she were a captured dryad subdued to the conventions of the drawing-room" (12). Selden's apartment frees her timeless tree-nymph-like nature, whereas the clock signals her return to the social prison, anticipating her initial encounter with Rosedale.

Shortly after this scene, Lily does catch the next train to Bellomont, while her marriage to milk-toast millionaire and collector of precious "Americana," Percy Gryce, is still imminent, her future wide open. Yet she no sooner planned to accompany Gryce to church on Sunday morning when she oversleeps, "the germs of rebellion" taking over at the sight of "the grey dress and the borrowed prayer book," which "flashed a long light down the years. She would have to go to church with Percy Gryce every Sunday" (47). If marriage is a tunnel of routinized time, Selden promises freedom from it. The day instead becomes "the accomplice of her mood . . . for impulse and truancy," resulting in a spontaneous secret tryst with Selden on an open ledge of rock in an otherwise secluded beech-grove (47). There, punctuated by a "sense of leisure and safety," Selden introduces Lily to the "republic of the spirit," an imaginary, ideal realm of "personal freedom," a "country one has to find the way to one's self," provided one knows "how to read" the "sign-posts" (55). Selden's "aesthetic amusement" is that of a "reflective man" because time has no hold on him—young, male, financially self-sufficient. But although the republic holds out the promise of freedom from social rules, from time itself, Lily cannot enter; it is closed to the married and rich, both of which Lily wants to be, and she is quick to note the hypocrisy that "one of the conditions of citizenship is not to think too much about money, and the only way not to think about money is to have a great deal of it" (56).

Although we see Lily as Selden does, disinterestedly, with an attitude of "admiring spectatorship," the scene also figures as one of gambling, riddled with the temporal language of providence and risk (55). As Lily and Selden flirt, banter about marriage, and take stock of one another and their values, mutual feelings, and trust, "something throbbed between them," though the scene does not deliver the anticipated marriage proposal. When she asks, "Do you want to marry me?" he responds, "No, I don't want to—but perhaps I should if you did!" leading to further sallies (58). Ultimately, they are both too cowardly to really propose—he to try and provide for her, she to take what little he could offer. Although "the exquisite influences of the hour trembled in their veins, and drew them to each other as the loosened leaves were drawn to earth," their romantic tension is abruptly broken by "a remote sound" when "a black object rushed across their vision," a carriage, a car, some mark of society, evidence that they had lost track of time. "I had no idea it was so late!" Lily says "impatiently" (59). Was Selden "serious," Lily inquires, to which he replies, "Why not? . . . I took no risks in being so" (60). The risk was all Lily's, as were all of the consequences: Percy Gryce's hasty departure from Bellomont, Gus Trenor's first advances toward her, and Trenor's interesting "discourse" with her about investments, which is "rudely interrupted by the mention of Mr. Rosedale's name" (65).

Unlike the republic of the spirit, time is a prison-house for women like Lily in *The House of Mirth*. Lily's bleak future is best foreshadowed by the childless Mrs. Peniston, a "small plump woman, with a colourless skin lined with trivial wrinkles" and "an air of being packed and ready to start; yet she never started" (84), who "kept her imagination shrouded, like the drawing-room furniture" (98). Mrs. Peniston's first action in the novel is to rise "abruptly" from her "glossy purple arm-chair" and take a lace handkerchief to the layer of dust upon the "ormulu clock surmounted by a helmeted Minerva" on her "chimney-piece" (85). If the impoverished Nettie Struthers represents the only regenerative future at the novel's end, Mrs. Peniston—with her gilded clock and "trivial wrinkles," vicarious appetite for others' weddings and balls, and vast storage house of saved "*menus*" and "cotillion favours" from her youth—is life petrified (84, 85). Though not quite a Miss Havisham, she embodies an encrusted nostalgia for a traditional past.[87] Lily's bedroom in her house is "as dreary as a prison," and when she later returns for the reading of Aunt Peniston's will, the house feels like a "well-kept family vault, in which the last corpse had just been decently deposited."[88] A figure of "empty, homogeneous time" if ever there was one, Mrs. Peniston, in death, produces the "last corpse" in the family, her disinheritance of Lily severing Lily from the past once and for all.

In Aunt Peniston, an impeccable slave to social decorum, we see how the mechanistic experience in society's "great gilt cage" unfolds in linear, homogeneous time, what Paul Ricoeur would call the "prefigured time" of the novel. This temporality, however, is "refigured" narratively when intersected and "configured" by the heterogeneous, repetitive temporality of chance.[89] Lily's plot is fueled by the chance that she will escape her fate, her failure having begun well before the novel even begins: "But why had she failed? Was it her own fault or that of destiny?"[90] She recalls the time when the family lost its money, and her mother's "fierce vindictiveness" as she insisted, "But you'll get it all back—you'll get it all back, with your face" (25). Following Mr. Bart's death, Mrs. Bart and Lily wander hopelessly from relative to relative in disgrace and fear of friendly condescension, and "only one thought consoled" Mrs. Bart, "the contemplation of Lily's beauty" (29):

> She studied [Lily's face] with a kind of passion, as though
> it were some weapon she had slowly fashioned for her ven-
> geance. It was the last asset in their fortunes, the nucleus

around which their life was to be rebuilt. She watched it jealously, as though it were her own property and Lily its mere custodian; and she tried to instill into the latter a sense of the responsibility that such a charge involved. (29)

Lily's "face" is a source of hope for financial restitution, an "asset" to substitute for actual labor, and a "weapon" to relieve the indignation of newfound poverty before an unforgiving social world. Her beauty is held out as the only possibility for restoring their rightful wealth and stabilizing time.

Lily was "secretly ashamed" of her mother's "crude passion for money"; she would prefer symbolic over economic capital, "an English nobleman with political ambitions," an "Italian prince with a castle in the Apennines," or some other "lost cause" with the benefit of making claims on "an immemorial tradition" (30). She thus refuses to sell herself outright in marriage, even though she needs money to maintain her status. Caught up in a dialectic of economic and symbolic capital, Lily chooses to gamble rather than trade her one asset, her beauty. If trade is an even exchange, gambling, like speculation, holds out the possibility of gain without loss, though at the risk of complete loss. Put another way, gambling buys one time: with the completion of the transaction deferred into the future, the extension of time transforms that time into value.

For Lily, Rosedale's marriage proposal is too economic; it would too baldly reduce fragile human interactions to a brutal formula, a zero sum game akin to balancing a checkbook. After Selden's lover, Bertha Dorset, has thrown over Lily, a scapegoat for her own extramarital affairs, Rosedale suggests Lily use the evidence she possesses—a set of love letters from Bertha to Selden, sold to Lily by the shrewd char-woman of the Benedick—to blackmail Bertha, and in exchange, he will marry her. As it would restore Lily's tarnished reputation as accused accomplice in adultery with Bertha's husband, the deal has a certain appeal:

Put by Rosedale in terms of business-like give-and-take, this understanding took on the harmless air of a mutual accommodation, like a transfer of property or a revision of boundary lines. It certainly simplified life to view it as a perpetual adjustment, a play of party politics, in which every concession had its recognized equivalent: Lily's tired mind was fascinated by this escape from fluctuating ethical estimates into a region of concrete weights and measures. (202)

The marriage would provide security and put an end to Lily's endless and hopeless calculations: "All Jack [Stepney] has to do to get everything he wants is to keep quiet and let that girl marry him; whereas I have to calculate and contrive, and retreat and advance, as if I were going through an intricate dance, where one misstep would throw me hopelessly out of time" (40). Yet Lily initially rejects the deal, for, at the decisive moment, Rosedale suggested "the likelihood of her distrusting him and perhaps trying to cheat him of his share of the spoils. This glimpse of his inner mind seemed to present the whole transaction in a new aspect, and she saw that the essential baseness of the act lay in its *freedom from risk*" (203; emphasis mine). Ironically, in the name of risk, Lily rejects the one calculated transaction that would free her from all others. Her subsequent fall—like George Hurstwood's to Carrie Meeber—perhaps makes Lily noble, heroic, principled.[91] But it also suggests her—or Wharton's—unwillingness to allow business and leisure to come together, to let Lily step into economic modernity and form an intimate partnership with the "Jew."

Lily's seemingly principled rejection of economic calculation may also strike readers as naive, itself a retrograde stance, since we learn that someone always did labor to provide her leisure and luxury—her father, Hudson Bart. If Lily's mother embodies the timeless beauty she espoused to her daughter, Lily's father, by contrast, appears the very figure of *Chronos*:

> Ruling the turbulent element called home was the vigorous and determined figure of a mother still young enough to dance her ball-dresses to rags, while the hazy outline of a neutral-tinted father filled an indeterminate space between the butler and the man who came to wind the clocks. Even to the eyes of infancy, Mrs. Hudson Bart had appeared young; but Lily could not recall a time when her father had not been bald and slightly stooping, with streaks of grey in

his hair, and a tired walk. It was a shock to her to learn afterwards that he was but two years older than her mother.[92]

Lily's parents are nearly the same age, but while she remembers her mother as vigorously young and dancing away time, Mr. Bart seemed always to be old, colorless, overworked, "stooping" in posture, if not in status. His wife, meanwhile, climbed upon his bowed back into opulence. Lily recalls him as a placeholder between the "butler" and the one who kept time ticking, between physical labor and age itself. If Mr. Bart is Father Time, it is the time of labor, precisely what protected her mother *from time*. "Lily seldom saw her father by daylight," writes Wharton. "All day he was 'down town'; and in winter it was long after nightfall when she heard his fagged step on the stairs and his hand on the school-room door" (26). He disappeared even more in summer, when it even "seemed to tire him to rest" (26). When Mrs. Bart and Lily went abroad, no sooner did the steamer reach the halfway point than Mr. Bart effectively "dipped below the horizon," out of mind, save to be "denounced for having neglected to forward Mrs. Bart's remittances" (26). Among friends, Mrs. Bart was spoken of as a "wonderful manager" of her household, but when money was short, Lily's father "in some vague way . . . seemed always to blame for the deficiency" (26). Though a faithful and dependable breadwinner, when Mr. Bart was not providing or being chastised by Mrs. Bart for not doing so, he simply ceased to exist.

Lily's young life is described as shaped by manic-depressive extremes of elation and need, dependent upon yet detached from any sense of labor time: "a zig-zag broken course down which the family craft glided on a rapid current of amusement, tugged at by the underflow of a perpetual need—the need of more money" (26). Having never seen her father labor (much less seen him at all), "[s]he knew very little of the value of money," and so was raised as if money could be created *ex nihilo* (27). When her father finally announced to his bewildered family, "I'm ruined," it was as if he "had become extinct when he ceased to fulfil [*sic*] his purpose." Perhaps unsurprisingly, "[i]t was a relief to Lily when her father died" (28, 29). Yet, once fully orphaned and on her own, and lacking her father's work ethic, Lily cannot fulfill the dual roles of her parents: the laboring, aging, economic agent on one side and the timeless beneficiary of that labor on the other—the one subject to time, the other protected from it. In the ups and downs of her increasing "fits of angry rebellion against fate" and attempts to reach for the "bright pinnacles of success," Lily becomes instead caught between these two orders of time (33). As a poor economic agent who succumbs to age and increasing debt, Lily is trapped in the causality of linear time; meanwhile, the so-called real, true Lily, seen only in glimpses, lies outside time, in the eternal realm of art.

In the *tableaux vivants* scene, for example, the "eternal" essence of Lily's beauty is most evident to Selden; her beauty codified *through art*, only as art does she appear "the real Lily" (107). Posing as Reynolds's "Mrs. Lloyd" to entertain the Welly Brys's parlor guests, Lily's tableau produced a breathless, "unanimous 'Oh!'" among the spectators. Only Lily "could embody the person represented without ceasing to be herself" (106). To a "responsive fancy" like Selden's, such scenes gave "magic glimpses of the boundary world between fact and imagination" (105)—in other words, to an eternal aesthetic realm beyond the material, temporal one:

> The noble buoyancy of her attitude, its suggestion of soaring grace, revealed the touch of poetry in her beauty that Selden always felt in her presence, yet lost the sense of when he was not with her. Its expression was now so vivid that for the first time he seemed to see before him *the real Lily Bart*, divested of the trivialities of her little world, and catching for a moment a note of that *eternal harmony* of which her beauty was a part. (106; emphasis mine)

This "touch of poetry," this "eternal harmony" barely glimpsed, encompasses for Selden "the whole tragedy of her life": "it was as though her beauty, thus detached from all that cheapened and vulgarized it, had held out suppliant hands to [Selden] from the world in which he and she had once met for a moment" (107). For Elaine Showalter, Selden is "enraptured" by the "carefully constructed Lily of his desire," the "dryad-like" nature he would make of her "vivid plastic sense."[93] Showalter is right, but further, this "Lily" is detached from the "cheapening" realm of the economic, in which Lily is commodified. When time stands still, by contrast, as Gerty Farish agrees, the tableau "'makes her look like the real Lily.'"[94] The tragedy in this scene is the timeless vision Lily's admirers impose upon her, foreshadowing how in death—her complete passage out of time—Lily again reveals through her "delicate impalpable mask" the "real Lily" (253). Scholars such as Showalter and Cynthia Griffin Wolff have tended to read the split in Lily's character here in aesthetic, feminist, and economic terms: she is both artist and art object; brutal speculator and victim of financial speculation.[95] Yet whether the "real Lily" is one who rises above market calculations, as Wai-Chee Dimock contends, or is squarely in the thick of them, as according to Walter Benn Michaels, Lily is both subject to the inexorable passage of time and, only for brief, ultimately fatal, moments of total risk, does she get beyond it.[96]

While Selden grieves Lily's compromised ideals, Rosedale promises to rescue Lily from her relentless debt, her most practical, material burden. Marrying Percy Gryce might have meant a way out, but "it was the idea of the gambling debt that frightened" him.[97] Instead, Lily faces a "mounting tide of indebtedness" (62). If usury is the crime of selling time that is not one's own, then debt means working to pay off the time now owned by another. Debt is the real monkey on Lily's back; it ages her in servitude to her creditors to pay off an already-mortgaged future, and renders her vulnerable to a predator like Gus Trenor. When he describes how he profits from speculation, Lily fancies a "means of escape from her dreary predicament":

> "You don't know how a fellow has to hustle to keep this kind of thing going." He waved his whip in the direction of the Bellomont acres, which lay outspread before them in opulent undulations. "Judy has no idea of what she spends—not that there isn't plenty to keep the thing going," he interrupted himself, "but a man has got to keep his eyes open and pick up all the tips he can . . . the truth is it takes a devilish lot of hard work to keep the machinery running." (65)

Lily is baffled over this "hustle," the mystified workings of speculative capitalism; to her, the economy is magical, where something can be made from nothing, a secular creation *ex nihilo*. Trenor abuses this ignorance, pretending to help Lily by investing her money, only to invest more of his own with an expectation of reciprocation.

Rosedale may be at the center of the novel's speculative economy, but Gus Trenor is the real Shylock. When Lily fails to return his "kindness" in kind, he traps her in his house to extort his pound of flesh—her intimacy—in terms of time. The novel's turning point amounts to a near-rape scene: "Look here, Lily: won't you give me five minutes of your own accord?" And when she demurs, he replies, "Very good, then: I'll take 'em. And as many more as I want" (113). Trenor's demands for the time to which he feels entitled show implicit connections between time and usury:

> . . . a man's got his feelings, and you've played with mine too long . . . thought you could turn me inside out and chuck me in the gutter like an empty purse. But, by gad, that ain't playing fair: that's dodging the rules of the game. Of course I know now what you wanted—it wasn't my beautiful eyes you were after—but I tell you what, Miss Lily, you've got to pay up for making me think so— . . . Oh, I'm not asking for payment in kind. But there's such a thing as fair play—and interest on one's money—and hang me if I've had as much as a look from you. . . . (114–16)

Trenor, not Rosedale, reinvents the "rules of the game," demands sexual "interest," and thus silently and secretly embodies the parasitism fueled by an economic system of speculation. At this climactic moment, Trenor retreats from committing sexual violence, but Lily's physical terror and subsequent shame make clear the damaging effects of his attempts to extort her time: "Over and over her the sea of humiliation broke—wave crashing on wave so close that the moral shame was one with the physical dread" (116). As she begs him to ring for a servant and a cab, she "heard herself [do so] in a voice that was her own yet outside herself," and once safely inside the cab, "reaction came, and shuddering darkness closed on her. . . . She seemed a stranger to herself, or rather *there were two selves in her*, the one she had always known, and a new abhorrent being to which it found itself chained" (117; emphasis mine). Irrevocably divided yet chained to herself, Lily is reembodied as the "real Lily Bart," but imprisoned in homogeneous time: "There was a great gulf fixed between today and yesterday. . . . Her eyes fell on an illuminated clock at a street corner, and she saw that the hands marked the half hour after eleven" (117). Clock time here marks the long hours Lily would lie "alone, shuddering sleepless on her bed" following her "ordeal," but also the "lateness of the hour" (117). And yet, in spite of Trenor, remarkably, the blame goes to Rosedale, as Lily has "a vague sense of [Rosedale] being somehow connected with her lucky speculations" (89).

By the novel's final chapters, Lily is fully twain—a social, physical being, subjugated by the ravages of *Chronos*, and a spiritual, eternal one who exists perhaps only for Selden in the form of their shared yet unarticulated love:

> "You have something to tell me—do you mean to marry?" he said abruptly.
>
> Lily's eyes did not falter, but a look of wonder, of puzzled self-interrogation, formed itself slowly in their depths. In the light of his question, she had paused to ask herself if her decision had really been taken when she entered the room.
>
> "You always told me I should have to come to it sooner or later!" she said with a faint smile.
>
> "And you have come to it now?"
>
> "I shall have come to it—presently. But there is something else I must come to first." She paused again, trying to transmit to her voice the steadiness of her recovered smile. "There is some one I must say goodbye to. Oh, not you—we are sure to see each other again—but the Lily Bart you knew. I have kept her with me all this time, but now we are going to part, and I have brought her back to you—I am going to leave her here. When I go out presently she will not go with me. I shall like to think that she has stayed with you—and she'll be no trouble, she'll take up no room." (240)

Lily herewith deposits in Selden's hands the cherished ideal self: she drops Bertha's letters, her sole weapon of revenge and calculation for power, into the fire. Sacrificing any chance of social rehabilitation and any potential marital deal with Rosedale, she enters the republic of the spirit by a marriage of death, foreshadowed in Selden's scrutiny, "with a strange sense of foreboding," of "how thin her hands looked against the rising light of the flames," and how, "under the loose lines of her dress . . . the curves of her figure had shrunk to angularity" (241). With Lily's death imminent, the present becomes a significant future past for Selden: "*he remembered long afterward* how the red play of the flame sharpened the depression of her nostrils, and intensified the blackness of the shadows which struck up from her cheekbones to her eyes" (241; emphasis mine). "Afterward"— after death, a nameless future time—Selden will recollect this moment as pregnant with signs of Lily's mortal decline.

Retrospectively cast, the penultimate moment of the novel is certainly suffused with the affective traces that Lily's death will leave on Selden. But perhaps more importantly in this scene, Lily squares her financial accounts. Having finally received a belated inheritance check, she resolves to pay off Trenor. Yet even this belated influx of cash frees her from neither moral compromise nor the pressures of time. She quickly calculates that the $10,000 would be too little to live on after settling up, and in any case, could never compensate for her "deeper impoverishment," an "inner destitution" that no amount of money could repay, and of which each new moment seems a reminder:

> . . . there was something more miserable still [than being poor]—it was the clutch of solitude at her heart, the sense of being swept like a stray uprooted growth down the heedless current of the years. That was the feeling that possessed her now—the feeling of being something rootless and ephemeral, mere spin-drift of the whirling surface of existence. . . . And as she looked back she saw that there had never been a time when she had had any relation to life. (248)

In her "rootless and ephemeral" state, Lily's past, her debt, is irredeemable. If there was never a time within the "whirling surface of existence" that she felt "any relation to life," the only way to find it now, she concludes, is to step out of the "spin-drift" altogether, to stop moving, stop calculating, and rest. As it grows late into the night, Lily fears that to go on as before would be to "slip into gradual tolerance of the debt," and she "could feel the countless hands of habit dragging her back into some fresh compromise with fate" (249). These "countless hands of habit" may suggest the addictive temptations of her gambling, but they also personify the future, which could only consist of an endless series of repetitions of the past.[98] In this way, the march of time becomes Lily's tangible enemy, from which she would escape, had she anything left to wager. In her sleepless delirium, manifesting what Wharton determined from the start, she recalls her "fate": "the terrible silence and emptiness seemed to symbolize her future— she felt as though the house, the street, the world were all empty, and she alone left sentient in a lifeless universe."[99] In this "multiplication of wakefulness," she feels "her whole past . . . reenacting itself at a hundred points of consciousness," and cannot bear the infinite repetition of days to come, the inexorable pressure of linear time itself: "Perspective had disappeared— the next day pressed close upon her, and on its heels came the days that were to follow—they swarmed about her like a shrieking mob" (250). Like a crowd closing in upon her, the past penetrates the future at all points and the present disappears.

Lily Bart escapes the onslaught of future days with a fatal chloral overdose, but the tragedy is less about suicide, though the novel flirts with this, than her desire to escape time itself, even if to enjoy a "brief bath of oblivion," involving a "slight risk," she knew, but only "one chance in a hundred" (250). In Lily's last calculated gamble, wagering her life, she drifts into the peaceful "subjugation" of soothed nerves, as the narrator reflects, "Tomorrow would not be so difficult after all" (251). Drifting into unconsciousness, fantasizing about Nettie Struther's babe in her arms, she recalls something that she must tell Selden—"some word she had found that should make life clear between them" (251)—but we never hear it. Lily finds relief but loses the bet. Her last act culminates in a silent, timeless, painterly tableau of mother and child, in which the "the real Lily" escapes social and clock time at once (253).[100]

Chance, Gambling, and the Jewish Future

The alternative future that the novel posits for Lily Bart lay ostensibly with Simon Rosedale, even if a marriage to him—though a sensible, mutually beneficial, business deal—is for Lily the ultimate sign of degradation. Such a union would signal that timeless traditions and values of beauty, grace, nobility, and honor that the character Selden represents have been reduced to their monetary equivalent by the likes of the "Seligman 'Jews.'" In rejecting Rosedale's offer, however, and perhaps ironically, Lily becomes all the more quickly subject to the ravages of time, resulting in her inevitable death, as she passes out of time altogether. Presuming we can take *The House of Mirth* to be a naturalist novel, what does this novel say about Jewish-Gentile intermarriage in naturalism?

Since its publication, debates have ensued over whether *The House of Mirth* is a novel of sentiment, a determinist naturalist novel, a tragedy, a realist novel, or something else, taking on even greater force in 1967, when the Wharton papers in the Yale archive were first released to scholars.[101] Though early critics focused on the novel's moral implications, it was Henry James who, according to Helen Killoran, opened the debate about its genre in 1905, when he commented that the novel is "not one, but two books."[102] The book seemed confused to James, and for many readers since it lacked a standard plot, relying on an episodic structure.[103] Given the readings above, I would suggest that, rather than a sign of a defect, this disjointed, episodic structure signals the novel's temporal tensions. Lily Bart confronts repeated opportunities, or chances, to make choices that could alter her fate. Yet these instances of chance, possibility, and open-ended futurity are foreclosed by the linear time of determinism—her death was a given for the author from the start. These two temporal dynamics—naturalism's "pessimistic determinism" and the cycles and temporal distensions of chance—are inextricably linked to create cycles of readerly desire, even when we know she will ultimately die.

Although Wharton has been admitted to the naturalist canon relatively recently, these temporal tensions either disqualify the novel for naturalism or ask us to look at the genre as temporally heterogeneous. Lily's death as a progression out of time seems in accord with conceptions of naturalism as a determinist genre operating in linear time, in which a cruel social machine—reflecting the economics of the age, the forces of industrialization and rationalization, or a contingent universe more broadly—chews up and spits out its helpless victims and rewards its survivors.[104] While critics have differed on the issue of the genre's determinism, they agree on its linear temporality: June Howard regards the "tension between determinism and reform [as] intrinsic" to the genre, while Donald Pizer sees "tragic irony" in its conflict between individual autonomy and social contingency.[105] Critics in the 1930s like Wilson Follett judged *The House of Mirth* as a set of nostalgic chronicles, "curiosities" of a bygone era.[106] But, even later, Dimock (1985) and Benn Michaels (1987) read Lily as utterly determined by the modern economic marketplace: Dimock sees her rebelling against a totalizing "exchange system," however feebly, while Benn Michaels sees her embodying, even in her moments of greatest distaste for Wall Street commerce, a "complete commitment to the practices of speculation" that define modern market logic.[107]

Jennifer Fleissner escapes this (in many ways, temporal) binary by reading naturalism's "most characteristic plot" as marked not by the linear movements of either resistance or resignation to broader systemic forces but by "an ongoing, nonlinear, repetitive motion—back and forth, around and around, on and on," the rhythms not of determinism but of "compulsion."[108] Fleissner's work is crucial in how it redefines naturalist temporality; she challenges the linearity of deterministic plots and a critical canon that has not only ignored female authorship but remained "limited by a tendency to reduce its meanings" to two "polarized responses": "either fatalistic or nostalgic in the face of modern life."[109] Lily's death only illuminates how critics, like Lily's peers, punish her precisely for her acts of spontaneity, her moments of indecision, and breaks from the proscribed course of securing a husband, as we saw in the narrator's lament, "Why must a girl pay so dearly for her least escape from routine?"[110] Fleissner rightly argues that Lily is punished not just for her spontaneity but for challenging a gendered temporality in her "attempts to stop time in its tracks," rather than succumb to the linear path of the "biological clock."[111] Compulsive as Lily's acts appear, in her vacillation between "the whirling surface of existence" and her deep desire for stasis and love that would transcend the whirling, she also points to an analogous aesthetic problem of narrative form: how to maintain a heightened readerly experience, and keep that affective dimension present for the reader in the face of Lily's inexorable fate.

As noted earlier, Fredric Jameson argues that realism is the dialectical manifestation of the tension between just such affective dimensions and narrative itself, such that moments of affect disrupt and suspend narrative's linear flow in the moment of "ekphrasis." For Jameson, description opens up what he calls "the eternal present," a "realm of affect" that opposes narrative linearity.[112] Goran Blix's clarification is helpful here: the nontemporal quality Jameson attributes to affect "might redeem . . . the oppressive impression of fate and closure that haunts the social trajectories of the novel's characters."[113] This "clash" between prescription and possibility sounds remarkably close to what I have been describing as the conflicting temporalities that only get intensified in literary naturalism: the linearity of determinism and the unpredictable futurity of chance.

With the spread of the "probabilistic revolution," Maurice Lee has recently shown, nineteenth-century American literature took part in broad intellectual and cultural shifts to try and control chance, the "expansion of stock markets, the growth of the insurance industry, the spread of numerical literacy and statistical thinking, and the application of probability theory to travel, politics, health, consumerism and other aspects of daily experience."[114] Given the themes of gambling and speculation in *The House of Mirth*, it is possible to explain its temporal tensions between fate and chance as a collision of what Jackson Lears calls the "culture of chance" and the "culture of control," a "face-off between the confidence man, the devotee of Fortuna, and the self-made man, the herald of Providence."[115] Cultures of control, such as the American protestant or managerial traditions, Lears asserts, "dismiss chance as a demon to be denied or a difficulty to be minimized" (7). Cultures of chance, by contrast, "encourage reverence for grace, luck and fortune—powers beyond human mastery whose favor may nonetheless be courted" (7). Lears makes historical links between gambling and grace, the latter perceived "as a kind of spiritual luck, a free gift from God," an idea that "lies at the heart of gambling's larger cultural significance" (9), and traces the culture of chance to its roots in the Greek god of chance, the trickster Hermes, who presided over the crossroads where "chance and choice merge" (10).

In a discussion of determinism, one might view this crossroads as the locus of free will, but to read it in temporal terms, it becomes a function of *Chronos* and *Kairos*. Hermes, after all, serves as emissary between limitation and possibility: between *Chronos*, here the temporal register for linear determinism, and *Kairos*, the magical, seemingly fateful, decisive moments. Because fiction relies on the interventions of Kairotic time, it participates in, and helps preserve, a very old religious tradition of providential thinking. As the forces of control and chance compete in Wharton's novel, Lily's gambling, loans, and debts are folded into the linear narrative of decline. This conflict registers aesthetically by creating two temporal, structural orders, as I have been suggesting: linear determinism—whether guided by Darwinist encoding or providence—and chance's unpredictability, in the forms of gambling and financial speculation. If the eighteenth-century invention of clock time severed time from space, as Anthony Giddens contends, only to reconnect it though the social organization of time—calendars and timetables, key markers of modernity—then money only intensifies the gap as a mode of deferral.[116] Money connects "credit and liability in circumstances where immediate exchange of products is impossible," Giddens insists, and speculation widens the temporal gap even further into the future (24). What is remarkable about these competing temporalities in *The House of Mirth* is how Rosedale, as noted above, appears at these crucial Kairotic moments at the crossroads of its heroine's fate.

In Wharton, chance thus opens up the specific affect of "suspense" in both senses of the word—anticipation and promise of fulfillment, but also suspension of the narrative itself—and this disrupts the temporality of narrative "fate." Lily wages a battle against fate's homogeneous time, but her gambling opens up time-spaces, projecting possible futures. Moments foreshadowing her death also incite our desire to read in spite of a known outcome, creating affective tension between hope and hopelessness, between an investment in Lily Bart's future and a gamble we know we will lose. Even though the character's fate is determined, chance provides textual moments in which time is suspended, moments of respite from its onward march. The forces of chance—gambling, speculation, borrowing on credit—provide the character and the reader with renewed hope from episode to episode, whereas the ethos of control puts the reader into a more distanced position of sympathy. Since control can only be evaluated in retrospect, via consequences, chance orients the reader toward the future—of possibility, of indeterminacy. Determining the outcomes of both requires a backward glance. As Lears notes, providentialist assumptions tend to have an "ex post facto quality": "In theater as in real estate or stocks, success made it easy to match reward and merit—but only in retrospect."[117] Control, based on rational calculation, is teleological and linear, but chance has the magical ability to renew infinite future possibilities.

Rosedale has his hands on the economic future, but Wharton makes Lily's potential marriage to him not an opportunity or risk but a consequence, a punishment. Unwilling to bank on her future security, Lily pays far more at the capricious hands of luck. Gambling, in the form of bridge, is socially inescapable, increasing her obligations to others, as she has so little to wager and so much to lose. For the Trenors and their guests, bridge is an act of supreme leisure that Lily "knew she could not afford" and that leaves her "little gold purse" three hundred dollars lighter at the end of the day.[118] Lily feared passing "under the spell of the terrible god of chance," but participating at the card table was "one of the taxes" her hostesses expected her "to pay for their prolonged hospitality, and for the dresses and trinkets which occasionally replenished her insufficient wardrobe," so she is driven to "risk higher stakes at each fresh venture" (24). Lily must play her hand, yet even when "the gambling passion was upon her," the text is unclear as to whether her losses result from Providence or bad choices:

> . . . she had so many uses for [the three hundred dollars] that its very insufficiency had caused her to play high in the hope of doubling it. But of course she had lost—she who needed every penny, while Bertha Dorset, whose husband showered money on her, must have pocketed at least five hundred, and Judy Trenor, who could have afforded to lose a thousand a night, had left the table clutching such a heap

of bills that she had been unable to shake hands with her guests when they bade her good night.

A world in which such things could be seemed a miserable place to Lily Bart; but then she had never been able to understand the laws of a universe which was so ready to leave her out of its calculations. (24)

If gambling favors the rich, Lily's bad luck resolves into a narrative of fate, of the "calculations" of the "universe" before which she is helpless.[119] Gambling ages Lily, most visibly in her face: "As she sat before the mirror brushing her hair, her face looked hollow and pale, and she was frightened by two little lines near her mouth, faint flaws in the smooth curve of the cheek . . . it seemed an added injustice that petty cares should leave a trace on the beauty which was her only defense against them."[120] Gambling is also precisely the moral crime for which her Aunt Peniston later disinherits her. Nothing at that point can mitigate the contamination of the "contagious illness" of gossip Lily's gambling brings into Mrs. Peniston's house: "it was horrible of a girl to let herself be talked about; however unfounded the charges against her, she must be to blame for their having been made" (100).

Subject to time as Lily is, Selden only appreciates the ephemeral, timeless qualities of her beauty; Rosedale, by contrast, appreciates Lily as a woman *in time*. Even in her tired, overworked condition, "Rosedale was seized afresh by the poignant surprise of her beauty . . . a forgotten enemy that had lain in ambush and now sprang out on him unawares" (226). If Selden appreciates Lily like a work of art, Rosedale admires her as a woman. In encouraging her to clear her name, he also supports her role as an equal business partner of sorts, one who could act in her own economic self-interest. If only she would let him, he would clear her mounting debt and her battle against time. If *The House of Mirth* is tragic, the tragedy is that while Lily could anchor value for Rosedale, Rosedale could stabilize time for Lily; they are aligned, but they never meet.

Rosedale's *interest* in Lily is what, therefore, makes him finally emerge as the more sympathetic character. So why can't she marry him? Lily's physical revulsion clearly sounds like plain old racist antisemitism. Dale Bauer takes this view, arguing that "Rosedale is everything that Selden is not" and this is precisely about his abject "Jewishness":

> Selden comes from an established family; Rosedale is an interloper. Selden enjoys a fineness of feeling and enjoins Lily Bart to be a citizen in the "republic of the spirit"; Rosedale is perceived as vulgar and materialistic, exhorting Lily to blackmail her way back into society. Selden cannot bear to acknowledge the presence of passion; Rosedale actually tells Lily how much he wants her. Lily first rebuffs Rosedale's proposal of marriage, then contemplates the prospect, but when her night thoughts turn to an image of herself with Rosedale, she finds the idea of sex with him too revolting. Lily's principle objection to Simon Rosedale is not that he is materialistic or vulgar or sexually aggressive, *but that he is all those things, a Jew.* His Jewishness marks, in the context of the reigning prejudices, just how steeply Lily's status has declined.[121]

Other critics have argued that Lily refuses to marry Rosedale for principled reasons of value and tradition, for example, "not because he is a social climbing Jew," but because she refuses to engage in revenge.[122] She refuses to adopt the calculating nature of market mentality, so that "each decisive moment in [Lily's] social decline turns on her unwillingness to elevate her own social position at someone else's expense."[123]

It is easy to reproduce the characters' facile use of Jewishness as a catchall term for the complicated problems "the Jew" reflects about Gentile society, or even to ascribe their antisemitic views to Wharton; however, the novel seems to challenge this logic, as Christian Reigel argues, leaving readers with a sense of uncertainty as to Wharton's actual feelings toward Jews.[124] Her negative portrait of Rosedale, after all, is reversed by the end of the novel, when he becomes the only one to express compassion toward Lily in her fallen state. It is not Selden but Rosedale who finally bewails her abject poverty as a "crazy farce" and a "damnable outrage."[125] The novel thus critiques an irrational fear of new-moneyed individuals like Rosedale on the economic and social rise, even as it mourns the increasingly obsolete values and forms of the past that Lily and Selden embody.

Inasmuch as Wharton's portrayal of Rosedale is, at times, unkind, to become mired in the antisemitic debate elides the structural tensions of time and value that he mediates. Wharton creates in Rosedale an abject figure of the market, but his function in the novel challenges the very stereotypes she establishes. In spite of his "polished baldness" and sense of having mastered society manners, he remains the most honest character in that set (76). He may never be "the real thing," as Henry James would put it—a born and bred gentleman—but unlike Selden, a paralyzed spectator, Rosedale acts in time.[126] In this respect, if *The House of Mirth* is shaped by what Nancy Bentley calls "an internalized modernity," its temporal sensibility links Jewishness to the modern future as it critiques an untenable, antiquated, and romantic nostalgia for values and traditions of the past.[127] The character Rosedale thus complicates the racially determined position of the "Seligman 'Jew'" of naturalism. Neither noble Hebrew nor avaricious "Jew," reflecting neither purely philosemitic nor antisemitic feeling, he instead reconfigures this inherited duality of literary Jewishness and promises to integrate the splintering versions of time that cause Lily's demise. In Rosedale, the figure of the "Jew" is not that of a debased past but of the promising future of modernity.[128]

These last two chapters have elucidated how "Jewishness" is expected to absorb and explain away modern social and economic problems of value, and mediate conflicts between leisure time and business. Placing the "Seligman 'Jew'" at the forefront of modernity, *The House of Mirth* provides an important precedent for the ideologies of improvement and success put forth in Anzia Yezierska's novels examined in the next chapter. In literary naturalism, we have seen, for every rise there is a fall; the New World economy of opportunity is restricted, taking its toll on the spiritual and material riches of the Old. For Jacob Riis, the encounter with immigrant "aliens" of "Jewtown" represented un-Christian stubbornness and, hence, moral decline in America. For Henry James, a similar encounter represents cultural decline, but possible promise for a New Jerusalem in New York (one to which he nonetheless bids his own farewell). For Wharton, however, the encounter with the rising classes of "cultured" Jewish immigrants is only life threatening for old-moneyed culture because that culture is already defunct, in decline. As those like Simon Rosedale fortify their New World roots—he is the only character about to become a father—those like Lily Bart become uprooted, a generation passing away. The rise of Simon Rosedale and coincident fall of Lily Bart thus mark a changing of the social and economic guards, a future for two social groups—Jewish and Gentile—now intimately intertwined socially and financially. In the next chapter, Yezierska picks up in her novels where Wharton leaves off, with fictional experiments in a deeper form of Jewish-Gentile intimacy, intermarriage, which, in the context of Christian philosemitism, is figured as a benign, voluntary, highly incentivized form of conversion, Progressive-era immigrant assimilation.

4

The Melting Pot, Intermarriage, and Progressive Reform

> The mighty tide of immigration to our shores has brought in its train much of good and much of evil; and whether the good or the evil shall predominate depends mainly on whether these newcomers do or do not throw themselves heartily into our national life, cease to be Europeans, and become Americans like the rest of us. But where immigrants, or the sons of immigrants, do not heartily and in good faith throw in their lot with us, but cling to the speech, the customs, the ways of life, and the habits of thought of the Old World which they have left, they thereby harm both themselves and us. . . . Above all, the immigrant must learn to talk and think and *be* United States.
>
> —Theodore Roosevelt, "True Americanism" (1894)

> My age alone, my true age, would be reason enough for my writing. I began life in the Middle Ages, as I shall prove, and here am I still, your contemporary in the twentieth century, thrilling with your latest thought.
>
> —Mary Antin, *The Promised Land* (1912)

ISRAEL ZANGWILL'S 1908 PLAY, *The Melting-Pot*, a drama of assimilation through religious intermarriage, opened at the Comedy Theatre in New York on September 6, 1909, and ran for 136 performances, not many for a play that provided the most iconic image in American self-definition, shaping American discourse on immigration and ethnicity for over a century.[1] Written by perhaps "the most famous Jew in the English-speaking

183

world," Zangwill's play popularized the notion that the path into the American future would be cleared when immigrants relinquished the past—namely their prior cultural and ethnic identities—through marriages of choice.[2] The play's drama unfolds around a troubled affair between David Quixano, orphaned Jewish immigrant and prodigious musical composer, and Vera Davenport, Russian revolutionary turned immigrant settlement house worker. Vera's father turns out to have been the antisemitic Russian baron responsible for the murder of David's parents in the 1903 Kishinev pogrom. As both are warned against defying the ties of blood, the lovers must overcome racial, religious, and class differences—that is, their various ties to the past, and the parochial hatred these ties could engender between them. Envisioning America as God's "melting-pot," however, David overcomes these obstacles, and the two lovers unite atop an immigrant settlement house in New York, with the irregular skyline on one side and the harbor with its Statue of Liberty on the other, before a glorious sunset charged with sacred meaning:

DAVID

> [*Prophetically exalted by the spectacle.*]

It is the fires of God round His Crucible.
> [*He drops her hand and points downward.*]

There she lies, the great Melting-Pot—listen! Can't you hear the
> roaring and bubbling? There gapes her mouth
> [*He points east.*]

—the harbor where a thousand mammoth feeders come from the
> ends of the earth to pour in their human freight. Ah, what
> a stirring and seething! Celt and Latin, Slav and Teuton,
> Greek and Syrian,—black and yellow—

VERA

> [*Softly, nestling to him.*]

Jew and Gentile—

DAVID

Yes, East and West, and North and South, the palm and the pine,
the pole and the equator, the crescent and the cross—how
the great Alchemist melts and fuses them with his purging
flame! Here shall they all unite to build the Republic of
Man and the Kingdom of God. Ah, Vera, what is the glory
of Rome and Jerusalem where all nations and races come to
worship and look back, compared with the glory of America, where all races and nations come to labour and look
forward!

[*He raises his hand in benediction over the shining city.*]

Peace, peace, to all ye unborn millions, fated to fill this giant
continent—the God of our children give you Peace.[3]

As the curtain falls to the soft accompaniment of "My Country, 'tis of
Thee," the play's final scene crystallizes the symbol of "the Melting-Pot," as
Werner Sollors puts it, the "crucible" for ethnic assimilation in the United
States.[4] The alchemical metaphors of "melting" and "fusing" have long been
taken to signify in racial terms: "Celt and Latin, Slav and Teuton, Greek
and Syrian,—black and yellow," but also "Jew and Gentile," as nineteenth-
century racial logic would have it. The play's setting, however, the settlement
house, is the site not only of "racial" fusing but also of a social experiment
that will pave the way for a sacred, redemptive American future. There, all
"nations and races" of the earth will come together to America to "build the
Republic of Man and the Kingdom of God." As the language of alchemy
combines with that of eschatology, the scene captures how America represented for Progressives—as it once did for Puritans—the New Jerusalem
on earth. In America, the "human freight" from all "ends of the earth" will
be guided not by the God of our fathers—of family, tradition, and the
past—but the "God of our children," those born of democratic choice and
love. This new America, built on ethnic and religious intermarriage, public
education, and Progressive reform, offers not the promises of the past, "the
glory of Rome and Jerusalem," but keys to the future, "where all races and
nations come to labour and look forward."[5]

Zangwill fondly dedicated his play to Theodore Roosevelt, whose advocacy of nationalist assimilation and critique of "hyphenated" American identities prefigured the metaphorical meaning of the "melting pot" that gave the play its title. Roosevelt had insisted that for American Jews (and all immigrants) the future lay in cultural assimilation and intermarriage.[6] He made a strong case for the kind of liberal state that Marx derided, one in which "we have as little use for people who carry religious prejudices into our politics as for those who carry prejudices of caste or nationality," even as "we demand that all citizens, Protestant and Catholic, Jew and Gentile, shall have fair treatment in every way."[7] In other words, we shall have religious freedom, but we must also "merge" our "Old World religious race and national antipathies . . . into a love for our common country" (28). Invoking the notion of national "love," Roosevelt likened the process of Americanization to one of matrimony: a secular repetition of the demand for religious conversion, or at the very least apostasy, but now as a freely chosen form of loyalty to the new American nation. Roosevelt's exceptionalist vision of America revised Puritan claims for American settlement as divine errand. For Jews to choose the predominantly Protestant nation and become Americans, therefore, such "melting" would require a renunciation of the Jewish past. Roosevelt insisted, after all, that Americans declare a singular loyalty to the customs, language, and political and cultural institutions of the United States, likening national loyalty to monogamous, marital fidelity. It may be, he argued, that in remote ages hence, philosophers will no longer regard patriotism as a virtue, but then again, they may also "look down upon and disregard monogamic marriage" (20). Building a comparison between marriage and nation, Roosevelt added that, for now, the words "'home'" and "'country'" still mean a "great deal," so that "treason, like adultery, ranks as one of the worst of all possible crimes" (20). Whereas the abuse of patriotism makes one a "scoundrel," a lack of patriotism is worse, so that cosmopolitanism of any form was deplorable and, to extend the metaphor above, akin to spousal infidelity as a form of treason (21).

With these values in mind, Roosevelt urged that we "Americanize" immigrants, the primary motivation for Progressive ventures like the settlement house movement. During its peak years, between 1893 and 1922, the movement's agenda was largely that of the entire Progressive reform movement, including "access for all Americans to excellent public education, protective labor laws for women and children, woman's suffrage, municipal reform, recreational facilities, affordable housing for low-income people, and city planning."[8] In 1892, the same year that Roosevelt published "True Americanism" in the *Forum*, Jane Addams, who established Chicago's Hull House in 1889, published two influential speeches in the same journal and emerged as the movement's leader.[9] Addams stressed the idea of the "social settlement," rather than the "settlement as laboratory," emphasizing community building over research, and the "twin goals of social reform and self-reformation," key Protestant themes in the movement.[10] Roosevelt, however, emphasized the individual: the fundamental aim of reform was for immigrants to choose to be Americans first. They must "cease to be Europeans, and become Americans like the rest of us"; abandon all ways of the "Old World"; and "talk and think and *be* United States."[11] Roosevelt punctuated his theory by quoting a happily assimilated new American, the Honorable Richard Guenther of Wisconsin, who invoked, like Zangwill, the alchemical metaphor for the process of assimilation:

> After passing through the crucible of naturalization, we are no longer Germans; we are Americans. Our attachment to America cannot be measured by the length of our residence here. We are Americans from the moment we touch the American shore until we are laid in American graves. We will fight for American whenever necessary. America, first, last, and all the time. America against Germany, America against the world; America, right or wrong; always America. We are Americans. (30–31)

Guenther's effusive repetition of "America" suggests the anxiety of rhetorically proving one's loyalty, love, and monogamous devotion in this "marriage" of choice, as opposed to one by arrangement or birth. But his rhetoric also mystifies the ground-level social processes, painstaking commitments to public education, and Protestant values learned therein, which promised immigrants upward mobility, even if at the cost of maintaining their ties to the past.

These choices had high stakes for immigrant Jews, and the level of national devotion Zangwill dramatized was believed by many to be difficult, if not impossible, for Jews to achieve. The basic thrust of the "Jewish Problem" in America was, after all, the question: Are Jews assimilable? Are they loyal and can they be trusted to put national affiliation before international or religious ones? These doubts projected into the future the outcome of the American experiment to which immigrants were expected to wed themselves. For immigrant Jews already committed to the nation but seeking to prove their loyalty, the debate posed particular problems: given the premise of American religious freedom, how were they to remain religiously observant, and maintain a sense of Jewishness that was for so long defined in relation to the past—an ancient, biblical, typologically rewritten past—yet still find their place in a Protestant Progressive-Era America that essentially asked them to divorce themselves from it?

If Progressive-Era arguments for intermarriage promised one solution to the "Jewish Problem," in the works of Mary Antin and Anzia Yezierska we see (real and fictional) Jewish women make their own marital choices; thereby affirm or critique American assimilationist politics and Jewish patriarchy; and negotiate, if not reconcile, Jewish traditions of the past with the modern, American future. This chapter thus takes a close look at how literature figured intermarriage and public education as paths into modernity for Jewish women, those whose religious and cultural heritage offered them limited, scripted roles within a biblical tradition regarded in the Gentile world as outmoded and unmodern. In line with the efforts of Roosevelt and Zangwill, as well as Progressive reformers like Edward Everett Hale, John Dewey, and Addams (an avid fan of Zangwill's play), a spate of proassimilationist narratives and novels addressing religious intermarriage were published and popularized in the first decades of the twentieth century: by Elias Tobenkin, M. E. Ravage, Sidney Nyburg, Ezra Brudno, John Cournos, and Henry Harland (aka, Sidney Luska), among others.[12] Jewish novels of intermarriage, in particular, responded to the weight of a burdensome past, to create what Adam Sol describes as the "ultimate expression of liberation from an antiquated tradition."[13] Sol goes on, "early Progressive scholars and representatives of immigrant groups believed that a rapid integration into mainstream American life would be best for

America as a whole, as well as for the immigrant groups themselves, and intermarriage was seen as the culmination of these efforts."[14] Writing these fictions, literary authors engaged in broader debates over the relationship between religion and American cultural citizenship, their narratives mediating the Jewish past with the American future.

Writing within and against this tradition, Antin and Yezierska extolled the virtues of public education, but they took different views of exogamous marriage and the settlement house movement. Both authors began their early careers in settlement houses, those charitable institutions of Progressive-era reform designed to provide new immigrants economic and practical support in return for their participation in Americanization programs, such as learning English, job preparation and, for women, domestic training.[15] Antin owed much of her success to these institutions: her early work in two philanthropic social agencies in Boston, Hale House and the Hebrew Immigration Aid Society (HIAS), connected her with paleontologist Amadeus Grabau (Gentile man and future husband); with Zangwill, who wrote the foreword to her first book, *From Plotzk to Boston* (1899); and with Philip Cowen, founder and publisher of the weekly, genteel, New York City magazine *American Hebrew*, who helped her publish *From Plotzk*.[16] Of particular significance, at Hale House Antin discovered the Natural History Club, which introduced her to "zoölogy, botany, geology, ornithology, and an infinite number of other ologies," in a word, to science.[17] Her "restless questioning of the universe" had actually begun long before in Russia, but at Hale House these problems "ceased to torment" her (280). She now learned how "life and death, beginning and end, were all parts of the process of being," so that "it mattered less what particular ripple of the flux of existence [in which she] found herself"; she had discovered the "promised land of evolution," with which she "rebuilt the world" (280–81). As one of the youngest members among the natural scientists there, Antin enjoyed the "freedom of outdoors," the "society of congenial friends," and an "exuberance" of happiness "like unto the iridescent dews" (281).

Yezierska took a different, far less poetic view than Antin of the settlement house movement in New York's Lower East Side. While she was earning her Columbia's Teachers College certificate in home economics in 1904, John Dewey—soon to be major twentieth-century intellectual, Progressive pragmatist philosopher, psychologist, and educational reformer—was studying at the University of Chicago, flourishing in the world of social change embodied in Jane Addams's Hull House. Dewey's goals of Progressive education became directly intertwined with those of Addams and the settlement house movement, both aimed at shaping the values of children and immigrants in order to transform society.[18] When looking for a solid teaching position in 1916, it was on Dewey's office door that Yezierska knocked (he was now dean of the Teaching College), subsequently enrolling in his Columbia University philosophy seminar.[19] Dewey's papers from Columbia at that time reveal numerous love poems he wrote to Yezierska, evidence of a passionate affair between the two that apparently began with her participation as a translator on his research project about a Philadelphia Polish community.[20] Literary critics agree that the "Dewey figure" subsequently appears as a love interest throughout Yezierska's fiction, for example, in *Bread Givers* (1925) as Mr. Edman at the "American College" that Sara Smolinsky attends.[21] Most notably, as we will see, the Puritanical millionaire-philanthropist John Manning in *Salome of the Tenements* (1923) has been read as a composite of Dewey and actual millionaire Graham Stokes, who married Jewish immigrant Rose Pastor Stokes. As Mary Dearborn puts it, "Yezierska wrote about Dewey in love because the idea of America in love with the immigrant was a compelling and vivid image for her, a vision of the immigrant's acceptance by the New World."[22] Perhaps so; yet, heroine Sonya Vrunsky also derides Manning's conventional scientific methodology as idealistic and out of touch. In Manning, the Dewey figure is marked by cold detachment, insensitivity to the poor, and, as Lori Jirousek argues, a tendency to sexually fetishize Jewish women as "exotic."[23] Natalie Freidman rightly calls *Salome* a distinctly "anti-assimilationist" text, which depicts in Manning a Dewey who "represents the worst of the Americanization movement and a hypocritical 'educational' approach that purports to help immigrants assimilate," yet actually, like the "laboratory" model against which Jane Addams defined her settlement house, patronizes the poor and exploits them for data.[24] If Manning is metonymic for Protestant-American Progressive reform, Yezierska makes clear that women like the fictional Sonya will not so easily "melt" into the nation without tremendous conflict and resistance on all sides.

Despite the two authors' differences on the settlements, however, both Antin and Yezierska redirect the question and push us to rethink the critical framework of cultural assimilation by framing their otherwise secular narratives in biblical Hebraic terms. Both authors depict Jewish women coming of age in a Progressive-Era culture of political and philanthropic reform, one in which each author was personally involved. Examined through the operative lens of this study—of Jewish and Protestant temporalities, messianic and eschatological—their texts offer distinct, yet profound ways of negotiating the Jewish female relationship to time, particularly the future, in the context of a Protestant culture of conversion and assimilation.[25] As the "Jewish Problem" became increasingly understood within larger debates about the future of the American "race," both authors moved beyond the "dual image" of the male figure of the Jew rehearsed earlier, by reviving and revising biblical Hebraic women as redemptive models for a future that they, themselves, could inhabit.

INTERMARRIAGE AND THE JEWISH PROBLEM

Although Judaism has always been a minority religion in the United States, its existence, argues Hasia Diner, has nonetheless challenged the way Americans think about religion. Americans, though committed to the separation of church and state, have prioritized protecting the health of Christianity in America (meaning Protestantism). Consequently, legal declarations of the sanctity of the Christian Sabbath, like that by the Supreme Court of Georgia in 1871, which forbid mercantile activity on the Lord's Day, were perceived by Jewish leaders as directed at Jews. Well through the 1870s, evangelicals pushed for a constitutional amendment to acknowledge Christianity as America's religion. Though it died in the House Judiciary Committee in 1874, the amendment received wide endorsement by many influential Americans, including several governors, college professors, and a Supreme Court justice.[26] Although American Protestants "shared no single view of the prospects for Judaism in America," Diner writes, they all seemed to stress "the unbroken chains that bound the Jews of the nineteenth century with ancient ideas and forms" (179). And while this may sound positive, it also meant ignoring the reform of Judaism in order to preserve both this image of a religion out of step with modernity, and the very idea of

America as a modern Protestant nation. By the end of the nineteenth century, many laws aimed generally, such as those focused on immigration restriction, adversely affected Jewish populations.

On April 4, 1890, Philip Cowen, publisher and editor of the *American Hebrew*, asked a host of non-Jewish educators, clergyman, politicians, and intellectuals to offer their frank views on the growing anti-Jewish sentiment in the United States, in a specially published symposium titled "Prejudice Against the Jew: its nature, its causes and remedies: a symposium by foremost Christians."[27] The *American Hebrew* had already established the career of Jewish poet Emma Lazarus, publishing under its auspices her tragedy *The Dance to Death* (1882), her poetry and essays beginning in 1883, and a special issue commemorating her death in 1887. Here, three years later, Cowen asked prominent public figures to respond to the following questions:

> I. Can you, of your own personal experience, find any justification whatever for the entertainment of prejudice towards individuals solely because they are Jews? II. Is this prejudice not due largely to the religious instruction that is given by the church and Sunday-school? For instance, the teachings that the Jews crucified Jesus; that they rejected him, and can only secure salvation by belief in him, and similar matters that are calculated to excite in the impressionable mind of the child an aversion, if not a loathing, for members of "the despised race." III. Have you observed in the social or business life of the Jew, so far as your personal experience has gone, any different standard of conduct than prevails among Christians of the same social status? IV. Can you suggest what should be done to dispel the existing prejudice?[28]

Cowen's questions imply religious sources for antisemitism, although by this time, according to Jacob Rader Marcus, anti-Jewish stereotypes in the theater and the press abounded, exemplified by popular caricatures in humor magazines: "The Jewish arsonist was Mr. Burnheim, the usurer Loanstein, the crook, Swindelbaum."[29] Among the educated prevailed the belief that if there was a "Jewish Problem," it was due to ineradicable racial qualities. This led to racially motivated immigration restriction laws and journalistic anti-Jewish attacks, Marcus notes, such as the founding of the (albeit unsuccessful) Minerva Press by Telemachus T. Timayenis in 1888, depicting Jews as avaricious murderers of Christians (170). The Protestant elite of New England was perhaps more "anti-foreigner" than anti-Jewish; Nathaniel S. Shaler, for example, writing on the "Hebrew Problem," saw Jews as a highly intellectual and able people, although different, unliked, unduly acquisitive; like James Russell Lowell, MIT and Harvard economist William S. Ripley, and Henry Cabot Lodge, he found them difficult to assimilate. According to Marcus, Shaler recommended "blending, intermarriage of course, and the disappearance of the Jew qua Jew" (173). Meanwhile, academicians, eugenicists, historians, sociologists and others worked hard for immigration restrictions. Several groups invested in protecting American Anglo-Saxon stock, for example, were born in the 1890s, like the Daughters of the American Revolution, the General Society of Colonial Wars, the Colonial Dames of America, and the Immigration Restriction League formed by New England Brahmins in 1894 (174).

In light of these collectively xenophobic developments came Cowen's request, responses to which, Marcus writes, were "cautiously phrased; many reported what others believed, not what they themselves believed," creating an overall portrait of Jews who were said to be "clannish, unproductive, economic exploiters, vulgar, morally inadequate, socially unacceptable, Christ-killers, unassimilable" (172). Oliver Wendell Holmes, who had years earlier protested the 1877 Seligman-Hilton affair (see chapter 3, above), was among the more tolerant whom Cowen asked to respond.[30] In a subsequently published version of his conversation in *Over the Teacups* (1890), Holmes admitted that, as a child, he had learned "the traditional idea that [the Jews] were a race lying under a curse for their obstinacy in refusing the gospel," believers in a "false" religion whose "principal use . . . seemed to be to lend money, and to fulfill the predictions of the old prophets of their race."[31] He recalled further, "No doubt the individual sons of Abraham whom we found in our ill-favoured and ill-flavored streets were apt to be unpleasing specimens of the race" (194). It was thus against all odds that the great Jewish "philosophers, the musicians, the financiers, the statesmen of the last centuries forced the world to recognize and accept them" for their achievements, that is, despite religious prejudice (194). Holmes's changing views may reflect his personal growth in tolerance toward Jews, but his views are underwritten by the "philosemitic" Hebraic myth we have been tracing. Roosevelt perhaps summed it up best, when he, alone among responders solemnly admitted, "Some of my most valued friends are Hebrews."[32]

Responses from others, like Burton J. Hendrick, a sensational newspaper muckraker who won the Pulitzer Prize three times, illustrate how tied up the Jewish Problem was with a more pernicious use of the Hebraic myth, that is, with how the issue of religious intermarriage became increasingly articulated as a racial problem that divorced living Jews—mainly Russian and East European—from an ever-more-idealized version of mythical Hebrews. Hendrick wrote many pieces on the Jewish Problem, including several for *World's Work* later collected as a book, *The Jews in America* (1922).[33] If, in the 1870s, the likes of Judge Henry Hilton distinguished "Seligman 'Jews'" from noble "Hebrews"—that is, specifically Orthodox Jews against whom the vulgar, German parvenus were judged as dirty, loud, and "disgusting" (see chapter 3, above)—for Hendrick, thirty to forty years later, the problematic Jewish "race" had expanded now to *include* the Orthodox. Hendrick denigrated the Russian and Polish "stock" in particular as inassimilable medieval holdovers, but he did so in comparison to ever-more-abstract "notional Jews," to recall Zygmunt Bauman's term—the mythical "sons of Israel." The legal and cultural fates of actual Jews thus continued to be debated in theoretical terms, so that the racialization and denigration of living Jewish people was underwritten by praise for their noble, idealized—effectively nonexistent—coreligionists, the latter who seemed to represent not philosemitic admiration but, as Eliane Glaser puts it, a "Judaism without Jews."[34]

In "The Great Jewish Invasion" (1907), Hendrick casts the Jews as parasitic, marked by "intense ambition and individualism," as witnessed in their complete domination of the real estate market and ready-to-wear clothing manufacturing trade ("They have turned the whole East Side into one huge workshop").[35] If the material prosperity of the Russian Jew was unquestionable, the real question was: "[I]s he assimilable?" (319). For

Hendrick the answer was yes, provided Jews continued to Americanize and intermarry, in effect, to suppress their Jewishness. In "Will the Jews Disappear?" published in the *American Hebrew* on August 3, 1917, Hendrick argued that perhaps they would, since intermarriage, in his view, was the only viable solution to the Jewish Problem. This would not be damaging to the American "race," however: "Whatever consequences the wholesale amalgamation of our Jewish stock will have, it will not debase the long-heralded composite American."[36]

Hendrick maintained the same racial views in *The Jews in America* (1922), except now he saw the "Jewish Problem" of assimilation to be posed only by Russian and Polish Jews (not the Spanish or German Jews of previous waves of immigration).[37] Describing a history of the Jews in America, he argued that the "aristocracy of Israel," or Sephardim of the first American settlement, outside of their shared religion were racially superior to "their Russian co-religionists," upon whom they look down with even "greater aversion" than any "anti-Semite among the native American stock" (7, 17). This superior breed, most of them also married to Christians, "are not pawn-brokers or peddlers or rag-pickers," and thus present no "Jewish 'problem'" (17–19). Nor were the German Jews of the second wave a "'problem'" (19). Although they were seen as racially inferior to the Sephardim, at least the German Ashkenazim established themselves in retail and banking, rising from humble beginnings to wealth and success (22). They adapted their practice of Judaism to the larger Christian culture, moreover (through the Reform Judaism movement), and thus assimilated well.

The real issue, he contended, was with those who neither intermarried nor blended "racially," the "Eastern" Jewish immigrants whose "religious orthodoxy" was medieval and atavistic (31). For Hendrick, it was thus "the year 1881 that marks the beginning of the American Jewish 'problem' as that word is commonly understood," for that was the year of the Russian pogroms and onset of refugee emigration from Russia and Eastern Europe (27). The Russian Jewish "type," almost of "an entirely different race," is best recognized by its Orthodox religious trappings (30):

> The long, unkempt beards, the trailing hair, the little
> curls about the ears—these carefully preserved stigmata of

traditional Israel were merely the outward signs of lives that were lived strictly according to the teachings of rabbinical law. . . . *These new Jewish immigrants came from a country that was still living in the Middle Ages.* . . . [H]is life was still a squalid and poverty-stricken routine; he was totally illiterate. . . . [T]hat industrialism which is the great feature of modern life had made practically no progress. (31–33; emphasis mine)

Unlike their Spanish and German coreligionists, these Jews spoke no identifiable European language (only "an outlandish jargon . . . known as Yiddish") and were clearly holdovers of a previous, distinctly medieval era, outside industrial modernity and the march of progress, their religious trappings "stigmata" of an outmoded life (34). The Russian Jew lacked American "creative genius" in technology, progress, and competition, which he never "encountered in his more than two thousand years of wanderings" (66). The "Polish Jew" was even more of a "menace" than the Russian, Hendrick insisted, since he "had never been a citizen," but for thousands of years merely "the member of a tribe, governed by tribal laws and tribal chiefs" (93). In his view, these Jews segregated themselves, living by their own customs and laws, using their own language, and functioning according to their own sense of time. With their "orthodox faith" posing an "almost complete impediment to . . . industrialization," Polish Jews were hardly noble; they were racially moribund (103). As Arnold Eisen and others have long proven (see chapter 1, above), the boundaries of real *shtetls* (unlike their fictional counterparts) were not impermeable but porous, with Jews like Antin modernizing, as we will see, well before emigrating.[38] Yet in Hendrick's claims we see a persistent stereotype of "Old World"—namely Orthodox—Jews who were not just unmodern and immune to progress but actually frozen in time for millennia, an argument deploying a key strain of the Hebraic myth.

With his belief in a Jewish racial hierarchy, a Protestant ethic of productive labor, and immigration restriction, Hendrick shared much with his even more overtly racist and antisemitic eugenicist contemporaries Edward Alsworth Ross and Madison Grant. Ross, a Wisconsin sociologist and political economist, agreed that East European Jews would not make good citizens; they were unconscionable moral cripples, exploiters, arsonists, and white slave traders and, save for a few good intellectuals, a menace. Even he did not deny, however, the possibility of their ultimate assimilation.[39] In *Passing of the Great Race in America* (1916), Grant—lawyer, eugenicist, zoologist, traveler, explore, and hunter—took his racist claims even further: he not only argued that American cultural strains were being diluted by foreigners, he also retroactively racialized biblical history. Yes, Jesus was a Jew, he conceded, but probably not a racial "Semite"; like Houston Stewart Chamberlain, he argued that Jesus was a "Nordic."[40]

These painstaking attempts to parse racial, religious, evolutionary, and social Darwinian ideologies reflect some of the most significant efforts of the era to distinguish Jews (specifically "Eastern" Jews in Hendrick's case) from Gentiles in "scientific" terms, and to argue for their inability to become "true" Americans. Eugenicist arguments like those of Ross and Grant warned of the polluting dangers such racial strains would bring to the national body politic and brought religious typology to bear on their arguments. According to them, there was no viable future in America for religious—inherently medieval—Jews of this sort. Such arguments had great implications for questions of marriage and sexual reproduction, specifically for Jewish women's contributions to the "future" of the American "race," concerns only thinly veiled beneath the more benign discourse of religious intermarriage.

If these accounts are any indication of how racialized the "Jewish Problem" had become, they also show how the myth of the noble Hebrew nonetheless persisted, now divorced even from visibly Orthodox Jews, in a form abstracted to the point of nonrecognition. If Orthodox Jews once represented a return of the typologically, pre-Christian repressed past, they now returned here, in the United States, to face real cultural and political repression. Writing within this climate of nativist xenophobia, it is no wonder that neither Antin nor Yezierska engaged in narrative nostalgia about the Jewish past. On the contrary, their stories face the future—narratives of passion and love, of young women trying to wrest their destinies free from the chains of patriarchal tradition, as they forge a path forward in the face of an increasingly racialized political debate over the Jewish Problem.

Bridging Time in the Promised Land: Mary Antin

Perhaps the most famous story critics have taken as that of assimilation, transformation, and East European immigrant experience, Mary Antin's autobiography *The Promised Land* (1912) was an immediate bestseller that launched Antin into national fame. First serialized in the *Atlantic Monthly* in 1911 under the editorship of Ellery Sedgwick, the subsequent book sold over a hundred thousand copies in its first year, when Antin was a mere thirty-one years old. The book is commonly remembered as a distinctive argument for the Russian immigrant's right and ability to become fully American in an era of rampant nativism. In it, Antin argued for the Progressive Party tenet of unrestricted immigration, expressed admiration for Roosevelt, and constructed her own life story as one of conversion from Russian Jew to acculturated, patriotic American and immigrant reformer, through the powers of education, schools, teachers, and the mastery of English. For these reasons, her wildly successful book has been read as idealizing America, as a paradigmatic example of the assimilation narrative.[41] Maria Karifilis goes so far as claim that Antin's story redefines Americanness as "an orientation, a system of beliefs, and a commitment to individual self-improvement through education," embodied as much in Antin, a "'vain, boastful, curly-headed little Jew' with a desire to educate herself as in any other citizen in the nation."[42] Like Abraham Cahan and others who told their American immigrant stories as narratives of rebirth—Andrew Carnegie, Jacob Riis, Edward Bok—Antin claimed for herself, and thus for all immigrants, a rebirth in the New World, as if embodying Zangwill's "melting-pot" ideal.[43] She even wanted to title it "Americans in the Making," but felt "robbed," as she wrote to Sedgwick, because Jacob Riis had made this impossible with his autobiography, titled "Making of an American."[44]

As Antin celebrated the birth of her new American self, she tellingly emphasized her profound journey in temporal terms, as Jules Chametzky puts it, one from "medieval Old World superstition and backwardness" to "modernity and enlightenment."[45] Her story was to have the sweep of ages: in search of the precise phrase that "tells what America does for the immigrant," she considered such titles as "Out of the Land of Egypt" and "The Heir of the Ages," before settling on "The Promised Land."[46] Framed thus as a spiritual autobiography, Antin's conversion narrative follows such models as St. Paul, Augustine, Phyllis Wheatley, Benjamin Franklin, Booker T. Washington, Frederick Douglass, and others—many of whom find their analogue in Protestant narratives like John Winthrop's "city on a hill." But Antin's has a distinct Hebraic note: an ocean of time and experience separate her "then" and "now," her "Old World" and the "New," as expressed in the autobiography's opening lines:

> I was born, I have lived, and I have been made over. Is it not time to write my life's story? I am just as much out of the way as if I were dead, for I am absolutely other than the person whose story I have to tell. Physical continuity with my earlier self is no disadvantage. I could speak in the third person and not feel that I was masquerading. I can analyze my subject, I can reveal everything; for she, and not I, is my real heroine. My life I have still to live; her life ended when mine began.[47]

Her opening declaration of spiritual death, rebirth, and secular reinvention on American soil perhaps seems audacious. For the conviction of her patriotism to come through, however, such a dramatic declaration was necessary: her old, Russian Orthodox Jewish self, she claimed, had perished so that her new American self could be born.

Critics have tended to emphasize these profound initial claims, as well as the second half of the book where she challenges xenophobic and anti-immigrant arguments that were gaining legislative traction by this time.[48] What critics tend to overlook, however, is that the first 150-odd pages comprise perhaps the most detailed, elaborate portrait of "Old World" East European life ever to be published. The sections devoted to her life in the Russian *shtetl* of Polotzk take up as much space, attention, and prominence as those devoted to America, preserving the "before" of her life story as much as the "after" for posterity.[49] More recently, critics have begun to note complexities and tensions within Antin's purported assimilationist ideology, however. Jolie A. Sheffer argues for "the significance of the incommensurable, and hence traumatic, break created by immigration" in Antin's book, and Sarah Sillin sees Antin drawing on both sentimental and realist literary conventions to portray herself "as an Americanized woman," but one whose "experience of immigration [is] fraught with conflict."[50] These conflicts complicate our sense of the text's structure, but also point to temporal breaks in Antin's experience that, in her narration, she aims to heal with biblical Hebraic tropes—that is, with use of the Hebraic myth. For example, Antin adapts the spiritual autobiography model to a Jewish narrative by using explicitly Hebraic chapter headings. Titles like "The Tree of Knowledge," "The Exodus," "Manna," and "The Burning Bush" illustrate how, for all of her professions to leaving the past behind, Antin was deeply committed to preserving that Jewish religious past, which, in turn, structured her sense of literary form. Charting profound transformations—like her "Exodus" from Old World violence, persecution, and religious intolerance to New World freedom—Antin writes her contemporary journey akin to a Pilgrim's landing in America, itself a typological revision of the biblical Hebrews' entry into Canaan, the original "Promised Land."

Antin opens her conversion story with the declaration, "I think I have thoroughly assimilated my past—I have done its bidding—I want now to be of to-day. It is painful to be consciously of two worlds. The Wandering Jew in me seeks forgetfulness. I am not afraid to live on and on, if only I do not have to remember too much. A long past vividly remembered is like a heavy garment that clings to your limbs when you would run."[51] This claim accords with her life at the time of the book's publication, namely that when writing it, she was a successful writer already married for eleven years to Gentile Grabau.[52] Her implicit endorsement of religious intermarriage and explicit emphasis on forgetting, assimilation, and apostasy, have thus provoked derision by some Jewish literary critics. Sarah Blacher Cohen, for example, condemns Antin's hurried "race for assimilation" as a "religio-cultural striptease."[53] Others, like Michael Kramer, agree she was an assimilationist, but praise her for it.[54] But as Evelyn Salz shows, Antin's life was complicated: she went on to embrace political Zionism in 1912 when Louis Brandeis began to promote that movement.[55] Later still, Salz describes how, after World War One, having divorced Grabau, Antin suffered a mental breakdown and became attached to a Protestant minister, Will Gould of Gould Farm, with whom she began to explore Christianity (xx).

Then, writing as late as 1941, eight years before her death, in the face of Nazi fascism she was still negotiating her relationship to her "thoroughly assimilated" Jewish past, as Salz quotes her: "I can no more return to the Jewish fold than I can return to my mother's womb; neither can I in decency continue to enjoy my accidental personal immunity from the penalties of being a Jew in a time of virulent anti-Semitism. The least I can do, in my need to share the suffering of my people, is to declare that I am as one of them" (xxiii). Antin's conversions, in other words, were multiple, her life story far more complex than her book reveals.

Salz's *Selected Letters of Mary Antin* (2000) best illustrates this complexity, how Antin's life was hardly defined by a clear "Old World" before and a "New World" after. The letters collected there instead reveal a more complicated, less resolved Antin, a Progressive with a strong belief in open immigration who came to believe strongly in Zionism, but also a woman with a deep concern to portray accurately Russian Jewish history, Polotzk *shtetl* life, and a fundamental preoccupation with her Jewishness (xxii–xxiii). This is illustrated clearly in Antin's 1911 letter to Sedgwick regarding the first 150 pages of her manuscript for *The Promised Land* devoted to her Polotzk past. Sedwick wanted her "to use more of the American than the Russian material," like another of her readers, who apparently "proposed that I sum up the whole Russian matter in one chapter . . . and concentrate on the theme of the immigrant in America, calling the story "My Country"! It would make an intense story, but would leave *me* out of the book, and some of the best things in the book, if I am my judge, only count because they are true of an individual; namely, the author."[56] Antin's life, as indicated in her letters perhaps more than in her autobiography, thus betrays signs that the melting-pot model of American national identity, particularly as achieved through exogamous marriage, failed to bridge time and was itself more myth than reality. The "heavy garment" of the past was not so easily shed.

EDUCATION AND THE "CONTINUITY OF TIME"

If Antin's life proved that religious intermarriage could not resolve the temporal disparities of past and future, of Jewish and Protestant American life, *The Promised Land* clearly argues that secular education provided her the space, the means, and the opportunity for negotiating, and then writing about, these temporally defined experiences for posterity. Secular education was particularly crucial for Jewish girls and women like Antin, because religious Jewish education, patriarchal at its core, expressly excluded them. Antin's own educational journey began in Polotzk, well before her "Exodus" to America, where her parents, *Haskalah* adherents, had embraced the idea of a "liberal education" for their young daughters, Mary (then Maryashe, or Mashke) and her sister Fetchke. The girls were to learn Hebrew like their brother, but also Russian, German, and "arithmetic."[57] Antin notes how otherwise, education for Jewish girls, both as Jews and as women, was doubly restricted, and the forced assimilation of Jews only promoted more extreme religious Orthodoxy:

> History shows that in all countries where Jews have equal rights with the rest of the people, they lose their fear of secular science, and learn how to take their ancient religion with them from century to awakening century, dropping nothing by the way but what their growing spirit has outgrown. In countries where progress is to be bought only at the price of apostasy, they shut themselves up in their synagogues, and raise the wall of extreme separateness between themselves and their Gentile neighbors. (98)

In Russia, she argues, "medieval injustice to Jews" was thus to blame for "the narrowness of educational standards in Polotzk"; any inflexible penchant on the part of Jews themselves was simply a reaction to their oppression. Compounding the problem of Russian restrictions on Jewish life was Jewish patriarchy: "in the medieval position of the women of Polotzk education really had no place," so that even for Jews who pursued a narrow religious education, Jewish women were left behind (98). Antin's parents were thus exceptional for educating their daughters with both a "rebbe" and a "*lehrer*" in biblical and secular subjects alike (102–3). Unfortunately, the girls' education was cut short by their parents' illnesses and their rejection from private schools, likely due to their religion. As Antin makes clear, the dividing line in Polotzk between Jews and Gentiles was stark, leaving little room for secular Jewishness: "One was a Jew, leading a righteous life, or one was a Gentile, existing to harass the Jews, while making a living off Jewish enterprise. In the vocabulary of the more intelligent part of Polotzk, there were no such words as freethinker or apostate" (106–7).

When Russian government authorities began to clear Jews out of cities like Moscow outside the Pale and persecution became real, Antin began to doubt God's existence in earnest, well before migrating to America. She began to undertake "tests" to "put God himself to the proof," such as the day she tested the "sacred admonition not to carry anything beyond the house-limits on the Sabbath day" (108). Placing a handkerchief in her pocket, she stepped into the street, "her heart beating so hard that it pained," and yet "Nothing happened!" (108). She felt bitter disappointment at God's fail-ure to manifest with some form of punishment; she subsequently returned home to find her mother and grandmother adorned in their Orthodox wigs and caps, looking "*different*," "*very* strange" (110). She questioned the Jew-ish God and also the Christian God ("what a foolish god was that who taught the stupid Gentiles that we drank the blood of a murdered child at our Passover feast!"), as well as her own authenticity as a Jew (111). As both religion and state failed her, America became her imagined "promised land." When at the Passover celebration they read the story of the Exodus, they seemed to "read a chapter of current history, only for [them] there was no deliverer and no promised land." At the end of the service they therefore replaced the traditional saying, "Next year in Jerusalem," with a new one: "Next year—in America!" (122).

These examples illustrate internal complications within Antin's conver-sion narrative, given that her secularization, and eventual apostasy, began long before America entered her consciousness. In Vitebsk, for example, both her Uncle Solomon and Cousin Hirshel, a high school student whom she "worshipped," introduced her to "secular literature," such as Defoe's *Robinson Crusoe* (135). Vitebsk also altered her sense of time: in contrast with the death and rebirth model of the text's opening chapter, Antin describes a different kind of transformative experience following a wedding she attended. The next day, riding in the train from Vitebsk, she reflects how the next adventure to come seemed to blend into the last one at the wedding: "When did yesterday end? Why was not this new day the same day continued?" (132). Her meditations on time continued as "the engine throbbed and lurched, and the wheels ground along," for she was "astonished to hear that they were keeping perfectly the time of the last waltz [she] had danced at the wedding" (132). Discovering that the "engine knew" and repeated that rhythm, she "forgot the problem of the Continuity of Time," and came to experience it as reality: now, whenever she hears a Danube waltz, she lives through "that entire experience: the festive night, the misty morning, the abnormal consciousness of time, as if I had existed forever, without a break" (132). Moments like this, which transcend linear time, belie the dual structure established by the narrative's opening, and also suggest that Antin understood how before and after, past and present, could be continuous. She may have anticipated America, or retrospectively figured it as the fulcrum of her life experience, but these details show how the "boundaries" of her world had "burst" out into the "wider world" well before she left Russia (139).

The autobiography nonetheless positions the start of her "second infancy" midway through the book upon her arrival in America, in the chapter "The Promised Land" (155). Here, "maiden aunts" in the "guise of immigrant officials, schoolteachers, settlement workers, and sundry other unprejudiced and critical observers" nurtured the "first breathless years" of her life in America (155). Yet her descriptions complicate even this crucial narrative midpoint: the moment of immigrant arrival also opens up a different order of time that transcends that of the individual life. The Jewish immigrants—be they "the creature with the untidy beard," the "cross-legged tailor," the "ragpicker's daughters," or the "greasy alien on the street"—she writes, were "born thousands of years before the oldest native American" (156). Rendering Jews bearers of time itself, her words echo Henry James's in *The American Scene* in which each individual Jewish immigrant carries the oldest of biblical, Hebraic histories, the "whole hard glitter" and "gathered past of Israel."[58] She tells her reader that the uncouth immigrant "may have something to communicate to you, when you two shall have learned a common language" (156). In other words, the Jewish immigrant stands to translate that vast and noble past to "native" Americans, and to bridge the wide gaps of time between biblical and modern, old and new orders of time.

Antin argued that the bridging of time, evident in her sacred transformation from ancient to modern, from "Mashke, the granddaughter of Raphael the Russian, born to a humble destiny" to Mary, "an American among Americans," took place nowhere more powerfully than in the free American public schools (168). The day she started public school represented for Antin "[t]he apex of [her] civic pride and personal contentment," a day, she writes, "I must always remember, even if I live to be so old that I cannot tell my name" (168–69). Her father may have failed at business and other New World ventures, but at least "[h]e could send his children to school" and "thus he would walk by proxy in the Elysian Fields of liberal learning" (173). Bringing his children to school was a holy rite for him, as if "an act of consecration" by a "foreigner" who "regarded the teacher of the primer class with reverence, who spoke of visions," and who, by educating his children, "took possession of America" itself (174). The chapter titled "Initiation" thus chronicles a "hundred-fold miracle," not of Moses but of how a "green"—or newly arrived—immigrant girl would go from "not knowing the days of the week in English" to "declaiming patriotic verses in honor of George Washington and Abraham Lincoln, with a foreign accent, indeed, but with plenty of enthusiasm" (175).

Antin makes her secular New World experiences in school sacred. Yet this reading might allow us to overlook the fact that these experiences were not, in fact, entirely secular. Antin was still expected to shed her Yiddish accent—to say "water" instead of "*vater*"—and to participate in the Christian religious rituals that took place in public school (178). For instance, she attributes her acquisition of the "beautiful" English language, her "earliest efforts at writing," and her "very first appearance in print" to a particular teacher, Miss Dillingham (176, 180). Miss Dillingham, after all, published Antin's first essay in English in an educational journal, thus starting the writer's career. But Antin also remembers Miss Dillingham for administering her first dose of discipline in a moment marked by religious difference. One day, when the class was "repeating in chorus the Lord's Prayer, heads bowed on desks," Antin was doing her best to keep up, but got stuck on "hallowed," a word whose meaning she didn't know. A Jewish boy got her attention and whispered:

> "You must not say that . . . it's Christian." I whispered back
> that it wasn't, and went on to the "Amen." I did not know

but what he was right, but the name of Christ was not in
the prayer, and I was bound to do everything that the class
did. If I had any Jewish scruples, they were lagging away
behind my interest in school affairs. How American was
this: two pupils side by side in the schoolroom, each holding to his own opinion, but both submitting to the common law; for the boy at least bowed his head as the teacher
ordered. (177–78)

Although Antin celebrates this moment as revealing the wonders of America, a liberal state where two Jews can maintain their private beliefs while
engaging in public prayer, it also illustrates the Protestant bent of American public education and the forced "conversion," however provisional or
performed, of its Jewish pupils. Miss Dillingham reinforced this with her
authority: all she knew was that two of her pupils "whispered during morning prayer," and so Antin was "degraded from the honor row to the lowest
row" (178). Apparently the teacher later let the two students defend themselves, but Antin still learned that "there was a time and place for religious
arguments, and she meant to help us remember the point" (178). In other
words, even if theoretically or spiritually the Jewish students were justified
in their actions, practically speaking, outward conformity with the Christian majority was mandatory, and any deviation punishable.

For Antin, the real "making of an American" happened in public schools
(188). Yet it was also in school that, for all of its Protestant leanings, Antin
wed American and Hebraic mythologies to create an alternate, noble heritage out of which her new future self could grow. She first found a new idol
for worship who taught her both "humility" and "dignity": George Washington, "the noble boy who would not tell a lie to save himself from punishment" (189–90). In her newly discovered relationship to Washington as
a "Fellow Citizen," she reinvented her line of kinship and wrote herself into
American national mythology (190). Studying the history of the American Revolution, she discovered the meaning of the phrase "*my* country":
"people all desiring noble things, and striving for them together, defying
their oppressors, giving their lives for each other" (190–91). She cultivated
pride and patriotism for her adopted nation, one that welcomed rather

than betrayed her, and shunned oppression at its very founding moment. Antin concludes, "Polotzk was not my country. It was *goluth*—exile" (191). America was her *real* home, its Revolution a *real* history, unlike the Exodus, which now seemed "a glorious myth" with "Holy Zion," "Palestine," and "Judea" all part of the "supernatural legends and hazy associations of Bible lore" (192).

Even as Antin seems to have dismissed the biblical Hebraic past, however, she harnessed its noble power in her first poem about Washington, composed of "the loftiest sentiments" and "the most abstract truths" of "'tyranny,' 'freedom,' and 'justice,'" which she, the proud young immigrant, was asked to recite before her entire school (193). In her poem, she reflects, "ran a special note":

> [A] thought that only Israel Rubenstein or Beckie Arono-
> vitch could have fully understood, besides myself. For I
> made myself the spokesman of the "luckless sons of Abra-
> ham," saying—

> > Then we weary Hebrew children at last found rest
> > In the land where reigned Freedom, and like a nest
> > To homeless birds your land proved to us, and therefore
> > Will we gratefully sing your praise evermore. (195)

Here Antin invents for herself a dual lineage: an American line through Washington and a Jewish one through Abraham. Apparently the poem did speak to her Gentile classmates, "the boys and girls who had never been turned away from any door because of their father's religion," because they "woke up and applauded heartily." (195). Her poem was subsequently published in a local paper, "testimony to the goodness of [Antin's] exalted hero [and] to the greatness of [her] adopted country" (201). But above all, it represents her first literary employment of Hebraic mythology with which to bridge and preserve the wide expanse of time between biblical Jewish past and American future, particularly poignant as the very next chapter announces Antin's total apostasy and rejection of God. Anzia Yezierska, we will see, perhaps took cues from Antin, but also learned from her mistakes:

secular education may take the place of proper religious practice, but the Jewish past is not so easily left behind.

Cultural Pluralism and Intermarriage

If Antin's autobiography implicitly endorses religious intermarriage, Yezierska's novels ultimately reject it, mirroring a broad social and political shift that took place from the early 1900s "melting pot" model of American citizenship to what Horace Kallen called "cultural pluralism." Just three years after Antin published her 1912 autobiography, Horace Kallen, a German Jewish immigrant who arrived in the United States in 1887, claimed that the melting pot had failed.[59] Kallen argued that democracy was being altered by rising nativism (he named E. A. Ross specifically), which, with its ultimate fear of ethnic differences, reasserted racial hierarchies that the founding fathers sought to destabilize in the name of equality. The proclaimed "American" cultural standards of Progressives and others, he argued, had really become Anglo-Saxon standards, so that Americanization amounted to immigrants adopting the tradition and culture descended from Puritan New England, which, though considered "representative," was really just that of the oldest "rooted" economic settlement.[60] Americanization of the kind Roosevelt and others advocated, moreover, was an *external* process—"the adopting of English speech, of American clothes and manners, of the American attitude in politics" (192). Americanization certainly *connoted* the internal "fusion of the various bloods" by intermarriage, a "transmutation by 'the miracle of assimilation'" into "the Anglo-Saxon stock," to create a "new 'American race,'" but Kallen rejected this possibility as more hope than reality (192, 193).

In his essay "Democracy Versus the Melting Pot" (1915), published in two installments in the *Nation*, Kallen contended that the "instrument especially devised" for the purpose of creating a purportedly "newer and better" race is "the public school," best illustrated in the "biographical testimony" of writers like Riis and Antin, and promulgated as "a principle and an aspiration" by Israel Zangwill as "the melting-pot" (193). But what one acquired in the public school or settlement, he claimed, is "not really a *life*, it is an abstraction" (194). In other words, Americanization is superficial. His argument is clear: Antin, Riis, they "protest too much, they are too self-conscious and self-centered, their 'Americanization' . . . too much like an achievement, a *tour de force*, too little like a growth" (193). Despite their claims for assimilation, what persists is a "dualism" of "ethnic disparities," of differences that Kallen claims are inherited, intrinsic; the "most durable" expression of group identity, the "*natio*," or national identity, cannot be changed, even if one is cut off from the past (194). What preserves this durable ethnicity, above all, is religion, which can be "modified, even inverted, by race place and time," but remains the "sole repository of the national spirit" and "conservator of . . . the tradition that is passed on with the language to succeeding generations."[61] Such "ethnic disparity" therefore only fosters *more* group self-consciousness and "solidarity"; it cannot simply be melted away, particularly not through efforts at social control like immigration restriction, which only restrict entrepreneurial greed.[62] Americanization efforts, Kallen concludes, only lead to a hardening of "ethnic dualism" (193). We are *all*, he implies, hyphenated Americans.

If being American for Kallen meant the acceptance of ineradicable ethnic (and religious) differences, then the best exemplars of nationhood (understood as persistent ethnicity), he argued, were the Jews. Yiddish culture on the Lower East Side illustrated his maxim that "On the whole Americanization has not repressed nationality. Americanization has liberated nationality."[63] In his use of the Jewish example, we see, again, claims about the Jewish preservation of time, the "the oldest civilized tradition," maintained by a "flexible and accommodating" religion, taught in parochial schools that succeed by supplementing public ones (218). "In sum," the Jews, "the most eagerly American of the immigrant groups are also the most autonomous and self-conscious in spirit and culture" (218). Kallen's model of cultural pluralism therefore privileges the musical metaphor of "harmony" over the "unison" advocated by Roosevelt, since the latter only led to the kind of violence witnessed in the Russian Pale of Settlement. Rather than cutting off the past in the enforced manner of "True Americanism," harmony requires public action to protect all group differences, to create a "democracy of nationalities, cooperating voluntarily and autonomously in the enterprise of self-realization through the perfection of men according to their kind" (220).

For all that it improved upon the conversionist ethos of the "melting pot," Kallen's model had some obvious limits, particularly in terms of gender. Here and elsewhere—with "the perfection of men"—Kallen's argument for the path of ethnic "inheritance" is notably gendered male, as in this summative claim: "Men may change their clothes, their politics, their wives, their religions, their philosophies, to a greater or lesser extent: they cannot change their grandfathers" (220). If Jewish ethnic inheritance is patriarchal—wives, not grandfathers, can be changed—then what about husbands? Where does this leave Jewish women seeking to articulate a place in Protestant American culture? Antin's spiritual autobiography engaged assimilationist logic and took religious intermarriage for granted (even if later complicated by her failed marriage and changing relationship to Judaism and Protestantism). Yezierska's novels, by contrast, thwart religious intermarriage in the service of Jewish cultural preservation, in line with Kallen's cultural pluralism and reflecting the evolving historical realities of the era. Yet Yezierska's novels also revise Kallen's claims by suggesting that *women*, too, may change their clothes, their politics, their *husbands*, their religions, their philosophies, to a greater or lesser extent, even if they cannot change their fathers. Yezierska's heroines choose their own (notably) Jewish husbands, and they also choose professions in Progressive-Era education, or in the service of an artistic calling, with which to construct bridges between past and future.

JOHN DEWEY, EDUCATIONAL REFORM, AND YEZIERSKA'S *SALOME OF THE TENEMENTS*

Public education was central for Yezierska, as for Antin, as a means to a successful life, but also as a valuable end in itself. John Dewey, who greatly influenced Yeziersa's views of public education, was arguably the most important figure in Progressive-Era educational reform, best known for providing the philosophical foundation for "progressive education." In such works as *My Pedagogic Creed* (1897), *The School and Society* (1900), *The Child and the Curriculum* (1902), *Democracy and Education* (1916), and *Experience and Education* (1938), Dewey extolled the social and civic virtues of public schools, and of the classroom as a place of learning and socialization, a training ground for democratic citizenship. In a 1916 address to the National Education Association, "Nationalizing Education," Dewey expressed fears of jingoistic nationalist arguments, and argued for how to develop inclusiveness, or "the good aspect of nationalism without its evil side—of developing a nationalism which is the friend and not the foe of internationalism."[64] Dewey ranked the public school as the most important institution among educational agencies for achieving diverse nationhood, central to a thriving democracy, because rather than appealing to fears, jealousies, and sectional divisions, as war and warmongering do, it promotes a "real nationalism, a real Americanism" (210). In a direct rebuke of Roosevelt's "True Americanism," Dewey advocated the kind of "harmony" that formed the cornerstone of Kallen's notion of cultural pluralism:

> No matter how loudly any one proclaims his Americanism, if he assumes that any one racial strain, any one component culture, no matter how early settled it was in our territory, or how effective it has proved in its own land, is to furnish a pattern to which all other strains and cultures are to conform, he is a traitor to an American nationalism. Our unity cannot be a homogeneous thing like that of the separate states of Europe from which our population is drawn; *it must be a unity created by drawing out and composing into a harmonious whole the best, the most characteristic, which each contributing race and people has to offer.* (210)

Dewey echoes Kallen in direct response to Roosevelt's critique of "hyphenated" identities, by arguing we should welcome them, "in the sense of extracting from each people its special good, so that it shall surrender into a common fund of wisdom and experience what it especially has to contribute" (210). The problem, he argued, is when the hyphen itself becomes the focus, for it then becomes the thing *"which separates one people from other peoples,* and thereby prevents American nationalism" (210). Dewey's point is that there is no need to emphasize the hyphen, because "America" is already hyphenated, pragmatically speaking:

> Such terms as Irish-American or Hebrew-American or German-American are false terms because they seem to

assume something which is already in existence called America, to which the other factor may be externally hitched on. The fact is, the genuine American, the typical American, is himself a hyphenated character . . . the American is himself Pole-German-English-French-Spanish-Italian-Greek-Irish-Scandinavian-Bohemian-Jew- and so on. (211)

The "national idea" that Dewey believed our educational systems should promote, therefore, is not one of cultural homogeneity but diverse democracy—essentially, a liberal state of tolerance, united by a collective investment in the greater, shared good (211). This liberal model, Dewey believed, is what made the United States progressive among nations.

It is easy to see the appeal that Dewey's ideas would have had for a writer like Yezierska, who in *Bread Givers* (1925), we will see, wildly celebrated the American educational system as an avenue for immigrants to achieve Emersonian freedom, cultural adaptation, and economic success. Yezierska's relationship to Dewey began when he became her ethnographic mentor in 1918, and she joined his team studying Philadelphia's Polish immigrants, the day-to-day experience of which she fictionally recreated in her novel *All I Could Never Be* (1932).[65] From Dewey, Yezierska learned to conduct empirical study of individuals and their social environment, with a particular emphasis on self-directed education. She graduated from Columbia's Teachers College in 1904, the year Dewey joined Columbia's philosophy department, but returned to audit his 1918 graduate seminar in social and political philosophy, beginning their significant personal and professional relationship.[66] In Yezierska's fictions, Dewey became a model for her heroine's love interests, but also, significantly, for the idealistic, sometimes condescending figures of educational and Progressive reform, well-intended at best, hypocritical at worst, unable to connect with the practical needs of the people they sought to help.[67] In these characters, we see Yezierska's fascination with, but also critique of, Progressive-Era reforms aimed at "intractable" immigrant Jews.

The negative Dewey figure is best elaborated in *Salome of the Tenements* (1923), in which poor, Jewish immigrant Sonya Vrunsky falls in love with the opulent John Manning, a Protestant millionaire philanthropist whose pet project is a Lower East Side settlement house.[68] In search of a better life, Sonya seduces the head of Manning Settlement House, "the temple of her new faith," where she hopes to achieve her reformist goals and, together with Manning, save the East Side (82). She succeeds at marrying the millionaire, only to find him finally cold and unfeeling, the members of his family and class condescending toward the poor at best, disgusted at worst, particularly when confronted with the likes of Sonya up close. Consequently, she risks the complete social scandal of divorce, and leaves him for successful entrepreneur and clothing designer Jacques Hollins (né Jaky Solomon), a modernist aesthete with Jewish immigrant roots.

The initial consummation of Sonya and Manning's Jewish-Gentile love is figured as a sacred fusing, the beginning of a melting-pot marriage that, like the one between Zangwill's hero and heroine, would overcome all racial and religious differences. Manning himself is described in religious terms as Sonya's "deliverer," a Christ-like redeemer of the "cheapness" that surrounds her, one who will bring her "the high things of heaven and the beauty and abundance of the earth" (5, 7). Sonya reveres him like a god—she goes so far as to profess that "she would give her last drop of blood just to be the footstool on which he stepped" (99)—their mutual passion figured in racial stereotypes. She is savage—the passionate, biblical Jewess; he is civilized—the cold Anglo-Saxon, embodiment of her American Dream. Sonya muses, "The beauty, culture of all ages is in him. To have him is to possess all—the deepest, the finest of all America" (99). In Manning's presence, Sonya typically "burns," and he, for his part, sees her as "a fluid flame that merged into the rapt ardor of his mood" (103). For Manning, Sonya combines "the primitive fascination of the oriental" with "the intensity of spirit of the oppressed races" (101).[69] When they ultimately consummate their passion, Manning "crushes her to him," "a flame of life—a vivid exotic—a miraculous priestess of romance who had brought release for the ice of his New England heart."[70] The narrator likens this consummation to a "Miracle" at Manning's estate, Greenwold, now "God's own Eden," where, in the forest surrounding them, reminiscent of Moses's meeting on Mount Sinai, "every bush had a million pulses" (106, 107). Unlike the older meeting, though, this one is overtly sexual, their "melting" having clear racial implications: "the flesh merging their hearts into one consuming flame of love" (107). "Are we not the mingling of races?" Manning asks, "The oriental mystery and the Anglo-Saxon clarity that will pioneer a new race of men?" (108). Sonya responds, "Races and classes and creeds, the religion of your people and my people melt like mist in our togetherness" (108).

This audacious sexual literalization of "melting," and thus of eugenicist logic, however, comes to an abrupt halt after their actual wedding. Unlike a conventional marriage plot, this wedding occurs not at the novel's end but two-thirds of the way through, and between chapters, as if the event itself is insignificant. The exotic fantasy of interracial love is instead transformed into practical reality in "The Days After" of the chapter's title, when the "first veil of illusion fell between" the two lovers (109). Only then does Sonya see a truer Manning, a boring "higher-up," cold, impersonal, and (the narrator notes no less than three times) "placidly reading an article in the Atlantic Monthly!" (110–11). Antin's autobiography, we may recall, was initially published in this very New England venue for high culture. Yet here, Yezierska critiques the periodical's snobbishness as the epitome of chilly WASP culture, one to whose expectations of high realism and local color, we may also recall, Jewish authors like Cahan were expected to conform. When Sonya complains that she feels like a "steerage passenger" traveling in Manning's "first class" house, and rightly worries that his society will reject her, Manning becomes a virtual satire of Dewey, mouthing Progressive platitudes like "democratic understanding," a "belief in the brotherhood of man," and "the elimination of all artificial class barriers," and accusing Sonya of causing all their problems with her harping on "class differences" (119, 120). Although the wedding itself is elided, the reception scene couldn't have been better written by the likes of a Woody Allen, with Sonya's alternately gaudy and careworn East Side friends rubbing elbows with New York's "Four Hundred" society. In a virtual parody of class collision, Yezierska highlights in ways Zangwill failed to do the quixotic nature of the whole idea of religious and class intermarriage.

When Manning, Sonya's "savior," fails her, the honeymoon over, the narrator frames Sonya's disillusionment in expressly biblical Hebraic terms, suggesting Sonya's return, after a long Mosaic "Exodus" in Gentile country, to a familiar Jewish framework: "She was an outsider in her own house.

She was lost among Manning's people like a stranger in a strange land" (122). The narrator here recalls the biblical Exodus of formerly enslaved Israelites, led by Moses under God's guidance into the wilderness in search of the Promised Land. Sonya is exiled from Manning's estate, "Griswold—'God's Own Eden,'" as the chapter title announces, and disabused of her false, Christ-like messiah, only to depart in search of a real one (103). It is here that we may recall how, contrary to other plots of women marrying up—the likes of a Carrie Meeber or an Undine Spragg—Sonya's interest never really was in Manning's wealth, but in aesthetic redemption. Her "worship" of him is wrapped up in a desire to live (and subsequently provide the poor) with beauty, to be lifted out of the "sordidness of haggling and bargaining" into a realm of quiet grace and elegance (12, 13). Upon leaving Manning, then, Sonya's first, exogamous marriage of choice is followed by a second, endogamous one, with Jacques Hollins, the extraordinarily successful, Paris-trained, Fifth-Avenue fashion designer, formerly Jaky Solomon, Russian Jewish immigrant of East Broadway. What thus begins as an intermarriage plot of Protestant conversion is disrupted and reclaimed as Sonya embarks on a second, entirely different, plot of aesthetic passion with the Jewish artist.

Yezierska thus undoes the assimilationist marriage plot in this novel, and she does so in the language of biblical Hebraism, only here the noble Hebrew is gendered female. In the first half of the novel, Sonya is cast in the typological language of the New Testament as an oriental seductress, a biblical femme fatale—"Salome" to Manning's "John the Baptist," the "high-souled saint . . . without blood in his veins" (95–96). Manning's fetishization of Sonya as an exotic "Jewess" representing the "pulse of the people" (32) is ironic in contrast with her aspiration to shed her Jewishness and her past: "with the ardor of an adolescent convert Sonya had made of Manning the ideal of what she aspired to be. . . . [S]he had adapted herself to a new race, a new culture, a new religion!" (84). Though temporary, her conversion is best captured in an artistic metaphor, "a Salome of the tenements striving to be a Mona Lisa" (84). Like the famous painting that hung over Manning's desk, with her "inscrutable eyes," Sonya aspired to be like the "eternal ancestress of Manning and his kind," marked by "generations of self-control," even though to the very end of the novel Manning exoticizes and fetishizes Sonya's sexual and emotional force, with all her "oriental" difference (84).

In the novel's latter chapters, however, it is precisely Sonya's *artistic*, rather than sexual, passion that Jacques Hollins appreciates, her Jewishness now rendered in "philosemitic" metaphorical terms as the female Hebraic myth. Sonya seems to seduce and fake her way to impressing Manning, forging cultural capital on loan. With the power of Manning's name, which she liberally drops, and by hinting at sexual favors, she tricks her miserly landlord Rosenblat into repainting her apartment. She then borrows money from a diabolical pawnbroker, "Honest Abe," who subsequently extorts from her the promise of payment in her millionaire husband's name. It is that very loan, in fact, that irreparably sullies Manning's image of Sonya and leads him to utter antisemitic slurs, suggesting his true colors, and prompting Sonja to leave him. By contrast, she wins Hollins over immediately with vital energy and aesthetic force: "Not since Jacques Hollins had left the dark tenement in Division Street had he seen such naked, passionate youth. Here was inspiration, stimulus—an ardor for beauty that he had not believed anyone but himself possessed. How starved he had been these years of Fifth Avenue Success, starved for something more than the appreciation of his art in terms of money!" (23). If marriage to the Protestant American millionaire leads Sonya to debase herself sexually and economically, and to shed the trappings of her ethnic past, with Hollins, by contrast, she finds middle-class upward mobility through her own efforts and talents, and precisely as a figure connected to the Lower East Side.

Sonya brings Hollins back to his recent Jaky Solomon past, but she also links their present and future together to a deeper, Hebraic sense of time: "One minute she talked like an East Side *yenteh*—the next minute the rhythm of the Bible flowed from her lips" (23). This way of bridging epochs of time is what makes her extraordinary in Hollins's eyes. Particularly when draped in his magnificent clothing, Sonya becomes a vital, noble Hebrew of the future: "A pleading thing of youth and flame reached up to him. Her hands fluttered up and down his arm like antennae of rapacious famine. It brought back to him the thrill of his own emotion when he first touched fine silk. It was irresistible. She pierced to the core of him. Everything he had was hers . . ." (23). Whereas Hollins's other, wealthy clients are like bodies of "dead wood," Sonya is all youth, all vitality (24). She seems, like Pater's notion of the aesthetic, to "burn always with this hard gem-like flame."[71] With her neck "like the stalk of a flower," and her "bud-like breasts," she is to him "electric radiance divinely formed of flesh and blood," all fire and sacred flame. Unlike Manning's stoic Mona Lisa, in Hollins's artistic hands Sonya blossoms to life. Yezierska figures her as the iconic Jewish modernist dancer, "a Bernhardt in her youth," yet simultaneously as a "new Esther, dazzling the King of the Persians."[72] "You, Sonya," Hollins tells her, "are my first real work of art" (27). Between marriages, furthermore, Sonya talks a successful manufacturer into hiring her, and she learns the art of design herself, by practice, feel, instinct, and the "passion of creation" that is released when she once begins to make dresses. Hollins rediscovers Sonya there in the shop, now a gifted clothing designer, and his heart melts—for her passion and talent, but also, simultaneously, for this modern Hebraic Jewess.

The novel thus ends with a merging of past and future: the newly married lovers travel to Paris—the site of the avant-garde, the cultural future—and return to New York with what they've learned there, to "open up on the side a little shop on Grand Street" and offer "beauty for those that love it, beauty that is not for profit" (178). Whereas Manning made Sonya burn only physically, her shop with Hollins presents perhaps a deeper, more meaningful artistic passion, as we see in Sonya's reply: "I never burned so for something in my life like I burn for this. In the midst of the ready-mades of Grand Street, a shop of the beautiful—that's to be my settlement!" (178). Manning's Settlement House taught poor women how to make "[m]ilkless, butterless, eggless cake," what Sonya judges to be "faked, futile home economy," because it presumes the poor don't have "a palate in their mouth" (134–35). There they were expected to improve themselves by denying themselves the pleasure of the good and the beautiful. Her shop with Hollins, by contrast, will provide the poor a truly democratic enjoyment of a beauty that, as Hollins puts it, "belongs to no one class" (178). Yezierska critiques the settlement house movement and religious intermarriage simultaneously, but she does so through yet another iteration of the Hebraic myth.

In *Salome of the Tenements*, two Jewish artists—Jacques Hollins and Sonya Vrunsky—navigate aesthetics and business to achieve a marriage of choice not across religion but figuratively across time, linking a shared Jewish past to the modernist American future. The novel not only leaves behind the melting-pot marriage, in several places it also takes direct aim at Zangwill's play. The narrator compares Solomon to Zangwill himself, the prodigious Jewish artist, rather than to the hero of his ideologically charged play:

> Every now and then the Ghetto gives birth to an embry-
> onic virtuoso. Out of the crucible of privation and want,
> from hovels, basements, and black tenement holes, the
> unconquerable soul of the Jewish race rises in defiance of
> its environment.
>
> As Zangwill emerged from the abyss of London's East
> Side, as Heifitz strove for self-expression on the violin, and
> Pinsky wrestled in his Bowery printing shop with ghosts of
> his future dramas, so Jaky Solomon struggled blindly in a
> sweatshop as a designer in the dress trade to create clothes
> that would voice his love for color and line. (17)

Rather than religious intermarriage, poverty, suffering, and the artistic inspiration they create will form the redemptive "crucible" out of which can emerge an American Jewish future. Jaky's love of color and line, of art for art's sake—recalling the quintessential modernist mantra, "*l'art pour l'art*"—distinguishes "the Jewish race" for Yezierska. More than once, leading up to her pursuit of Manning, Sonya is compared to Quixote, interesting not least for the implications of the Cervantes reference but also as a clever pun on the name of Zangwill's hero, David Quixano. "Sonya was a being from another world—one bound by invisible laws of her own making," a real "Don Quixote" (8). Just prior to her reunion with Hollins, having run from Manning, shunned even by her East Side friends, we read: "As Don Quixote once tilted at windmills, so Sonya Vrunsky flung out her arms in battle with the deaf and dumb air" (162). Alone, Sonya consoles herself, "I am I. Now that I've no one to hold on to, I have me, myself. In me is my strength. I alone will yet beat them all" (162). Sonya's proud idealism and ultimate Emersonian self-reliance do seem quixotic, but she is rewarded by the novel's end, not in the fulfillment of an assimilationist marital dream. Rather, in a version of Hebraic myth, Yezierska's heroine enjoys the power of her passion and integrity as an artist, whose marriage to Hollins achieves what Lily Bart never could, the merging of business interests and idealism, of past and future.

Becoming a "*Teacherin*": Public Education in *Bread Givers*

Yezierska's second novel, *Bread Givers* (1925), is commonly read as one of assimilation, charting in heroine Sara Smolinsky's story the complex negotiations of cultural, ethnic, and economic forces that the process of assimilation implies. Subtitled "A Struggle between a father of the Old World and a daughter of the New," *Bread Givers* makes the passage across time explicit and central to the novel, suggesting another, albeit fictional, conversion narrative. Yet, whereas Antin's story bridges the actual time and space between the "Old" and "New" Worlds—moving, that is, across actual continents, oceans, and cultures—with the exception of her journey to the "Midwestern college," Sara's takes place entirely within New York. Neither does it involve religious intermarriage. Rather, Sara's transformation, her journey, is internal, private, even metaphorical. The novel's division into three "books" makes this clear: "Hester Street," "Between Two Worlds," and "The New World" chart the path of a *bildungsroman*, of Sara's movement away from home, her education, and her subsequent return to Hester Street as a college graduate. Sara's "new world" is not a new place, therefore, but a new status, that of an educated woman, an established "teacher in the schools" in the Lower East Side.[73] If the fulcrum point of Antin's narrative is her journey across the Atlantic "from Plotzk to Boston," where she is reborn in "The Promised Land" of America, Sara is reborn in a quintessential American Midwest college.

Likewise, Antin's metaphorical Egypt was Russia, a place of modern Jewish oppression, but Sara's Egypt is her own home, with Pharaoh as her own father. Her exodus midway through the novel thus takes her away from the metaphorical "old world" that is the Lower East Side, a place dominated by poverty and the Jewish patriarchal past, embodied in her father, Reb Smolinsky ("Reb" being the title "Mister" for an Orthodox

Jewish man). Sara is raised according to the biblical notion, upheld by both of her parents, that the prayers of women "didn't count because God didn't listen to women. Heaven and the next world were only for men. Women could get into Heaven because they were wives and daughters of men" (9). In other words, Sara's only hope for the World-to-Come rests upon her supporting her father in this world; his piety, not her own, will guarantee her salvation. Within a sacred Jewish economy, the Jewish woman may be a spectator, but her real role is to be the "bread giver" of the family, with education reserved explicitly for men.[74]

Sara's ambitions to learn, therefore, are obstructed by the character of Reb Smolinsky, in whom Yezierska reproduces in the extreme the dichotomy of male Jewishness we have been elaborating. At one moment, Sara describes her father praying with his "black satin skullcap" and his eyes "raised to God," looking as though "he just stepped out of the Bible."[75] At other moments, she sees him as a selfish tyrant; the pejoratives she hurls at his second wife, a leech, a "blackmailer," a "blood-sucker," are also aimed indirectly at him (274). Acting as Talmudic scholar as well as pawnbroker, gambler, and speculator, in whose hands marriage becomes less a sacred institution than a way of selling his daughters into "white slavery," Smolinsky is both ancient noble Hebrew and suspect modern "Jew" at once.[76] Though he remains a "Father with his eyes on the past," who never gives up the idea that "a woman without a man is less than nothing," Sara escapes him, and by the novel's end, unable to adapt to the world of American work, Smolinsky seems the object of Yezierska's punishment—alone, destitute, ill, no longer even a peddler of chewing gum on the street.[77]

For all that Yezierska reduces the position of the Orthodox Jewish patriarch in this novel, she jettisons neither the noble Hebrew nor the institution of marriage; rather, she recuperates both "racial" and religious categories of Jewishness in a fictional marriage of Jewish equals that transcends temporal divisions of "Old" and "New" Worlds, ancient and modern. Once on her own, Sara chooses a mate for herself based on love and what she calls a "blood" connection, Hugo Seelig, the principal of the school that hires her. Seelig not only shares her interest in education, he also looks forward and backward in time at once: he has "a Jewish face," one of "a dreamer, set free in the new air of America," yet, who, like Hollins "had found his work among us of the East Side" (273). She and Seelig, Sara also discovers, are "*Landsleute*—countrymen!" with a shared past, who "talked one language," who "had sprung from one soil," and thus are "of one blood" (277, 278). In her marriage to Seelig, Sara is therefore able to mediate her past as a Jewish woman with her future identity as an American. Rather than allowing Reb Smolinsky to die the martyr, moreover, they bring the poor father in to live with them, agree to keep an Orthodox home, and, above all, Hugo asks Smolinsky to teach him Hebrew. The novel thus preserves Smolinsky as a figure of sentimental pathos, of nostalgia, a noble Hebrew as collectible relic: "In a world where all is changed, he alone remained unchanged—as tragically isolate [*sic*] as the rocks" (296). The novel recuperates in him both the Jewish past and the messianic faith in a redemptive world to come, but in the form of a relatively impotent nostalgic literary figure, preserved as such by the novel in American Jewish literary culture.

Sara's future, likewise, depends upon reconciliation with the past, and this occurs not just through her marriage but also through her education and the various male Dewey figures that enable it. Sara initially rejects her traditional Jewish upbringing and defies the wishes of her parents by leaving home for school, but even as she creates a path for a meaningful future, in the novel's concluding lines, she is inescapably burdened by the heavy "shadow" of the past: "It wasn't just my father, but the generations who made my father whose weight was still upon me" (297). Unlike Antin, who proclaims, like the Ancient Mariner, to tell "his tale in order to be rid of it," Yezierska makes shedding the "heavy garment" of the past impossible.[78] Instead, in the Midwest college Sara finds ways to harness and convert her noble Jewish past into the stuff of narrative and social distinction. She learns to become, in effect, the writer and hero of her own story, one she delivers first as a successful graduation address and second as her first-person narrative, allowing her, as in Antin's Washington poem, to wed American and Hebraic mythologies into a meaningful dual lineage.

Upon leaving for college, Sara leaves behind her connection to Old World tradition, one that claims a woman without a man is "[l]ess than nothing—a blotted-out existence. No life on earth and no hope of Heaven."[79] At college, she not only acquires proper *bildung*—the Protestant values of "spick-and-span cleanliness" and proper "self-control" (212,

223)—she also solidifies her connection to a distinctly American narrative of the past. As she prepares for her journey, Sara compares herself to Columbus and to the Puritans: "I felt like the pilgrim fathers who had left their homeland and all their kin behind them and trailed out in search of the New World" (209). With these profound metaphors of American origin, Yezierska echoes Antin, except that her "New America" is the college itself, where she will find "the real Americans" (210). They are not found in the Lower East Side; rather, they are white, wealthy Protestants: "their faces were not worn with the hunger for things they never could have in their lives. There was in them that sure, settled look of those who belong to the world in which they were born," the look of generations of possession on American soil (211). Sara notes their "hands and necks white like milk," the men "all shaved up with pink, clean skins" (212). She looks at these "children of joy" and sees "their shiny freshness, their carefreeness," so that it becomes clear to Sara, by contrast, that with her "gray pushcart clothes," she "was nothing and nobody," worse than being ignored she was "an outcast. I simply didn't belong" (213, 212, 219).

Sara reconciles her poor, Jewish outsider status with the Protestant American world around her through the efforts of two male Dewey figures. The first, her psychology teacher, Mr. Edman, asks the class to "give an example from your own experience showing how anger or any strong emotion interferes with your thinking" (222). With this, Sara finds her voice, and a way to share with her peers the many anecdotes of her Hester Street past, which now seem "treasure chests of insight" (223). She also develops a dialogue with Mr. Edman outside school, personalizing her experience; the "power of logic and reason" she learns from him opens her to a "wider understanding of life" (226). The most significant moment at college, however, occurs when Sara befriends the benevolent dean of the college, who sympathizes with her concern that she must become "terribly hard" in order to become someone (231).

> "All pioneers have to get hard to survive," he said. He pointed to a faded oil painting of his grandmother. "Look! My grandmother came to the wilderness in an ox cart and with a gun on her lap. She had to chop down trees to build a

shelter for herself and her children. I'm more than a little ashamed to realize if I had to contend with the wilderness I'd perish with the unfit. But you, child—your place is with the pioneers. And you're going to survive." (232)

Here, Sara, the modern urban pioneer, is given a new ancestry in the dean's Protestant grandmother. Laura Wexler reads the dean as a Dewey figure, but no more than the replacement of the Old World patriarch with the New World patriarch, the "figure of the rational, comforting WASP."[80] She sees this passage in particular as a sign of the kind of Americanization that demands the obliteration of memory, of the "ominous process of erasure of [Sara's] own experience and interpretation and substitution of the values of another" (169). Indeed, Sara finds a historical narrative of rugged femininity available to her, but although she takes comfort in the dean's words, she does not in fact adopt this identity. Rather, she returns to her Jewishness by the novel's end.

Sara's college experience has less to do with forgetting the past than with offering her a form and framework through which to make her past meaningful in the American present and for the future. Above all, her experience grants her the recognition she craves but will never receive from her father. In addition to her college diploma, Sara wins a one-thousand-dollar prize for writing the best essay on "What the College Has Done For Me."[81] Although we never see the actual content of this essay, we can imagine it building upon the stories of her Hester Street past that she told in Mr. Edman's class. She proclaims, "Perhaps more than all the others, I had something to write about. Maybe they wouldn't understand. But if truth was what they wanted—here they had it" (232–33). As Antin's poem does for her, college provides Sara with an opportunity to tell her story to "real Americans," that is, to Gentiles, a story that she "poured . . . out as it came from [her] heart" (233). Her crowning moment of recognition occurs when she receives her graduation award: "all the students rose to their feet, cheering and waving and calling my name, like a triumph, 'Sara Smolinsky—Sara Smolinsky!'" (234). It is as though having her name chanted aloud hails Sara as an American, one now accepted not in spite of, but precisely for, her Jewishness.

The prize money, moreover, gives Sara her first experience of economic independence, enabling her to ride a Pullman home, eat good food, and indulge in that most definitive of bourgeois activities, shopping on Fifth Avenue. But shopping for Sara is no leisure pursuit; rather, it is the means by which to recreate her public image as the "*teacherin*" she is about to become. She chooses a look of "graceful quietness. That's what a school teacher ought to wear" (239). She rejects furs and "a pink ball gown," deciding that she must be "plain" as she is, "without ornaments" (238). Sara's "honeymoon" with herself becomes a love affair with the self she is constructing in the image of the austere Protestant teacher who taught her as a child: "A place for everything, and everything in its place" (8). In contrast with the hypocrisy of her father, whose pious appearance belies a selfish nature, Sara constructs herself as the truly transparent, sentimental heroine with solid Republican virtues. She has enough money to earn respectability, but she maintains an ascetic sensibility when it comes to consumption: "I furnished my room very simply. A table, a bed, a bureau, a few comfortable chairs. No carpet on the floors. No pictures on the wall. Nothing but a clean, airy emptiness. But when I thought of the crowded dirt from where I came, this simplicity was rich and fragrant with unutterable beauty" (240–41). This simple beauty extends to her new clothes: a dark blue and in "plain serge," with "more style in its plainness than the richest velvet," so that she muses, "for the first time in my life I was perfect from head to foot" (239, 240). Rather than becoming one addicted to consumerism like a Carrie Meeber or even a Lily Bart, Sara maintains a solid Protestant work ethic: "Life was all before me because my work was before me" (241).

If it seems that Sara's postgraduate rebirth is as a deracinated, Protestant American, it is also as a woman with the freedom to work and to choose her own destiny, and who also chooses to reunite with her Jewish past. The third book of the novel, entitled "The New World," marks Sara's return to Hester Street with her new status as a "person," now a college-educated teacher. She exclaims, "Home! Back to New York! Sara Smolinsky, from Hester Street, changed into a person! . . . I was a college graduate!" (237). Unlike her three sisters, Sara will choose her own husband, and, more importantly, as the chapter title "My Honeymoon With Myself" suggests, she will first reunite with the past self she left behind, now with new clothes and a room of her own. This return fundamentally involves reconciliation with her father, as mediated by Hugo Seelig. Marriage by choice therefore allows Sara to negotiate between her Jewish past and her American future, defined by Republican virtues, Emersonian individualism, and personal fulfillment, but also Protestant ethics. Following Cahan's Shaya Golub and David Levinsky, Sara emerges as a Jew who cannot seem to escape the reach of the Pale, which for her is more oppression and suffering than nostalgia. If *Salome* looks forward to Paris, to modernist art, here Yezierska registers the inescapable weight of the past. In the union of Sara Smolinsky and Hugo Seelig, East Side public school teacher and principal, respectively, *Bread Givers* illustrates the unfinished burden of reconciling, however imperfect, past and future, Jewish and Protestant American, religious and secular experiences, and preserves that struggle as the mark of the modern Jewish realist novel.

Coda

Emma Lazarus and the Future of the Jewish Problem

ON THURSDAY, JULY 25, 1867, eighteen-year-old Emma Lazarus visited and signed the visitors' log at the Touro Synagogue, the same one in which her own Seixas ancestors had prayed, among the first to bring Judaism to the New World in 1654.[1] Dedicated on the first day of Hanukkah, December 7, 1763, the Touro Synagogue in Newport was closed in 1791, its Torah scrolls sent to New York City, beginning a long, post-Revolutionary period of disuse.[2] It was therefore closed when Henry Wadsworth Longfellow visited Newport with his family on July 2, 1852, noted in the first draft of his poem, "The Jewish Cemetery at Newport" (1854): "And near them stands the vacant Synagogue; / But prayers and psalms no more its silent break, / Nor Rabbi reads the ancient Decalogue / In the grand dialect that Moses spake."[3] Coming to Newport when she did, however, Lazarus arrived among the wealthy for whom Newport, Rhode Island, was now a fashionable summering locale of choice. This visit led to her writing "In the Jewish Synagogue at Newport" (1867), a direct response to Longfellow, and the first of many poems Lazarus would write on Jewish themes.[4]

In his poetic take on the Newport cemetery, Longfellow fully embraces the Hebraic myth: the Jews are not only symbols of tradition but of a dead one, unfit for the modern world. As with the fate of American Indians in his poem "Hiawatha" (1855), no matter their natural wonder, Longfellow saw the disappearance of the Jewish people as inevitable. Their tombstones are "like the tablets of the Law, thrown down / And broken by Moses at the mountain's base" (lines 11–12). These shards of the holy Ten Commandments serve as signs of the disobedience and punishment of the Jews

227

for disregarding Moses's instruction. In these symbolic tablets, he tries to find some sort of Jewish essence, a narrative of Jewishness that will not disrupt but confirm Christian typology. He finds, however, only strange names, of "foreign accent, and of different climes," evidence of a people once transplanted from another place and time, at home here only in death (line 14). In Spanish, Portuguese, and Hebrew writing, the modern world commingles with the biblical, as historical time collapses in the engraved names. Although it is tradition that helped the Jews survive persecution over time, here that same tradition, in Esther Schor's words, "grasps them in a death lock"[5]:

> And thus forever with reverted look
> The mystic volume of the world they read
> Spelling it backward, like a Hebrew book,
> Till life became a Legend of the Dead. (lines 53–56)

In Longfellow's poem, the Jews are a "backward" people. Like their language, read from right to left, they, too, face toward the past. As Schor writes, it is unclear whether for Longfellow, they "turn away from Christian revelation, modernity, or both."[6] What is clear is that, in both cases, sacred and secular, they turn away from the present and future.

Above all, the poem emphasizes their passing as a "race" of people: the "portals" of the synagogue, Longfellow's speaker assumes, are now closed, no "Psalms of David" break the silence, "No Rabbi reads the ancient Decalogue" (lines 22, 23). Rather, the Jews live on only in memory: "a hand unseen" preserves their graves with a touch of care and beauty (line 26). He notes their former lives of persecution, running from ghetto to ghetto and living on the "bitter herbs of exile and its fears," a reference to those herbs eaten during the Jewish Passover Seder, intended to remind the observant of the sacrifices of their biblical ancestors (line 38). In a second draft of this much-revised poem, Longfellow made a protest against the bitter fate of the Jews, but it was later omitted:

> Is there no hope? no end of all their wrongs?
> No rest—no Truce of God to intervene,

For those who gave the world its noblest songs,
The only perfect man this world hath seen?[7]

With the omission of this passage, we lose a sense of Longfellow's reverence for the Jews as bearers of "the only perfect man," Jesus Christ, and thus of his overt use of the typological aesthetic. Without it, the poem nonetheless reduces Jewish civilization to a history of noble suffering. Since "dead nations never rise again," Longfellow immortalizes for memory this noble but vanished race through the Hebraic myth (line 60).

Lazarus responded to Longfellow's poem almost stanza for stanza, taking the same tone and form; however, her poem focuses not on the cemetery, the house of the dead, but on the synagogue itself, the house of vital worship. Rather than noting the strange silences of the graves, her speaker marks a place of welcome tranquility, where "the noises of the busy town, / The ocean's plunge and roar can enter not" (lines 1–2). Like Longfellow, she sees "no signs of life," and reads the Hebrew inscriptions on the walls as "in a language dead" (lines 4–5). She, too, mourns and exalts the "lone exiles of a thousand years," who in this temple "offered up" prayers that were "wrung from sad hearts that knew no joy on earth" (lines 11, 9, 10). But Lazarus's empathetic vision connects the exiles of the past with those of the present. She sees not strange, foreign, and displaced outsiders but signs of an unfortunate people, her own ancestors, scattered far "From the fair sunrise land that gave them birth" (line 12). Gazing "in this new world of light" upon a "relic of the days of old," invoking notions of both the "Old" and unenlightened and "New" and modern worlds, Lazarus muses on the romantic biblical past of "the patriarch with his flocks" (lines 13, 14, 17). Whereas Longfellow emphasizes the shattered nature of the holy tablets, however, Lazarus recalls Moses, who "reads Jehovah's written law, / 'Midst blinding glory and effulgence rare, / Unto a people prone with reverent awe" (lines 22–24). This is a scene of glory, not of failure, as Lazarus resurrects, rather than mourns, the noble Hebrew.

If Longfellow's speaker remains outside the Newport synagogue, Lazarus celebrates what happens inside: Jewish prayer, song, and the "chant of praise" (line 36). She writes herself into a centuries-old tradition of biblical poetry, claiming a place for herself as one who sanctifies the temple: here

"The weary ones, the sad, the suffering, / All found their comfort," and the "funeral and the marriage" were consecrated (lines 33–34, 37). Although now "green grass lieth over all," she insists, "the sacred shrine is holy yet" (lines 40, 41). In the last two lines of the poem, her speaker therefore commands us: "Take off your shoes as by the burning bush, / Before the mystery of death and God" (lines 43–44). In Lazarus's hands, death becomes not an occasion for finality and eulogy but a starting point for memory, ritual, and spiritual renewal. Her brief, finite poem invokes and channels the very "mystery" of the infinite: "death and God" alike. Although Lazarus extols the noble virtues of the suffering ancient Hebrews as Longfellow does, she uniquely transposes a vital Jewish force onto the present for her readers to experience in the here and now.

Lazarus was certainly influenced by the Fireside Poets and heir to their Hebraic mythology. As we have seen, Oliver Wendell Holmes, a Unitarian free of the proselytizing zeal of his Calvinist father, expressed genuine interest in the Jews; yet even if he accepted "the Jew as a Jew," in his poetry, like Longfellow, he invoked the Hebraic myth to create a typological prefiguration for the Christian present.[8] James Russell Lowell, also discussed earlier, was notable for having been unable to square his typological understanding of noble Hebrews with the Jewish reality in his midst, with "their invasion and despoilment of the few remaining patrician asylums."[9] It is worth noting, too, that these poets themselves had inherited the Hebraic myth from an earlier generation of American writers. The postrevolutionary poet Philip Freneau frequently invoked mythical biblical Hebrews, in some cases critically, as in "Sketches in American History" (1784), where a geographically confused Columbus is likened to "old Moses, the Jew," who "led his wrong-headed crew."[10] In other poems, Hebrews figure more sympathetically, as in "The Jewish Lamentation at the Euphrates" (1779), a rewriting of Psalm 137 expressing the yearnings and vengeful anger of the newly exiled Jewish people, best known for its opening, "By the waters of Babylon . . ."[11] The Hebraic myth makes frequent appearances in antebellum poetry: in William Croswell's conversion poem "The Synagogue" (1842), and in more or less sympathetic fashion in poems by Jones Very, western poet Johnson Pierson, and William Wetmore Story, to name just a few.[12] The postbellum Fireside Poets—William Cullen Bryant and John

Greenleaf Whittier, as well as Holmes, Lowell, and Longfellow—continued this tradition into later parts of the nineteenth century, when mythical Hebraism became complicated by Jewish immigration and the consequent political, social conversations surrounding the Jewish Problem.[13]

Emma Lazarus is perhaps best known for immortalizing the "tired," the "poor," and "huddled masses yearning to be free" in her now-famous poem of America as a great haven for immigrants, "The New Colossus" (1883), but her story provides a significant bookend to this study for other reasons. Daughter of Moses and Esther Nathan Lazarus, she was born in 1849 to one of the best-known and oldest Jewish families in New York, having been established there for four generations.[14] Descending from the first twenty-three Jewish New Amsterdam settlers of 1654, the Nathan family was prolific in social, political, and literary life. Moses Lazarus was a prosperous sugar refiner said to have amassed a fortune and, along with John Jacob, William Astor, John Hay, August Belmont, and William Vanderbilt, was a founder of the exclusive Knickerbocker Club in New York in 1871.[15] Lazarus was thus part of the old-moneyed class of Sephardic Jews, the quite acceptable class of "Hebrews" that, as discussed earlier, Henry Hilton in his official New York Times "Statement" distinguished from the vulgar and unacceptable "Seligman Jew."[16] As president of Congregation Emanu-El, the first Reform synagogue in New York City, Seligman had helped Felix Adler incorporate the Society of Ethical Culture in February 1877, devoted to good works and social welfare over Orthodox creed or ritual, so that Hilton could dismiss them both as "Liberals" and illegitimate "Hebrews."[17] The hotel was meant for men of the "exclusive classes of society," that is, for families like Lazarus's.[18] Hilton might have viewed Lazarus as a noble Hebrew, but this would necessarily have been a class, rather than a religious, distinction. She was hardly an Orthodox Jew; as Schor shows, she was indifferent to Jewish piety and prayer, expressing her Jewishness within her elite, secular upbringing rather through commitments to family, community, and synagogue membership, and eventually in her poetry, where, as we have seen, the noble Hebrew was already a common figure.[19] When she began her career in the 1860s, publishing her first volume of poetry, *Poems and Translations* (1866), at just seventeen years old, Lazarus was influenced by Longfellow and would also have discovered the idea of the noble Hebrew in the works of German Romantic poet Heinrich Heine, a Christian convert born Jewish, whose lyrics she translated as early as 1866.[20]

But 1876 represented a shift: on the eve of the 1877 Seligman-Hilton affair, Lazarus began publishing original poems with biblical Hebraic themes that not only celebrate Jewish antiquity but also criticize modern antisemitism. Following her second book, *Admetus and Other Poems* (1871), in 1876 Lazarus began to translate those poems of Heine's specifically on themes of his own predicament as a cultured, assimilated, baptized Jew (though he later recanted it), such as "Donna Clara," about a self-hating Spanish Jew. She also translated poems about persecuted Sephardic rabbis by Medieval Spanish and Portuguese poets like Judah Ben Ha-Levi, Solomon Ben Judah Gabirol, Moses Ben Ezra, and others, with a fervent sense of humanism.[21] One major event that year was the publication of George Eliot's iconic "philosemitic" novel *Daniel Deronda* (1876). This novel had a profound effect on Lazarus: she began to write political essays on the Jewish Problem, and became a fierce advocate of national Jewish resettlement in Palestine, as dramatized in Eliot's novel. Lazarus even dedicated her first book of Jewish poems, *Songs of a Semite* (1882), to "the memory of George Eliot, the illustrious writer, who did most among the artists of our day toward elevating and ennobling the spirit of Jewish nationality."[22]

What is crucial about Lazarus's emergent Jewish poetry in this later period is how it engages Hebraic myths—noble Jewish figures of the distant past—but now in order to satirize and eviscerate modern Christian antisemitism in the present and for the future. "Raschi in Prague" (1880), for example, tells the legendary story of the renowned medieval biblical commentator who was put to death by a mob while visiting the Jewish community in Prague. In Lazarus's hands, Raschi becomes a tragic, noble hero, martyred by the very Christians whose own Saviour once faced a similar fate: "others had seized and bound, / And gagged from speech, the helpless, aged man; / . . . He struggled not while his free limbs were tied, / His beard plucked, torn and spat upon his robe."[23] In "The Guardian of the Red Disc," a monologue set in fourteenth-century Malta, the speaker is an antisemitic Christian "Citizen" praising the bishop of Malta for requiring

Jews to wear identifying badges.[24] These poems use satire and irony to expose Christian antisemitism and the hypocrisy of Christian charity and forgiveness. By implication, they also not only render modern Christian antisemites unmodern and retrograde, but show their bigoted violence to be the obvious medieval atavism. In these poems, Lazarus maps noble stories from actual Jewish history onto present circumstances to highlight and challenge the stuck-ness of Christian antisemitism in the medieval past, in stories forgotten by or unknown to contemporary anti-Jewish agitators of the "Jewish Problem" in the literary press, like Madame Z. Ragozin and Telemachus T. Timayenis, as I discuss below.[25]

Following the arrival of the first crowds of Russian Jewish refugees fleeing *shtetl* pogroms in New York in 1881 and prompting what would soon become a refugee crisis, Lazarus became a philanthropist and aid worker. Her poems argued vociferously that we were seeing a historical repetition of Jewish persecution from the Middle Ages to modern nineteenth-century Europe, now that she was witnessing the effects of these violent outbreaks firsthand. By the autumn of 1882, after visiting Ward's Island, where 250 Jewish refugees were being held, she started teaching English to immigrant girls and volunteering in the newly founded Hebrew Emigrant Aid Society (HEAS).[26] Her play *The Dance to Death: A Historical Tragedy in Five Acts* (1882), serialized in Philip Cowen's *American Hebrew* during that year, reads as her most sustained poetic attack on modern antisemitism. Set in plague-ridden Germany in 1359, the play is based on the May 1348 mass execution by fire of a German village's Jewish population.[27] According to Schor, it draws on at least two sources, both of which feature a young Jewish woman and a Christian noble against a backdrop of violent antisemitism: Richard Reinhard's *Der Tanz zum Tode* (1877), about martyred Jews in Nordhausen accused of spreading the plague, and Fromental Halévy's five-act opera *La Juive* (1835) ("The Jewess"), set to a French libretto by Eugène Scribe, one of the most popular operas of the nineteenth century.[28] Like the Halévy-Scribe opera, Lazarus's drama unfolds a plot of concealed Christian identity. A Jewish father hides the terrible secret that his adopted daughter is actually born of a powerful Christian, complicit with the Jewish persecution. In Reinhard's original narrative, when the Jews are condemned to die the daughter is given the chance to convert to

Christianity but she chooses death, leaving her act of loyalty unclear as to what it proves: a commitment to Jewish values or a deeply Christian soul.

Lazarus's revision follows the fashion of her Jewish poetic predecessors, Penina Moïse (1797–1880) and Adah Isaacs Menken (1835–68), who reinterpreted biblical female characters to assert women's political and religious power.[29] Here in *The Dance to Death*, the daughter's motives are also pointedly redemptive: learning that her birth father is the enemy to the Jews, Liebhaid firmly declares loyalty to her Jewish family—"Never! If I be offspring to that kite, / I here deny my race, forsake my father . . . Thy God is mine, / Thy people are my people"—illustrating how Lazarus harnesses the power of the noble Jewish past to confront contemporary persecution.[30] As in the Purim story to which the play alludes, Liebhaid's father, Susskind, encourages her, the Esther figure, to use her connection to the oppressor for the good of the Jewish people. When she refuses in the lines above, as Schor notes, the Book of Esther subtext transforms into the Book of Ruth, echoing Ruth's speech to her mother-in-law, "Whither thou goest, I shall go . . ." (Ruth 1:16).[31] Susskind's final speech, as the Jews are led into the fire, projects into the future, prophesying that their deaths will be avenged by "Jew-priest, Jew-poet, Jew-singer, or Jew-saint."[32] Perhaps that "Jew-poet" is Lazarus herself as she rewrites these biblical myths, so that in the play's final consuming fire, the poet makes us feel "in ancient flames, a modern pain."[33]

R. Barbara Gitenstein has argued that only after the publication of *Daniel Deronda* "did Lazarus become a Jewish poet."[34] Yet Ranen Omer-Sherman challenges the idea of Lazarus's "unqualified conversion" to Judaism and Jewish themes as the center of her work. He argues, rather, that we must understand her "Jewish ambivalence," particularly given her early silence on Judaism. For Omer-Sherman, Lazarus was instead a "harbinger of the modern ethnic Jew," who, anticipating Horace Kallen, "embraced *ethnicity*, not religion, as the key to Jewish survival."[35] Omer-Sherman's argument is entirely compelling, yet it also creates a sacred/secular binary of Jewishness, the conversion trope suggesting Lazarus was either "Hebrew" or "Jew," at one point one and then the other (although of a better sort than Judge Hilton surmised). Yet Lazarus's life and career challenge this binary logic by modernizing the antiquated image of the noble Hebrew and harnessing the Hebraic myth to disrupt typology. In other words, Lazarus makes a sacred narrative of the past secular and modern. And by drawing the past into the present, she also gives the secular story a sacred significance, one derived not from God but from the collective memory of a vitally relevant Jewish past that her poem engenders. Lazarus thereby undoes the logic of typology. Instead of the mythical Hebraic past prefiguring a Christian present, it *refigures* it: she proves that present-day, modern antisemitic persecution is the real atavistic phenomenon, experienced by Jewish people as a repetition of a past to which they are repeatedly subjected, against and out of which they themselves must create a modern, livable experience. If Liebhaid's conversion to Judaism is an allegory for Lazarus's life, it tells of her political-poetical conversion, which we see in the literary transformation of Jewish myth into living population in her poetry, a conscientious declaration of her "solidarity with the Jewish people."[36] Lazarus's art becomes a mode of "public intervention": she becomes, in Julian Levinson's view, "herself an 'Esther' who, like the figure of Liebhaid in the play, moves in the gentile world as a loyal Jewish emissary."[37]

Lazarus's work thus narrows and mediates the broad temporal gaps of Jewishness created by her poetic forbears, between an ancient biblical Hebraic culture and the contemporary modern world.[38] In the last years of her life (cut short by Hodgkin's disease at age thirty-eight), she explicitly linked the Hebraic myth to current political issues in her prose writing on the Jewish Problem.[39] Her first essay on the subject, "Was the Earl of Beaconsfield a Representative Jew?" praised Benjamin Disraeli for the "faculty which enables this [Jewish] people, not only to perceive and make the most of every advantage of their situation and temperament, but also, with marvelous adroitness, to transform their very disabilities into new instruments of power."[40] Although, defensively, she noted the Jews' "commercial prosperity," that which makes others jealous and hateful of them, but she maintained that it was a direct result of the "stupid, not to say cruel, policy of those very nations in confining them for years to the practice of usury" (940). As Mary Antin would do three decades later in large swaths of her autobiography *The Promised Land* (1912), Lazarus explained away perceived "backward" Jewish behaviors as reactions to antisemitic discrimination. Jews may be accused of clannishness, she concedes, but it is persecution that has driven them to form their own close, small communities and to be distrustful of others. Lazarus emphasized their "patient humility" as they accepted these blows, not as "the inertia of a broken will, but the calculating, self-control of a nature imbued with persistent and unconquerable energy" (940). Lazarus's rehearsal of both philosemitic and antisemitic stereotypes may illustrate "the tug-of-war between [her] assimilationist desires and her group loyalty," as Omer-Sherman contends, but it also illustrates her participation in a literary tradition of the typological aesthetic, in which these stereotypes not only appear simultaneously but also flow from the same temporal logic.[41] Lazarus's argument uniquely works to complicate, if not to reverse, the temporal logic of typology: in her hands, it is a persistent, medieval Christian antisemitism that stands in the way of modern Jewish redemption.

Side by side with the previous essay, the *Century* also printed "Russian Jews and Gentiles: from a Russian point of view," in which Russian social scientist Madame Zénaïde A. Ragozin defended the mob perpetrators of the violent pogroms against Russian Jews.[42] Ragozin attacked the Jews as "notorious usurers," part of a broad Jewish conspiracy, "enslaving" Russian peasants, a "parasitical race who, producing nothing, fasten on the produce of the land and labor, and live on it, choking the breath of life out of commerce and industry as sure as the creeper throttles the tree that holds it"; hence, these parasites deserved the treatment they received.[43] Ragozin advocated for assimilation as a solution to the Jewish Problem: with it, "the number of Jews who discard the Talmud and keep to the simple Mosaic law in its wider and more liberal application would annually increase" (920). The "simple Mosaic law," that is, the ethical values of the noble Hebrew, would be fine; actual living, worshipping Jews, however—also conceived of as usurious, parasitical speculators—are the problem. Like Judge Hilton, Ragozin separated out "notional," noble "Hebrews" abstracted from actual "Jews," as if the Hebraic myth could not only be disembodied and made atemporal but also be used simultaneously to justify denigrating a living Jewish people.

Lazarus was shown Ragozin's piece before it went to print and was horrified. In spite of her protests, however, the magazine printed it, but subsequently published her retort, "Russian Christianity Versus Modern

Judaism," in which Lazarus refuted Ragozin point by point and educated readers on East European Jewish life and the medieval brutality of the Russian pogroms.[44] In February 1883, *Century* then published Lazarus's second full-length piece on the subject, "The Jewish Problem," a chauvinistic appeal for sympathy among the magazine's Christian readership.[45] Here Lazarus made her strongest appeal for Zionism, quoting George Eliot in her advocacy for political nationality and a Jewish homeland as an "organic center" for this besieged "race."[46] Lazarus still exalted the heroic pride of her people, as she did in her first Hebraic ponderings on the Jewish synagogue in Newport, but by this point Lazarus had come to understand modern antisemitism as a persistent, racially charged problem of the present, not mythical but political and economic in nature, and, like many Jews and non-Jews alike at this time, she viewed it as a problem that would be solved by political nationhood.

In the face of historical Jewish persecution, here but mostly abroad, Lazarus ultimately became an American spokesperson for Jewish resettlement, advocating Zionism more than a decade before Theodor Herzl convened the First Zionist Congress in Basel in 1897.[47] Yet even as the Zionist ideal transformed into a modern political movement for a Jewish nation, one with both secular and religious strands, it found strange bedfellows with those millennial Christians engaged in their own profoundly typological eschatology, as we have seen. It was precisely in this period, after all, that William Blackstone, with his most famous tract, *Jesus is Coming* (1878), also began to espouse Jewish resettlement as part of the broader movement of Protestant dispensationalism, that is, the unfolding of God's redemptive plan.[48] Blackstone believed that "Jewish people everywhere were the objects of biblical prophecy. The Jews had rejected Jesus as Messiah during his first earthly manifestation, but they now had the opportunity to place their faith in his imminent return to earth and the establishment of a millennial kingdom." Blackstone espoused that the Second Coming "would be preceded by a massive return of Jews to Israel, their rightful homeland."[49] Lazarus must have known that her advocacy for a Jewish return to Palestine put her in a tricky place vis-à-vis such expressions of Christian Zionism, which viewed Jews not as a diasporic people in search of a homeland in their own right but as foundational to the Christian redemptive mission, a logic that is alive and kicking today among evangelical Christians, heirs to the late-nineteenth-century dispensationalist movement, and thus natural lovers of Zionism—of Israel as key to past, present, and future redemptive history.[50]

The poetic noble Hebrew of the past and the Christian Zionist vision of the future constitute the two temporal ends of the spectrum of Hebraic mythology. This mythology authenticated and justified Christian self-definition, but in doing so subordinated the significance of Jews and Jewish culture to a different order of time. By contrast, Emma Lazarus, in her poetry and prose alike, revised this inherited tradition of contested Christian identity by recasting Christianity as ancient and reclaiming Hebraic Jewishness as modern and central to the future in its own terms. Perhaps it was the historical events that catalyzed Lazarus into action and urged her to revise her poetic approach to the past. Perhaps it was, as it would be for her literary successors Mary Antin and Anzia Yezierska—Jewish women who also rejected the patriarchal oppressiveness of Jewish tradition—a matter of gender. After all, we see the redemptive Jewish female voice extend well into the works of mid-twentieth-century writers like Grace Paley and Tillie Olsen.

Paley gave women voices that, though inflected by Yiddish intonation and humor, find little grounding in the past. Faith Darwin in "Faith in the Afternoon" meditates on the question, "Who are her antecedents?" only to have her aging father, whom she rarely visits, turn away from her in "an explosion of nausea, absolute digestive disgust."[51] Victoria Aarons reads Paley "as indelibly a Jewish writer" in relation to the past, her fiction full of characters "bracketed by history," "by a shared past and by the mythology of the outsider characteristic to the Jewish protagonist."[52] And certainly Rose Leiber in "Goodbye and Good Luck" (1956), Paley's first published story, narrates and reclaims her past from the shame and judgment into which actual young, attractive, unmarried women were undoubtedly cast—particularly those who, like Rose, may have allowed a married man (Volodya Vlashkin) to come live with them.[53] But even as Rose redeems her past with her pending marriage to Vlashkin, she also anticipates the future by telling her young niece, Lillie—the occasion for the story—such details as Lillie's mother wouldn't dare hear ("I'll faint! I'll faint!" [21]).

In other words, Rose harnesses the mythology of her past to shape Lillie's future, perhaps that of all young girls, urging Lillie, "tell this story to your mama from your young mouth" (21). The story concludes by looking ahead, with Rosie's words of benediction for an open-ended, unknown, yet hopeful future: "Hug Mama, tell her from Aunt Rose, goodbye and good luck" (22). Lazarus's poetry also looks backward, to the biblical past, in order to look forward to the future she envisioned, one of a national homeland for Jews free of modern antisemitic persecution. Likewise, her career stretches across time to link Jewish female poets of the past, like Moïse and Menken, to writers of the future who, like Paley, similarly redeem the power of Jewish female voices. If Lazarus was "by far the most influential Jewish-American literary figure of the nineteenth century," then her poetry and meditations on the Jewish Problem offer a complex example of how Jewishness in American literature could and did transition from myth to reality to put "the Jew" back in time.[54]

NOTES

INTRODUCTION

Jacques Le Goff, *Time, Work and Culture in the Middle Ages* (Chicago: University of Chicago Press, 1980), 29; Jacob Riis, *How the Other Half Lives: Studies Among the Tenements of New York* (New York: Hill and Wang, 1957), 83.

1. Henry James, *The American Scene* (New York: Penguin, 1994).
2. James, *American Scene*, 82–83. Alan Trachtenberg suggests that in the "aliens" James sees a mirror for his own state of "homelessness and worldseeking," and an "insecurity about American identity," which is not a condition "one is born into or ever confidently arrives at but . . . a steady process of exchange, of reinvention and revision." See Alan Trachtenberg, "Conceivable Aliens," *Yale Review* 82, no. 4 (1994): 49, 50, 63.
3. James, *American Scene*, 99–100.
4. I treat this in more depth in chapter 2. See, for example, Ross Posnock, *The Trial of Curiosity* (New York: Oxford University Press, 1991); Greg Zacharias, "Henry James' Fictional Jew," in *Representations of Jews Through the Ages*, ed. Leonard Jay Greenspoon and Bryan F. Le Beau (Omaha, NE: Creighton University Press, 1996); and Jonathan Freedman, "Henry James and the Discourses of Antisemitism," in *Between "Race" and Culture: Representations of "the Jew" in English and American Literature*, ed. Bryan Cheyette (Stanford, CA: Stanford University Press, 1996).
5. James, *American Scene*, 101.
6. See, for example, Jean M. O'Brien, *Firsting and Lasting: Writing Indians Out of Existence in New England* (Minneapolis: University of Minnesota Press, 2010), esp. chapter 3, "Lasting."
7. Alan Trachtenberg makes explicit the connections in this era between US policy toward tribal Native Americans and that toward immigrants seeking citizenship. See Trachtenberg, *Shades of Hiawatha: Staging Indians, Making Americans, 1880–1930* (New York: Hill and Wang, 2004).

8. See Ezek. 48:35 and Rev. 3:12 and 21:2. In Judaism, it is commonly believed that the New Jerusalem will be here on earth; in Christianity, some see it in the future, others believe it a metaphor for heaven, others see it as a current reality, and still others believe it will be a literal city.

9. James, *American Scene*, 101–2.

10. "But ah! what once has been shall be no more! / The groaning earth in travail and in pain / Brings forth its races, but does not restore, / And the dead nations never rise again." Henry Wadsworth Longfellow, "The Jewish Cemetery at Newport" (1852), lines 57–60, *The Complete Poetical Works of Henry Wadsworth Longfellow* (Boston: Houghton Mifflin, 1893).

11. Harold Fisch, *The Dual Image: The Figure of the Jew in English and American Literature* (New York: Ktav Publishing, 1971), 13. Fisch is helpful for parsing "the 'good' Jew of Biblical times, and the 'bad' Jew of today" (89), but the scope of his study is limited. He dismisses writers like Cahan and Henry Roth in a single sentence: "There is little in American Jewish writing prior to the Second World War to prepare us for the extraordinary flowering of talent which has since placed the Jews, especially of New York, in a position of literary supremacy unknown before in the history of the Diaspora," and makes no mention of Jewish women writers at all (111). For an account of how anti-Jewish stereotypes functioned as projections of political polemics in the postrevolutionary period, see William Pencak, *Jews and Gentiles in Early America: 1654–1800* (Ann Arbor: University of Michigan Press, 2005), 6–18.

12. Kathleen Biddick, *The Typological Imaginary: Circumcision, Technology, History* (Philadelphia: University of Pennsylvania Press, 2003), 1.

13. Yosef Hayim Yerushalmi, *Zakhor: Jewish History and Jewish Memory* (Seattle: University of Washington Press, 1982), xxxv.

14. The actual dates are unclear, as accounts vary as to whether or not Seligman actually took the journey to the Grand Union Hotel in defiance of the policy against "Israelites." See Stephen Birmingham, *Our Crowd: The Great Jewish Families of New York* (New York: Harper and Row, 1967), 143–44.

15. "A Sensation at Saratoga," *New York Times*, June 19, 1877, 1. The reference is to Felix Adler, who established the Society for Ethical Culture in February 1877 with the help of Seligman, then president of the reform Temple Emanu-El. See Howard Radest, *Toward Common Ground: The Story of the Ethical Societies in the United States* (New York: Fredrick Unger, 1969).

16. "Sensation at Saratoga," 1.

17. An excellent example is Eric Lott, *Love and Theft: Blackface Minstrelsy and the American Working Class* (Oxford: Oxford University Press, 1995).

18. For an account of this phase, and the return to religion in early American literary studies in the first decade of the twenty-first century, see Sarah Rivett, "Early American Religion in a Postsecular Age," *PMLA* 128, no. 4 (2013): 990–91.

19. For Bauer, all religion needed to be abolished in the secular state, particularly hard for Jews to achieve since Judaism was a "primitive" stage in the unfolding of Christianity, a Hegelian version of Protestant typology. For Marx, however, Jewish "particularism" couldn't be abolished, as it had already become a practical, "worldly religion," one of "huckstering" and economic self-interest, the "Spirit" of the Christian nation that sociologists Werner Sombart and Max Weber would later more fully theorize. Marx's arguably antisemitic claims in that essay reached their sinister apogee one hundred years later in the "Final Solution" to the Jewish Question in Europe. Bruno Bauer, *Die Judenfrage* (Braunschweig, 1843); see *Stanford Encyclopedia of Philosophy* (Winter 2017 ed.), s.v. "Bruno Bauer," https://plato.stanford.edu/archives/win2017/entries/bauer/; and Karl Marx, *Selected Writings*, ed. David McLellan (Oxford: Oxford University Press, 2000), 46–63.

20. Amanda Anderson, "George Eliot and the Jewish Question," *Yale Journal of Criticism*, 10, no. 1 (1997): 39.

21. Shmuel Feiner, *The Jewish Enlightenment*, trans. Chaya Naor (Philadelphia: University of Pennsylvania Press, 2002), xi. For Feiner, this revolution in thought was no less significant for the Jews as the French Revolution was for the French, for it effectively created a modern, secular Jewish public sphere (1–2, 13, 35). Feiner insists this movement began among a small number of elite Jewish scholars trying to overcome their sense of intellectual inferiority in relation to European scholars, and to challenge rabbinical orthodoxy in the name of Enlightenment values (7, 25).

22. Anderson, "George Eliot and the Jewish Question," 39–40. See also David Patterson, *Emil L. Fackenheim: A Jewish Philosopher's Response to the Holocaust* (Syracuse, NY: Syracuse University Press, 2008), 63.

23. The Jewish Reform movement was greatly shaped by the work of Bohemian immigrant Rabbi Isaac Mayer Wise in Cincinnati, who wrote the first prayer book for American worshipers, *Minhag American* (1857), and founded the Union of American Hebrew Congregations in 1873, the Hebrew Union College in Cincinnati in 1875, and the Central Conference of American Rabbis

(CCAR) in 1889. See Jonathan Sarna, *American Judaism* (New Haven, CT: Yale University Press, 2004), 96–98, 125, 132, 195.

24. Challenging the commonly accepted periodizations, or "waves," of Jewish immigration—the idea of a Sephardic era (1645–1820), a German era (1820–80), and an age dominated by East European Jewish immigrants beginning in 1880, Hasia Diner argues that the more than two and a half million immigrants arriving between 1880 and 1925 proved to be simply an extension and intensification of what had already begun in Jewish American communities. See Hasia Diner, *A Time for Gathering: The Second Migration, 1820–1880* (Baltimore: Johns Hopkins University Press, 1992), 4–5, 213–35.

25. Diner, *A Time for Gathering*, 234.

26. Over five million immigrants entered the United States from 1880 to 1890. The Chinese Exclusion Act of 1882 and Alien Contract Labor laws of 1885 and 1887 prohibited certain laborers from immigrating to the United States. In 1888, expelling "aliens" became legally possible. In 1891, the Bureau of Immigration, newly established in the Treasury Department, forced steamship companies to return ineligible passengers to countries of origin; the federal government assumed direct control of inspecting, admitting, rejecting, and processing all immigrants seeking admission to the United States with the Immigration Act of 1891. The 1891 Immigration Act also expanded the list of excludable classes to include polygamists, persons convicted of crimes of moral turpitude, and those suffering loathsome or contagious diseases. In 1892, Ellis Island opened. In 1903, anarchists were ruled inadmissible to the United States. See Roger Daniels, *Coming to America: A History of Immigration and Ethnicity in American Life* (New York: Perennial, 2002), 124; and John Higham, *Strangers in the Land* (New York: Athenaeum, 1963), 48–49; 99–100, 112–13.

27. Theodore Roosevelt, "True Americanism," In *The Works of Theodore Roosevelt* (New York: Charles Scribner & Sons, 1925), 25, 26.

28. Burton J. Hendrick, "The Great Jewish Invasion," *McClure's Magazine* 28 (January 1907): 319.

29. Louis Brandeis, "Speech to the Conference of Eastern Council of Reform Rabbis, April 25, 1915," www.zionism-israel.com/hdoc/Brandeis_Jewish_Problem .htm. Brandeis cites the Dreyfus affair in France, the Aliens Act in England, and the Seligman affair in the United States as watershed moments of modern antisemitism.

30. East European Jewish immigration to the United States peaked in the year 1908, but between 1900 and 1909, as a result of a second wave of Russian

pogroms against Jewish shtetls, over one million Jews arrived. Distinct from other immigrant groups of the period, the Jews were not "birds of passage," but here to remain permanently. See Alan M. Kraut, *The Huddled Masses: The Immigrant in American Society, 1880–1921* (Arlington Heights, IL: Harlan Davidson, 1982), 8–41. On Jews, race, and whiteness, see Karen Brodkin, *How Jews Became White Folks, and What That Says about Race in America* (New Brunswick: Rutgers University Press, 1998); and Matthew Frye Jacobson, *Whiteness of a Different Color: European Immigrants and the Alchemy of Race* (Cambridge, MA: Harvard University Press, 1998).

31. See Jonathan Boyarin and Daniel Boyarin, eds., *Jews and Other Differences: The New Jewish Cultural Studies* (Minneapolis: University of Minnesota Press, 1997).

32. See, for example, Carey McWilliams, *A Mask for Privilege: Anti-Semitism in America* (Boston: Little, Brown and Company, 1948); John Higham, *Send These to Me: Immigrants in Urban America* (New York: Athenaeum, 1975); Michael Dobkowski, *The Tarnished Dream: The Basis of American Anti-Semitism* (Westport, CT: Greenwood, 1979); Leonard Dinnerstein, *Anti-Semitism in America* (New York: Oxford, 1994); and Frank Felsenstein, *Anti-Semitic Stereotypes: A Paradigm of Otherness in English Popular Culture, 1660–1830* (Baltimore: Johns Hopkins University Press, 1995).

33. Oscar Handlin, "American Views of the Jew at the Opening of the Twentieth Century," *Publications of the American Jewish Historical Society* 40 (June 1951): 325. Scholars have debated over whether American antisemitism is a late-nineteenth- and early-twentieth-century phenomenon, or if it dates back to the colonial period. Handlin did not see pre-1900 antisemitism in US literature; his case for a prevalent philosemitism in this period has led Dobkowski to call him an apologist. See Dobkowski, *Tarnished Dream*, 6. Louis Harap, by contrast, proves the opposite: that pernicious images of the "rascally" Jew persisted throughout the nineteenth century, beginning in the Early Republic. See Louis Harap, *The Image of the Jew in American Literature: From Early Republic to Mass Immigration* (Syracuse, NY: Syracuse University Press, 2003), 5. Overviews of the history of philosemitism include Salomon Rappaport, *Jew and Gentile: The Philosemitic Aspect* (New York: Philosophical Library, 1980); Alan Edelstein, *An Unacknowledged Harmony: Philo-Semitism and the Survival of European Jewry* (Westport, CT: Greenwood, 1982); William D. Rubinstein and Hilary Rubinstein, *Philosemitism: Admiration and Support for Jews in the English-Speaking World, 1840–1939* (Basingstoke, UK: Palgrave Macmillan,

1999); Tony Kushner and Nadia Valman, eds., *Philosemitism, Antisemitism and "the Jews": Perspectives from the Middle Ages to the Twentieth Century* (Aldershot: Ashgate, 2004); Jonathan Karp and Adam Sutcliffe, *Philosemitism in History* (Cambridge: Cambridge University Press, 2011); and Gertrude Himmelfarb, *The People of the Book: Philosemitism in England, From Cromwell to Churchill* (New York: Encounter Books, 2011).

34. Adam Sutcliffe and Jonathan Karp, "Introduction: A Brief History of Philosemitism," in Karp and Sutcliffe, *Philosemitism in History*, 3.

35. Sutcliffe and Karp, "Introduction," 1. Anti-Jewish German ideologists coined the term "anti*semitism*," its purported opposite, to distinguish themselves from religious bigots (the term "semite" denoting many postbiblical linguistic groups), but many of the anti-Jewish views that now fall under that rubric have circulated across the Americas, Europe, and Asia for centuries.

36. Sutcliffe and Karp, 1.

37. Sutcliffe and Karp, 4.

38. The term was coined by the Polish-Jewish literary historian and critic Arthur Sandauer. See Zygmunt Bauman, "Allosemitism: Premodern, Modern, Postmodern" in *Modernity, Culture and "The Jew,"* ed. Bryan Cheyette and Laura Marcus (Palo Alto, CA: Stanford University Press, 1998), 143. Bryan Cheyette suggests "semitic discourse" in Cheyette, *Constructions of "the Jew" in English Literature and Society: Racial Representations, 1875–1945* (Cambridge: Cambridge University Press, 1993), 8–12, 268–75.

39. Sutcliffe and Karp, 5.

40. For the origin and attitudinal nature of "Christian Zionism," in particular his final chapter on American evangelicals at the end of the nineteenth century, see Shalom Goldman, *Zeal for Zion: Christians, Jews and the Idea of the Promised Land* (Chapel Hill: University of North Carolina Press, 2009).

41. Sutcliffe and Karp, 3.

42. Ariel Levy, "Prodigal Son: Is the Wayward Republican Mike Huckabee Now His Party's Best Hope?" *New Yorker*, June 28, 2010, www.newyorker.com/magazine/2010/06/28/prodigal-son.

43. Yaakov Ariel, "'It's All in the Bible': Evangelical Christians, Biblical Literalism, and Philosemitism in Our Times," in Karp and Sutcliffe, *Philosemitism in History*, 257–61.

44. See Shalom Goldman, ed., *Hebrew and the Bible in America: The First Two Centuries* (Hanover, NH: University Press of New England, 1993); and Shalom Goldman, *God's Sacred Tongue: Hebrew and the American Imagination* (Chapel

Hill: University of North Carolina Press, 2004). For a study of the importance of Palestine to nineteenth-century secular American Holy Land literature such as Melville's *Clarel* and Mark Twain's *Innocents Abroad*, see Hilton Obenzinger, *American Palestine: Melville, Twain, and the Holy Land Mania* (Princeton, NJ: Princeton University Press, 1999).

45. Hasia Diner, *The Jews of the United States, 1654–2000* (Berkeley: University of California Press, 2004), 24. Diner charts a shift from doctrinal anti-Judaism during the colonial era to a commercially based antipathy, but such attitudes and rights accorded Jews also varied regionally among Eastern seaboard states (22–26, 39).

46. Dobkowski, *Tarnished Dream*, 10. The logic of conversion resurfaced with late-nineteenth-century evangelical Protestants like William Blackstone (1841–1935), founder of "dispensationalism" and Christian Zionism, for whom the Jew—or, rather, the "Israelite" or "Hebrew"—is central to Christian eschatology. See John Fea, "Blackstone, William E.," American National Biography Online, February 2000, www.anb.org/articles/08/08-01994.html.

47. Egal Felman, "American Protestant Theologians on the Frontiers of Jewish-Christian Relations, 1922–82," in David A. Gerber, ed., *Anti-Semitism in American History* (Urbana: University of Illinois Press, 1986), 363–64.

48. The apostle Paul, the great architect of the faith, himself set the standard for an enlightened Judaism. As a Jewish patrician who led violent mobs against the early Christians, he underwent one of the most dramatic and inspiring conversions in Christian history. Paul's central concern was to overcome religious particularities, namely Jewish distinctiveness, "to reformulate Judaism as a universalistic message, open to all" by interpreting the Jewish law "as an allegorical prefiguring of the coming of Christ, which he regarded as having annulled its validity." See Sutcliffe and Karp, "Introduction," 10.

49. Mather, cited in Sacvan Bercovitch, introduction to *The American Puritan Imagination: Essays in Revaluation*, ed. Sacvan Bercovitch (London: Cambridge University Press, 1974), 16.

50. Sacvan Bercovitch, *The American Jeremiad* (Madison: University of Wisconsin Press, 1978), 15.

51. Bercovitch, *American Jeremiad*, 15. Just as Augustine saw "God's hand and God's purposes" as "equally present and equally hidden" in history, the Puritan project, as a model of the reformed Christian church and the New Jerusalem to come, reworked Augustine's fusion of sacred and secular histories in an effort to consecrate the fledgling American settlement. See R. A. Markus, *Saeculum:*

History and Society in the Theology of Augustine, rev. ed. (New York: Cambridge University Press, 1988), 23.

52. Bercovitch, *American Jeremiad*, 73–80. See also Sarah Rivett, *The Science of the Soul in Colonial New England* (Chapel Hill: University of North Carolina Press, 2011).

53. Harap, *Image of the Jew*, 136. Despite the Hebraistic foundations of Smith's Mormonism, the Mormons showed little interest in embracing the increased Jewish-centrism of other millennial faith groups that made Jewish conversion part of their millennial plan. See Joseph Smith, *The Book of Mormon* (1829).

54. See Arthur Hertzberg, "The New England Puritans and the Jews," in Goldman, *Hebrew and the Bible in America*, 105–21.

55. Ariel, "It's All in the Bible," 259. On Jewish messianism, see Abraham Duker, "The Tarniks," in *Joshua Starr Memorial Volume* (New York: Conference on Jewish Relations, 1953), 191–201; Michal Gałas, "Sabbatianism in the 17th-Century Polish-Lithuanian Commonwealth," in *The Sabbatian Movement and Its Aftermath*, ed. Rachel Elior (Jerusalem: Posner and Sons, 2001), 2:51–63; Harris Lenowitz, *The Jewish Messiahs* (New York, 1998); Aviezer Ravitzky, *Messianism, Zionism, and Jewish Religious Radicalism*, trans. Michael Swirsky and Jonathan Chipman (Chicago: University of Chicago Press, 1996); Gershom Scholem, *The Messianic Idea in Judaism and Other Essays on Jewish Spirituality* (New York: Schocken, 1971); Martin Kavka, *Jewish Messianism and the History of Philosophy* (Cambridge: Cambridge University Press, 2004). For an excellent synopsis of conversionist literature, see Felsenstein, *Anti-Semitic Stereotypes*, 90–122.

56. See Bercovitch, *American Jeremiad*, 74; and Menassah ben Israel, quoted in Bercovitch, *American Jeremiad*, 74.

57. Ariel, "It's All in the Bible," 258.

58. Ariel, 259.

59. Harap, *Image of the Jew*, 135.

60. Fea, "Blackstone, William E."

61. Signatories included Melville W. Fuller, chief justice of the US Supreme Court; congressman and future president William McKinley; J. P. Morgan; Charles Scribner; and John D. Rockefeller. Fea, "Blackstone, William E."

62. Such "solutions" reached their apotheosis in the Final Solution, which, as Alon Confino has recently argued, was an effort to undo time and history by eliminating the Jews. See Confino, *A World Without Jews: The Nazi Imagination from Persecution to Genocide* (New Haven, CT: Yale University Press, 2014).

63. See Dobkowski, *Tarnished Dream*, 14; and Harap, *Image of the Jew*, 135–88.

64. John Kitto, *An Illustrated History of the Holy Bible* (Norwich: H. Bill, 1868), 496–97, 556, 560, 574, 631–32; quoted in Dobkowski, *Tarnished Dream*, 14, 36, n. 11.

65. Joseph Holt Ingraham, *The Throne of David; From the Consecration of the Shepherd of Bethlehem, to the Rebellion of Prince Absalom* (Philadelphia: G. G. Evans, 1860), 10, https://archive.org/stream/thronedavidfrom01ingrgoog#page/n2/mode/2up.

66. Ingraham, *The Throne of David*, 7.

67. This is the dedication to Ingraham, *The Throne of David* (1860). The trilogy includes *The Prince of the House of David; Or, Three Years in the Holy City* (1855), which is dedicated to "The Daughters of Israel, The Country-Women of Mary, The Mother of Jesus"; and *The Pillar of Fire; Or, Israel in Bondage* (1859), dedicated to "The Men of Israel, Sons of Abraham, Isaac, and Jacob, Kindred of Moses, The Great Lawgiver and Friend of God."

68. Longfellow, "The Jewish Cemetery at Newport" line 8.

69. Oliver Wendell Holmes, *The Complete Poetical Works of Oliver Wendell Holmes.* Cambridge Edition (Boston: Houghton Mifflin, 1895), 26–28, lines 34, 3, 59, 95–96. https://archive.org/stream/complete00holm#page/n7/mode/2up.

70. Oliver Wendell Holmes, "At the Pantomime," revised from "A Hebrew Tale" (1856), in *Complete Poetical Works*, 189.

71. Jonathan Freedman reads these lines as emblematic of the poem's "wildly overwrought symbolic power" of the Jew in relation to Christian culture, seen in the speaker's "labile and wildly disproportionate affect, ranging from disgust to identification and passing at just about every point in between." Perhaps so, but the affective reading omits the central feature of the scene and the speaker's logic, which is typological and thus, temporal. See *Klezmer America: Jewishness, Ethnicity, Modernity* (New York: Columbia University Press, 2008), 5. See also Freedman, "Do American and Ethnic American Studies Have a Jewish Problem; or, When Is an Ethnic Not an Ethnic, and What Should We Do about It?" *MELUS* 37, no. 2 (2012): 28.

72. Dobkowski, *Tarnished Dream*, 115.

73. On the Christian Hebraism of the founders of Harvard, see Thomas J. Siegel, "Professor Stephen Sewall and the Transformation of Hebrew at Harvard," in Shalom Goldman, ed., *Hebrew and the Bible in America: The First Two Centuries* (Hanover, NH: University Press of New England, 1993), 228–45.

74. Dobkowski, *Tarnished Dream*, 116–17.

75. Oscar Handlin, *Adventures in Freedom: Three Hundred Years of Jewish Life in America* (New York: McGraw Hill, 1954), 176–77. Louis Harap makes this point about conversion as well; see Harap, *Image of the Jew*, 541.

76. In her conversion novel, *The Jewish Twins* (1860), Sarah Baker (under the pseudonym Aunt Friendly) argues that only Christ can redeem the Jews' inherent failings. Harriette N. Baker's heroine of *Rebecca the Jewess* (1879), Rebecca Stickney, transforms from a superficial Jewish materialist to a devoted charity worker through her encounter with Christianity. In doing so, she stands in contrast to her father, Aaron, who, as a strict Orthodox Jew, is only concerned with the accumulation of wealth and prestige. See Harap, *Image of the Jew*, 541. Other examples include James Freeman Clarke, *Legend of Thomas Didymus, the Jewish Sceptic* (1881); Elbridge Streeter Brooks, *A Son of Issachar; A Romance of the Days of Messias* (1890); Edgar Saltus, *Mary Magdalen: A Chronicle* (1891); Mary Elizabeth Jennings, *Asa of Bethlehem and His Household* (1895); Caroline Atwater Mason, *The Quiet King: A Story of Christ* (1895); Florence M. Kingsley, *Titus* (1894), *Stephen* (1896), *Paul* (1897), and *The Cross Triumphant* (1898); and Elizabeth Stuart Phelps Ward, *The Story of Jesus Christ, An Interpretation* (1898). Kingsley published in the New Sabbath Library Series along with authors Fannie E. Neberry, William A. Hammond, Anna May Wilson, the Reverend Enoch Burr, the Reverend George Anson Jackson, Edmund Berry, and Eliza Lee, among others. For plot summaries, see Dobkowski, *Tarnished Dream*, 16–20.

77. See Edward Bellamy, *Looking Backward, 2000–1887* (Oxford: Oxford University Press, 2007); Reverend Jesse H. Jones, *Joshua Davidson, Christian* (New York: Grafton, 1907); Albion W. Tourgee, *Murvale Eastman: Christian Socialist* (New York: Fords, Howard and Hulbert, 1891), Caroline Atwater Mason, *A Woman of Yesterday* (New York: Doubleday, Page & Co, 1900); Joaquin Miller, *The Building of the City Beautiful* (Trenton, NJ: Albert Brandt, 1905); Alexander Craig, *Ionia; Land of Wise Men and Fair Women* (Chicago: E. A. Weeks, 1898).

78. See Harap, *Image of the Jew*, 404–5.

79. Miller, *Building of the City Beautiful*, 6, 12.

80. Dobkowski, *Tarnished Dream*, 20.

81. Matthew Arnold, "Hebraism and Hellenism," in *Culture and Anarchy and Other Writings*, ed. Stefan Collini (Cambridge: Cambridge University Press, 1993), 128.

82. Editor Moses Rischin notes that "*The Spirit of the Ghetto* appears as much the work of [Abraham] Cahan as it was of Hapgood," because Hapgood, like

William Dean Howells, became acquainted with Russian literary realism and life on the Yiddish-speaking Lower East Side through Cahan. Rischin describes the book as "the first authentic study by an outsider of the inner life of an American immigrant community, devoid of stereotypes or sentimentality, intimate yet judicious and restrained." See Rischin, introduction to *The Spirit of the Ghetto*, by Hutchins Hapgood, ed. Moses Rischin (Cambridge, MA: Harvard University Press, 1967), x, vii. I discuss Cahan's relation to Hapgood further in chapter 1.

83. Hapgood, *The Spirit of the Ghetto: Studies of the Jewish Quarter in New York* (New York: Funk and Wagnalls, 1902), 60. According to Isidore S. Meyer, "Hapgood wrote of the invisible East Side, of its essential humanity and its quest for justice, truth and beauty." See Meyer, review of *The Spirit of the Ghetto*, ed. Moses Rischin, *American Jewish Historical Quarterly* 59, no. 4 (1970): 545.

84. Riis, *How the Other Half Lives*, 83.

85. Felsenstein, *Anti-Semitic Stereotypes*, 90–91.

86. Felsenstein, 90–91.

87. Benjamin Schreier, *The Impossible Jew: Identity and the Reconstruction of Jewish American Literary History* (New York: New York University Press, 2015).

88. Dean Franco, *Race, Rights and Recognition: Jewish American Literature Since 1969* (Ithaca, NY: Cornell University Press, 2012), 17; Freedman, *Klezmer America*.

89. See Cheyette, *Constructions of "the Jew"*; and also Cheyette, ed., *Between 'Race' and Culture: Representations of 'the Jew' in English and American Literature* (Stanford, CA: Stanford University Press, 1996); and Boyarin and Boyarin, *Jews and Other Differences*.

90. Svetlana Boym, *The Future of Nostalgia* (New York: Basic Books, 2001), 55.

91. The argument that the realist novel, in particular, is secular begins with Ian Watt. See Watt, *The Rise of the Novel: Studies in Defoe, Richardson, and Fielding* (London: Peregrine, 1968), 14, 16.

92. See Vincent P. Pecora, *Secularization and Cultural Criticism* (Chicago: University of Chicago Press, 2006); Charles Taylor, *A Secular Age* (Cambridge, MA: Harvard University Press, 2007), Talal Asad, *Formations of the Secular: Christianity, Islam, Modernity* (Stanford, CA: Stanford University Press, 2003), and Tracy Fessenden, *Culture and Redemption: Religion, the Secular, and American Literature* (Princeton, NJ: Princeton University Press, 2007).

93. Pecora, *Secularization and Cultural Criticism*, 26.

94. Pecora, *Secularization and Cultural Criticism*, 26; Taylor, *Secular Age*, 5.

95. Vincent Pecora, *Households of the Soul* (Baltimore: Johns Hopkins University Press, 1997); Pericles Lewis, *Religious Experience and the Modernist Novel* (Cambridge: Cambridge University Press, 2010).

96. Georg Lukacs, *Theory of the Novel*, trans. Anna Bostock (Cambridge, MA: MIT Press, 1999), 88.

97. Gregory S. Jackson, *The Word and Its Witness* (Chicago: University of Chicago Press, 2008). In the twentieth-century literary context, see Amy Hungerford, *Postmodern Belief: American Literature and Religion since 1960* (Princeton, NJ: Princeton University Press, 2010).

98. Jackson, *The Word and Its Witness*, 240.

99. Cindy Weinstein, *Time, Tense, and American Literature: When Is Now?* (New York: Cambridge University Press, 2015), 12. Other recent studies of time in literature include Anthony Giddens, *The Consequences of Modernity* (Stanford, CA: Stanford University Press, 1990); Thomas M. Allen, *A Republic in Time: Temporality and Social Imagination in Nineteenth-Century America* (Chapel Hill: University of North Carolina Press, 2008); Boym, *The Future of Nostalgia*; Mark Currie, *About Time: Narrative, Fiction and the Philosophy of Time* (Edinburgh: Edinburgh University Press, 2007); Lauren Berlant, *Cruel Optimism* (Durham, NC: Duke University Press, 2011).

100. Elizabeth Freeman, *Time Binds: Queer Temporalities, Queer Histories* (Durham, NC: Duke University Press, 2010); Dana Luciano, *Arranging Grief: Sacred Time and the Body in Nineteenth-Century America* (New York: New York University Press, 2007).

101. Freeman, *Time Binds*, xi.

102. Wai-Chee Dimock, *Through Other Continents: American Literature across Deep Time* (Princeton, NJ: Princeton University Press, 2006), 6.

103. Lloyd Pratt, *Archives of American Time: Literature and Modernity in the Nineteenth Century* (Philadelphia: University of Pennsylvania Press, 2010), 5.

104. Frederic Jameson, *The Antinomies of Realism* (London: Verso, 2013), 6, 26. Jameson charts the story of realism through its rise and dissolution, although critics cannot pinpoint a decisive [realist] moment; through Erich Auerbach's "mimesis," although the Frankfurt school rendered the idea of the "mimetic impulse" idiosyncratic; through reductive binaries about what realism is and what it isn't; through periodization, a stage between Romanticism and modernism; and through identification with the novel and its history, as with Luckács, who sees it as the form that best registers the "irreconcilable contradictions of a purely secular modernity" (4).

105. Goran Blix, "Story, Affect, Style," in special issue, "Jameson's *Antinomies of Realism*," *Nonsite.org* 11 (March 14, 2014): http://nonsite.org/the-tank/jamesons-the-antinomies-of-realism.

106. Jameson, *Antinomies of Realism*, 24, 26. For Danielle Follett, Jameson's claim suggests a "pessimistic view" that relies upon a "postmodern celebration of delirious meaninglessness." See Follett, "Is the Cheese Meaningless? The Distension of Dialectics in Jameson's *The Antinomies of Realism*," in special issue, "Jameson's *Antinomies of Realism*," *Nonsite.org* 11 (March 14, 2014): http://nonsite.org/the-tank/jamesons-the-antinomies-of-realism.

CHAPTER 1

1. Shmuel Feiner, *The Jewish Enlightenment*, trans. Chaya Naor (Philadelphia, University of Pennsylvania Press, 2002), xi.

2. For Feiner, this revolution in thought was no less significant for the Jews than the French Revolution was for the French, for it effectively created a modern, secular Jewish public sphere (Feiner, *Jewish Enlightenment*, 1–2, 13, 35). Feiner insists this movement began among a small number of elite Jewish scholars trying to overcome their sense of *intellectual* inferiority in relation to European scholars, and to challenge rabbinical orthodoxy in the name of Enlightenment values (Feiner, 7, 25).

3. *Feiner, 16.*

4. Dan Miron, "Sholem Aleichem," *YIVO Encyclopedia*, www.yivoencyclopedia.org/article.aspx/Sholem_Aleichem; and "Abramovitsh, Sholem Yankev," *YIVO Encyclopedia*, www.yivoencyclopedia.org/article.aspx/Abramovitsh_Sholem_Yankev.

5. Dan Miron, "The Literary Image of the Shtetl," *Jewish Social Studies*, 1, no. 3 (1995): 4.

6. Barbara Kirshenblatt-Gimblett, introduction to *Life Is with People: The Culture of the Shtetl*, ed. Mark Zborowski and Elizabeth Herzog (New York: Schocken, 1995), xii–xiv. For a brief account of the historically changing political, social, and economic status of Russian Jews, see Kirshenblatt-Gimblett, introduction, xix–xxv.

7. Kirshenblatt-Gimblett notes that "shtetl" connotes "little town," but also the hermetically sealed timeless Jewish world conjured by Yiddish literature; real shtetls were actually complex, fluid social structures, and not the only places that Jews lived; (introduction, xviii, xix). For Zborowski and Herzog, the term offers textual "coherence, totality, and authority," a "heuristic device for presenting the research findings" on a lost culture (*Life Is with People*, xxxiii). The 1952 subtitle

was "the Jewish Little-Town in Europe"; the 1962 subtitle ushered the term "shtetl" into the English language (xxxi). The entry "shtetl" only appeared in the *Encyclopedia Judaica* in 1971, written by Zborowski (*Life Is with People*, xxxi). The nostalgic *shtetl*-vision then became a staple of American Jewish culture in Jerome Robbins's iconic Broadway musical, *Fiddler on the Roof*, which opened on September 22, 1964, starred Tony Award–winner Zero Mostel as Tevye, and ultimately ran for a record-setting 3,242 performances. Following multiple runs in London, and Broadway revivals in 1976, 1981, 1990, and 2004, the play was immortalized in the 1971 film adaptation by Norman Jewison, starring Topol as Tevye. https://en.wikipedia.org/wiki/Fiddler_on_the_Roof.

8. Bernard G. Richards, introduction to Abraham Cahan, *Yekl and the Imported Bridegroom and Other Stories of Yiddish New York* (Mineola, NY: Dover, 1970), vi. This is a reprint of *Yekl* (1896) and *The Imported Bridegroom and Other Stories of the New York Ghetto* (1898).

9. David Roskies, *The Jewish Search for a Usable Past* (Bloomington: Indiana University Press, 1999), 1–3.

10. Abraham Cahan, *Yekl and the Imported Bridegroom and Other Stories of Yiddish New York* (Mineola, NY: Dover, 1970), 98.

11. Immanuel Kant, *Anthropology from a Pragmatic Point of View*, ed. Robert B. Louden (Cambridge: Cambridge University Press, 2006), 71. See also Jean Starobinski and William S. Kemp, "The Idea of Nostalgia," *Diogenes: An International Review of Philosophy* 14 (1966): 94–95.

12. This "Place" represents both symbolic bookends of Jewish history and theodicy: the pre-exilic Eden, and the place of exile's end. See Zali Guravitch and Gideon Aran, "The Land of Israel: Myth and Phenomenon," in *Reshaping the Past: Jewish History and the Historians*, ed. Jonathan Frankel (New York: Oxford University Press, 1994), 195–96. See also Sidra Dekoven Ezrahi, *Booking Passage: Exile and Homecoming in the Modern Jewish Imagination* (Berkeley: University of California Press, 2000), 29, 3; and Miron, "Literary Image of the Shtetl," 18–22.

13. Ezrahi, *Booking Passage*, 30.

14. Jules Chametzky, *From the Ghetto: The Fiction of Abraham Cahan* (Amherst: University of Massachusetts Press, 1977), 13, 8. Cahan first published freelance Yiddish articles in 1886 for the socialist weekly, the *Neie Zeit* ("New Era"), and later the *Arbeiter Zeitung* ("Workers Times"); Ronald Sanders, *The Lower East Side Jews: An Immigrant Generation* (Mineola, NY: Dover, 1999), 98–99, 103–25, 203, 206.

15. Howells's review for the *New York World* in Howells, "New York Low Life in Fiction" [1896], *American Jewish Historical Quarterly.* 52, no. 1 (1962): 51–52.

16. Quoted in Irving Howe, *The World of Our Fathers* (New York: Simon and Schuster, 1976), 396.

17. Sanders, *Lower East Side Jews,* 109.

18. Sanders, 109–10. From 1906 on, he published "The Bintel Brief," a column offering advice on manners and other types of social concerns, As *Forward* editor, he also published the first Yiddish literature in America, including the stories of I. L. Peretz, Sholem Aleichem, Sholem Asch, I. J. Singer, and I. B. Singer. See Chametzky, *From the Ghetto,* 21–22.

19. Donald Pizer, "Introduction, 1874–1914," *Documents of American Realism and Naturalism,* ed. Donald Pizer (Carbondale: Southern Illinois University Press, 1998), 4. On Cahan's relationship to Howells, see Hana Wirth-Nesher, "'Shpeaking Plain' and Writing Foreign: Abraham Cahan's *Yekl,*" *Poetics Today* 22, no. 1 (2001): 41–63.

20. Sanders, *Lower East Side Jews,* 193. Their relationship culminated with Cahan's obituary of Howells on May 16, 1920, in the *Jewish Daily Forward.* See Rudolph Kirk and Clara M. Kirk, "Abraham Cahan and William Dean Howells: The Story of a Friendship," *American Jewish Historical Quarterly* 52, no. 1 (1962): 30. For debates on the social function of realism, see George Parsons Lathrop, "The Novel and Its Future," and Charles Dudley Warner, "Modern Fiction," in Pizer, *Documents,* 18–32, 33–44.

21. Abraham Cahan, *The Education of Abraham Cahan,* trans. Leon Stein, et al. (Philadelphia: Jewish Publication Society of America, 1969), 404–5.

22. The speech was published on March 15, 1889, in the *Workmen's Advocate;* Sanders, *Lower East Side Jews,* 182–84. Clarence Darrow defended a socialist realism in "Realism in Literature in Art" (1893) in Pizer, *Documents,* 132–43.

23. Phillip Barrish, *American Literary Realism, Critical Theory, and Intellectual Prestige, 1880–1995* (Cambridge: Cambridge University Press, 2001), 74.

24. Kirk and Kirk, "Abraham Cahan and William Dean Howells," 29.

25. Kirk and Kirk, 29.

26. Cahan translated "A Providential Match" from an 1891 Yiddish story, "Mottke Arbel and His Romance," published in *Short Story* in 1895; Sanders, *Lower East Side Jews,* 189–90. Cahan was later invited to contribute "ghetto" pieces for *Cosmopolitan* ("Circumstances" in April 1897) and *The Atlantic Monthly* ("A Ghetto Wedding" in February 1898); Sanford E. Marovitz, *Abraham Cahan* (New York: Twayne, 1996), 85–96.

27. Kirk and Kirk, "Abraham Cahan and William Dean Howells," 32.

28. Pizer, "Introduction, 1874–1914," 4.

29. Hana Wirth-Nesher notes, "Cahan performed as ethnic writer just as Howells had intended him to do." Wirth-Nesher, "Shpeaking Plain," 61.

30. Quoted in Chametzky, *From the Ghetto*, 67. Distressed by such responses, Cahan translated *Yekl* into Yiddish for the *Arbeiter Zeitung* in 1895 as "Yankel the Yankee" (Chametzky, 68).

31. Richard Brodhead, *Cultures of Letters: Scenes of Reading and Writing in Nineteenth-Century America* (Chicago: University of Chicago Press, 1993), 133.

32. Quoted in Sanders, *Lower East Side Jews*, 201.

33. Howells, quoted in Wirth-Nesher, "Shpeaking Plain," 47. *The Imported Bridegroom*, first published in 1898 by the Riverside Press, was subtitled, "and Other Stories of the New York Ghetto." For reformers, see Jacob A. Riis, *How the Other Half Lives: Studies Among the Tenements of New York* (New York: Hill and Wang, 1957); Helen Campbell, *The Problem of the Poor: A Record of Quiet Work in Unquiet Places* (New York, 1882); Campbell, *Prisoners of Poverty: Women Wage-Workers, Their Trades and Their Lives* (Boston, 1889); and Campbell, *Women Wage-Earners: Their Past, Their Present, and Their Future* (Boston, 1893).

34. Howells, "Low Life," 51.

35. By 1911, *McClure's* requested sketches on Jewish immigrant cloak makers, which became his novel, *The Rise of David Levinsky*; Marovitz, *Abraham Cahan*, 85–96.

36. Sanders, *Lower East Side Jews*, 220.

37. Cahan, *Education of Abraham Cahan*, 294; and Sanders, *Lower East Side Jews*, 181–87.

38. Cahan, *Education of Abraham Cahan*, 354–55. On the history of the term "ghetto" and its transformation in use from denoting Jewish to denoting African American places, see Mitchell Duneier, *Ghetto: The Invention of a Place, the History of an Idea* (New York: Farrar, Straus and Giroux, 2016).

39. Cahan, *Education of Abraham Cahan*, 355.

40. Moses Rischin, "Abraham Cahan and the New York *Commercial Advertiser: A Study in Acculturation*," *Publication of the American Jewish Historical Society* 43 (1953): 11; Sanders, *Lower East Side Jews*, 210.

41. Chametzky, *From the Ghetto*, 16–17.

42. Rischin, "Abraham Cahan and the New York *Commercial Advertiser*," 12–13; Sanders, *Lower East Side Jews*, 210–11.

43. Hutchins Hapgood, *The Spirit of the Ghetto: Studies of the Jewish Quarter of New York*, illustrated by Jacob Epstein (1902; repr., New York: Funk and Wagnalls, 1965).

44. Sanders, *Lower East Side Jews*, 214.

45. Rischin, "Abraham Cahan and the New York *Commercial Advertiser*," 18; Lincoln Steffens, *The Autobiography of Lincoln Steffens* (1931; repr., Berkeley, CA: Heyday, 2005), 311–12. See also Justin Kaplan, *Lincoln Steffens: A Biography* (New York: Simon and Schuster, 1974), 83–85.

46. Kaplan, *Lincoln Steffens*, 84.

47. Rischin, "Abraham Cahan and the New York *Commercial Advertiser*," 13–14.

48. Steffens, *Autobiography*, 321.

49. The basic point of Moses Rischin's argument is also important: Cahan's "journalistic apprenticeship" at the *Commercial Advertiser* brought about his "Americanization" and dramatically contributed to his authority in the immigrant Jewish community and his subsequent ability to transform successfully the *Jewish Daily Forward* when he left the American press behind and returned as its editor in 1902. Simultaneously, Rischin attributes Steffens's rise as "King of the Muckrakers" in the early 1900s, in part, to Cahan's political influence. See Rischin, "Abraham Cahan and the New York *Commercial Advertiser*."

50. Steffens, *Autobiography*, 24.

51. This informed Hapgood's *The Spirit of the Ghetto*.

52. Steffens, *Autobiography*, 318.

53. Steffens, 243.

54. Steffens, 244, 312–13. See also Kaplan, *Lincoln Steffens*, 83–88.

55. Kaplan, *Lincoln Steffens*, 85.

56. Cited in Kaplan, *Lincoln Steffens*, 85.

57. Steffens, *Autobiography*, 244.

58. Lincoln Steffens, "Schloma, the Daughter of Schmuhl," *Chap-Book Semi-Monthly* 5 (May 15–November 1, 1896), 128–32.

59. I am indebted to Janet Hadda for this observation.

60. The Babylonian Jews of late antiquity, for example, opposed popular music making as "unsuitable for a nation in distress," and permitted it only at wedding festivities. Given the influence of *halakhah*, or religious law, both instrument playing and the female voice were rejected from the synagogue service. In the rabbinical tradition of the twelfth through the fourteenth centuries, "the ethical potential of music was esteemed above its aesthetic values." *Encyclopaedia Judaica*, 1st ed. (1972), s.v. *"Music: The Roots of Synagogue Song in the Near*

Eastern Communities (c. 70–950 CE)," "Music: The Formation of Concepts of Jewish Music (12th–14th Centuries)."

61. Steffens, "Schloma," 128.

62. Steffens, "Schloma," 131. Deep gratitude to Janet Hadda for her assistance in translating the Yiddish portions of Steffens's text.

63. Matthew Arnold, "Hebraism and Hellenism," in *Culture and Anarchy and Other Writings*, ed. Stefan Collini (Cambridge: Cambridge University Press, 1993), 128.

64. In his autobiography, Steffens narrates how he acted as a kind of ambassador of the Lower East Side for Israel Zangwill, as Cahan had been for him, and takes credit for contributing to Zangwill's play *The Melting Pot*: "When Israel Zangwill . . . came from London to visit New York, he heard about me from Jews and asked me to be his guide for a survey of the East Side; and he saw and he went home and wrote *The Melting Pot.*" See Steffens, *Autobiography*, 243–44. Zangwill's play coined the now-famous titular expression in its dramatization of the assimilationist solution to "The Jewish Problem," as discussed in chapter 4.

65. Oscar Handlin, "American Views of the Jew at the Opening of the Twentieth Century," *Publications of the American Jewish Historical Society* 40 (June 1951): 325. In this essay, Handlin's case for prevalent philosemitism has caused one critic to call him an apologist who overlooks the ideology of antisemitism. See Michael Dobkowski, *The Tarnished Dream: The Basis of American Anti-Semitism* (Westport, CT: Greenwood, 1979), 6.

66. Cited in Howe, *World of Our Fathers*, 396.

67. Jacob Riis charts the history of housing regulations and reforms for which he tirelessly battled in *How the Other Half Lives*.

68. As Irving Howe describes, "While free, as a rule, of explicit Jew-baiting, the journalism of these years betrays a nervous anticipation that the immigrant Jews, despite their momentary wretchedness, will yet come to exercise powers of the uncanny. The Jew is treated as a stranger not merely to the American experience or the Protestant imagination, but to the whole of the Western tradition; and thereby he comes to seem a source of possible infection, a carrier of unwanted complications—as if the Europe that had been left behind decades or centuries ago were approaching too closely" (Howe, *World of Our Fathers*, 395–96).

69. Priscilla Wald, "Communicable Americanism: Contagion, Geographic Fictions and the Sociological Legacy of Robert E. Park," *American Literary History* 14, no. 4 (2002): 654.

70. Kaplan, *Lincoln Steffens*, 115–16.

71. The full title of the first article was "The Shame of Minneapolis: The Rescue and Redemption of a City That Was Sold Out," published in January 1903; "The Shamelessness of St. Louis" appeared in the March 1903 *McClure's*. See Kaplan, *Lincoln Steffens*, 110.

72. See Kaplan, *Lincoln Steffens*, 132.

73. Jacob Riis, *How the Other Half Lives: Studies Among the Tenements of New York* (New York: Hill and Wang, 1957).

74. It is difficult to see how Cahan fits in to this particular tradition. Gregory S. Jackson, "Cultivating Spiritual Sight: Jacob Riis's Virtual-Tour Narrative and the Visual Modernization of Protestant Homiletics," *Representations* 83 (Summer 2003): 130–31.

75. See, for example, Riis's autobiography, *The Making of an American* (New York: Macmillan, 1970).

76. Riis, preface to *How the Other Half Lives*, 1.

77. Roosevelt, "True Americanism," in *The Works of Theodore Roosevelt* (New York: Charles Scribner & Sons, 1925), 15:29.

78. Riis, *How the Other Half Lives*, 78–79.

79. Riis is perhaps most famous for his photographs of denizens on the Lower East Side. However, his first edition of *How the Other Half Lives*, published by Charles Scribner's Sons in 1890, included only illustrated versions by Kenyon Cox. In photos where Riis's subjects looked directly into the camera—that is, at the photographer and viewer—such gazes were averted in their respective drawings. Consequently, the photographer's presence disappears from the drawings; the subjects of the photos lose their agency; and perhaps most importantly, those depicted become more picturesque as types. Thanks to the Huntington Library in San Marino for access to the first edition of *How the Other Half Lives*. Subsequent editions containing Riis's original photos include that edited by Sam Bass Warner Jr. (Cambridge, MA: Belknap Press, 1970).

80. Howe, *World of Our Fathers*, 398. Perhaps the most elaborate example of such "fashionable philo-semitism" is George Eliot's novel *Daniel Deronda* (1876), which combines the ancient glory of the Jews with a contemporary Protestant work ethic in the figure of Ezra Cohen, who then ordains Deronda with his sacred Zionist mission. George Eliot, *Daniel Deronda* (London: Penguin, 1995).

81. Howe, *World of Our Fathers*, 398.

82. For their relevance, I have selected a few exemplary pieces from among a survey of approximately one hundred articles representing Jews and Jewishness in the *Atlantic Monthly*, *Century Magazine*, and *Harper's New Monthly Magazine* from the 1860s to roughly 1900.

83. Charles Dawson Shanly, "The Bowery at Night," *Atlantic Monthly* 20, no. 121 (1867): 602–8.

84. Henry Moscow, *The Street Book: An Encyclopedia of Manhattan's Street Names and Their Origins* (New York: Fordham University Press, 1990), 29.

85. The Bowery, the street, was named for the late-seventeenth-century farm, or *bouwerij*, of the Dutch governor Peter Stuyvesant, to which the road then led (Moscow, *Street Book*, 29).

86. Running from Chatham Square to Cooper Square, the Bowery, originally the *bouwerij*, Dutch for "farm," is one of Manhattan's oldest streets, associated in the post–Civil War era with poverty, crime, alcoholism, and loneliness. Although it was a fine residential neighborhood in the early nineteenth century, the lower streets surrounding the Bowery soon became a center for slaughterhouses and factories for lard, soap, and candles, and by the 1870s, slum life seemed to encroach upon it from both sides. It subsequently began to slide into poverty with the arrival of beer halls and cheap lodgings, making it the den of sin that alarmed reformers like Jacob Riis. The Bowery did, however, enjoy a brief period of glamour, as it "glittered with the lights of theaters," in the midnineteenth century, witnessing the first blackface minstrelsy show in New York City, the first stage version of *Uncle Tom's Cabin*, and, in 1892, the first Yiddish theater production. See Carol Von Pressentin Wright, Stuart Miller, and Sharon Seitz, *The Blue Guide: New York* (London: A&C Black Limited, 2002), 231.

87. Shanly, "The Bowery at Night," 602.

88. As I note in chapter 2, James refers to himself variously as the "restless analyst," the "story-seeker," the "ancient contemplative person," and, at one point, an "indiscreet listener," all of which amount to the construction of a narrative persona at once probing, intrusive, curiously on the hunt for "impressions," and a kind of passive receptacle through which passes what the "other" James, William, calls the "stream of experience." See Henry James, *The American Scene* (New York: Penguin, 1994), 12, 13, 33; and William James, "What Pragmatism Means," in *William James: Writings 1902–1910*, ed. Bruce Kuklick (New York: Library of America, 1987), 509.

89. Stephanie Foote, *Regional Fictions: Culture and Identity in Nineteenth-Century American Literature* (Madison: University of Wisconsin Press, 2001), 124–25.

90. Shanly, "The Bowery at Night," 605–7.

91. Moses Rischin, *The Promised City* (Cambridge: Harvard University Press, 1962), 8. Rischin attributes this correlation to the fact that immigrants often flocked to their own when looking for work, out of both convenience and necessity, given language barriers and specific skills. Some industries experienced greater turnover, especially those requiring a lesser degree of skill. Thus, whereas German immigrants dominated piano manufacturing, a highly skilled trade, their dominance of the less-skilled trade of clothing manufacturing was taken over in the 1880s by East European Jews, who were, in turn, replaced by Italians and Lithuanians at the turn of the century (8–9).

92. According to Irving Howe, in the 1900 census, 40 percent of the "Russian-born" female and 20 percent of the "Russian-born" male immigrants were listed as garment workers. See Howe, *World of Our Fathers*, 154–55. On the role of women in that industry, see Andrew Heinze, *Adapting to Abundance: Jewish Immigrants, Mass Consumption, and the Search for American Identity* (New York: Columbia University Press, 1990), 98–99.

93. Shanly, "The Bowery at Night," 603.

94. Shanly, 603. By 1904, New York's Lower East Side had become so crowded with tenement dwellers and sweatshop laborers spilling out onto the streets that business and domestic life became for Henry James virtually indistinguishable. He thus laments the loss of privacy, "the highest luxury of all, the supremely expensive thing," and claims that without it, "in such conditions there couldn't *be* any manners to speak of" *(American Scene*, 11, 10).

95. Jacob Riis notes that in 1890, there were 37,316 tenements in New York, with an estimated population of 1,250,000. The old-style tenement apartments tended to be roughly two rooms, the living rooms 10 x 12 feet, and the bedrooms 6.5 x 7 feet. See Riis, *How the Other Half Lives*, 231.

96. Shanly, "The Bowery at Night," 603.

97. In *The American Scene*, James rhetorically asks of the Jews in the Lower East Side, "Who can ever tell [. . .] in any conditions and in presence of any anomaly, what the genius of Israel may, or may not, really be 'up to'?" (103).

98. Shanly, "The Bowery at Night," 605. Stuyvesant, incidentally, was no champion of the Jews. Rather, he claimed that "the deceitful race,—such hateful enemies and blasphemers of the name of Christ,—be not allowed further to infect and trouble this new colony." Cited in Morris Schappes, ed., *A Documentary History of Jews in the United States, 1654–1875* (New York: Schocken, 1950, 1971), 1–2.

99. Shanly, "The Bowery at Night," 608.

100. Tolerance for the twenty-three Jews who came to the Dutch colony in 1654 came gradually. At first, however, they "were denied even the most elementary economic and religious rights by the choleric governor and the Dutch West India Company." By the 1660s, "they achieved the right to settle and own land, but it was not until the 1690s, under British rule, that they were accorded the privilege of holding public worship and selling at retail." Michael Dobkowski, *Tarnished Dream*, 12.

101. Calvin E. Stowe, "The Talmud," *Atlantic Monthly* 21, no. 128 (1868): 673.

102. Stowe was also influenced by Henry Ward Beecher, an active religious reformer who praised the industriousness of Jews on the one hand but harshly condemned the practices of gambling and speculation on the other, duplicitous economic practices with which Jews came to be associated. See Sol Liptzin, *The Jew in American Literature* (New York: Bloch Publishing., 1966).

103. Stowe, "Talmud," 673. A classic text of the higher criticism, *The Life of Jesus* dealt with Jesus the man, an eternal inspiration, in whom "was condensed all that is good and elevated in our nature." Of Jesus's Jewishness, Renan asked the following: "Is it more just to say that Jesus owes all to Judaism, and that his greatness is only that of the Jewish people? No one is more disposed than myself to place high this unique people, whose particular gift seems to have been to contain in its midst the extremes of good and evil. No doubt, Jesus proceeded from Judaism; but he proceeded from it as Socrates proceeded from the schools of the Sophists, as Luther proceeded from the Middle Ages, as Lamennais from Catholicism, as Rousseau from the eighteenth century. A man is of his age and his race even when he reacts against his age and his race. *Far from Jesus having continued Judaism, he represents the rupture with the Jewish spirit.* The general direction of Christianity after him does not permit the supposition that his idea in this respect could lead to any misunderstanding. The general march of Christianity has been to remove itself more and more from Judaism. It will become perfect in returning to Jesus, but certainly not in returning to Judaism. The great originality of the founder remains then undiminished; his glory admits no legitimate sharer" (Ernest Renan, *The Life of Jesus* [London: Trubner and Company, 1864], 309, 310, emphasis mine).

104. Stowe, "Talmud," 673, emphasis in original.

105. Stowe, "Talmud," 674.

106. Within Judaism, the Talmud is essentially the summary and interpretive debate of Jewish oral law, in written form, that evolved for centuries in Palestine and

Babylonia until the Middle Ages. It is composed of thousands of years of Jewish wisdom, as well as logic, philosophy, humor, legend, anecdotes, history, and science. Because the Talmud comprises the "oral law," or collective interpretation of God's Word, it is considered just as important as the Jewish written law, the Torah itself. See Adin Steinsaltz, *The Essential Talmud*, trans. Chaya Galai (New York: Basic Books, 1976), 3–4.

107. The Hebrew root of the word "Talmud" is the same as that of words like *talmid*, student; *melamed*, teacher; and *lalemed*, to study.

108. Steinsaltz, *Essential Talmud*, 5–9.

109. Stowe, "Talmud," 674.

110. Dobkowski, *Tarnished Dream*, 9–10.

111. Dobkowski, 10–11.

112. Pierre Nora, "Between Memory and History: Les Lieux de Memoire," *Representations*, Special Issue: Memory and Counter-Memory 26 (Spring 1989): 19.

113. Nora, "Between Memory and History," 19.

114. Charles Taylor, *A Secular Age* (Cambridge, MA: Harvard University Press, 2007), 5.

115. Hana Wirth-Nesher, "Shpeaking Plain," 50. See Chametzky, *From the Ghetto*, 61; and Eric Sundquist, "Realism and Regionalism," in *The Columbia Literary History of the United States*, ed. Emory Elliott (New York: Columbia University Press, 1988), 520–21.

116. Howe, *World of Our Fathers*, 585.

117. Sanders, *Lower East Side Jews*, 195. Recent critics who see Cahan as anti-nostalgic include David Engel, "The 'Discrepancies' of the Modern: Towards a Revaluation of Abraham Cahan's *The Rise of David Levinsky*," *Studies in American Jewish Literature* 2 (1982): 58; Sara Blair, "Whose Modernism Is It? Abraham Cahan, Fictions of Yiddish, and the Contest of Modernity," *Modern Fiction Studies* 51 (Summer 2005): 258–84; and Donald Weber, *Haunted in the New World: Jewish American Culture from Cahan to The Goldbergs* (Bloomington: Indiana University Press, 2005), 10–23. For a queer reading of *The Rise of David Levinsky*, see Warren Hoffman's *The Passing Game: Queering Jewish American Culture* (Syracuse, NY: Syracuse University Press 2009), 45–66.

118. Nina Baym, et al., introduction to *The Norton Anthology of American Literature* (New York: Norton, 2012), 2:11. Josephine Donovan, *New England Local Color Literature: A Women's Tradition* (New York: Frederick Ungar Publishing, 1983), 1, 3, 8.

119. Brodhead, *Cultures of Letters*, 115–16. For Clifford Geertz, religion is one aspect of "culture," just one of many "historically transmitted pattern[s] of meanings embodied in symbols." Geertz, *The Interpretation of Cultures: Selected Essays* (New York: Basic Books, 1973, 2000), 89.

120. Amy Kaplan, "Nation, Region, and Empire," in *The Columbia History of the American Novel*, ed. Emory Elliott (New York: Columbia University Press, 1991), 252, 254; and Foote, *Regional Fictions*, 124–25.

121. See Tom Lutz, *Cosmopolitan Vistas: American Regionalism and Literary Value* (Ithaca, NY: Cornell University Press, 2004), 123, 165–67; Priscilla Wald, "Communicable Americanism," 669, 672; and Dalia Kandiyoti, "Comparative Diasporas: The Local and the Mobile in Abraham Cahan and Alberto Gerchunoff." *Modern Fiction Studies* 44 (Spring 1998): 86.

122. Hamlin Garland, *Crumbling Idols: Twelve Essays on Art Dealing Chiefly with Literature Painting and the Drama*, ed. Jane Johnson (Cambridge, MA: Belknap Press, 1960), 53–54. Garland first delivered this as a lecture, "Local Color in Fiction," at the 1893 World's Columbian Exposition, and later published it in *Crumbling Idols* (1894).

123. Garland, *Crumbling Idols*, 54. Garland was criticized for "so many explosions of literary Jingoism and anarchy" in "New Figures in Literature and Art," *Atlantic Monthly* 76 (December 1895): 842.

124. See Kandiyoti, "Comparative Diasporas," 80.

125. Kandiyoti, 78.

126. Foote, *Regional Fictions*, 124–25.

127. Nora, "Between Memory and History," 23.

128. Fred Davis, *Yearning for Yesterday: A Sociology of Nostalgia* (New York: Free Press, 1979), 49.

129. Alan Trachtenberg notes how the discipline of history itself emerged with Turner's Frontier Thesis, a secular narrative of America's sacred providential destiny. For him, Turner's Thesis, delivered at the 1893 World's Columbian Expo in Chicago, had "transposed the prophesied destiny [of America] into a different discourse," a "coherent, integrated story of its beginnings and its development," gathered up and offered in "the language of historical interpretation." Trachtenberg, *The Incorporation of America: Culture and Society in the Gilded Age* (New York: Hill and Wang, 1994), 13.

130. Nora, "Between Memory and History," 9.

131. Nora, 22.

132. As Eric Hayot once suggested to me, Cahan chooses the cyclorama, but what if "the cyclorama also chooses Cahan"? The sheer availability to Cahan of this phenomenon as a cultural metaphor enacts a reciprocal effect on Cahan's figurations of Jewish time and place, specific to this American popular cultural moment.

133. Miron, "Literary Image of the Shtetl," 1.

134. On this period of anti-Jewish violence in Eastern Europe and Russia, see Hasia Diner, *The Jews of the United States, 1654 to 2000* (Berkeley: University of California Press, 2004), 89–99. Immigration historian Reed Ueda refers to an "international force field of displacing 'push' and attractive 'pull' factors" that shape immigration patterns to the United States. Common "push" factors include population growth, economic stagnation, and shifts in economic, labor, and production practices. See Ueda, *Postwar Immigrant America: A Social History* (New York: Bedford St. Martins, 1994), 7–9.

135. The stories first appeared in 1884 in the Warsaw periodical *Der Hoyz-fraynd* and continued in installments over a twenty-year period. See Dan Miron, introduction to *Tevye the Dairyman: And, Motl the Cantor's Son* (New York: Penguin, 2009), xiii. See also Miron, "Sholem Aleichem"; and Rachel K. Fischer, "Tevye the Dairyman, Publication History," http://tevyethedairyman .weebly.com/publication-history.html.

136. Dan Miron, introduction to *Tevye the Dairyman*, xiii. See also Ezra Glinter, "Will the Real Sholem Aleichem Please Stand Up?" *Forward*, November 24, 2013, http://forward.com/culture/188007/will-the-real-sholem-aleichem-please -stand-up/.

137. *Lekh-Lekho* (also spelled *Lekh L'kha; Lech Lecha*) refers to Genesis 12:1–17:27, the third weekly Torah portion in the annual cycle of Jewish Torah reading, which deals expressly with the theme of diaspora. Miron argues that, contrary to the modern secular Jewish culture that reprimanded traditional Jews for their weakness, Sholem Aleichem, in his "moments of true greatness," embraced an acceptance of "Jewish passivity," rather than a critique of it (Miron, introduction to *Tevye the Dairyman*, xxv).

138. Cahan, *Imported Bridegroom*, 104.

139. For Ezrahi, this expression captures postwar European "*reliquaries*" of the Jewish past, "constructed outside of the Holy Land by a modern imagination increasingly intoxicated by the sanctification of *place*," a diasporic "substitution" for the lost Jerusalem (*Booking Passage*, 17). With the onslaught of violent pogroms under Czar Alexander III, Jews fled to cities and followed the mass

exodus to American shores. More than two million Jews would remain permanently in the United States by 1920, suggesting the near extinction of *shtetls*. See Diner, *Jews of the United States*, 89–99.

140. Cahan, *Imported Bridegroom*, 117.

141. On museum culture in this period, see Steven Conn, *Museums and American Intellectual Life, 1876–1926* (Chicago: University of Chicago Press, 2000).

142. Re-created by William Wehler's American Panorama Company in Milwaukee, the "Battle of Atlanta" cyclorama, a twenty-thousand-square-foot painting, toured Detroit and Minneapolis before Atlanta took ownership of it. In the largest cyclorama, a three-mile-long depiction of the Mississippi River, spectators would walk 1.5 miles through a tunnel painted on either side. See "Atlanta Cyclorama," Atlanta History Center, www.atlantahistorycenter.com/explore/destinations/atlanta-cyclorama.

143. "The Battle of Gettysburg in Art," *National Park Service*, December 2, 2015, www.nps.gov/gett/learn/historyculture/gettysburg-cyclorama.htm.

144. The "Battle" was reconstructed in 1882 in Paris by French artist Paul Philippoteaux and his team from field sketches, panoramic site photographs, and veteran interviews. The Boston version was likely the one displayed at the Chicago World's Fair in 1892; Chris Brenneman and Sue Boardman, *The Gettysburg Cyclorama: The Turning Point of the Civil War on Canvas* (El Dorado Hills, CA: Savas Beatie, 2015), 20–24. Since 1962, a version resides at the Gettysburg National Military Park Cyclorama Center in Gettysburg, Pennsylvania, one of the last in the United States. See "The Battle of Gettysburg in Art." Other cycloramas include the Cyclorama of Jerusalem, Quebec, Canada, www.cyclorama.com/eng/index.htm. The 1899 Broadway dramatization of *Ben Hur* that ran for twenty-one consecutive years, featured a live chariot race with real horses and chariots upon a stage surrounded by a revolving cyclorama backdrop (the Art and Popular Culture Encyclopedia, www.artandpopularculture.com/Cyclorama).

145. A. J. Donnelle, *The Battle of Gettysburg Cyclorama* (Boston, 1886), 4.

146. Angela Miller, "The Panorama, the Cinema, and the Emergence of the Spectacular." *Wide Angle* 18 (April 1996): 41.

147. Larzer Ziff, *The American 1890s: Life and Times of a Lost Generation* (Lincoln: University of Nebraska Press, 1979), 4; Erik Larsen, *The Devil in the White City* (New York: Crown 2003), 160, 207–8, 267; and Julie K. Rose, "The World's Columbian Exposition: Idea, Experience, Aftermath," Crossroads at the University of Virginia, 1996, http://xroads.virginia.edu/~ma96/WCE/title.html.

148. Miller, "Panorama," 41.

149. *Compact Oxford English Dictionary*, 2nd ed. 1991, s.v. "nostalgia."

150. Svetlana Boym, *The Future of Nostalgia* (New York: Basic Books, 2001), xiv.

151. Boym, *Future of Nostalgia*, xviii, 55.

152. Beth Wenger, "Memory as Identity: The Invention of the Lower East Side," *American Jewish History* 85 (March 1997): 4. On the spatialization of memory, see David Lowenthal, *The Past Is a Foreign Country* (Cambridge: Cambridge University Press, 1985).

153. Jonathan Boyarin, *Storm from Paradise: The Politics of Jewish Memory* (Minneapolis: University of Minnesota Press, 1992), 1–8. On the mythical qualities of the shtetl, see Roskies, *Jewish Search for a Usable Past*, 43, 44.

154. Boyarin, *Storm*, 3.

155. Rabbi Neil Gillman, *The Death of Death: Resurrection and Immortality in Jewish Thought* (Woodstock, VT: Jewish Lights Publishing), 22.

156. Cahan, *Yekl and the Imported Bridegroom*, 110.

157. Yosef Hayim Yerushalmi, *Zakhor: Jewish History and Jewish Memory* (Seattle: University of Washington Press, 1982), xxxv.

158. Yerushalmi, *Zakhor*, 9, 11, 15.

159. Gillman, "Death of Death," 284n1. See *Encyclopaedia Judaica (1972)*, s.v. "Resurrection," "Eschatology," and "Olam Ha-ba." See also *The Encyclopedia of Judaism (1999)*, s.v. "Death and Afterlife, Judaic Doctrines of."

160. Yerushalmi, *Zakhor*, 24. See also *The Encyclopedia of Judaism* (1999), s.v. "Death and Afterlife."

161. Yerushalmi, *Zakhor*, 86.

162. See Shmuel Feiner, *Haskalah and History: The Emergence of a Modern Jewish Historical Consciousness* (Portland, OR: Littman Library of Jewish Civilization, 2002), 274–95.

163. Feiner, *Haskalah and History*, 281, 283–84.

164. Feiner, 287–88.

165. Feiner, 288–89.

166. Mark Currie, *About Time: Narrative, Fiction and the Philosophy of Time* (Edinburgh: Edinburgh University Press, 2007), 6.

167. M. M. Bakhtin, *The Dialogic Imagination*, ed. Michael Holquist, trans. Caryl Emerson and Michael Holquist (Austin: University of Texas Press, 1981), 250. Bakhtin speaks of such novelistic chronotopes as scenes, meetings, and "well delineated spatial areas" where "time becomes, in effect, palpable and visible," and narrative events "take on flesh" (250).

168. Bakhtin, *Dialogic Imagination*, 254.

169. Abraham Cahan, *The Rise of David Levinsky* (New York: Harper and Row, 1960), 530.

170. Cahan, *Yekl and the Imported Bridegroom*, 119, 122.

171. Susan Stewart, *On Longing: Narratives of the Miniature, the Gigantic, the Souvenir, and the Collection* (Durham, NC: Duke University Press, 1993), 23.

172. Cahan, *Yekl and the Imported Bridegroom*, 120, 150. An "apikoros," first used in the Mishnah, forfeits his "share in the world to come" (Sanhedrin 10:1). Linked to Greek Epicureanism, it is one who ignores the commandments, derides the Torah, or its representatives; Maimonides defined it as one who denies prophecy, the possibility of God's communion with man, or divine revelation; later it was extended to those who disobey rabbis; now, the heterodox. See *Encyclopaedia Judaica* (1972), s.v. "apikoros." As Barbara Packer once pointed out to me, the subplot of Shaya's apostasy anticipates Chaim Potok's *The Chosen* (1967).

173. Cahan, *Yekl and the Imported Bridegroom*, 149, 147.

174. Cahan, *Yekl and the Imported Bridegroom*, 124. Embracing the attendant privileges of American whiteness, Flora absorbs the racial hierarchies of the period, uttering a disturbing racial slur in the midst of her insistent flirtations with Shaya:

> "You'll make a daisy of a college boy, too—you bet. Would you like to wear a high hat, and spec's, and ride in a buggy, with a little nigger for a driver?—would you, would you, bad boy, you? Hello, Doctor Golub! How are you?"
> She presented her lips, and they kissed again and again.

This first edition passage—excised in subsequent editions and unnoticed by critics—links the seductions of whiteness to a provincial, "place-oriented" version of cosmopolitanism: Flora wants a "worldly" husband, literally, one with a high social place in the world, regardless of cultural or intellectual experience. Cahan, *The Imported Bridegroom and Other Stories of the New York Ghetto* (Boston: Houghton, Mifflin and Co., 1898), 82–83. First edition courtesy of the Huntington Library, San Marino.

175. Guravitch and Aran, "The Land of Israel," 195–96.

176. Cahan, *Yekl and the Imported Bridegroom*, 152.

177. Barbara Mann, *Space and Place in Jewish Studies* (New Brunswick, NJ: Rutgers University Press, 2012), 5.

178. So important is the Destruction that remembering it is part of the Judaic calendar, commemorated by the annual fasting day, *Tisha B'Av*. Human geographer Yi-Fu Tuan distinguishes "space" as "that which allows movement" from "place," which is "pause." *Space and Place: The Perspective of Experience* (Minneapolis: University of Minnesota Press, 1977), 6.

179. Irving Howe and Eliezer Greenberg, eds. *A Treasury of Yiddish Stories* (New York: Penguin, 1990), 9.

180. William Scott Green and Jed Silverstein, "The Doctrine of the Messiah," in *The Blackwell Companion to Judaism, ed. Jacob Neusner and Alan J. Avery-Peck* (Oxford: Wiley-Blackwell, 2000), 260.

181. The Hasidic sense of history saw an endless, passive expectation of the Messiah, his advent hastened by our honoring God's commandments. Modern orthodoxy, by contrast, adhered to the rabbinic prohibition against "forcing" divine redemption, which is in God's hands only; we can only transform the here and now through Torah observance. Nascent Zionism, whether national or spiritual, exposed these tensions about messianic time (Green and Silverstein, "The Doctrine of the Messiah," 260). In Chaim Potok's *The Chosen*, the tzaddik Reb Saunders argues that while "*goyim*" and "*apikorsim*" try to build a Jewish land, which is God's job, only the Messiah can bring about a homeland (New York: Ballantine, 1967), 197.

182. Zionist pioneer Theodor Herzl (1860–1904) published arguments for a national solution to the "Jewish Question"—a modern, secular enlightened state—in *Der Judenstaat* (*The Jewish State*, 1896).

183. Mann explains that the Hebrew word for "place" in biblical discourse is frequently a synonym for God (Mann, *Space and Place*, 5).

184. Cahan, *Yekl and the Imported Bridegroom*, 131.

185. The 1989 film adaptation of "The Imported Bridegroom," produced and directed by Pamela Berger, places visual and symbolic emphasis upon Shaya's Talmudic gesticulations. Whereas they represent all that Flora initially cannot bear in Shaya, in a dramatically romantic and happy rewriting of the story's conclusion, it is the gesticulations that Flora comes to appreciate most, now signs of Shaya's enthusiasm for Western philosophy.

186. Feiner notes that even among the radical *maskilim* there were divisions between "realists" like Moses Lilienblum and socialists and materialists like Aaron Samuel Lieberman and Morris Vinchevsky, whom Lilienblum took to task for their "utopian-messianic ideas." His and others' pessimistic views marked the decline of the *Haskalah*. (Feiner *Haskalah and History*, 287, 289).

187. Cahan, *Yekl and the Imported Bridegroom*, 159.

188. Philip Joseph, "Literary Migration: Abraham Cahan's *The Imported Bridegroom* and the Alternative of American Fiction," *MELUS* 27, no. 4 (2002): 20.

189. Very few still exist today. See, e.g., Jonathan Boyarin, *Thinking in Jewish* (Chicago: University of Chicago Press, 1996), chapter 1, "Waiting for a Jew: Marginal Redemption at the Eight Street Shul," 8–33.

190. General George A. Sheridan, "Address of General George A. Sheridan, delivered upon May 22nd, 1886, at the opening of the Cyclorama of Vicksburg, New York City," (New York, 1886), 12.

191. As noted above, over five million immigrants entered the United States from 1880 to 1890; the Chinese Exclusion Act was passed on May 6, 1882; the 1885 Contract Labor Law forbade importing unskilled laborers from overseas; in 1888, expelling "aliens" became legally possible; in 1891 the newly established Bureau of Immigration forced steamship companies to return ineligible passengers to countries of origin, deporting illegal aliens, the poor, and polygamists; in 1892, Ellis Island opened; and in 1903, anarchists were ruled inadmissible to the United States. See Roger Daniels, *Coming to America: A History of Immigration and Ethnicity in American Life* (New York: Perennial, 2002), 124; and John Higham, *Strangers in the Land* (New York: Athenaeum, 1963), 48–49; 99–100, 112–13.

192. Kant, *Anthropology*, 257, 259.

CHAPTER 2

Marcel Mauss, *The Gift: The Form and Reason for Exchange in Archaic Societies*, trans. W. D. Halls (New York: Norton, 1990), 20.

1. Henry James, preface to *The Portrait of a Lady* (London: Penguin, 1986), 51.

2. Leon Edel, quoted in David McWhirter, ed., *Henry James's New York Edition: The Construction of Authorship* (Stanford, CA: Stanford University Press, 1995), 2.

3. See Walter P. Zenner, *Minorities in the Middle: A Cross-Cultural Analysis* (Albany: SUNY Press, 1991). As explored in the following chapter, the 1890s witnessed the rise of a prominent class of German-Jewish American and international bankers.

4. James, preface to *The Portrait of a Lady*, 47.

5. James praised the Isabella Steward Gardner collection in Boston, as Beverly Haviland notes, because the "'spoils'" that constitute it "are restored to a living

tradition rather than taken out of circulation and hoarded" (Haviland, *Henry James's Last Romance: Making Sense of the Past and the American Scene* [Cambridge: Cambridge University Press, 1997], 90). But he most certainly and dramatically rejects the hoarding of "spoils"—particularly at the expense of familial relations—in the great sacrificial potlatch with which Poynton goes up in smoke at the conclusion to *The Spoils of Poynton* (1897).

6. See Edel, "Henry James: The Dramatic Years," in *The Complete Plays of Henry James* (Philadelphia: Lippincott, 1949), 43, 51; and Edel, *Henry James: The Middle Years, 1881–1895* (Philadelphia, Lipincott, 1953), 262–67, 335–40.

7. Michael Anesko, *"Friction with the Market": Henry James and the Profession of Authorship* (New York: Oxford University Press, 1986), vii, 11–24.

8. Georg Simmel explains value in the following way: "the object thus formed, which is characterized by its separation from the subject, who at the same time establishes it and seeks to overcome it by his desire, is for us a value" (*The Philosophy of Money*, ed. David Frisby, trans. Tom Bottomore and David Frisby [London: Routledge, 1990], 66). In effect, value does not inhere in objects but is a projection of judgment made by subjects who desire them.

9. Simmel, *Philosophy of Money*, 120.

10. Simmel, *Philosophy of Money*, 277–79; Simmel, "The Conflict in Modern Culture," in *On Individuality and Social Forms*, ed. Donald N. Levine (Chicago: University of Chicago Press, 1971), 376.

11. Arjun Appadurai, "Introduction: Commodities and the Politics of Value," in *The Social Life of Things: Commodities in Cultural Perspective*, ed. Arjun Appadurai (Cambridge: Cambridge University Press, 1986), 3.

12. Mauss, *Gift*, 13.

13. Mary Douglas, foreword to *The Gift* by Marcel Mauss (New York: Norton, 1990), vii.

14. Mauss, *Gift*, 3.

15. The sea change began most notably when, in 1990, Jonathan Freedman broke from the reigning notion of James the expatriate aesthete *tout court*, and from Foucauldian readings of Jamesian knowledge and power, to offer us James as the literary professional embroiled in commodity culture. See Jonathan Freedman, *Professions of Taste: Henry James, British Aestheticism, and Commodity Culture* (Stanford, CA: Stanford University Press, 1990); and also Nancy Bentley, *The Ethnography of Manners: Hawthorne, James, Wharton* (Cambridge: Cambridge University Press, 1995). For Foucauldian readings of James, see Carolyn Porter, *Seeing and Being: The Plight of the Participant Observer in Emerson,*

James, Adams, and Faulkner (Middletown, CT.: Wesleyan University Press, 1981); and Mark Seltzer, *Henry James and the Art of Power* (Ithaca, NY: Cornell University Press, 1984). Equally groundbreaking was Ross Posnock's 1991 reconsideration of *The American Scene* as a pragmatic text, one that "constitutes a calculated act of affiliation with the new century and its endless possibilities" (Posnock, *The Trial of Curiosity* [New York: Oxford University Press, 1991], 12). Subsequent studies suggest a new James of the "major phase," at once aloof and curious; antimodern yet protomodernist; and in *The American Scene*, a genteel elitist who is alienated yet intrigued by impoverished Ellis Island aliens. See Haviland, *Henry James's Last Romance*; and Sara Blair, *Henry James and the Writing of Race and Nation* (Cambridge: Cambridge University Press, 1996).

16. Ross Posnock apologetically sees James's curiosity toward the Lower East Side denizens as redemptive, indicative of James's open-ended stance toward the world, nontotalizing and ever-questioning. He sees James's search for "Otherness . . . what James finds rare and most precious in the American scene" satisfied in his encounter with the Jewish immigrants. See Posnock, *Trial of Curiosity*, 285, 278. Greg Zacharias characterizes these same pages as a reaction to Theodore Roosevelt's call for total assimilation, as James's "declaration to those immigrants *not* to abandon their deeply held cultural and thus personal identities, but to develop a Jamesian public performance, which would enable their integration into the larger culture without forcing them to renounce their identities." See Zacharias, "Henry James' Fictional Jew," in *Representations of Jews Through the Ages*, ed. Leonard Jay Greenspoon and Bryan F. Le Beau (Omaha, NE: Creighton University Press, 1996), 191–93; and Freedman, "Henry James and the Discourses of Antisemitism," in *Between "Race" and Culture: Representations of "the Jew" in English and American Literature*, ed. Bryan Cheyette (Stanford, CA: Stanford University Press, 1996), 65.

17. Sara Blair, "In the House of Fiction: Henry James and the Engendering of Literary Mastery," in McWhirter, *Henry James's New York Edition*, 59.

18. See Barbara Herrnstein Smith, *Contingencies of Value: Alternative Perspectives for Critical Theory* (Cambridge: Harvard University Press, 1988).

19. James, *Portrait of a Lady*, 248; *The Golden Bowl* (New York: Penguin, 1985), 119.

20. William Spengemann, introduction to *The American*, by Henry James (New York: Penguin, 1981), 24–25.

21. This reading of value is indebted to Georg Simmel's theory of value production understood through Hegel's formulation of *Sittlichkeit*. See Simmel, *Philosophy*

of Money; and Georg Wilhelm Friedrich Hegel, *Elements of the Philosophy of Right*, ed. Allen Woods, trans. H. B. Nisbet (Cambridge: Cambridge University Press, 1991).

22. See, for example, Harold Fisch, *The Dual Image: The Figure of the Jew in English and American Literature* (New York: Ktav Publishing, 1971); and Louise Mayo, *The Ambivalent Image: Nineteenth-Century America's Perception of the Jew* (Cranbury, NJ: Associated University Press, 1988).

23. Henry James, *The American Scene* (New York: Penguin. 1994), 100. For the most direct and virulent charge of James's antisemitism, see Maxwell Geismar, *Henry James and the Jacobites* (New York: Hill and Wang, 1965). Eli Ben-Joseph also presumes James an antisemite, often conflating the most bigoted views of characters with those of the author. See Eli Ben-Joseph, *Aesthetic Persuasion: Henry James, the Jews, and Race* (Lanham, MD: University Press of America, 1996). See also Louis Harap, *The Image of the Jew in American Literature: From Early Republic to Mass Immigration* (Syracuse, NY: Syracuse University Press, 2003.) For arguments on "constructed" Jewishness in James, see Posnock; Zacharias; and Freedman, *"Discourses of Antisemitism" and The Temple of Culture* (London: Oxford University Press, 2000).

24. In 1848, the number of Jews in the United States was about 50,000. By 1880, that number had jumped to about 230,000. And by 1924, the national number was 4,000,000. See Morris Schappes, ed., *Emma Lazarus: Selections from her Poetry and Prose* (New York: Cooperative Book League, 1944), 12; and Karen Brodkin, *How Jews Became White Folks, and What That Says about Race in America* (New Brunswick, NJ: Rutgers University Press, 1998), 34. See also John Higham, *Send These to Me: Immigrants in Urban America (New York: Atheneum, 1975)*; and Roger Daniels, *Coming to America: A History of Immigration and Ethnicity in American Life* (New York: Perennial, 2002), 223–32.

25. Henry James, "The Art of Fiction," in Henry James, *The Critical Muse: Selected Literary Criticism*, ed. Roger Gard (London: Penguin, 1987), 189.

26. James, "Art of Fiction," 192.

27. James, *American Scene*, 67.

28. Haviland, *Henry James's Last Romance*, 148–54.

29. James, *American Scene*, 100.

30. James, "Daniel Deronda," in Henry James, *Critical Muse: Selected Literary Criticism*, ed. Roger Gard (London: Penguin, 1987), 116. Critics have referred to this piece in debates over James's use of Eliot's characters from *Deronda*, Gwendolyn Harleth and Henleigh Grandcourt, as models for Isabel Archer

and Gilbert Osmond, in *The Portrait of a Lady*. See F. R. Leavis, *The Great Tradition* (New York: Doubleday, 1954), 316; and George Levine, "Isabel, Gwendolyn and Dorothea," *ELH* 30, no. 3 (1963): 244–57.

31. James, "Daniel Deronda," 121. See Sander Gilman, *The Jew's Body* (New York: Routledge, 1991).

32. James, "The Art of Fiction," in *Critical Muse*, 193–95.

33. James, *American Scene*, 101.

34. James, *American Scene*, 103. See Hutchins Hapgood, *The Spirit of the Ghetto* (Cambridge: Belknap Press: 1967).

35. Creating the dichotomy upon which he constructed his entire notion of "culture," Matthew Arnold characterized Hellenism by its tendency toward "sweetness and light" and freedom from the bondage of Hebraism, which is marked, conversely, by its slavish adherence to the law, and to Benthamite utilitarianism. See Arnold, *Culture and Anarchy and Other Writings*, ed. Stefan Collini (Cambridge: Cambridge University Press, 1993), 77–79, 126–37.

36. Max Weber, *The Protestant Ethic and the Spirit of Capitalism*, trans. Talcott Parsons (London: Harper Collins Academic, 1991); Mark Twain, quoted in Justin Kaplan, *Mr. Clemens and Mark Twain: A Biography* (New York: Simon and Schuster, 1966), 158.

37. James, "Honoré de Balzac," in Henry James, *Critical Muse: Selected Literary Criticism*, ed. Roger Gard (London: Penguin, 1987), 356–57.

38. William Dean Howells, "The Man of Letters as a Man of Business," in *Criticism and Fiction and Other Essays*, ed. Clara Marburg Kirk and Rudolf Kirk (New York: New York University Press, 1959), 298, 309; James, "Honoré de Balzac," 355.

39. This idea is considered basic to literary critical accounts of the realist novel, attributable to Ian Watt's foundational study, *The Rise of the Novel: Studies in Defoe, Richardson, and Fielding* (London: Peregrine, 1968). See also Robert Shulman, "Realism," in *The Columbia History of the American Novel*, ed. Emory Elliott (New York, Columbia University Press, 1991), 160–88.

40. James, *American Scene*, 100.

41. Freedman draws this conclusion in light of the translation into English in 1895 of Max Nordau's *Degeneration*, and the practice of eugenics in the early part of the twentieth century. See Freedman, "Henry James and the Discourses of Antisemitism," 65.

42. James, *American Scene*, 100.

43. See George Eliot, *Daniel Deronda* (London: Penguin, 1995); and James, *Golden Bowl*, 190.

44. Daniel Boyarin and Jonathan Boyarin, "Diaspora: Generation and the Ground of Jewish Identity," *Critical Inquiry* 19 (1993): 723.

45. Boyarin and Boyarin, "Diaspora," 720.

46. See Jonathan Boyarin and Daniel Boyarin, eds., *Jews and Other Differences: The New Jewish Cultural Studies* (Minneapolis: University of Minnesota Press, 1997). To late-nineteenth-century nativists and nationalists alike, the cosmopolitan posed a grave threat to both national identity and national values.

47. Amanda Anderson, "Cosmopolitanism, Universalism, and the Divided Legacies of Modernity," in *Cosmopolitics: Thinking and Feeling beyond the Nation*, ed. Pheng Cheah and Bruce Robbins (Minneapolis: University of Minnesota Press, 1998), 266, 267. See also Anderson, *The Powers of Distance: Cosmopolitanism and the Cultivation of Detachment* (Princeton, NJ: Princeton University Press, 2001).

48. Anderson notes how Bruce Robbins, for example, defends cosmopolitanism as a "self-conscious professionalism among academics that acknowledges its own privileges and interests, but without imagining that such an acknowledgement irrevocably taints its practices, or fundamentally disarms its attempts to forward progressive principles and strive against prejudice and partiality." See Anderson, "Cosmopolitanism, Universalism, and the Divided Legacies of Modernity," in *Cosmopolitics*, 269. Robbins elsewhere refers to "actually existing cosmopolitanisms," a category that, in the context of postcoloniality, recognizes social and political conditions of oppression without resorting to the restrictive localism of identity politics. See Robbins, "Introduction Part I: Actually Existing Cosmopolitanism," in Cheah and Robbins, *Cosmopolitics*, 1–19. James Clifford describes what he calls "discrepant cosmopolitanisms": neither "overly global" nor "excessively local," they are generated by diaspora cultures "inseparable from specific, often violent, histories of economic, political, and cultural interaction." See Clifford, "Traveling Cultures," in *Cultural Studies*, ed. Lawrence Grossberg, Cary Nelson, and Paula A. Treichler (New York: Routledge, 1992), 108. For a study that retains cosmopolitanism's ideological utopianism, see David Hollinger, *Postethnic America* (New York: Basic Books, 1995). See also Kwame Anthony Appiah, *Cosmopolitanism: Ethics in a World of Strangers* (New York: Norton, 2006).

49. Immanuel Kant, *Anthropology from a Pragmatic Point of View*, ed. Robert B. Louden (Cambridge: Cambridge University Press, 2006), 254, 260.

50. Mill, quoted in Robbins, "Comparative Cosmopolitanism," 171.

51. Malachi Haim Hacohen, "Dilemmas of Cosmopolitanism: Karl Popper, Jewish Identity, and 'Central European Culture,'" *Journal of Modern History* 71 (1999): 119.

52. David Hollinger, "Ethnic Diversity, Cosmopolitanism and the Emergence of the American Liberal Intelligentsia," *American Quarterly* 27 (1975): 139.

53. See Michael Dobkowski, *The Tarnished Dream: The Basis of American Anti-Semitism* (Westport, CT: Greenwood, 1979), 196; and, more recently, Robert Rockaway and Arnon Gutfeld, "Demonic Images of the Jew in the Nineteenth Century United States," *American Jewish History* 89 (2001): 355–81.

54. J. Hector St. John de Crèvecoeur, Letter III: "What is an American?" in *Letters from an American Farmer*, ed. Susan Manning (Oxford: Oxford University Press, 1998), 40–82.

55. Theodore Roosevelt, "True Americanism" (1894), in *The Works of Theodore Roosevelt, National Edition*, ed. Hermann Hagedorn (New York: Scribner's, 1926), 13:19, 20–22.

56. Henry James, "Democracy and Theodore Roosevelt," in *Henry James: The American Essays, ed. Leon Edel (1898; repr., New York: Vintage, 1956), 213.*

57. Henry James, "The Pupil," in *The Complete Tales of Henry James*, ed. Leon Edel (Philadelphia: J. B. Lippincott, 1963), 7:409, 414.

58. James, "Pupil," 414.

59. Most studies of "queerness" in James are, of course, related to sexuality and sexual difference, including John Carlos Rowe, *The Other Henry James* (Durham, NC: Duke University Press, 1998), especially chapter 4, "Textual Preference: James's Literary Defenses against Sexuality in 'The Middle Years' and 'The Death of the Lion'"; Hugh Stevens, "Queer Henry in the Cage," in *The Cambridge Companion to Henry James*, ed. Jonathan Freedman (Cambridge: Cambridge University Press, 1998); Hugh Stevens, "Homoeroticism, Identity, and Agency in James's Late Tales," in *Enacting History in Henry James: Narrative, Power, and Ethics*, ed. Gert Buelens (Cambridge: Cambridge University Press, 1997); and Melissa Solomon, "The Female World of Exorcism and Displacement (or, Relations Between Women in Henry James Nineteenth-Century *The Portrait of a Lady*)," in *Novel Gazing: Queer Reading in Fiction*, ed. Eve Kosofsky Sedgwick (Durham, NC: Duke University Press, 1997).

60. Erving Goffman, *The Presentation of Self in Everyday Life* (Woodstock, NY: Overlook Press, 1973). Goffman insists there is a moral character to self-presentation: "[s]ociety is organized on the principle that any individual who

possesses certain social characteristics has a moral right to expect that others will value and treat him in an appropriate way. Connected with this principle is a second, namely that an individual who implicitly or explicitly signifies that he has certain social characteristics ought in fact to be what he claims he is" (Goffman, 13). "Appearance" and "manner" for Goffman, like Hegelian "habit" or "custom," thus take on an ethical valence.

61. Pierre Bourdieu, *Distinction: A Social Critique of the Judgment of Taste*, trans. Richard Nice (Cambridge: Harvard University Press, 1984), 6.

62. James, "Pupil," 416.

63. James, "Pupil," 418. Matthew Arnold lays out a new nomenclature to replace the "awkward and tiresome" terms "aristocratic class, the middle class, the working class" with "the Barbarians," "the Philistines," and "the Populace," respectively. See Arnold, "Barbarians, Philistines, Populace" in *Culture and Anarchy and Other Writings*, ed. Stefan Collini (Cambridge: Cambridge University Press, 1993), 102–25.

64. James, "Pupil," 442.

65. James, *American Scene*, 132, 133.

66. James, "Pupil," 414–15.

67. See, for example, Hans Christian Andersen's haunting tale of modernity and duplicity, "The Shadow"; for a longer exploration of this trope, see Judith Jackson Fawcett, *Illuminated Darkness: Slavery and Its Shadow in the Long Nineteenth Century* (Chapel Hill: University of North Carolina Press, 2010).

68. James, *The American* (New York: Penguin, 1981), 54.

69. James, *Golden Bowl*, 143.

70. James, *American*, 71.

71. As Arnold warned in 1869, one year after Christopher Newman arrives in Paris, the challenge for democracy is essentially "how to find and keep high ideals," that is, to value "the best that is known and thought in the world" above the worldliness of bourgeois philistinism, to replace interest with disinterestedness. For Arnold, culture "goes beyond religion" in its ability to aid us in this task of human perfection (Arnold, *Culture and Anarchy*, 62, 63). See also Arnold, *Culture and Anarchy*, 14, 36.

72. James, *Golden Bowl*, 49, 56.

73. Martha Banta, introduction to *New Essays on* The American (Cambridge: Cambridge University Press, 1987), 17. Here Banta is quoting James from an 1878 essay, "Americans Abroad," *Nation* 27 (October 3, 1878): 208–9.

74. James, *American*, 33.

75. See Donald Weber, "Outsiders and Greenhorns: Christopher Newman in the Old World, David Levinsky in the New," *American Literature*, 67, no. 4 (1995): 728.

76. James, *American*, 51.

77. James, *American Scene*, 44.

78. Carolyn Porter, "Gender and Value in *The American*," in *New Essays on* The American, ed. Martha Banta (New York: Cambridge University Press, 1987), 107.

79. James, *American*, 89.

80. Georges Bataille, *The Accursed Share, Volume I*, trans. Robert Hurley (New York: Zone Books, 1988), 25. Writing in 1949, Bataille wanted to operate in a general economy, where surplus of any kind was consumed by forms of pure expenditure, ranging from suicide and sacrifice to less violent forms such as conspicuous consumption, nonreproductive sex, and the potlatch. Yet even Bataille had trouble escaping the restricted economy; even the notion of expenditure has use-value in a broader sense, whether it is the pleasure gained in orgiastic effervescence or in the immediate consumption of a beautiful object.

81. James, *American*, 75.

82. Porter, "Gender and Value," 107.

83. Spengemann, introduction to *The American*, 21.

84. Porter, "Gender and Value," 100.

85. See Alan Trachtenberg, *The Incorporation of America: Culture and Society in the Gilded Age* (New York: Hill and Wang, 1982); Amy Kaplan, *The Social Construction of American Realism* (Chicago: University of Chicago Press, 1988); Richard Brodhead, *Cultures of Letters: Scenes of Reading and Writing in Nineteenth-Century America* (Chicago: University of Chicago Press, 1993); Daniel H. Borus, *Writing Realism: Howells, James, and Norris in the Mass Market* (Chapel Hill: North Carolina University Press, 1989); Richard Wightman Fox and T. J. Jackson Lears, *The Culture of Consumption: Critical Essays in American History, 1880–1890* (New York: Pantheon, 1983); Jay Martin, *Harvests of Change: American Literature, 1865–1914* (Englewood Cliffs, NJ: Prentice-Hall, 1967); and Seltzer, *Henry James and the Art of Power*.

86. Eric J. Sundquist, "The Country of the Blue," in *American Realism: New Essays*, ed. Eric J. Sundquist (Baltimore: Johns Hopkins University Press, 1982), 19.

87. On Beecher and other critics of speculation and credit, see Karen Halttunen, *Confidence Men and Painted Women: A Study of Middle-Class Culture in America*,

1830–1870 (New Haven, CT: Yale University Press, 1982); and Ann Fabian, *Card Sharps, Dream Books, and Bucket Shops: Gambling in 19th-Century America* (Ithaca, NY: Cornell University Press, 1990). On the populist critique of speculators, see Trachtenberg, *Incorporation of America*.

88. Susan Mizruchi, "Fiction and the Science of Society," in *The Columbia History of the American Novel*, ed. Emory Elliott (New York: Columbia University Press, 1991), 191. Other sociological readings of James include Bentley, *Ethnography of Manners*; Phillip Barrish, *American Literary Realism, Critical Theory, and Intellectual Prestige, 1880–1995* (Cambridge: Cambridge University Press, 2001); and Kendall Johnson, "'Dark Spot' in the Picturesque: The Aesthetics of Polygenism and Henry James's 'A Landscape-Painter,'" *American Literature* 74 (2002): 59–87.

89. Georg Simmel, *The Philosophy of Money*, 277–79.

90. James, "Art of Fiction," 190.

91. Marc Shell makes the functional connection between money and literary language explicit: "Credit, or belief, involves the very ground of aesthetic experience, and the same medium that seems to confer belief in fiduciary money (bank notes) and in scriptural money (created by the process of bookkeeping) also seems to confer it in literature. That medium is writing" (*Money, Language, and Thought: Literary and Philosophic Economies from the Medieval to the Modern Era* [Baltimore: Johns Hopkins University Press, 1982], 7).

92. Albert W. Aiken. *The Genteel Spotter; or, The Night Hawks of New York, A Tale of the Lawless*. Beadle's Dime Library, vol. 25, no. 320 (New York: Beadle and Adams, December 10, 1884), 6, 11.

93. "Conspicuously over the door hung the pawnbroker's sign, the same all over the world, no matter the country, nor the language, the three golden balls, the old-time arms of the Florentine house of the Medicis, who long years ago in the land of sunny Italy lent money to their brother nobles, took usury and security, and so founded the numerous if not noble line of pawnbrokers" (Aiken, *Genteel Spotter*, 11).

94. Vincent P. Pecora, *Households of the Soul* (Baltimore: Johns Hopkins University Press, 1997), 8.

95. In *The Golden Bowl*, James uses the term "shopman"; however, whereas a shopkeeper buys and sells wares for profit, James's "shopman" is more like a pawnbroker, operating within a social system of deposit and credit, honor and loyalty. It is the pawnbroker, after all, who both reveals and eases the burden of those who have fallen on hard times by accepting their treasured possessions for cash,

and who later restores them or, in time, passes them on to become someone else's unique treasures.

96. James, preface to *The Portrait of a Lady*, 47.

97. James, *Golden Bowl*, 123, 122–23.

98. What I am calling "age-value" can be likened to what Walter Benjamin calls the "aura" of the work of art, the uniqueness and "authenticity" of the original, predicated on its "presence" and unique history: "all that is transmissible from its beginning, ranging from its substantive duration to its testimony to the history which it has experienced." What gets lost in modern reproduction for Benjamin is the object's "ritual function," or "cult value." The biblical Hebrew-turned-immigrant Jew—though paradoxically the ultimate figure of market exchange—seems to possess for James just such a "cult value," a value that, once appropriated, enables James to reenchant the very marketplace that he, himself, cannot escape. See "The Work of Art in the Age of Mechanical Reproduction" in *Illuminations*, ed. Hannah Arendt, trans. Harry Zohn (New York: Schocken Books, 1968), 221 and 243n5. Thank you to Jim Berkley for bringing this connection to my attention.

99. James, *Golden Bowl*, 115.

100. Noting the Prince's social malleability within his new family, Adam Verver tells the Prince: "You're round, my boy, . . . you're all, you're variously and inexhaustibly round, when you might, by all the chances, have been abominably square. . . . It's the sort of thing one feels—at least I do—with one's hand. Say you had been formed all over in a lot of little pyramidal lozenges like that wonderful side of the Ducal Palace in Venice . . . all the architectural diamonds. . . . One would have been scratched by diamonds. . . . As it is . . . you're a pure and perfect crystal" (James, *Golden Bowl*, 137–38).

101. James, *American Scene*, 176.

102. Simmel, "Modern Culture," 376.

103. Appadurai, "Introduction," 3.

104. James, *Golden Bowl*, 432.

105. The "souvenir," according to Susan Stewart, acts as a trace of an authentic experience that is "reportable," but not repeatable, of "events whose materiality has escaped us . . . that thereby exist only through the invention of narrative" (*On Longing: Narratives of the Miniature, the Gigantic, the Souvenir, and the Collection* [Durham, NC: Duke University Press, 1993], 135).

106. Anderson, "Cosmopolitanism," 266.

107. Georges Bataille, *Accursed Share*, 25.

108. James, *Golden Bowl*, 460; emphasis mine.

109. Repentance is linear and unidirectional, involving the acceptance of guilt and the demonstration of remorse or regret, but not necessarily a change of heart, as with the repentance of Judas. See Matthew George Easton, *Easton's Bible Dictionary*, 3rd ed. (1897), s.v. "repentance," www.ccel.org/ccel/easton/ebd2.html ?term=Repentance. Atonement, however, is a form of reparation, amends, or compensation: for Christians, the "reconciliation of God and humans brought about by the redemptive life and death of Jesus" (*The American Heritage Dictionary, 4th ed., s.v. "atonement" def. 2b*). Jewish atonement also involves reconciliation with a God one has abandoned with sin, but, once rooted in the priestly rite of blood sacrifice—the symbolic offering of life for life—was replaced after the destruction of the Temple with repentance, reparation, prayer, fasting, charity, and suffering in exile. See Kaufmann Kohler, "Atonement," in *The Jewish Encyclopedia*, 1906, www.jewishencyclopedia.com/articles/2092-atonement.

110. James, *Golden Bowl*, 460.

111. Porter, "Gender and Value," 105.

112. James, *Golden Bowl*, 292.

113. Pecora describes Émile Durkheim's notion of "social solidarity" as "the free exchange of goods and services warranted and enabled by increasing division of labor and social difference." See *Households of the Soul*, 115.

114. James, *Golden Bowl*, 437.

115. In his 1909 preface to the New York edition of *The Golden Bowl*, James describes the act of revision variously as that of "re-reading," "re-accepting," "re-tasting," "re-assimilating," and "re-enjoying," deeming the entire process "a *living* affair" (*Golden Bowl*, 29, 30, 31). Likewise, in "The Art of Fiction," James calls the novel "a living thing" (196).

116. Émile Durkheim, *The Elementary Forms of the Religious Life*, trans. Joseph Ward Swain (New York: Free Press, 1965), 251.

117. James, *American Scene*, 101.

118. See Mauss, *Gift*, 13.

119. James, preface to *The Portrait of a Lady*, 47.

120. See Dobkowski, *Tarnished Dream*, 7, 8n16. On the Seligman case, see also Higham, *Send These to Me*, 150–51. Other milestones include the 1902 attack on Rabbi Jacob Joseph by Irish factory workers during a funeral procession, and subsequently by the largely Irish New York City police force. See Higham, 135.

121. Higham, *Send These to Me*, 130.

122. Higham attributes this event to the insecurities of industrial capitalism, the ascendance of biological racial determinism, and a sweeping ethnocentrism in response to immigration. See Higham, 172–73, 185–86.

123. For example, Ford republished the antisemitic forgery, *The Protocols of the Elders of Zion*, in his paper, the *Dearborn Independent*, as well as a series of articles on a purported Jewish conspiracy, later collected into four volumes titled *The International Jew* (1920). See Higham, 187–88. See also Dobkowski, *Tarnished Dream*, 196–200. On American antisemitism, see Leonard Dinnerstein, *Antisemitism in America* (New York: Oxford University Press, 1994). For a Marxist perspective, see Carey McWilliams, *A Mask for Privilege: Anti-Semitism in America* (Boston: Little Brown, 1948); for the populist origins of American antisemitism, see Richard Hofstadter, *The Age of Reform; from Bryan to F.D.R.* (New York: Knopf, 1956); and for antisemitic images in literature, see Harap, *Image of the Jew*; and Mayo, *Ambivalent Image*.

124. James, *American Scene*, 192.

125. Gert Buelens, *Henry James and the "Aliens" in Possession of the American Scene* (Amsterdam: Rodopi, 2002), 9.

126. James, *American Scene*, 194.

127. James, "Art of Fiction," 189.

128. James, "Art of Fiction," 196.

129. James, *Golden Bowl*, 35.

CHAPTER 3

1. Stephen Birmingham, *Our Crowd: The Jewish Families of New York* (London: Futura, 1967), 17. Seligman even hired Alger to tutor his young boys (Birmingham, 150–51).

2. Birmingham, *Our Crowd*, 86. Birmingham comments, "By the war's end, though he may not have actually 'won the war,' Joseph Seligman was very dear to Washington's heart" (Birmingham, 89); Cyrus Adler and Joseph Jacobs, "Seligman," in *The Jewish Encyclopedia*, 1906, www.jewishencyclopedia.com/articles/13403-seligman.

3. He turned the position down, possibly out of shyness on the public stage. Birmingham, *Our Crowd*, 115.

4. Birmingham, *Our Crowd*, 153–58. According to the *Jewish Encyclopedia*, by 1879, the Seligmans and Rothschilds took on a whopping $150 million in US bonds. See Adler Jacobs, "Seligman."

5. Deemed the most practical of the submissions, Seligman's plan was to build up a reserve of gold totaling approximately 40 percent of the greenbacks through the sale of bonds for coin. See Birmingham, *Our Crowd*, 115, 160–61.

6. Birmingham, 160–61.

7. Lee Livney, "Let Us Now Praise Self-Made Men: A Reexamination of the Hilton-Seligman Affair," *New York History* 75, no. 1 (1994): 70. On Hilton and the Union League Club, see "A Reply to Judge Hilton," *New York Times*, June 20, 1877.

8. See, for example, James Livingston, *The Concise Princeton Encyclopedia of American Political History, Volume 2* (2011), s.v. "Economy and Politics: 1860–1920."

9. See Birmingham, *Our Crowd*, 8. The Guggenheims alone among them were from German-speaking Switzerland.

10. "A Sensation at Saratoga" *New York Times*, June 19, 1877, 1.

11. It is unclear if the Seligmans actually showed up and were sent away from the hotel, or were notified in advance that they would not be admitted, but either way the "affair" caused a great public stir. Birmingham, *Our Crowd*, 162–65; Livney, "Let Us Now Praise Self-Made Men," 76–77.

12. These are Livney's reasons for why the affair received so much attention in the press. See "Let Us Now Praise Self-Made Men," 95–98.

13. "A Reply to Judge Hilton" *New York Times*, June 20, 1877.

14. "A Reply to Judge Hilton" *New York Times*, June 20, 1877.

15. "Judge Hilton's Position," *New York Times*, June 20, 1877.

16. "No Jews Need Apply," *New York Tribune*, June 20, 1877.

17. "Jewish Clothiers of One Mind," *New York Times*, June 22, 1877.

18. "Jewish Clothiers of One Mind."

19. Henry Ward Beecher, "Jew and Gentile," sermon delivered on June 24, 1877, printed first in the *Christian Union* and reprinted in *An Hour with the "American Hebrew"* (New York: Jesse Haney and Company, 1879), 51–76. https://babel.hathitrust.org/cgi/pt?id=loc.ark:/13960/t6b28nr3f;view=1up;seq=1 accessed July 8, 2016.

20. Irene C. Goldman-Price suggests this in "The 'Perfect Jew' and *The House of Mirth*: A Study in Point of View," in *Edith Wharton's The House of Mirth: A Casebook*, ed. Carol J. Singley (Oxford: Oxford University Press, 2003), 167.

21. Birmingham, *Our Crowd*, 158.

22. Goldman-Price, "'Perfect Jew,'" 165–67.

23. Goldman-Price sees Rosedale's ultimate acceptance into the Gentile power elite as an ironic indictment of a society that is "*so* frivolous, *so* irresponsible, *so* wasteful, cruel, and self-serving, that even a vulgar Jew is better than they

are." See Goldman-Price, "'Perfect Jew,'" 176; see also Joan Lidoff, "Another Sleeping Beauty: Narcissism in *The House of Mirth*," in *American Realism: New Essays*, ed. Eric Sundquist (Baltimore: Johns Hopkins University Press, 1982), 238–58; and Elaine Showalter, "The Death of the Lady (Novelist): Wharton's *House of Mirth*," *Representations* 9 (Winter 1985): 142–43. Donald Pizer explores Rosedale and Darwinian themes in "The Naturalism of Edith Wharton's *House of Mirth*," *Twentieth-Century Literature*, 41, no. 2 (1955): 241–48; and briefly in *American Naturalism and the Jews: Garland, Norris, Dreiser, Wharton and Cather* (Urbana: University of Illinois Press, 2008), 50–58. For readings of Rosedale and Wharton's patrician racism, see Elizabeth Ammons, *Edith Wharton's Argument with America* (Athens: University of Georgia Press, 1980); Hildegard Hoeller, *Edith Wharton's Dialogue with Realism and Sentimental Fiction* (Gainesville: University Press of Florida, 2000); Jennie A. Kassanoff, *Edith Wharton and the Politics of Race* (Cambridge: Cambridge University Press, 2004); Gary Martin Levine, *Merchant of Modernism: The Economic Jew in Anglo-American Literature, 1864–1939* (New York: Routledge, 2003); and Christian Riegel, "Rosedale and Anti-Semitism in House of Mirth," *Studies in American Fiction* 20, no. 2 (1992): 219–24. On Rosedale as the embodiment of stock exchange logic, see Wayne Westbrook, "Lily-Bartering on the New York Social Exchange in *The House of Mirth*," *Ball State University Forum* 20 (1979): 59–64; and Wai-Chee Dimock, "Debasing Exchange: Edith Wharton's *The House of Mirth*," *PMLA* 100 (1985): 783–92.

24. Beecher, "Jew and Gentile," 74.

25. Birmingham, *Our Crowd*, 75; emphasis mine.

26. Martha Banta, "In Fashion, In History, Out of Time," in *A Historical Guide to Edith Wharton*, ed. Carol J. Singley (New York: Oxford University Press, 2003), 51–88. Banta suggests, "Wharton presents women whose narratives question their ability to share the same time-scheme which their adversaries enlist to define rules of the game that Wharton's heroines are expected to obey" (Banta, 56).

27. Edith Wharton, *The House of Mirth* (New York: Norton, 1990), 10.

28. Johannes Fabian, *Time and the Other* (New York: Columbia University Press, 1983), 24.

29. Elaine Showalter quotes nineteenth-century feminist novelist Elizabeth Oakes Smith, who noted in her diary, "How few women have any history after the age of thirty!" in Showalter, "Death of the Lady (Novelist)," 133.

For Showalter, Wharton situates Lily on the verge of a "crisis of adulthood" (Showalter, 134).

30. Wharton, *House of Mirth*, 106.

31. Pierre Bourdieu defines symbolic capital as follows: "for those who, like the professionals, live on the sale of cultural services to a clientele, the accumulation of economic capital merges with the accumulation of symbolic capital, that is, with the acquisition of a reputation for competence and an image of respectability and honourability that are easily converted into political positions as a local or national *notable*. It is therefore understandable that they should identify with the established (moral) order to which they make daily contributions, of which their political positions and actions . . . are only the most visible form." See Bourdieu, *Distinction: A Social Critique of the Judgment of Taste*, trans. Richard Nice (Cambridge: Harvard University Press, 1984), 291.

32. Edith Wharton, *A Backward Glance* (New York: D. Appleton-Century, 1934), 208.

33. This is essentially Lidoff's argument: "Lily is a victim predestined to sacrifice to a deterministic sense of the inevitability of spiritual destruction by social institutions' collective necessities. Wharton's declared intent was to show, in the only way possible, the tragic possibilities of the idle society of the wealthy by showing what that society destroys." See Lidoff, "Another Sleeping Beauty: Narcissism in The House of Mirth," 239.

34. *Chronos* (from the ancient Greek χρόνος, "time") is the personification of time itself. *Kairos* (derived from the Greek καιρός, "right or proper time") is the "fullness of time; the propitious moment for the performance of an action or the coming into being of a new state." See Henry George Liddell, Robert Scott, *A Greek English Lexicon* (Oxford: Clarendon Press, 1940); www.oed .com/view/Entry/102356?redirectedFrom=kairos#eid.

35. Wharton, *House of Mirth*, 13.

36. In the 1930s, Wilson Follett judged Wharton's work as a set of nostalgic chronicles, "curiosities" of a bygone era (Wilson Follett, "What Edith Wharton Did—And Might Have Done." *New York Times Book Review* 5 [September 1937]; quoted in Shari Benstock, ed., *The House of Mirth* [Case Studies in Contemporary Criticism] [Boston: Bedford St. Martin, 1994], 315).

37. Anthony Giddens, *The Consequences of Modernity* (Stanford, CA: Stanford University Press, 1990), 20–26. As the bearer of stock market "tips," Rosedale is part of an "expert system" that challenges "traditional social systems" by removing

"the social relations from the immediacies of context," and separating time from the space of the agents involved inherently involves trust (Giddens, 28–29).

38. Wharton, *House of Mirth*, 140.

39. Goldman-Price, "'Perfect Jew,'" 27–28. As discussed in my Introduction, Hilton did not consider Seligman a "Hebrew" because he was not religious. Hilton distinguished acceptable Sephardim from "these 'Jews' (not Hebrews), of whom Joseph Seligman is a representative, [who] are not wanted any more at any of the first-class Summer hotels" (*New York Times*, June 21, 1877, 8; quoted in Esther Schor, *Emma Lazarus* [New York: Schocken, 2006], 81–82).

40. Lidoff argues that "unlike any of the other voices in the novel, including the narrator's, Rosedale does not confuse the language of love and money, but talks of money when he means money, and love when he means love" (Lidoff, "Another Sleeping Beauty," 250).

41. Wharton, *House of Mirth*, 187.

42. See Goldman-Price, "'Perfect' Jew," 31.

43. Jennifer Baker, *Securing the Commonwealth: Debt, Speculation, and Writing in the Making of Early America* (Baltimore: Johns Hopkins University Press, 2005), 2.

44. Baker, *Securing the Commonwealth*, 16.

45. Marc Shell, *Money, Language, and Thought: Literary and Philosophical Economies from the Medieval to the Modern Era* (Baltimore: Johns Hopkins University Press, 1982), 6. Shell dates the relationship between "fact value (intellectual currency) and substantial value (material currency)" to the institution of coinage by the Greeks in the sixth and fifth centuries BCE (Shell, 1).

46. Mary Poovey argues that British economic and literary writing share common concerns with representation, which the modern credit economy makes visible by deferring its "authenticating ground." If the gap between money and the value it represents widens with the credit economy, jeopardizing "prevailing modes of value" and conventions of trust, then both economic and literary writing helped to manage these effects by "creating a nonfactual form of representation that was nevertheless *not a lie*." See Poovey, *Genres of the Credit Economy: Mediating Value in Eighteenth- and Nineteenth-Century Britain* (Chicago: University of Chicago Press, 2008), 5–6.

47. See Sandra Sherman, *Finance and Fictionality in the Early Eighteenth Century: Accounting for Defoe* (Cambridge: Cambridge University Press, 1996) and Patrick Brantlinger, *Fictions of State: Culture and Credit in Britain, 1694–1994* (Ithaca, NY: Cornell University Press, 1996) Anthony Giddens argues that

credit exacerbates the condition already created by money, a symbolic token that couples "instantaneity and deferral, presence and absence" (Giddens, *Consequences of Modernity*, 25). For a more recent take on cultural representations and the "horror" of the recent housing credit crisis, see Annie McClanahan, "Dead Pledges: Debt, Horror, and the Credit Crisis," *Post45*, May 7, 2012, http://post45.research.yale.edu/2012/05/dead-pledges-debt-horror-and-the -credit-crisis/.

48. Terry Mulcaire, "Public Credit; or, The Feminization of Virtue in the Marketplace," *PMLA* 114 (October 1999): 1030. See also Brantlinger, *Fictions of State*, 144–45; J. G. A. Pocock, *Virtue, Commerce, and History: Essays on Political Thought and History, Chiefly in the Eighteenth Century* (Cambridge: Cambridge University Press, 1985), 91–102.

49. Brantlinger, *Fictions of State*, 139, 144.

50. Marc Shell describes how both paper money and art could thus be "taken for the real thing by a willing suspension of belief," which was further complicated by the problem of counterfeiting passed off by "confidence men" (Shell, 6–7). This confusion troubled literary writers like Herman Melville, for example, because "credit, or belief, involves the very ground of aesthetic experience, and the same medium that seems to confer belief in fiduciary money (bank notes) and in scriptural money (created by the process of bookkeeping) also seems to confer it in literature. That medium is writing" (7).

51. Karen Halttunen, *Confidence Men and Painted Women: A Study of Middle-Class Culture in America, 1830–1870* (New Haven, CT: Yale University Press, 1982).

52. This figure was perhaps most fully embodied in Herman Melville's famous novel *The Confidence Man* (1857).

53. Halttunen, *Confidence Men*, 19.

54. Mulcaire, "Public Credit," 1034.

55. Cited in Halttunen, *Confidence Men*, 19.

56. Henry Ward Beecher, cited in Halttunen, *Confidence Men*, 17.

57. Beecher, cited in Halttunen, *Confidence Men*, 17–18; Halttunen, *Confidence Men*, 19. "Character," Halttunen makes clear here, is to be understood in the eighteenth-century sense of the etching on a Lockean lump of wax.

58. Emile Durkheim studied primitive dances and festivals devoted to religious totems, since these communal activities generated the core impulses of full-blown religion in nascent form. Just as these rituals became replaced by more complex ones, speculation and gambling survive as atavistic remnants of primitive ecstatic religious formations, uncontrollable tendencies that erupt with

"contagion" throughout the nineteenth century. Distinguished by sacrifice and risk, gambling is a ritual of collective life that produces what Durkheim described as an effervescence that leaves in one "the conviction that there really exist two heterogeneous and mutually incomparable worlds": one where "daily life drags wearily along"; the other of "relations with extraordinary powers that excite [one] to the point of frenzy. The first is the profane world, the second, that of sacred things" (250). See Émile Durkheim, *The Elementary Forms of the Religious Life*, trans. Joseph Ward Swain (1915; repr., New York: Free Press, 1965), 249–51.

59. Horatio Alger, *Ragged Dick, or Street Life in New York with Boot Blacks* (New York: Norton, 2008).

60. Halttunen, *Confidence Men*, 30–32.

61. Of course this method was already being employed in the Revolutionary period, best detailed by Benjamin Franklin in his advice manuals on how to get ahead in a tricky colonial economy.

62. Poovey argues, "It is a truth universally acknowledged that mid-nineteenth-century novelists represented financial matters in ethical and moral terms": "as part of their generally critical relation to market society . . . [they] used a character's attitude toward money to indicate moral worth, and, more often than not, only a character's indifference to—or even repudiation of—money can signal virtue." *Genres of the Credit Economy*, 373.

63. One usage of the word "trust" dating from 1882 came from the counting house. A similar usage relating to finance dating from 1825 denotes "A group of companies, industries, etc., organized to reduce or eliminate competition, or to control production and distribution for their common advantage"; and also "such a group with a governing body of trustees holding a majority of the stock of each participating company, and therefore having a controlling vote in their conduct." OED online (January 2018), s.v. "trust, n." 8 a.b. www.oed.com/view/Entry/207004 ?rskey=YSXm29&result=1&isAdvanced=false (accessed February 26, 2018).

64. From as early as the sixteenth century, the verb "to trust" had a specifically economic usage: "to give (a person) credit" *for* "money or goods supplied"; "to supply *with* goods on credit." *OED* online (January 2018) s.v. "trust, v." 6a. www.oed.com/view/Entry/207006?rskey=YSXm29&result=3 (accessed February 26, 2018).

65. Ann Fabian, *Card Sharps, Dream Books and Bucket Shops: Gambling in 19th-Century America* (Ithaca, NY: Cornell University Press, 1990), 2. Fabian reformulates nineteenth-century economic change as a shift from an economy of

production to a speculative economy as she traces the histories of gambling and resistance to it in the United States.

66. Daniel Defoe remarked of Lady Credit that she has the power to "turn paper into money" but can as easily turn "money" back "into dross." Daniel Defoe, *The Best of Defoe's Review*, ed. William Payne (New York: Columbia University Press, 1951), 118; cited in Mulcaire, "Public Credit," 1033.

67. Fabian, *Card Sharps*, 6–7.

68. Fabian, *Card Sharps*, 9.

69. John Higham, *Send These to Me: Immigrants in Urban America* (New York: Atheneum, 1975), 180–81.

70. June Howard, *Form and History in American Literary Naturalism* (Chapel Hill: University of North Carolina Press, 1985), 119, 117.

71. Birmingham, *Our Crowd*, 119–29, 179–83, 188–94, 225–38.

72. Pizer bases the case for this connection on two texts by William H. Harvey, *Coin's Financial School* (1894), a study that blamed foreign (British) banks for keeping money in short supply and which featured a cartoon of the famous Jewish British banker Rothschild as an octopus, and *A Tale of Two Nations* (1894), an antisemitic novel demonstrating the silver standard as a Jewish conspiracy. Pizer then puts this portrait into the context of Norris's commitment to Anglo-Saxon racial superiority and use of stock antisemitic stereotypes in "A Case for Lambroso," and in particular with the character Zerkov in *McTeague*, whom Louis Harap considers "a really vicious stereotype." See Pizer, *American Naturalism and the Jews*, 4–5, 22, 28–29; and Louis Harap, *The Image of the Jew in American Literature: From Early Republic to Mass Immigration* (Syracuse, NY: Syracuse University Press, 2003), 392.

73. See Keith Newlin, *Hamlin Garland: A Life* (Lincoln: University of Nebraska Press, 2008), 102–15; and Hamlin Garland, "'Single Tax' and Woman Suffrage" in *Hamlin Garland, Prairie Radical: Writings from the 1890s*, ed. Donald Pizer (Urbana: University of Illinois Press, 2010), 96–99.

74. Pizer, *American Naturalism and the Jews*, 9.

75. John Higham, *Strangers in the Land: Patterns of American Nativism 1860–1925* (New York: Athenaeum, 1963). 159. See especially chapter 7, "Anti-Semitism and American Culture," 153–74.

76. Le Goff, *Time, Work and Culture in the Middle Ages* (Chicago: University of Chicago Press, 1980), 29 (emphasis mine).

77. E. P. Thompson, "Time, Work-Discipline, and Industrial Capitalism," *Past & Present* 38 (December 1967): 95.

78. Richard Baxter, *A Christian Directory* (London, 1673), 274–75; quoted in Thompson, "Time, Work-Discipline, and Industrial Capitalism," 87.

79. Thompson, "Time, Work-Discipline, and Industrial Capitalism," 90. As Max Weber argues, Baxter's real moral objection was the "relaxation in the security of possession, the enjoyment of wealth with the consequence of idleness and the temptations of the flesh, above all of distraction from the pursuit of a righteous life." In other words, wasting time was the "first and in principle the deadliest of sins," since time was valued in terms of its being spent "in labour for the Glory of God." See Max Weber, *The Protestant Ethic and the Spirit of Capitalism*, trans. Talcott Parsons (London: Routledge, 1992), 104.

80. See Weber, *The Protestant Ethic.*

81. June Howard calls the "brute Other" in naturalism the menacing character who has little self-consciousness about his actions, who "can only be observed and analyzed" by "a self-conscious, purposeful agent." See Howard, *Form and History*, 104.

82. Theodore Dreiser, *The Hand of the Potter: A Tragedy in Four Acts* (New York: Boni and Liveright, 1918), 193, https://archive.org/details/handofpotter00drei.

83. Abraham Cahan, "Unusual Jewish Tragedy in an Unusual Theater," *Forward*, quoted in Pizer, *American Naturalism and the Jews*, 34n9, 72.

84. Wharton, *House of Mirth*, 235.

85. Halttunen, *Confidence Men*, 25.

86. Wharton, *House of Mirth*, 12.

87. Miss Havisham is the aging, childless woman in Charles Dickens's *Great Expectations* (1861) who lives alone in a decaying old mansion, perennially in her faded wedding dress, and one shoe, and who has had all the clocks stopped at the exact time on her wedding day, twenty minutes to nine, when she received the letter that her husband-to-be had defrauded her and was leaving her at the altar.

88. Wharton, *House of Mirth*, 86, 175.

89. Paul Ricoeur, *Time and Narrative, Volume I*, trans. Kathleen McLaughlin and David Pellauer (Chicago: University of Chicago Press, 1984), 54.

90. Wharton, *House of Mirth*, 25.

91. Carrie Meeber is the self-interested heroine of Theodore Dreiser's *Sister Carrie* (1900), whose rise from rural poverty to some measure of fame and comfort in urban Chicago is predicated on her lover-turned-husband, George Hurstwood's, bitter fall into destitution.

92. Wharton, *House of Mirth*, 25–26.

93. Showalter, "Death of the Lady (Novelist)," 140; Wharton, *House of Mirth*, 106, 103.

94. Wharton, *House of Mirth*, 107.

95. Cynthia Griffin Wolff argues that *The House of Mirth* is a critique of the aestheticization of women for male pleasure as Wharton's "first *kunstlerroman*." Wolff, *A Feast of Words: The Triumph of Edith Wharton* (London: Oxford University Press, 1977), 107. Elaine Showalter agrees and suggests that the novel is a "fictional house of birth for the woman novelist." See Showalter, "Death of the Lady (Novelist)," 135. Other feminist critics have argued that the "new abhorrent being" Lily discovers in herself is a "female personality produced by a patriarchal society and a capitalist economy" (Showalter, 140). On this, see Ammons, *Edith Wharton's Argument with America*.

96. Walter Benn Michaels concludes *The Gold Standard* with a contentious rereading of the tableau vivant scene in *The House of Mirth*. Lily's "Mrs. Lloyd" had been read by feminist scholars as the reduction of Lily to an "ornamental victim of patriarchy and capitalism," but in Benn Michaels's rereading, it is "a moment of speculation." "If Lily is a victim of patriarchal capitalism," he argues, then "so are Rosedale and Gus Trenor and all the other speculators. Only in the risk-free republic of the spirit can such victimization be escaped" (240). For Benn Michaels, risk illustrates "an irreducible discrepancy between intention and effect" so that Lily's overdose represents a decision "neither to live nor die," but "only to take a chance" (230). To equate Lily's victimization with that of Rosedale and Trenor is absurd. On the contrary, I read Lily's addiction to chance, and to risk, particularly in the final scene, as a desire to escape time, under patriarchal control. Both gambling and speculation involve a projection into the future that suspends the outcome. To escape the world of cause/effect, of action/consequence, and of judgment—that is the real realm of freedom. The republic of the spirit is only free for Lily because it is entirely circumscribed by risk.

97. Wharton, *House of Mirth*, 61.

98. Dale Bauer makes the case for Lily Bart's drug addiction to chloral, linking it with intimacy in *The House of Mirth*. See "Wharton's 'Others': Addiction and Intimacy," in *A Historical Guide to Edith Wharton*, ed. Carol Singley (New York: Oxford University Press, 2003).

99. Wharton, *House of Mirth*, 250.

100. Cynthia Griffin Wolff sees this final scene as Lily arranging herself once more as an "object of aesthetic attention" for Nettie's benefit. See Wolff, *A Feast of Words*, 130–31. See also Showalter, "Death of the Lady (Novelist)," 145.

101. Shari Benstock points out how the novel suffered dire critical consequences in the wake of the New Criticism in the 1940s and 1950s; the aesthetic, formalist grounds of its approach was "ruinous to a novel like *The House of Mirth*, with its strong thematic and moral emphasis" (Benstock, *The House of Mirth*, 316). Blake Nevius's *Edith Wharton: A Study of Her Fiction* (Berkeley: University of California Press, 1953) represented the first major reassessment of her work after her death; and Richard Poirier's 1965 reexamination of American literary history made a strong case for Wharton's distinction from Henry James and her artistic originality (Benstock, 316–17). See Richard Poirier, "Edith Wharton's *The House of Mirth*." *The American Novel: From James Fenimore Cooper to William Faulkner* (New York: Basic Books, 1965), expanded and reprinted as *A World Elsewhere. The Place of Style in American Literature* (New York: Oxford University Press, 1966).

102. Helen Killoran, *The Critical Reception of Edith Wharton* (Rochester, NY: Camden House, 2001), 30. Henry James, "The Younger Generation," review of *The Custom of the Country,* by Edith Wharton, *Times Literary Supplement* (England) (April 2, 1914), 157–58; "Review of *The Custom of the Country,*" *Bookman* (England) 45 (March 9, 1914): 330.

103. Killoran, *Critical Reception*, 30.

104. Pizer dates the earliest suggestion of Wharton's novel as one of naturalist determinism to Blake Nevius, *Edith Wharton: A Study of Her Fiction* (1953), an idea then taken up more fully by Larry Rubin (1957) and Alan Price (1980). See Pizer, "The Naturalism of Edith Wharton's *House of Mirth*," 241–42, 247n1. Subsequent studies by Wai-Chee Dimock (1985), Walter Benn Michaels (1987), Amy Kaplan (1988), and Ruth Yeazell (1992) have rendered Wharton's inclusion in the naturalist canon commonplace.

105. Howard, *Form and History*, 117; Donald Pizer, *The Theory and Practice of American Literary Naturalism* (Carbondale: Southern Illinois University Press, 1993), 165.

106. Follett, "What Edith Wharton Did—And Might Have Done," 2.

107. Dimock (1985); Walter Benn Michaels, *The Gold Standard and the Logic of Naturalism* (Berkeley: University of California Press, 1987), 228.

108. Jennifer L. Fleissner, *Women, Compulsion, Modernity: The Moment of American Naturalism* (Chicago: University of Chicago Press, 2004), 9. Fleissner's account of Lily's compulsive, whirling oscillation—both her recurring indecisiveness and her ongoing circumstantial highs and lows—is itself compelling not least for how it makes the novel's conclusion the symptom rather than the problem

of what Elaine Showalter calls the "novel of the woman of thirty" (Showalter, "Death of the Lady [Novelist]," 39).

109. Fleissner, *Women, Compulsion, Modernity*, 6.

110. Wharton, *House of Mirth*, 16.

111. Fleissner, *Women, Compulsion, Modernity*, 200. Certainly no figure points more to that clock than Rosedale, the only character depicted as sexually reproductive, or remotely fatherly. In a poignant moment when Lily observes him unawares, "kneeling domestically on the drawing-room hearth before his hostess's [Carry Fisher's] little girl," she notices "a quality of homely goodness" in his gestures; they "were not, at any rate, the premeditated and perfunctory endearments of the guest under his hostess's eye . . . something in his attitude made him seem a simple and kindly being compared to the small critical creature who endured his homage" (Wharton, *House of Mirth*, 195).

112. Frederic Jameson, *The Antinomies of Realism* (London: Verso, 2013), 24, 10.

113. See Goran Blix, "Story, Affect, Style," in special issue, "Jameson's *Antinomies of Realism*," Nonsite.org 11 (March 14, 2014), http://nonsite.org/the-tank/jamesons-the-antinomies-of-realism.

114. Maurice Lee, *Uncertain Chances: Science, Skepticism, and Belief in Nineteenth-Century American Literature* (New York: Oxford University Press, 2012), 4–6. Lee asserts that the Civil War is the dividing point, after which the teleological confidence of Americans was upset, and providence was invoked only ironically, for example, in Melville, thus revising Jackson Lears's claim that dialectical tensions between chance and control occurred throughout American history (Lee, 11, 16).

115. Jackson Lears, *Something for Nothing: Luck in America* (New York: Viking Penguin, 2003), 6.

116. Giddens, *Consequences of Modernity*, 18.

117. Lears, *Something for Nothing*, 155.

118. Wharton, *House of Mirth*, 23, 24.

119. Martha Banta argues that Lily "did not know how to win playing at bridge as the truly modern girl does," comparing her to Audrey De Peyster, the successful heroine of Wharton's *Vanity Fair* sketch of October 1916, "Getting on in New York Society." Audrey "smokes, drinks, and plays 'cut throat,'" and unlike Lily is free to choose to marry, free from that "fatal determinant," as Banta calls it, of "must." See Banta, "In Fashion, In History, Out of Time," 80.

120. Wharton, *House of Mirth*, 25.

121. Dale M. Bauer, "Wharton's 'Others,'" 119; emphasis mine.

122. Nancy Armstrong, "Structuralism's Unfinished Business: Lily Bart and Lady Credit," an as-yet-unpublished conference paper delivered at the *Arizona Quarterly* Annual Symposium, Tucson, Arizona, July 2002. I thank her for sharing it with me.

123. Armstrong, "Structuralism's Unfinished Business."

124. Riegel, "Rosedale and Anti-Semitism," 223.

125. Wharton, *House of Mirth*, 233.

126. See Henry James, "The Real Thing," in *The Real Thing and Other Tales* (New York: Macmillan, 1922).

127. Nancy Bentley, "Wharton, Travel and Modernity," in *A Historical Guide to Edith Wharton*, ed. Carol Singley (New York: Oxford University Press, 2003), 149.

128. As Anthony Giddens puts it, the "future-oriented character of modernity is largely structured by trust vested in abstract systems." Rosedale mediates just such trust in the stock market for the novel's characters. See Giddens, *Consequences of Modernity*, 84.

Chapter 4

1. Israel Zangwill, *The Melting-Pot* in *Works of Israel Zangwill* (New York: American Jewish Book Co., 1919), https://archive.org/stream/worksofisraelzan06 zanguoft#page/n3/mode/2up. See also Edna Nahshon, *From the Ghetto to the Melting Pot: Israel Zangwill's Jewish Plays* (Detroit: Wayne State University Press, 2006), 211.

2. Meri-Jane Rochelson, *A Jew in the Public Arena: The Career of Israel Zangwill* (Detroit: Wayne State University Press, 2008), 1. Zangwill also figures prominently in five essays in the collection by Eitan Bar-Yosef and Nadia Valman, eds., *The Jew in Late-Victorian and Edwardian Culture: Between the East End and East Africa* (London: Palgrave Macmillan, 2009). On Jewish religious intermarriage, see Keren R. McGinity, *Still Jewish: A History of Women and Intermarriage in America* (New York: New York University Press, 2009) and Marshall Sklare, "Intermarriage and the Jewish Future," *Commentary*, April 1, 1964, www .commentarymagazine.com/article/intermarriage-the-jewish-future/; see also Julius Drachsler, *Democracy and Assimilation: The Blending of Immigrant Heritages in America* (New York: Macmillan, 1920).

3. Zangwill, *The Melting Pot*, 184–85.

4. Werner Sollors, *Beyond Ethnicity: Consent and Descent in American Culture* (New York: Oxford University Press, 1986), 66.

5. For Sollors, the play "sacrilizes loving consent as the abolition of prejudices of descent" (*Beyond Ethnicity*, 72).

6. Roosevelt, "True Americanism," in *The Works of Theodore Roosevelt, Vol. XV* (New York: Charles Scribner's Sons, 1925), 15–31.

7. Roosevelt, "True Americanism," 24, 25.

8. Louise W. Knight, "Jane Addams and the Settlement House Movement," in *Against the Tide: Women Reformers in American Society*, ed. Paul A. Cimbala and Randall M. Miller (Westport, CT: Praeger, 1997), 85.

9. Jane Addams, "Hull House, Chicago: An Effort Toward Social Democracy," *Forum* (October 1892): 226–41; and "A New Impulse to an Old Gospel," *Forum* (November 1892): 345–58.

10. Knight, "Jane Addams," 91–93. See also, Jane Addams, "The Subjective Necessity for Social Settlements" and "The Objective Value of a Social Settlement," in *Philanthropy and Social Progress* (New York: Thomas Y. Crowell and Co., 1893), 1–56.

11. Roosevelt, "True Americanism," 28.

12. See, e.g., Bruno Lessing, *Children of Men* (1903); Ezra Selig Brudno, *The Tether* (1908); Elias Tobenkin, *Witte Arrives* (1916) and *House of Conrad* (1918); M. E. Ravage, *An American in the Making: The Life Story of an Immigrant* (1917); Sidney Nyburg, *The Chosen People* (1917); John Cournos, *The Mask* (1919); and Fanny Hurst, *Humoresque* (1919). Henry Harland published several novels of "picturesque" Jewish life, some featuring intermarriage, under the pseudonym Sidney Luska: *As It Was Written—A Jewish Musician's Story* (1885), *Mrs. Peixada* (1886), *The Yoke of Thorah* (1887), *My Uncle Florimond* (1888), and *Mr. Sonnenschein's Inheritance* (1888).

13. Adam Sol, "Longings and Renunciation: Attitudes Toward Intermarriage in Early Twentieth Century Jewish American Novels," *American Jewish History* 89, no. 2 (2001): 215.

14. Sol, "Longings and Renunciation," 216.

15. See, e.g., Judith Ann Trolander, *Professionalism and Social Change: From the Settlement House Movement to Neighborhood Centers, 1886 to the Present* (New York: Columbia University Press, 1987), 7–21.

16. Founded in 1895 at 6 and 8 Garland Street in Boston, Hale House takes its name from Dr. Edward Everett Hale (1822–1909), Unitarian clergyman, philanthropist, and author. See Antin, The *Promised Land*, 325, ch. 18, n.2; and Evelyn Salz, *Selected Letters of Mary Antin* (Syracuse, NY: Syracuse University Press, 2000), xiv–xv. On the *American Hebrew*, established in New

York in 1879 as a highbrow newspaper designed "for the perpetuation and elevation of Judaism," see Jonathan Sarna, *American Judaism* (New Haven, CT: Yale University Press, 2004), 136.

17. Antin, *Promised Land*, 277.

18. Mary V. Dearborn, *Love in the Promised Land: The Story of Anzia Yezierska and John Dewey* (New York: Free Press, 1988), 51–66.

19. Dearborn, *Love in the Promised Land*, 107, 122–26.

20. Dearborn, *Love in the Promised Land*, 110–21. These papers were discovered only in 1974. See Louise Levitas Henriksen, *Anzia Yezierska: A Writer's Life* (New Brunswick, NJ: Rutgers University Press, 1988), 6–7.

21. Most critics take their cue from Dearborn; see *Love in the Promised Land*, 68–69, 108–17, 136–38. See also Henriksen, *Anzia Yezierska*, 172; Laura Wexler, "Looking at Yezierska," in *Woman of the Word: Jewish Women and Jewish Writing*, ed. Judith Baskin (Detroit: Wayne State University Press, 1994), 153–81; Thomas J. Ferraro, *Ethnic Passages: Literary Immigrants in Twentieth-Century America* (Chicago: University of Chicago Press, 1993); Alice Kessler-Harris, introduction to *Bread Givers*, by Anzia Yezierska (New York: Persea, 1975), v–xviii; Carol B. Schoen, *Anzia Yezierska* (Boston: Twayne, 1982), 99–101; Natalie Friedman, "Marriage and the Immigrant Narrative: Anzia Yezierska's *Salome of the Tenements*," *Legacy* 22, no. 2 (2005) 176–86; Brooks E. Hefner, "'Slipping Back into the Vernacular': Anzia Yezierska's Vernacular Modernism," *MELUS* 36, no. 3 (2011): 198; Lori Jirousek, "Ethnics and Ethnographers: Zora Neale Hurston and Anzia Yezierska," *Journal of Modern Literature* 29, no. 2 (2006): 20.

22. Dearborn, *Love in the Promised Land*, 137–38.

23. Jirousek, "Ethnics and Ethnographers," 25.

24. Friedman, "Marriage and the Immigrant Narrative," 178, 181.

25. Sol sees Jewish writers looking on intermarriage "with ambivalence," in favor of some "continued identification with their ethnic heritage" ("Longings and Renunciation," 215). While I agree, as in other chapters, here I will argue that the language of affect, of "ambivalence," is a symptom of the temporal tensions these authors negotiate in their fictions.

26. Hasia Diner, *A Time for Gathering: The Second Migration, 1820–1880* (Baltimore: Johns Hopkins University Press, 1992), 173–74.

27. Jacob Rader Marcus, *United States Jewry, 1776–1985* (Detroit, Wayne State University Press, 1993), 3:171–72. The full title was "Prejudice Against

the Jew: its nature, its causes and remedies: a symposium by foremost
Christians published in the *American Hebrew*," April 4, 1890 (New York:
Philip Cowen, 1928). Contributors included President James McCosh of
Princeton University and Charles W. Eliot of Harvard University; Bish-
ops Potter, Littlejohn, and Coxe; literary men like John Burroughs, Oliver
Wendell Holmes, William Dean Howells, Thomas Wentworth Higginson
Sr., Washington Gladden, and George W. Curtis; and representing pub-
lic men and politicians, Zebulon B. Vance, Charles D. Warner, Theodore
Roosevelt, and others. See also Rochelson, *A Jew in the Public Arena*, 65,
110; and Frank H. Vizetelly, who writes that the symposium was called "A
Consensus on Prejudice" (Vizetelly, "The American Hebrew," in *The Jewish
Encyclopedia*, 1906, www.jewishencyclopedia.com/articles/1387-american
-hebrew-the#ixzz0yElrpynv).

28. Oliver Wendell Holmes, *Over the Teacups* (Boston: Houghton, Mifflin, 1891),
193.

29. Marcus, *United States Jewry*, 168.

30. As discussed in chapter 3, the Seligman-Hilton affair was the first public antisemitic scandal in the United States to date, considered with the Dreyfus affair in
France (1894–1906) to be a key manifestation of modern antisemitism. Joseph
Seligman and his family, although longtime patrons, were denied entrance into
the Grand Union Hotel in Saratoga, New York. As reported in the *New York
Times*, when the family entered the parlors, the manager said, "Mr. Seligman, I
am required to inform you that Mr. Hilton has given instructions that no Israelites shall be permitted in future to stop at this hotel." When asked why Jews
were thus persecuted, the manager told Seligman, "Christians did not like their
company." "A Sensation at Saratoga," *New York Times*, June 19, 1877, 8, www
.sekonassociation.com/files/NYTimes_June_19_1877_overall_article_about
_Hilton_affair.pdf.

31. Holmes, *Over the Teacups*, 194.

32. Marcus, *United States Jewry*, 172.

33. The first was "The Great Jewish Invasion" (1907), and later the "Jewish Inva-
sion of America" (1913), both published in *McClure's Magazine*. See Marcus,
United States Jewry, 177. *McClure's Magazine* was a muckraking magazine;
Lincoln Steffens, treated at greater length in chapter 1, worked and had a close
relationship with S. S. McClure. See Frank Luther Mott, *A History of American
Magazines*, 5 vols. (Cambridge: Belknap Press, 1968); and Harold Wilson,

McClure's Magazine and the Muckrakers (Princeton, NJ: Princeton University Press, 1970). I discuss "The Great Jewish Invasion" in more depth in this chapter and in chapter 1.

34. Eliane Glaser, *Judaism without Jews: Philosemitism and Christian Polemic in Early Modern England* (Basingstoke: Palgrave, 2007). Glaser's study brings early modern English and early modern Jewish history together to argue that the emergence of a Jewish community in England after four centuries can only be understood in the historical context of the readmission of the Jews.

35. Burton J. Hendrick, "The Great Jewish Invasion," *McClure's Magazine* 28 (January 1907), 314, 316–17.

36. Hendrick, "Will the Jews Disappear," *American Hebrew*, August 3, 1917, 337.

37. Hendrick, *The Jews in America* (New York: Doubleday, 1923), 2, https://archive.org/details/jewsinamerica00hend.

38. See Arnold Eisen, *Galut: Modern Jewish Reflection on Homelessness and Homecoming* (Bloomington: Indiana University Press, 1986). On the fictional shtetl in modern Yiddish literature, see Dan Miron, "The Literary Image of the Shtetl," *Jewish Social Studies* 1, no. 3 (1995): 1–43.

39. Marcus, *United States Jewry*, 177–78. See E. A. Ross, *The Old World in the New: The Significance of Past and Present Immigration to the American People* (1914).

40. Marcus, *United States Jewry*, 178. See also, Madison Grant, *Passing of the Great Race; Or, The Racial Basis of European History* (New York: Charles Scribner's Sons, 1936), https://archive.org/details/passingofgreatra00granuoft.

41. See Mary V. Dearborn, *Pocahontas's Daughters: Gender and Ethnicity in American Culture* (New York: Oxford University Press, 1986), 42; Matthew Frye Jacobson, *Barbarian Virtues: The United States Encounters Foreign Peoples at Home and Abroad, 1876–1917* (New York: Hill, 2000), 206; Sarah Blacher Cohen, "Mary Antin's *The Promised Land*: A Breach of Promise," *Studies in American Jewish Literature* 3, no. 2 (1977): 31–32; Babak Elahi, "The Heavy Garments of the Past: Mary and Frieda Antin in *The Promised Land*," *College Literature* 32, no. 4 (2005): 29–49; Michael P. Kramer, "Assimilation in *The Promised Land*: Mary Antin and the Jewish Origins of the American Self," *Prooftexts* 18, no. 2 (1998): 123–28.

42. Maria Karafilis, "The Jewish Ghetto and the Americanization of Space in Mary Antin and Her Contemporaries," *American Literary Realism* 42, no. 2 (2010): 147–48.

43. Zangwill was both Antin's mentor and her interlocutor. He wrote the foreword for her first published book, *From Plotzk to Boston* (1899), and exchanged

letters with her as she continued writing and publishing short stories and eventually *The Promised Land*, well through 1914. See Salz, *Selected Letters of Mary Antin*, 3. 4–39, 45, 47–50, 152.

44. Mary Antin, Letter to Ellery Sedgwick, July 19, 1911, in Salz, *Selected Letters of Mary Antin*, 52–53.

45. Jules Chametzky, introduction to *The Promised Land by Mary Antin* (New York: The Modern Library, 2001), xii.

46. Antin, Letter to Ellery Sedgwick, July 30, 1911, in Salz, *Selected Letters of Mary Antin*, 55.

47. Antin, *The Promised Land*, 3.

48. See Chametzky, introduction to *The Promised Land*, ix–xi. Chametzky also lingers over the descriptions in the "Exodus" chapter about the family's harrowing railroad journey from Russia to Germany and subsequent experience of mass delousing there, as seemingly prescient from a post–World War Two point of view. See Chametzky, introduction to *The Promised Land*, xvii–xviii. On xenophobia and immigration restriction, see John Higham, *Send These to Me: Immigrants in Urban America*, rev. ed. (New York: Atheneum, 1975), 43.

49. *The Promised Land* uses this spelling of Polotzk from the first edition onward, as opposed to that in the title of Antin's first book, *From Plotzk to Boston*. See Antin, *The Promised Land* (Boston: Houghton Mifflin, 1912), https://archive.org/stream/promisedland02antigoog#page/n11/mode/2up. All citations, however, are from the 2001 edition.

50. Jolie A. Sheffer, "Recollecting, Repeating, and Walking Through: Immigration, Trauma, and Space in Mary Antin's *The Promised Land*," *MELUS* 35, no. 1 (2010): 141; Sarah Sillin, "Heroine, Reformer, Citizen: Novelistic Conventions in Antin's *The Promised Land*," *MELUS* 38, no. 3 (2013): 25.

51. Antin, *Promised Land* (New York: Modern Library, 2001), 6.

52. Chametzky, introduction to *The Promised Land*, xi.

53. Sarah Blacher Cohen, "Mary Antin's *The Promised Land*: A Breach of Promise," *Studies in American Jewish Literature* 3, no. 2 (1977): 32.

54. Kramer thinks Antin's assimilationism should all the more "place her in the mainstream of Jewish-American literary history"; Michael P. Kramer, "Assimilation in *The Promised Land*," 124.

55. Salz, *Selected Letters of Mary Antin*, xviii–xix.

56. Antin, Letter to Ellery Sedgwick, July 31, 1911, in Salz, *Selected Letters of Mary Antin*, 56.

57. Antin, *Promised Land*, 99.

58. Henry James, *The American Scene* (New York: Penguin, 1994), 101.

59. Horace Kallen, "Democracy Versus the Melting Pot: A Study of American Nationality, Part I" *The Nation*, February 18, 1915, 190–94, http://www.unz.com/print/Nation-1915feb18-00190a02/, and "Democracy Versus the Melting Pot: A Study of American Nationality, Part II" *The Nation*, February 25, 1915, 217–20, http://www.unz.com/print/Nation-1915feb25-00217/.

60. Kallen, "Democracy Versus the Melting Pot," Part I, 192.

61. Kallen, "Democracy Versus the Melting Pot," Part II, 217.

62. Kallen, "Democracy Versus the Melting Pot," Part I, 191.

63. Kallen, "Democracy Versus the Melting Pot," Part II, 219.

64. John Dewey, "Nationalizing Education," in *From Many, One: Readings in American Political and Social Thought*, ed. Richard C. Sinopoli (Washington, D.C., Georgetown University Press, 1997), 209.

65. See Dearborn, *Love in the Promised Land*, 83–106, 107–39; and Jirousek, "Ethnics and Ethnographers," 19.

66. Jirousek, "Ethnics and Ethnographers," 20.

67. See Dearborn, *Love in the Promised Land*, 136–37; Friedman, "Marriage and the Immigrant Narrative," 176–86.

68. Anzia Yezierska, *Salome of the Tenements* (Urbana: University of Illinois Press, 1995).

69. For an extended study of the figure of the "Jewess" in British literature, see Nadia Valman, *The Jewess in Nineteenth-Century British Literary Culture* (Cambridge: Cambridge University Press, 2007).

70. Yezierska, *Salome of the Tenements*, 106.

71. Walter M. Pater, *Studies in the History of the Renaissance* (London: Macmillan, 1873), 210.

72. Yezierska, *Salome of the Tenements*, 24, 26.

73. Anzia Yezierska, *Bread Givers* (New York: Persea, 1999), 155.

74. Susan Glenn notes how even Eastern European Jewish women who were breadwinners were treated as second-class citizens: education and other higher pursuits were always reserved for men. See Susan Glenn, *Daughters of the Shtetl: Life and Labor in the Immigrant Generation* (Ithaca, NY: Cornell University Press, 1990), 8.

75. Yezierska, *Bread Givers*, 16.

76. On Jewish immigrant women and "white slavery," see Margit Stange, *Personal Property: Wives, White Slaves, and the Market in Women* (Baltimore: Johns Hopkins University Press, 1998).

77. Yezierska, *Bread Givers*, 273, 294.

78. Antin, *The Promised Land*, 6.

79. Yezierska, *Bread Givers*, 205.

80. Wexler, "Looking at Yezierska," 165.

81. Yezierska, *Bread Givers*, 232.

Coda

1. Esther Schor, *Emma Lazarus* (New York: Schocken, 2006), 15–16.

2. In 1850, however, it reopened for religious services only, for visitors and the children of those who lived in Newport, but not regularly during summers. Rabbi D. De Sola Pool, "Some Notes on the Touro Synagogue," *Touro Synagogue of Congregation Jeshuat Israel* (Newport, RI: Friends of Touro Synagogue, 1948), 10–11. According to De Sola Pool the Touro Synagogue was antedated in the western hemisphere only by Mikveh Israel Synagogue in Curacao (1732), and the Zedek ve Shalom Synagogue in Paramaribo, Surinam (1737). Since the first building ever erected for a synagogue in the United States, in New York in 1730, no longer exists, the Touro Synagogue represents the second oldest Jewish community in United States, and the oldest synagogue building. In its nearby cemetery, the tombstones are written in Hebrew, English, Spanish, Portuguese, and Latin, but the architecture of the building is Sephardic, like the mother one in Amsterdam (8). By 1881, it was used for services on High Holy days, and by 1883, the Jewish permanent settlers numbered large enough for regular Shabbat services (11). Scrolls were donated by Mr. Alfred A. Marcus, descendent of the Newport community of a century earlier, since until that point, scrolls were brought back and forth from New York. The year 1883 thus marks the synagogue's shift from a "historic shrine" to an active synagogue (12).

3. The first draft is published in Pool, *Touro Synagogue*, 44, 47–48. For the definitive version, see Henry Wadsworth Longfellow, "The Jewish Cemetery at Newport" (1852), in *The Complete Poetical Works of Henry Wadsworth Longfellow* (Boston: Houghton, Mifflin, 1893), 191–92, https://archive.org/stream/completepoeti00long#page/n11/mode/2up.

4. Emma Lazarus, *Admetus and Other Poems* (New York: Hurd and Houghton, 1871), 160–62, https://archive.org/stream/cu31924022036259#page/n5/mode/2up.

5. Schor, *Emma Lazarus*, 16.

6. Schor, *Emma Lazarus*, 17.

7. Pool, *Touro Synagogue*, 49.

8. Louis Harap sees Holmes's attitude as marked by "amiable tolerance," but I hope I have, by now, shown otherwise. See Harap, *The Image of the Jew in American Literature: From Early Republic to Mass Immigration* (Syracuse, NY: Syracuse University Press, 2003), 86.

9. Michael Dobkowski, *The Tarnished Dream: The Basis of American Anti-Semitism* (Westport, CT: Greenwood, 1979), 114.

10. Philip Freneau, *The Poems of Philip Freneau: Poet of the American Revolution*, ed. Fred Lewis Pattee, 3 vols. (Princeton, NJ: The University Library, 1902–7), 2:267, https://archive.org/details/poemsphilipfren02frengoog.

11. Freneau, *The Poems of Philip Freneau*, 1:270–71, https://archive.org/details/cu31924091302343.

12. See Harap, *Image of the Jew*, 136–44.

13. Bryant wrote no poems on Jewish themes, but in 1866 commented on Jews as noble Hebrews in a review of Edwin Booth's Shylock (Harap, *Image of the Jew*, 83–84). Whittier's early poems on biblical themes make little mention of Jews, but two late poems, "The Rabbi Ishmael" and "The Two Rabbins" (1881), praise Jews by Christianizing them (Harap, 86).

14. Bette Roth Young, *Emma Lazarus in her World: Life and Letters* (Philadelphia, Jewish Publication Society, 1995), 6.

15. Young, *Emma Lazarus in Her World*, 6.

16. "Judge Hilton's Statement," published together with "A Sensation at Saratoga," *New York Times*, June 19, 1877.

17. On Seligman and Emanu-El, see Howard Radest, *Toward Common Ground: The Story of the Ethical Societies in the United States* (New York: Fredrick Ungar, 1969). See also Benny Kraut, *From Reform Judaism to Ethical Culture: The Religious Evolution of Felix Adler* (Cincinnati: Hebrew Union College Press, 1979). On the popular ignorance of the Jewish Reform movement in the 1870s, see Hasia Diner, *A Time for Gathering: The Second Migration, 1820–1880* (Baltimore: Johns Hopkins University Press, 1992), 181–85.

18. "Judge Hilton's Statement," *New York Times*, June 19, 1877.

19. Schor, *Emma Lazarus*, 19.

20. Gregory Eiselein, introduction to *Emma Lazarus: Selected Poems and Other Writings* (Ontario: Broadview Press, 2002), 15. See also Schor, *Emma Lazarus*, 20–23.

21. Schor, *Emma Lazarus*, 65, 73–79. Lazarus's translation of Heinrich Heine, *Poems and Ballads of Heinrich Heine*, was published in 1881. The other

translated poems were collected in Emma Lazarus, *Songs of a Semite: The Dance to Death, and Other Poems* (New York: Office of "The American Hebrew," 1882).

22. Lazarus, *Songs of a Semite*, https://archive.org/stream/songsofsemite00lazarich #page/n1/mode/2up. Ranen Omer-Sherman goes even further, to call Lazarus's belated return to Judaism "an unqualified conversion," and powerfully illustrates the shaping impact on Lazarus's poetry of Eliot's blend of philosemitic utopianism and antisemitic stereotyping, Eliot's "relentlessly romantic dichotomizing between noble Jews and Jewesses and their shopkeeping brethren." See Ranen Omer-Sherman, *Diaspora and Zionism in Jewish American Literature: Lazarus, Syrkin, Reznikoff, and Roth* (Hanover, NH: Brandeis University Press, 2002), 16, 48–49.

23. "Raschi in Prague," in Emma Lazarus, *Poems of Emma Lazarus: Volume II: Jewish Poems and Translations*, ed. Susan L. Rattiner (Mineola, NY: Dover, 2015), 25–40.

24. Lazarus, *Poems of Emma Lazarus*, 12–14.

25. Timayenis would go on to found the antisemitic Minerva press in 1888. See Jacob Rader Marcus, *United States Jewry, 1776–1985* (Detroit, Wayne State University Press, 1993), 3:173.

26. Ranen Omer-Sherman, *Diaspora and Zionism*, 23. Lazarus chronicled her first visit to the refugees in "Among the Russian Jews," an unsigned article in the *New York Times*, March 26, 1881. See Schor, *Emma Lazarus*, 125, 147–50.

27. Eiselein, introduction to *Emma Lazarus*, 25. See also Lazarus, *The Dance to Death*, in *Songs of a Semite*, 5–48.

28. Schor, *Emma Lazarus*, 86–90. The plea for religious tolerance is also a theme in earlier influential works such as Gotthold Ephraim Lessing's *Nathan the Wise* (1779) and Sir Walter Scott's novel *Ivanhoe* (1813). As discussed in chapter 4, English-Jewish playwright Israel Zangwill picks up this theme in his famous play, *The Melting-Pot* (1908), reviving the profoundly redemptive ending in support of assimilationist ideology.

29. See Penina Moïse, "Miriam" (1845) and Adah Isaacs Menken, "Judith" (1868) in *Jewish American Literature: A Norton Anthology*, ed. Jules Chametzky et al. (New York: Norton, 2001), 70–71, 88–89.

30. Lazarus, *The Dance to Death*, act V, scene 1, in *Songs of a Semite*, 42; See Schor, *Emma Lazarus*, 86–90; and Julian Levinson, *Exiles on Main Street: Jewish American Writers and American Literary Culture* (Bloomington: Indiana University Press, 2008), 29–31.

31. Schor, *Emma Lazarus*, 90.

32. Lazarus, *The Dance to Death*, act V, scene 3, in *Songs of a Semite*, 46.

33. Julian Levinson argues that because the "redemptive conclusion" of the Book of Esther is here "preempted," its evocation "ironically belies the town's Jews' insistence on the remoteness of the biblical word and its hardships," so that ancient history repeats itself, only "without the saving intervention of God." See Levinson, *Exiles on Main Street*, 30.

34. R. Barbara Gitenstein, *Apocalyptic Messianism and Contemporary Jewish-American Poetry* (Albany, SUNY Press, 1986), 4–5.

35. Omer-Sherman, *Diaspora and Zionism*, 16, 48–49.

36. Schor, *Emma Lazarus*, 88.

37. Levinson, *Exiles on Main Street*, 31.

38. Lazarus's poems on Hebraic figures and biblical themes include "Remember" (1866), "In the Jewish Synagogue at Newport" (1867), and "The Valley of the Baca" (1872); 1877 translations of Yehuda Halevi's "Admonition," Solomon Ibn Gabirol's "Meditation on Death," and Moses Ben Ezra's "In the Night"; then later, "Raschi in Prague" (1880), "Death of Raschi" (1880), and "The Banner of the Jew" (1882).

39. Jonathan Sarna, *American Judaism* (New Haven, CT: Yale University Press, 2004), 140.

40. Emma Lazarus, "Was the Earl of Beaconsfield a Representative Jew?" *Century Magazine* 23, no. 6 (1882): 939–40.

41. Omer-Sherman, *Diaspora and Zionism*, 57.

42. Mme. Z. Ragozin, "Russian Jews and Gentiles: from a Russian point of view," *Century Magazine* 23, no. 6 (1882): 905–20.

43. Ragozin, "Russian Jews and Gentiles," 919.

44. Emma Lazarus, "Russian Christianity Versus Modern Judaism," *Century Magazine* 24 (May 1882): 48–56.

45. Emma Lazarus, "The Jewish Problem," *Century Magazine* 25 (February 1885): 602–11. See Young, *Emma Lazarus in her World*, 61–62.

46. Lazarus, "The Jewish Problem," 610.

47. See Theodor Herzl, *A Jewish State: An Attempt at a Modern Solution of the Jewish Question* (1896; repr., New York: Federation of American Zionists, 1917), https://archive.org/details/cu31924028579781.

48. John Fea, "Blackstone, William E." American National Biography Online, February 2000, www.anb.org/articles/08/08-01994.html.

49. Fea, "Blackstone."

50. For what promises to be an in-depth historical excavation and analysis of the phenomenon, see Samuel Goldman's forthcoming study, *God's Country: Christian Zionism in America* (Philadelphia: University of Pennsylvania Press, forthcoming).

51. Grace Paley, "Faith in the Afternoon," in *Enormous Changes at the Last Minute* (New York: Farrar, Straus and Giroux, 1985), 32, 49.

52. See Victoria Aarons, "Grace Paley," in *Jewish American Women Writers*, ed. Ann R. Shapiro, et al. (Westport, CT: Greenwood, 1994), 283.

53. Grace Paley, "Goodbye and Good Luck," in *The Little Disturbances of Man* (New York: Penguin, 1987), 10, 14.

54. Omer-Sherman, *Diaspora and Zionism*, 16.

BIBLIOGRAPHY

PRIMARY SOURCES

Addams, Jane. "Hull House, Chicago: An Effort Toward Social Democracy." *Forum* (October 1892): 226–41.

Addams, Jane. "A New Impulse to an Old Gospel." *Forum* (November 1892): 345–58.

Addams, Jane. "The Objective Value of a Social Settlement." In *Philanthropy and Social Progress*. New York: Thomas Y. Crowell and Co., 1893.

Addams, Jane. "The Subjective Necessity for Social Settlements." In *Philanthropy and Social Progress*. New York: Thomas Y. Crowell and Co., 1893.

Aiken, Albert W. *The Genteel Spotter or The Night Hawks of New York, A Tale of the Lawless*. Beadle's Dime Library 25, no. 320. New York: Beadle and Adams, December 10, 1884.

Alger, Horatio. *Ragged Dick, or Street Life in New York with Boot Blacks*. New York: Norton, 2008.

"Among the Russian Jews." *New York Times*, March 26, 1881.

Antin, Mary. *The Promised Land*. Boston: Houghton Mifflin, 1912. https://archive.org/stream/promisedland02antigoog#page/n11/mode/2up.

Antin, Mary. *The Promised Land*. New York: The Modern Library, 2001.

Arnold, Matthew. *Culture and Anarchy and Other Writings*. Edited by Stefan Collini. Cambridge: Cambridge University Press, 1993.

Arnold, Matthew. "Hebraism and Hellenism." In *Culture and Anarchy and Other Writings*, edited by Stefan Collini. Cambridge: Cambridge University Press, 1993.

Bauer, Bruno. *Die Judenfrage*. Braunschweig, 1843.

Beecher, Henry Ward. "Jew and Gentile." Sermon delivered on June 24, 1877, printed first in the *Christian Union* and reprinted in *An Hour with the "American Hebrew*," 51–76. New York: Jesse Haney and Company, 1879.

Bellamy, Edward. *Looking Backward, 2000–1887*. Oxford: Oxford University Press, 2007.

Brandeis, Louis. "Speech to the Conference of Eastern Council of Reform Rabbis, April 25, 1915." www.zionism-israel.com/hdoc/Brandeis_Jewish_Problem.htm.

Cahan, Abraham. *The Education of Abraham Cahan*. Translated by Leon Stein, et al. Philadelphia: Jewish Publication Society of America, 1969.

Cahan, Abraham. *The Imported Bridegroom, and Other Stories of the New York Ghetto.* Boston: Houghton, Mifflin and Co., 1898.

Cahan, Abraham. *The Rise of David Levinsky.* New York: Harper and Row, 1960.

Cahan, Abraham. *Yekl and the Imported Bridegroom and Other Stories of Yiddish New York.* Mineola, New York: Dover. 1970.

Campbell, Helen. *Prisoners of Poverty: Women Wage-Workers, Their Trades and Their Lives.* Boston, 1889.

Campbell, Helen. *The Problem of the Poor: A Record of Quiet Work in Unquiet Places.* New York, 1882.

Campbell, Helen. *Women Wage-Earners: Their Past, Their Present, and Their Future.* Boston, 1893.

Craig, Alexander. *Ionia; Land of Wise Men and Fair Women.* Chicago: E. A. Weeks, 1898.

Crèvecoeur, J. Hector St. John de. "What Is an American?" In *Letters from an American Farmer*, edited by Susan Manning. Oxford: Oxford University Press, 1998.

Defoe, Daniel. *The Best of Defoe's Review.* Edited by William Payne. New York: Columbia University Press, 1951.

Dewey, John. "Nationalizing Education." In *From Many, One: Readings in American Political and Social Thought*, edited by Richard C. Sinopoli. Washington, DC: Georgetown University Press, 1997.

Donnelle, A. J. *The Battle of Gettysburg Cyclorama.* Boston, 1886.

Dreiser, Theodore. *The Hand of the Potter: A Tragedy in Four Acts.* New York: Boni and Liveright, 1918.

Eliot, George. *Daniel Deronda.* London: Penguin, 1995.

Freneau, Philip. *The Poems of Philip Freneau: Poet of the American Revolution*, 3 vols. Edited by Fred Lewis Pattee. Princeton, NJ: The University Library, 1902–7. https://archive.org/details/cu31924091302343; https://archive.org/details/poemsphilipfren02frengoog; https://archive.org/details/poemsphilipfren01frengoog

Garland, Hamlin. *Crumbling Idols: Twelve Essays on Art Dealing Chiefly with Literature Painting and the Drama.* Edited by Jane Johnson. Cambridge, MA: Belknap Press, 1960.

Grant, Madison. *Passing of the Great Race; Or, The Racial Basis of European History.* New York: Charles Scribner's Sons, 1936. https://archive.org/details/passingofgreatra00granuoft.

Hapgood, Hutchins. *The Spirit of the Ghetto.* Edited and Introduction by Moses Rischin. Cambridge, MA: Belknap Press, 1967.

Hapgood, Hutchins. *The Spirit of the Ghetto: Studies of the Jewish Quarter of New York.* Illustrated by Jacob Epstein. 1902. New York: Funk and Wagnalls, 1965.

Hendrick, Burton J. "The Great Jewish Invasion," *McClure's Magazine* 28 (January 1907): 307–21.

Hendrick, Burton J. *The Jews in America*. New York: Doubleday, 1923. https://archive .org/details/jewsinamerica00hend.

Hendrick, Burton J. "Will the Jews Disappear?" *American Hebrew*, August 3, 1917.

Herzl, Theodor. *A Jewish State: An Attempt at a Modern Solution of the Jewish Question*. 1896. New York: Federation of American Zionists, 1917. https://archive.org/ details/cu31924028579781.

Holmes, Oliver Wendell. *The Complete Poetical Works of Oliver Wendell Holmes*. Cambridge Edition. Boston: Houghton Mifflin, 1895. https://archive.org/stream/ complete00holm#page/n7/mode/2up.

Holmes, Oliver Wendell. *Over the Teacups*. Boston: Houghton, Mifflin, 1891.

Howells, William Dean. "The Man of Letters as a Man of Business." In *Criticism and Fiction and Other Essays*, edited by Clara Marburg Kirk and Rudolf Kirk. New York: New York University Press, 1959.

Howells, William Dean. "New York Low Life in Fiction." *New York World*, July 26, 1896, 18.

Ingraham, Joseph Holt. *The Throne of David; From the Consecration of the Shepherd of Bethlehem, to the Rebellion of Prince Absalom*. Philadelphia: G. G. Evans, 1860. https://archive.org/stream/thronedavidfrom01ingrgoog#page/n2/mode/2up.

James, Henry. *The American*. New York: Penguin, 1981.

James, Henry. *The American Scene*. New York: Penguin, 1994.

James, Henry. "Americans Abroad." *Nation* 27 (October 3, 1878): 208–9.

James, Henry. "The Art of Fiction." In *Henry James, The Critical Muse: Selected Literary Criticism*, edited by Roger Gard. London: Penguin, 1987.

James, Henry. "Daniel Deronda." In *Henry James, The Critical Muse: Selected Literary Criticism*, edited by Roger Gard. London: Penguin, 1987.

James, Henry. "Democracy and Theodore Roosevelt." In *Henry James: The American Essays*, edited by Leon Edel. New York: Vintage, 1956.

James, Henry. *The Golden Bowl*. New York: Penguin, 1985.

James, Henry. "Honoré de Balzac." In *Henry James, The Critical Muse: Selected Literary Criticism*, edited by Roger Gard. London: Penguin, 1987.

James, Henry. *The Portrait of a Lady*. London: Penguin, 1986.

James, Henry. "The Pupil." In *The Complete Tales of Henry James*, edited by Leon Edel. Philadelphia: J. B. Lippincott, 1963.

James, Henry. "The Real Thing." In *The Real Thing and Other Tales*. New York: Macmillan, 1922.

James, Henry. "The Younger Generation." Review of *The Custom of Our Country*, by Edith Wharton. *Times Literary Supplement* (England), April 2, 1914, 157–58.

James, William. "What Pragmatism Means." In *William James: Writings 1902–1910*, edited by Bruce Kuklick. New York: Library of America, 1987.

"Jewish Clothiers of One Mind." *New York Times*, June 22, 1877.

Jones, Reverend Jesse H. *Joshua Davidson, Christian*. New York: Grafton, 1907.

"Judge Hilton's Position." New York Times, June 20, 1877.

"Judge Hilton's Statement." New York Times, June 19, 1877.

Kallen, Horace. "Democracy Versus the Melting Pot: A Study of American Nationality, Part I." *The Nation*, February 18, 1915, 190–94. www.unz.com/print/Nation-1915feb18-00190a02/.

Kallen, Horace. "Democracy Versus the Melting Pot: A Study of American Nationality, Part II" *The Nation*, February 25, 1915, 217–20, www.unz.com/print/Nation-1915feb25-00217/.

Kitto, John. *An Illustrated History of the Holy Bible*. Norwich: H. Bill, 1868.

Lazarus, Emma. *Admetus and Other Poems*. New York: Hurd and Houghton, 1871. https://archive.org/stream/cu31924022036259#page/n5/mode/2up.

Lazarus, Emma. "The Jewish Problem." *Century Magazine* 25 (February 1885): 602–11.

Lazarus, Emma. *Poems of Emma Lazarus: Volume II: Jewish Poems and Translations*. Edited by Susan L. Rattiner. Mineola, NY: Dover, 2015.

Lazarus, Emma. "Russian Christianity Versus Modern Judaism." *Century Magazine* 24 (May 1882): 48–56.

Lazarus, Emma. *Songs of a Semite: The Dance to Death, and Other Poems*. New York: Office of "The American Hebrew," 1882. https://archive.org/stream/songsofsemite00lazarich#page/n1/mode/2up.

Lazarus, Emma. "Was the Earl of Beaconsfield a Representative Jew?" *Century Magazine* 23, no. 6 (1882): 939–41.

Longfellow, Henry Wadsworth. "The Jewish Cemetery at Newport." In *The Complete Poetical Works of Henry Wadsworth Longfellow*. Boston: Houghton Mifflin, 1893. https://archive.org/stream/completepoeti00long#page/n11/mode/2up.

Marx, Karl. "On the Jewish Question." In *Selected Writings*, edited by David McLellan. Oxford: Oxford University Press, 2000, 46–63.

Mason, Caroline Atwater. *A Woman of Yesterday*. New York: Doubleday, Page & Co, 1900.

Menken, Adah Isaacs. "Judith." In *Jewish American Literature: A Norton Anthology*, edited by Jules Chametzky et al., 88–89. New York: Norton, 2001.

Miller, Joaquin. *The Building of the City Beautiful*. Trenton, NJ: Albert Brandt, 1905.

Moïse, Penina. "Miriam." In *Jewish American Literature: A Norton Anthology*, edited by Jules Chametzky et al., 70–71. New York: Norton, 2001.

"No Jews Need Apply." *New York Tribune*, June 20, 1877.

Paley, Grace. "Faith in the Afternoon." In *Enormous Changes at the Last Minute*. New York: Farrar, Straus and Giroux, 1985.

Paley, Grace. "Goodbye and Good Luck." In *The Little Disturbances of Man*. New York: Penguin, 1987.

Potok, Chaim. *The Chosen*. New York: Ballantine, 1967.

"Prejudice Against the Jew: its nature, its causes and remedies: a symposium by foremost Christians published in the *American Hebrew*." April 4, 1890. New York: Philip Cowen, 1928.

Ragozin, Mme. Z. "Russian Jews and Gentiles: From a Russian Point of View." *Century Magazine* 23, no. 6 (1882): 905–20.

Renan, Ernest. *The Life of Jesus*. London: Trubner and Company, 1864.

"A Reply to Judge Hilton." *New York Times*, June 20, 1877.

"Review of *The Custom of the Country*." *Bookman* (England) 45 (March 9, 1914): 330.

Riis, Jacob. *How the Other Half Lives: Studies Among the Tenements of New York*. New York: Hill and Wang, 1957.

Riis, Jacob. *The Making of an American*. New York: Macmillan, 1970.

Roosevelt, Theodore. "True Americanism." In *The Works of Theodore Roosevelt*. New York: Charles Scribner & Sons, 1925.

Ross, E. A. *The Old World in the New: The Significance of Past and Present Immigration to the American People*. 1914.

Salz, Evelyn. *Selected Letters of Mary Antin*. Syracuse, NY: Syracuse University Press, 2000.

Schappes, Morris, ed. *Emma Lazarus: Selections from her Poetry and Prose*. New York: Cooperative Book League, 1944.

"A Sensation at Saratoga." *New York Times*, June 19, 1877. www.sekonassociation .com/files/NYTimes_June_19_1877_overall_article_about_Hilton_affair.pdf.

Shanly, Charles Dawson. "The Bowery at Night." *Atlantic Monthly* 20, no. 121 (1867): 602–8.

Sheridan, General George A. "Address of General George A. Sheridan, delivered upon May 22nd, 1886, at the opening of the Cyclorama of Vicksburg, New York City." New York, 1886.

Stowe, Calvin E. "The Talmud." *Atlantic Monthly* 21, no. 128 (1868): 673–85.

Tourgee, Albion W. *Murvale Eastman: Christian Socialist*. New York: Fords, Howard and Hulbert, 1891.

Wharton, Edith. *A Backward Glance*. New York: D. Appleton-Century, 1934. https://archive.org/stream/backwardglance030620mbp#page/n9/mode/2up/search/my+last+page.

Wharton, Edith. *The House of Mirth*. New York: Norton, 1990.

Yezierska, Anzia. *Bread Givers*. New York: Persea, 1999.

Yezierska, Anzia. *Salome of the Tenements*. Urbana: University of Illinois Press, 1995.

Zangwill, Israel. "The Melting-Pot." In *Works of Israel Zangwill*. New York: American Jewish Book Co., 1919. https://archive.org/stream/worksofisraelzan06zanguoft#page/n3/mode/2up.

SECONDARY SOURCES

Aarons, Victoria. "Grace Paley." In *Jewish American Women Writers*, edited by Ann R. Shapiro, et al. Westport, CT: Greenwood, 1994.

Adler, Cyrus, and Joseph Jacobs, "Seligman." In *The Jewish Encyclopedia*, 1906, www.jewishencyclopedia.com/articles/13403-seligman.

Allen, Thomas M. *A Republic in Time: Temporality and Social Imagination in Nineteenth-Century America*. Chapel Hill: University of North Carolina Press, 2008.

Ammons, Elizabeth. *Edith Wharton's Argument with America*. Athens: University of Georgia Press, 1980.

Anderson, Amanda. "Cosmopolitanism, Universalism, and the Divided Legacies of Modernity." In *Cosmopolitics: Thinking and Feeling beyond the Nation*, edited by Pheng Cheah and Bruce Robbins. Minneapolis: University of Minnesota Press, 1998.

Anderson, Amanda. "George Eliot and the Jewish Question." *Yale Journal of Criticism* 10, no. 1 (1997): 39–61.

Anderson, Amanda. *The Powers of Distance: Cosmopolitanism and the Cultivation of Detachment*. Princeton, NJ: Princeton University Press, 2001.

Anesko, Michael. *"Friction with the Market": Henry James and the Profession of Authorship*. New York: Oxford University Press, 1986.

Appadurai, Arjun. "Introduction: Commodities and the Politics of Value." In *The Social Life of Things: Commodities in Cultural Perspective*, edited by Arjun Appadurai. Cambridge: Cambridge University Press, 1986.

Appiah, Kwame Anthony. *Cosmopolitanism: Ethics in a World of Strangers*. New York: Norton, 2006.

Ariel, Yaakov. "'It's All in the Bible': Evangelical Christians, Biblical Literalism, and Philosemitism in Our Times." In *Philosemitism in History*, edited by Jonathan Karp and Adam Sutcliffe. Cambridge: Cambridge University Press, 2011.

Asad, Talal. *Formations of the Secular: Christianity, Islam, Modernity.* Stanford, CA: Stanford University Press, 2003.

"Atlanta Cyclorama." Atlanta History Center. www.atlantahistorycenter.com/explore/destinations/atlanta-cyclorama.

Baker, Jennifer. *Securing the Commonwealth: Debt, Speculation, and Writing in the Making of Early America.* Baltimore: Johns Hopkins University Press, 2005.

Bakhtin, M. M. *The Dialogic Imagination.* Edited by Michael Holquist. Translated by Caryl Emerson and Michael Holquist. Austin: University of Texas Press, 1981.

Banta, Martha. "In Fashion, In History, Out of Time." In *A Historical Guide to Edith Wharton*, edited by Carol J. Singley. New York: Oxford University Press, 2003.

Banta, Martha. *New Essays on The American.* Cambridge: Cambridge University Press, 1987.

Barrish, Phillip. *American Literary Realism, Critical Theory, and Intellectual Prestige, 1880–1995.* Cambridge: Cambridge University Press, 2001.

Bar-Yosef, Eitan, and Nadia Valman, eds. *The Jew in Late-Victorian and Edwardian Culture: Between the East End and East Africa.* London: Palgrave Macmillan, 2009.

Bataille, Georges. *The Accursed Share, Volume I.* Translated by Robert Hurley. New York: Zone Books, 1988.

"The Battle of Gettysburg in Art." National Park Service, December 2, 2015. www.nps.gov/gett/learn/historyculture/gettysburg-cyclorama.htm.

Bauer, Dale. "Wharton's 'Others': Addiction and Intimacy." In *A Historical Guide to Edith Wharton*, edited by Carol Singley. New York: Oxford University Press, 2003.

Bauman, Zygmunt. "Allosemitism: Premodern, Modern, Postmodern." In *Modernity, Culture and "The Jew,"* edited by Bryan Cheyette and Laura Marcus. Palo Alto, CA: Stanford University Press, 1998.

Baym, Nina, et al. *The Norton Anthology of American Literature.* New York: Norton, 2012.

Benjamin, Walter. "The Work of Art in the Age of Mechanical Reproduction." In *Illuminations*, edited by Hannah Arendt, translated by Harry Zohn. New York: Schocken Books, 1968.

Ben-Joseph, Eli. *Aesthetic Persuasion: Henry James, the Jews, and Race.* Lanham, MD: University Press of America, 1996.

Benn-Michaels, Walter. *The Gold Standard and the Logic of Naturalism.* Berkeley: University of California Press, 1987.

Benstock, Shari. *The House of Mirth (Case Studies in Contemporary Criticism).* Boston: Bedford St. Martin, 1994.

Bentley, Nancy. *The Ethnography of Manners: Hawthorne, James, Wharton*. Cambridge: Cambridge University Press, 1995.

Bentley, Nancy. "Wharton, Travel and Modernity." In *A Historical Guide to Edith Wharton*, edited by Carol Singley. New York: Oxford University Press, 2003.

Bercovitch, Sacvan. *The American Jeremiad*. Madison: University of Wisconsin Press, 1978.

Bercovitch, Sacvan, ed. *The American Puritan Imagination: Essays in Revaluation*. London: Cambridge University Press, 1974.

Berlant, Lauren. *Cruel Optimism*. Durham, NC: Duke University Press, 2011.

Biddick, Kathleen. *The Typological Imaginary: Circumcision, Technology, History*. Philadelphia: University of Pennsylvania Press, 2003.

Birmingham, Stephen. *Our Crowd: The Great Jewish Families of New York*. London: Futura, 1967.

Blair, Sara. *Henry James and the Writing of Race and Nation*. Cambridge: Cambridge University Press, 1996.

Blair, Sara. "In the House of Fiction: Henry James and the Engendering of Literary Mastery." In *Henry James's New York Edition: The Construction of Authorship*, edited by David McWhirter. Stanford, CA: Stanford University Press, 1995.

Blair, Sara. "Whose Modernism Is It? Abraham Cahan, Fictions of Yiddish, and the Contest of Modernity." *Modern Fiction Studies* 51 (Summer 2005): 258–84.

Blix, Goran. "Story, Affect, Style." In *Jameson's Antinomies of Realism*. Nonsite.org. 11 (March 14, 2014): http://nonsite.org/the-tank/jamesons-the-antinomies-of-realism.

Borus, Daniel H. *Writing Realism: Howells, James, and Norris in the Mass Market*. Chapel Hill: North Carolina University Press, 1989.

Bourdieu, Pierre. *Distinction: A Social Critique of the Judgment of Taste*. Translated by Richard Nice. Cambridge: Harvard University Press, 1984.

Boyarin, Jonathan. *Storm from Paradise: The Politics of Jewish Memory*. Minneapolis: University of Minnesota Press, 1992.

Boyarin, Jonathan. *Thinking in Jewish*. Chicago: University of Chicago Press, 1996.

Boyarin Jonathan, and Daniel Boyarin. "Diaspora: Generation and the Ground of Jewish Identity." *Critical Inquiry* 19 (1993): 693–725.

Boyarin, Jonathan, and Daniel Boyarin, eds. *Jews and Other Differences: The New Jewish Cultural Studies*. Minneapolis: University of Minnesota Press, 1997.

Boym, Svetlana. *The Future of Nostalgia*. New York: Basic Books, 2001.

Brantlinger, Patrick. *Fictions of State: Culture and Credit in Britain, 1694–1994*. Ithaca, NY: Cornell University Press, 1996.

Brenneman, Chris and Sue Boardman. *The Gettysburg Cyclorama: The Turning Point of the Civil War on Canvas*. El Dorado Hills, CA: Savas Beatie, 2015.

Brodhead, Richard. *Cultures of Letters: Scenes of Reading and Writing in Nineteenth-Century America*. Chicago: University of Chicago Press, 1993.

Brodkin, Karen. *How Jews Became White Folks, and What That Says about Race in America*. New Brunswick, NJ: Rutgers University Press, 1998.

Buelens, Gert. *Henry James and the "Aliens" in Possession of the American Scene*. Amsterdam: Rodopi, 2002.

Chametzky, Jules. *From the Ghetto: The Fiction of Abraham Cahan*. Amherst: University of Massachusetts Press, 1977.

Chametzky, Jules. Introduction to *The Promised Land* by Mary Antin. New York: The Modern Library, 2001.

Cheah, Pheng, and Bruce Robbins, eds. *Cosmopolitics: Thinking and Feeling Beyond the Nation*. Minneapolis: University of Minnesota Press, 1998.

Cheyette, Bryan, ed. *Between "Race" and Culture: Representations of "the Jew" in English and American Literature*. Stanford, CA: Stanford University Press, 1996.

Cheyette, Bryan. *Constructions of "the Jew" in English Literature and Society: Racial Representations, 1875–1945*. Cambridge: Cambridge University Press, 1993.

Clifford, James. "Traveling Cultures." In *Cultural Studies*, edited by Lawrence Grossberg, Cary Nelson, and Paula A. Treichler. New York: Routledge, 1992.

Cohen, Sarah Blacher. "Mary Antin's *The Promised Land*: A Breach of Promise." *Studies in American Jewish Literature* 3, no. 2 (1977): 28–35.

Confino, Alon. *A World Without Jews: The Nazi Imagination from Persecution to Genocide*. New Haven, CT: Yale University Press, 2014.

Conn, Steven. *Museums and American Intellectual Life, 1876–1926*. Chicago: University of Chicago Press, 2000.

Currie, Mark. *About Time: Narrative, Fiction and the Philosophy of Time*. Edinburgh: Edinburgh University Press, 2007.

Daniels, Roger. *Coming to America: A History of Immigration and Ethnicity in American Life*. New York: Perennial, 2002.

Davis, Fred. *Yearning for Yesterday: A Sociology of Nostalgia*. New York: Free Press, 1979.

Dearborn, Mary V. *Love in the Promised Land: The Story of Anzia Yezierska and John Dewey*. New York: Free Press, 1988.

Dearborn, Mary V. *Pocahontas's Daughters: Gender and Ethnicity in American Culture*. New York: Oxford University Press, 1986.

De Sola Pool, Rabbi D. "Some Notes on the Touro Synagogue," In *Touro Synagogue of Congregation Jeshuat Israel*. Newport, RI: Friends of Touro Synagogue, 1948.

Dimock, Wai-Chee. "Debasing Exchange: Edith Wharton's *The House of Mirth*." *PMLA* 100 (1985): 783–92.

Dimock, Wai-Chee. *Through Other Continents: American Literature across Deep Time*. Princeton, NJ: Princeton University Press, 2006.

Diner, Hasia. *The Jews of the United States, 1654 to 2000*. Berkeley: University of California Press, 2004.

Diner, Hasia. *A Time for Gathering: The Second Migration, 1820–1880*. Baltimore: Johns Hopkins University Press, 1992.

Dinnerstein, Leonard. *Anti-Semitism in America*. New York: Oxford, 1994.

Dobkowski, Michael. *The Tarnished Dream: The Basis of American Anti-Semitism*. Westport, CT: Greenwood, 1979.

Donovan, Josephine. *New England Local Color Literature: A Women's Tradition*. New York: Frederick Ungar Publishing, 1983.

Douglas, Mary. Foreword to *The Gift* by Marcel Mauss. New York: Norton, 1990.

Drachsler, Julius. *Democracy and Assimilation: The Blending of Immigrant Heritages in America*. New York: Macmillan, 1920.

Duker, Abraham. "The Tarniks." In *Joshua Starr Memorial Volume*. New York: Conference on Jewish Relations, 1953.

Duneier, Mitchell. *Ghetto: The Invention of a Place, the History of an Idea*. New York: Farrar, Straus and Giroux, 2016.

Durkheim, Émile. *The Elementary Forms of the Religious Life*. Translated by Joseph Ward Swain. New York: Free Press, 1965.

Edel, Leon. "Henry James: The Dramatic Years." In *The Complete Plays of Henry James*. Philadelphia: Lippincott, 1949.

Edel, Leon. *Henry James: The Middle Years, 1881–1895*. Philadelphia, Lipincott, 1953.

Edelstein, Alan. *An Unacknowledged Harmony: Philo-Semitism and the Survival of European Jewry*. Westport, CT: Greenwood, 1982.

Eiselein, Gregory. Introduction to *Emma Lazarus: Selected Poems and Other Writings*. Ontario: Broadview Press, 2002.

Eisen, Arnold. *Galut: Modern Jewish Reflection on Homelessness and Homecoming*. Bloomington: Indiana University Press, 1986.

Elahi, Babak. "The Heavy Garments of the Past: Mary and Frieda Antin in *The Promised Land*." *College Literature* 32, no. 4 (2005): 29–49.

Engel, David. "The 'Discrepancies' of the Modern: Towards a Revaluation of Abraham Cahan's *The Rise of David Levinsky*." *Studies in American Jewish Literature* 2 (1982): 36–59.

Ezrahi, Sidra Dekoven. *Booking Passage: Exile and Homecoming in the Modern Jewish Imagination*. Berkeley: University of California Press, 2000.

Fabian, Ann. *Card Sharps, Dream Books, and Bucket Shops: Gambling in 19th-Century America*. Ithaca, NY: Cornell University Press, 1990.

Fabian, Johannes. *Time and the Other*. New York: Columbia University Press, 1983.

Fawcett, Judith Jackson. *Illuminated Darkness: Slavery and Its Shadow in the Long Nineteenth Century*. Chapel Hill: University of North Carolina Press, 2010.

Fea, John. "Blackstone, William E." American National Biography Online, February 2000. www.anb.org/articles/08/08-01994.html.

Feiner, Shmuel. *Haskalah and History: The Emergence of a Modern Jewish Historical Consciousness*. Portland, OR: Littman Library of Jewish Civilization, 2002.

Feiner, Shmuel. *The Jewish Enlightenment*. Translated by Chaya Naor. Philadelphia: University of Pennsylvania Press, 2002.

Felman, Egal. "American Protestant Theologians on the Frontiers of Jewish-Christian Relations, 1922–82." In *Anti-Semitism in American History*, edited by David A. Gerber. Urbana: University of Illinois Press, 1986.

Felsenstein, Frank. *Anti-Semitic Stereotypes: A Paradigm of Otherness in English Popular Culture, 1660–1830*. Baltimore: Johns Hopkins University Press, 1995.

Ferraro, Thomas J. *Ethnic Passages: Literary Immigrants in Twentieth-Century America*. Chicago: University of Chicago Press, 1993.

Fessenden, Tracy. *Culture and Redemption: Religion, the Secular, and American Literature*. Princeton, NJ: Princeton University Press, 2007.

Fisch, Harold. *The Dual Image: The Figure of the Jew in English and American Literature*. New York: Ktav Publishing, 1971.

Fischer, Rachel K. "Tevye the Dairyman, Publication History." http://tevyethe dairyman.weebly.com/publication-history.html.

Fleissner, Jennifer L. *Women, Compulsion, Modernity: The Moment of American Naturalism*. Chicago: University of Chicago Press, 2004.

Follett, Danielle. "Is the Cheese Meaningless? The Distension of Dialectics in Jameson's *The Antinomies of Realism*." In special issue "Jameson's *Antinomies of Realism*." Nonsite.org 11 (March 14, 2014), http://nonsite.org/the-tank/jamesons-the -antinomies-of-realism.

Follett, Wilson. "What Edith Wharton Did—And Might Have Done." *New York Times Book Review* 5 (September 1937).

Foote, Stephanie. *Regional Fictions: Culture and Identity in Nineteenth-Century American Literature*. Madison: University of Wisconsin Press, 2001.

Fox, Richard Wightman, and T. J. Jackson Lears. *The Culture of Consumption: Critical Essays in American History, 1880–1890*. New York: Pantheon, 1983.

Franco, Dean. *Race, Rights and Recognition: Jewish American Literature Since 1969*. Ithaca, NY: Cornell University Press, 2012.

Freedman, Jonathan. "Do American and Ethnic American Studies Have a Jewish Problem; or, When Is an Ethnic Not an Ethnic, and What Should We Do About It?" *MELUS* 37, no. 2 (2012): 19–40.

Freedman, Jonathan. "Henry James and the Discourses of Antisemitism." In *Between "Race" and Culture: Representations of "the Jew" in English and American Literature*, edited by Bryan Cheyette. Stanford, CA: Stanford University Press, 1996.

Freedman, Jonathan. *Klezmer America: Jewishness, Ethnicity, Modernity*. New York: Columbia University Press, 2008.

Freedman, Jonathan. *Professions of Taste: Henry James, British Aestheticism, and Commodity Culture*. Stanford, CA: Stanford University Press, 1990.

Freedman, Jonathan. *The Temple of Culture*. London: Oxford University Press, 2000.

Freeman, Elizabeth. *Time Binds: Queer Temporalities, Queer Histories*. Durham, NC: Duke University Press, 2010.

Friedman, Natalie. "Marriage and the Immigrant Narrative: Anzia Yezierska's *Salome of the Tenements*." *Legacy* 22, no. 2 (2005): 176–86.

Gałas, Michal. "Sabbatianism in the 17th-Century Polish-Lithuanian Commonwealth." In *The Sabbatian Movement and Its Aftermath*, edited by Rachel Elior. Jerusalem: Posner and Sons, 2001.

Garland, Hamlin. "'Single Tax' and Woman Suffrage." In *Hamlin Garland, Prairie Radical: Writings from the 1890s*, edited by Donald Pizer. Urbana: University of Illinois Press, 2010.

Geertz, Clifford. *The Interpretation of Cultures: Selected Essays*. New York: Basic Books, 1973, 2000.

Geismar, Maxwell. *Henry James and the Jacobites*. New York: Hill and Wang, 1965.

Giddens, Anthony. *The Consequences of Modernity*. Stanford, CA: Stanford University Press, 1990.

Gillman, Rabbi Neil. *The Death of Death: Resurrection and Immortality in Jewish Thought*. Woodstock, VT: Jewish Lights Publishing, 2011.

Gilman, Sander. *The Jew's Body*. New York: Routledge, 1991.

Gitenstein, R. Barbara. *Apocalyptic Messianism and Contemporary Jewish-American Poetry*. Albany: SUNY Press, 1986.

Glaser, Eliane. *Judaism without Jews: Philosemitism and Christian Polemic in Early Modern England*. Basingstoke: Palgrave, 2007.

Glenn, Susan. *Daughters of the Shtetl: Life and Labor in the Immigrant Generation.* Ithaca, NY: Cornell University Press, 1990.

Glinter, Ezra. "Will the Real Sholem Aleichem Please Stand Up?" *Forward*, November 24, 2013. http://forward.com/culture/188007/will-the-real-sholem-aleichem -please-stand-up/.

Goffman, Erving. *The Presentation of Self in Everyday Life.* Woodstock, NY: Overlook Press, 1973.

Goldman-Price, Irene C. "The 'Perfect Jew' and *The House of Mirth*: A Study in Point of View." In *Edith Wharton's* The House of Mirth: *A Casebook*, edited by Carol J. Singley. Oxford: Oxford University Press, 2003.

Goldman, Samuel. *God's Country: Christian Zionism in America.* Philadelphia: University of Pennsylvania Press, forthcoming.

Goldman, Shalom. *God's Sacred Tongue: Hebrew and the American Imagination.* Chapel Hill: University of North Carolina Press, 2004.

Goldman, Shalom, ed. *Hebrew and the Bible in America: The First Two Centuries.* Hanover, NH: University Press of New England, 1993.

Goldman, Shalom. *Zeal for Zion: Christians, Jews and the Idea of the Promised Land.* Chapel Hill: University of North Carolina Press, 2009.

Green, William Scott, and Jed Silverstein. "The Doctrine of the Messiah." In *The Blackwell Companion to Judaism*, edited by Jacob Neusner and Alan J. Avery-Peck. Oxford: Wiley-Blackwell, 2000.

Guravitch, Zali, and Gideon Aran, "The Land of Israel: Myth and Phenomenon." In *Reshaping the Past: Jewish History and the Historians*, edited by Jonathan Frankel. New York: Oxford University Press, 1994.

Hacohen, Malachi Haim. "Dilemmas of Cosmopolitanism: Karl Popper, Jewish Identity, and 'Central European Culture.'" *Journal of Modern History* 71 (1999): 105–49.

Halttunen, Karen. *Confidence Men and Painted Women: A Study of Middle-Class Culture in America, 1830–1870.* New Haven, CT: Yale University Press, 1982.

Handlin, Oscar. *Adventures in Freedom: Three Hundred Years of Jewish Life in America.* New York: McGraw Hill, 1954.

Handlin, Oscar. "American Views of the Jew at the Opening of the Twentieth Century." *Publications of the American Jewish Historical Society* 40 (June 1951): 323–44.

Harap, Louis. *The Image of the Jew in American Literature: From Early Republic to Mass Immigration.* Syracuse, NY: Syracuse University Press, 2003.

Haviland, Beverly. *Henry James's Last Romance: Making Sense of the Past and the American Scene.* Cambridge: Cambridge University Press, 1997.

Hefner, Brooks E. "'Slipping Back into the Vernacular': Anzia Yezierska's Vernacular Modernism." *MELUS* 36, no. 3 (2011): 187–211.

Hegel, Georg Wilhelm Friedrich. *Elements of the Philosophy of Right*, edited by Allen Woods, translated by H. B. Nisbet. Cambridge: Cambridge University Press, 1991.

Heinze, Andrew. *Adapting to Abundance: Jewish Immigrants, Mass Consumption, and the Search for American Identity*. New York: Columbia University Press, 1990.

Henriksen, Louise Levitas. *Anzia Yezierska: A Writer's Life*. New Brunswick, NJ: Rutgers University Press, 1988.

Hertzberg, Arthur. "The New England Puritans and the Jews." In *Hebrew and the Bible in America: The First Two Centuries*, edited by Shalom Goldman. Hanover, NH: University Press of New England, 1993.

Higham, John. *Send These to Me: Immigrants in Urban America*. New York: Atheneum, 1975.

Higham, John. *Strangers in the Land: Patterns of American Nativism, 1860–1925*. New York: Atheneum, 1963.

Himmelfarb, Gertrude. *The People of the Book: Philosemitism in England, From Cromwell to Churchill*. New York: Encounter Books, 2011.

Hoeller, Hildegard. *Edith Wharton's Dialogue with Realism and Sentimental Fiction*. Gainesville: University Press of Florida, 2000.

Hoffman, Warren. *The Passing Game: Queering Jewish American Culture*. Syracuse, NY: Syracuse University Press 2009.

Hofstadter, Richard. *The Age of Reform; from Bryan to F.D.R.* New York: Knopf, 1956.

Hollinger, David. "Ethnic Diversity, Cosmopolitanism and the Emergence of the American Liberal Intelligentsia." *American Quarterly* 27 (1975): 133–51.

Hollinger, David. *Postethnic America*. New York: Basic Books, 1995.

Howard, June. *Form and History in American Literary Naturalism*. Chapel Hill: University of North Carolina Press, 1985.

Howe, Irving. *The World of Our Fathers*. New York: Simon and Schuster, 1976.

Howe, Irving, and Eliezer Greenberg, eds. *A Treasury of Yiddish Stories*. New York: Penguin, 1990.

Hungerford, Amy. *Postmodern Belief: American Literature and Religion since 1960*. Princeton, NJ: Princeton University Press, 2010.

Jackson, Gregory S. "Cultivating Spiritual Sight: Jacob Riis's Virtual-Tour Narrative and the Visual Modernization of Protestant Homiletics," *Representations* 83 (Summer 2003): 126–66.

Jackson, Gregory S. *The Word and Its Witness: The Spiritualization of American Realism*. Chicago: University of Chicago Press, 2008.

Jacobson, Matthew Frye. *Barbarian Virtues: The United States Encounters Foreign Peoples at Home and Abroad, 1876–1917*. New York: Hill and Wang, 2000.

Jacobson, Matthew Frye. *Whiteness of a Different Color: European Immigrants and the Alchemy of Race*. Cambridge, MA: Harvard University Press, 1998.

Jameson, Fredric. *The Antinomies of Realism*. London: Verso, 2013.

Jirousek, Lori. "Ethnics and Ethnographers: Zora Neale Hurston and Anzia Yezierska." *Journal of Modern Literature* 29, no. 2 (2006): 19–32.

Johnson, Kendall. "'Dark Spot' in the Picturesque: The Aesthetics of Polygenism and Henry James's 'A Landscape-Painter.'" *American Literature* 74 (2002): 59–87.

Joseph, Phillip. "Literary Migration: Abraham Cahan's *The Imported Bridegroom* and the Alternative of American Fiction," *MELUS* 27, no. 4 (2002): 3–32.

Kandiyoti, Dalia. "Comparative Diasporas: The Local and the Mobile in Abraham Cahan and Alberto Gerchunoff." *Modern Fiction Studies* 44 (Spring 1998): 77–122.

Kant, Immanuel. *Anthropology from a Pragmatic Point of View*, edited by Robert B. Louden. Cambridge: Cambridge University Press, 2006.

Kaplan, Amy. "Nation, Region, and Empire." In *The Columbia History of the American Novel*, edited by Emory Elliott. New York: Columbia University Press, 1991.

Kaplan, Amy. *The Social Construction of American Realism*. Chicago: University of Chicago Press, 1988.

Kaplan, Justin. *Lincoln Steffens: A Biography*. New York: Simon and Schuster, 1974.

Kaplan, Justin. *Mr. Clemens and Mark Twain: A Biography*. New York: Simon and Schuster, 1966.

Karafilis, Maria. "The Jewish Ghetto and the Americanization of Space in Mary Antin and Her Contemporaries." *American Literary Realism* 42, no. 2 (2010): 129–50.

Karp, Jonathan, and Adam Sutcliffe, eds. *Philosemitism in History*. Cambridge: Cambridge University Press, 2011.

Kassanoff, Jennie A. *Edith Wharton and the Politics of Race*. Cambridge: Cambridge University Press, 2004.

Kavka, Martin. *Jewish Messianism and the History of Philosophy*. Cambridge: Cambridge University Press, 2004.

Kessler-Harris, Alice. Introduction to *Bread Givers* by Anzia Yezierska. New York: Persea, 1975.

Killoran, Helen. *The Critical Reception of Edith Wharton*. Rochester, NY: Camden House, 2001.

Kirk, Rudolph, and Clara M. Kirk. "Abraham Cahan and William Dean Howells: The Story of a Friendship." *American Jewish Historical Quarterly* 52, no. 1 (1962): 27–57.

Kirshenblatt-Gimblett, Barbara. Introduction to *Life Is with People: The Culture of the Shtetl*, edited by Mark Zborowski and Elizabeth Herzog. New York: Schocken, 1995.

Knight, Louise W. "Jane Addams and the Settlement House Movement." In *Against the Tide: Women Reformers in American Society*, edited by Paul A. Cimbala and Randall M. Miller. Westport, CT: Praeger, 1997.

Kohler, Kaufmann. "Atonement." In *The Jewish Encyclopedia*, 1906. www .jewishencyclopedia.com/articles/2092-atonement.

Kramer, Michael P. "Assimilation in *The Promised Land*: Mary Antin and the Jewish Origins of the American Self," *Prooftexts* 18, no. 2 (1998): 121–48.

Kraut, Alan M. *The Huddled Masses: The Immigrant in American Society, 1880–1921*. Arlington Heights, IL: Harlan Davidson, 1982.

Kraut, Benny. *From Reform Judaism to Ethical Culture: The Religious Evolution of Felix Adler*. Cincinnati: Hebrew Union College Press, 1979.

Kushner, Tony, and Nadia Valman, eds. *Philosemitism, Antisemitism and 'the Jews': Perspectives from the Middle Ages to the Twentieth Century*. Aldershot: Ashgate, 2004.

Larsen, Erik. *The Devil in the White City*. New York: Crown, 2003.

Lathrop, George Parsons. "The Novel and Its Future." In *Documents of American Realism and Naturalism*, edited by Donald Pizer. Carbondale: Southern Illinois University Press, 1998.

Lears, Jackson. *Something for Nothing: Luck in America*. New York: Viking Penguin, 2003.

Leavis, F. R. *The Great Tradition*. New York: Doubleday, 1954.

Lee, Maurice. *Uncertain Chances; Science, Skepticism, and Belief in Nineteenth-Century American Literature*. New York: Oxford University Press, 2012.

Le Goff, Jacques. *Time, Work and Culture in the Middle Ages*. Chicago: University of Chicago Press, 1980.

Lenowitz, Harris. *The Jewish Messiahs*. New York: Oxford University Press, 1998.

Levine, Gary Martin. *Merchant of Modernism: The Economic Jew in Anglo-American Literature, 1864–1939*. New York: Routledge, 2003.

Levine, George. "Isabel, Gwendolyn and Dorothea," *ELH* 30, no. 3 (1963): 244–57.

Levinson, Julian. *Exiles on Main Street: Jewish American Writers and American Literary Culture*. Bloomington: Indiana University Press, 2008.

Levy, Ariel. "Prodigal Son: Is the Wayward Republican Mike Huckabee Now His Party's Best Hope?" *New Yorker*, June 28, 2010. www.newyorker.com/magazine/ 2010/06/28/prodigal-son.

Lewis, Pericles. *Religious Experience and the Modernist Novel*. Cambridge: Cambridge University Press, 2010.

Lidoff, Joan. "Another Sleeping Beauty: Narcissism in *The House of Mirth*." In *American Realism: New Essays*, edited by Eric Sundquist. Baltimore: Johns Hopkins University Press, 1982.

Liptzin, Sol. *The Jew in American Literature*. New York: Bloch Publishing Co., 1966.

Livney, Lee. "Let Us Now Praise Self-Made Men: A Reexamination of the Hilton-Seligman Affair," *New York History* 75, no. 1 (1994): 66–98.

Lott, Eric. *Love and Theft: Blackface Minstrelsy and the American Working Class*. Oxford: Oxford University Press, 1995.

Lowenthal, David. *The Past Is a Foreign Country*. Cambridge: Cambridge University Press, 1985.

Luciano, Dana. *Arranging Grief: Sacred Time and the Body in Nineteenth-Century America*. New York: New York University Press, 2007.

Lukacs, Georg. *Theory of the Novel*. Translated by Anna Bostock. Cambridge, MA: MIT Press, 1999.

Lutz, Tom. *Cosmopolitan Vistas: American Regionalism and Literary Value*. Ithaca, NY: Cornell University Press, 2004.

Mann, Barbara. *Space and Place in Jewish Studies*. New Brunswick, NJ: Rutgers University Press, 2012.

Marcus, Jacob Rader. *United States Jewry, 1776–1985*. Detroit: Wayne State University Press, 1993.

Markus, R. A. *Saeculum: History and Society in the Theology of Augustine*. Rev. ed. New York: Cambridge University Press, 1988.

Marovitz, Sanford E. *Abraham Cahan*. New York: Twayne, 1996.

Martin, Jay. *Harvests of Change: American Literature, 1865–1914*. Englewood Cliffs, NJ: Prentice-Hall, 1967.

Mauss, Marcel. *The Gift: The Form and Reason for Exchange in Archaic Societies*. Translated by W. D. Halls. New York: Norton, 1990.

Mayo, Louise. *The Ambivalent Image: Nineteenth-Century America's Perception of the Jew*. Cranbury, NJ: Associated University Press, 1988.

McClanahan, Annie. "Dead Pledges: Debt, Horror, and the Credit Crisis." *Post45*, May 7, 2012. http://post45.research.yale.edu/2012/05/dead-pledges-debt-horror-and-the-credit-crisis/.

McGinity, Keren R. *Still Jewish: A History of Women and Intermarriage in America*. New York: New York University Press, 2009.

McWhirter, David, ed. *Henry James's New York Edition: The Construction of Authorship*. Stanford, CA: Stanford University Press, 1995.

McWilliams, Carey. *A Mask for Privilege: Anti-Semitism in America*. Boston: Little, Brown and Company, 1948.

Meyer, Isidore S. Review of *The Spirit of the Ghetto*, edited by Moses Rischin. *American Jewish Historical Quarterly* 59, no. 4 (1970): 545.

Miller, Angela. "The Panorama, the Cinema, and the Emergence of the Spectacular." *Wide Angle* 18 (April 1996): 34–69.

Miron, Dan. "Abramovitsh, Sholem Yankev." *YIVO Encyclopedia*. www.yivoencyclopedia .org/article.aspx/Abramovitsh_Sholem_Yankev.

Miron, Dan. "The Literary Image of the Shtetl." *Jewish Social Studies* 1, no. 3 (1995): 1–43.

Miron, Dan. "Sholem Aleichem." *YIVO Encyclopedia*. www.yivoencyclopedia.org/article .aspx/Sholem_Aleichem.

Miron, Dan. *Tevye the Dairyman: And, Motl the Cantor's Son*. New York: Penguin, 2009.

Mizruchi, Susan. "Fiction and the Science of Society." In *The Columbia History of the American Novel*, edited by Emory Elliott. New York: Columbia University Press, 1991.

Moscow, Henry. *The Street Book: An Encyclopedia of Manhattan's Street Names and Their Origins*. New York: Fordham University Press, 1990.

Mott, Frank Luther. *A History of American Magazines*. 5 vols. Cambridge: Belknap Press, 1968.

Mulcaire, Terry. "Public Credit; or, The Feminization of Virtue in the Marketplace." *PMLA* 114 (October 1999): 1029–42.

Nahshon, Edna. *From the Ghetto to the Melting Pot: Israel Zangwill's Jewish Plays*. Detroit: Wayne State University Press, 2006.

Nevius, Blake. *Edith Wharton: A Study of Her Fiction*. Berkeley: University of California Press, 1953.

"New Figures in Literature and Art," *Atlantic Monthly* 76 (December 1895), 842.

Newlin, Keith. *Hamlin Garland: A Life*. Lincoln: University of Nebraska Press, 2008.

Nora, Pierre. "Between Memory and History: Les Lieux de Memoire." *Representations*, Special Issue: Memory and Counter-Memory 26 (Spring 1989): 7–24.

O'Brien, Jean M. *Firsting and Lasting: Writing Indians Out of Existence in New England*. Minneapolis: University of Minnesota Press, 2010.

Obenzinger, Hilton. *American Palestine: Melville, Twain, and the Holy Land Mania*. Princeton, NJ: Princeton University Press, 1999.

Omer-Sherman, Ranen. *Diaspora and Zionism in Jewish American Literature: Lazarus, Syrkin, Reznikoff, and Roth*. Hanover, NH: Brandeis University Press, 2002.

Pater, Walter M. *Studies in the History of the Renaissance*. London: Macmillan, 1873.

Patterson, David. *Emil L. Fackenheim: A Jewish Philosopher's Response to the Holocaust*. Syracuse, NY: Syracuse University Press, 2008.

Pecora, Vincent P. *Households of the Soul*. Baltimore: Johns Hopkins University Press, 1997.

Pecora, Vincent P. *Secularization and Cultural Criticism*. Chicago: University of Chicago Press, 2006.

Pencak, William. *Jews and Gentiles in Early America: 1654–1800*. Ann Arbor: University of Michigan Press, 2005.

Pizer, Donald. *American Naturalism and the Jews: Garland, Norris, Dreiser, Wharton and Cather*. Urbana: University of Illinois Press, 2008.

Pizer, Donald. "Introduction, 1874–1914." In *Documents of American Realism and Naturalism*, edited by Donald Pizer. Carbondale: Southern Illinois University Press, 1998.

Pizer, Donald. "The Naturalism of Edith Wharton's *House of Mirth*." *Twentieth-Century Literature* 41, no. 2 (1955): 241–48.

Pizer, Donald. *The Theory and Practice of American Literary Naturalism*. Carbondale: Southern Illinois University Press, 1993.

Pocock, G. A. *Virtue, Commerce, and History: Essays on Political Thought and History, Chiefly in the Eighteenth Century*. Cambridge: Cambridge University Press, 1985.

Poirier, Richard. "Edith Wharton's *The House of Mirth*." In *The American Novel: From James Fenimore Cooper to William Faulkner*. New York: Basic Books, 1965. Expanded and reprinted as *A World Elsewhere: The Place of Style in American Literature*. New York: Oxford University Press, 1966.

Poovey, Mary. *Genres of the Credit Economy: Mediating Value in Eighteenth- and Nineteenth-Century Britain*. Chicago: University of Chicago Press, 2008.

Porter, Carolyn. "Gender and Value in *The American*." In *New Essays on* The American, edited by Marth Banta. New York: Cambridge University Press, 1987.

Porter, Carolyn. *Seeing and Being: The Plight of the Participant Observer in Emerson, James, Adams, and Faulkner*. Middletown, CT.: Wesleyan University Press, 1981.

Posnock, Ross. *The Trial of Curiosity: Henry James, William James, and the Challenge of Modernity*. New York: Oxford University Press, 1991.

Pratt, Lloyd. *Archives of American Time: Literature and Modernity in the Nineteenth Century*. Philadelphia: University of Pennsylvania Press, 2010.

Radest, Howard. *Toward Common Ground: The Story of the Ethical Societies in the United States*. New York: Fredrick Unger, 1969.

Rappaport, Salomon. *Jew and Gentile: The Philosemitic Aspect*. New York: Philosophical Library, 1980.

Ravitzky, Aviezer. *Messianism, Zionism, and Jewish Religious Radicalism*. Translated by Michael Swirsky and Jonathan Chipman. Chicago: University of Chicago Press, 1996.

Richards, Bernard G. Introduction to *Yekl and the Imported Bride-groom and Other Stories of Yiddish New York* by Abraham Cahan. Mineola, NY: Dover, 1970.

Ricoeur, Paul. *Time and Narrative, Volume I*. Translated by Kathleen McLaughlin and David Pellauer. Chicago: University of Chicago Press, 1984.

Riegel, Christian. "Rosedale and Anti-Semitism in *House of Mirth*." *Studies in American Fiction* 20, no. 2 (1992): 219–24.

Rischin, Moses. "Abraham Cahan and the New York *Commercial Advertiser*: A Study in Acculturation." *Publication of the American Jewish Historical Society* 43 (1953): 10–36.

Rischin, Moses. *The Promised City*. Cambridge: Harvard University Press, 1962.

Rivett, Sarah. "Early American Religion in a Postsecular Age." *PMLA* 128, no. 4 (2013): 989–96.

Rivett, Sarah. *The Science of the Soul in Colonial New England*. Chapel Hill: University of North Carolina Press, 2011.

Robbins, Bruce. "Comparative Cosmopolitanism." *Social Text* 10, no. 2–3 (1992): 169–86.

Rochelson, Meri-Jane. *A Jew in the Public Arena: The Career of Israel Zangwill*. Detroit: Wayne State University Press, 2008.

Rockaway, Robert, and Arnon Gutfeld. "Demonic Images of the Jew in the Nineteenth Century United States." *American Jewish History* 89 (2001): 355–81.

Rose, Julie K. "The World's Columbian Exposition: Idea, Experience, Aftermath." Crossroads at the University of Virginia, 1996. http://xroads.virginia.edu/~ma96/WCE/title.html.

Roskies, David. *The Jewish Search for a Usable Past*. Bloomington: Indiana University Press, 1999.

Rowe, John Carlos. *The Other Henry James*. Durham, NC: Duke University Press, 1998.

Rubinstein, William D., and Hilary Rubinstein. *Philosemitism: Admiration and Support for Jews in the English-Speaking World, 1840–1939*. Basingstoke, UK: Palgrave Macmillan, 1999.

Sanders, Ronald. *The Lower East Side Jews: An Immigrant Generation*. Mineola, NY: Dover, 1999.

Sarna, Jonathan. *American Judaism*. New Haven, CT: Yale University Press, 2004.

Schappes, Morris, ed. *A Documentary History of Jews in the United States, 1654–1875*. New York: Schocken, 1950, 1971.

Schoen, Carol B. *Anzia Yezierska*. Boston: Twayne, 1982.

Scholem, Gershom. *The Messianic Idea in Judaism and Other Essays on Jewish Spirituality*. New York: Schocken, 1971.

Schor, Esther. *Emma Lazarus*. New York: Schocken, 2006.

Schreier, Benjamin. *The Impossible Jew: Identity and the Reconstruction of Jewish American Literary History*. New York: New York University Press, 2015.

Seltzer, Mark. *Henry James and the Art of Power*. Ithaca, NY: Cornell University Press, 1984.

Sheffer, Jolie. "Recollecting, Repeating, and Walking Through: Immigration, Trauma, and Space in Mary Antin's *The Promised Land*." *MELUS* 35, no. 1 (2010): 141–66.

Shell, Marc. *Money, Language, and Thought: Literary and Philosophic Economies from the Medieval to the Modern Era*. Baltimore: Johns Hopkins University Press, 1982.

Sherman, Sandra. *Finance and Fictionality in the Early Eighteenth Century: Accounting for Defoe*. Cambridge: Cambridge University Press, 1996.

Showalter, Elaine, "The Death of the Lady (Novelist): Wharton's *House of Mirth*." *Representations* 9 (Winter 1985): 142–43.

Shulman, Robert. "Realism." In *The Columbia History of the American Novel*, edited by Emory Elliott. New York, Columbia University Press, 1991.

Siegel, Thomas J. "Professor Stephen Sewall and the Transformation of Hebrew at Harvard." In *Hebrew and the Bible in America: The First Two Centuries*, edited by Shalom Goldman. Hanover, NH: University Press of New England, 1993.

Sillin, Sarah. "Heroine, Reformer, Citizen: Novelistic Conventions in Antin's *The Promised Land*." *MELUS* 38, no. 3 (2013): 25–43.

Simmel, Georg. "The Conflict in Modern Culture." In *On Individuality and Social Forms*, ed. Donald N. Levine. Chicago: University of Chicago Press, 1971.

Simmel, Georg. *The Philosophy of Money*, edited by David Frisby, translated by Tom Bottomore and David Frisby. London: Routledge, 1990.

Sklare, Marshall. "Intermarriage and the Jewish Future." *Commentary*, April 1, 1964. www.commentarymagazine.com/article/intermarriage-the-jewish-future/.

Smith, Barbara Hernstein. *Contingencies of Value: Alternative Perspectives for Critical Theory*. Cambridge: Harvard University Press, 1988.

Sol, Adam. "Longings and Renunciation: Attitudes Toward Intermarriage in Early Twentieth Century Jewish American Novels." *American Jewish History* 89, no. 2 (2001): 215–30.

Sollors, Werner. *Beyond Ethnicity: Consent and Descent in American Culture.* New York: Oxford University Press, 1986.

Solomon, Melissa. "The Female World of Exorcism and Displacement (or, Relations Between Women in Henry James Nineteenth-Century *The Portrait of a Lady*)." In *Novel Gazing: Queer Reading in Fiction,* edited by Eve Kosofsky Sedgwick. Durham, NC: Duke University Press, 1997.

Spengemann, William. Introduction to *The American* by Henry James. New York: Penguin, 1981.

Stange, Margit. *Personal Property: Wives, White Slaves, and the Market in Women.* Baltimore: Johns Hopkins University Press, 1998.

Starobinski, Jean, and William S. Kemp, "The Idea of Nostalgia." *Diogenes: An International Review of Philosophy* 14 (1966): 81–103.

Steffens, Lincoln. *The Autobiography of Lincoln Steffens.* 1931. Berkeley, CA: Heyday, 2005.

Steffens, Lincoln. "Schloma, the Daughter of Schmuhl." *Chap-Book Semi-Monthly* 5 (May 15–November 1, 1896), 128–32.

Steinsaltz, Adin. *The Essential Talmud.* Translated by Chaya Galai. New York: Basic Books, 1976.

Stevens, Hugh. "Homoeroticism, Identity, and Agency in James's Late Tales." In *Enacting History in Henry James: Narrative, Power, and Ethics,* edited by Gert Buelens. Cambridge: Cambridge University Press, 1997.

Stevens, Hugh. "Queer Henry in the Cage." In *The Cambridge Companion to Henry James,* edited by Jonathan Freedman. Cambridge: Cambridge University Press, 1998.

Stewart, Susan. *On Longing: Narratives of the Miniature, the Gigantic, the Souvenir, and the Collection.* Durham, NC: Duke University Press, 1993.

Sundquist, Eric. "The Country of the Blue." In *American Realism: New Essays,* edited by Eric J. Sundquist. Baltimore: Johns Hopkins University Press, 1982.

Sundquist, Eric. "Realism and Regionalism." In *The Columbia Literary History of the United States,* edited by Emory Elliott. New York: Columbia University Press, 1988.

Sutcliffe, Adam, and Jonathan Karp. "Introduction: A Brief History of Philosemitism." In *Philosemitism in History,* edited by Jonathan Karp and Adam Sutcliffe. Cambridge: Cambridge University Press, 2011.

Taylor, Charles. *A Secular Age.* Cambridge, MA: Harvard University Press, 2007.

Thompson, E. P. "Time, Work-Discipline, and Industrial Capitalism." *Past & Present* 38 (December 1967): 56–97.

Trachtenberg, Alan. "Conceivable Aliens." *Yale Review* 82, no. 4 (1994): 42–64.

Trachtenberg, Alan. *The Incorporation of America: Culture and Society in the Gilded Age.* New York: Hill and Wang, 1994.

Trachtenberg, Alan. *Shades of Hiawatha: Staging Indians, Making Americans, 1880–1930.* New York: Hill and Wang, 2004.

Trolander, Judith Ann. *Professionalism and Social Change: From the Settlement House Movement to Neighborhood Centers, 1886 to the Present.* New York: Columbia University Press, 1987.

Tuan, Yi-Fu. *Space and Place: The Perspective of Experience.* Minneapolis: University of Minnesota Press, 1977.

Ueda, Reed. *Postwar Immigrant America: A Social History.* New York: Bedford St. Martins, 1994.

Valman, Nadia. *The Jewess in Nineteenth-Century British Literary Culture.* Cambridge: Cambridge University Press, 2007.

Vizetelly, Frank H. "The American Hebrew." In *The Jewish Encyclopedia*, 1906. www .jewishencyclopedia.com/articles/1387-american-hebrew-the#ixzz0yElrpynv.

Wald, Priscilla. "Communicable Americanism: Contagion, Geographic Fictions and the Sociological Legacy of Robert E. Park," *American Literary History* 14, no. 4 (2002): 653–85.

Warner, Charles Dudley, "Modern Fiction." *In Documents of American Realism and Naturalism*, edited by Donald Pizer. Carbondale: Southern Illinois University Press, 1998.

Watt, Ian. *The Rise of the Novel: Studies in Defoe, Richardson, and Fielding.* London: Peregrine, 1968.

Weber, Donald. *Haunted in the New World: Jewish American Culture from Cahan to The Goldbergs.* Bloomington: Indiana University Press, 2005.

Weber, Donald. "Outsiders and Greenhorns: Christopher Newman in the Old World, David Levinsky in the New." *American Literature* 67, no. 4 (1995): 725–45.

Weber, Max. *The Protestant Ethic and the Spirit of Capitalism.* Translated by Talcott Parsons. London: Harper Collins Academic, 1992.

Weinstein, Cindy. *Time, Tense, and American Literature: When Is Now?* New York: Cambridge University Press, 2015.

Wenger, Beth. "Memory as Identity: The Invention of the Lower East Side." *American Jewish History* 85 (March 1997): 3–27.

Westbrook, Wayne. "Lily-Bartering on the New York Social Exchange in *The House of Mirth*." *Ball State University Forum* 20 (1979): 59–64.

Wexler, Laura. "Looking at Yezierska." In *Woman of the Word: Jewish Women and Jewish Writing*, edited by Judith Baskin. Detroit: Wayne State University Press, 1994.

Wilson, Harold. *McClure's Magazine and the Muckrakers*. Princeton, NJ: Princeton University Press, 1970.

Wirth-Nesher, Hana. "'Shpeaking Plain' and Writing Foreign: Abraham Cahan's *Yekl*." *Poetics Today* 22, no. 1 (2001): 41–63.

Wolff, Cynthia Griffin. *A Feast of Words: The Triumph of Edith Wharton*. London: Oxford University Press, 1977.

Wright, Carol Von Pressentin, Stuart Miller, and Sharon Seitz. *The Blue Guide: New York*. London: A&C Black Limited, 2002.

Yerushalmi, Yosef Hayim. *Zakhor: Jewish History and Jewish Memory*. Seattle: University of Washington Press, 1982.

Young, Bette Roth. *Emma Lazarus in her World: Life and Letters*. Philadelphia: Jewish Publication Society, 1995.

Zacharias, Greg. "Henry James' Fictional Jew." In *Representations of Jews Through the Ages*, edited by Leonard Jay Greenspoon and Bryan F. Le Beau. Omaha, NE: Creighton University Press, 1996.

Zborowski, Mark, and Elizabeth Herzog. *Life Is with People: The Culture of the Shtetl*. New York: Schocken, 1995.

Zenner, Walter P. *Minorities in the Middle: A Cross-Cultural Analysis*. Albany: SUNY Press, 1991.

Ziff, Larzer. *The American 1890s: Life and Times of a Lost Generation*. Lincoln: University of Nebraska Press, 1979.

INDEX

Page numbers in *italics* indicate illustrations.

Ben Hur: dramatization with cyclorama (1899), 266n144; Lew Wallace novel (1880), 23

Benjamin, Walter, 27, 29, 79, 118, 131, 280n98

Ben-Joseph, Eli, 273n23

Benn Michaels, Walter, 169, 175, 291n96, 292n104

Benstock, Shari, 291–92n101

Bentley, Nancy, 181

Bercovitch, Sacvan, 18

Berger, Pamela, 269n185

Berry, Edmund, 250n7

Biddick, Kathleen, 6–7

binary frameworks: of antisemitism and philosemitism, 3, 9, 14–15; "noble Hebrew" versus "avaricious Jew," 4.7–8, 31, 34–35, 141–44, 181, 194, 220, 231, 234, 286n39

Birmingham, Stephen, 139, 282n2; *Our Crowd* (1967), 144

Blackstone, William, 19, 247n46; *Jesus is Coming* (1878), 237

Blix, Goran, 30, 176

Bok, Edward, 198

Booth, Edwin, 302n13

Bourdieu, Pierre, 112, 113, 285n31

the Bowery (NYC), 57–60, 260nn85–86

Boyarin, Daniel and Jonathan, 26, 79, 88, 104, 105

Boym, Svetlana, 26, 27, 76

Brandeis, Louis, 13, 200, 244n29

Brantlinger, Patrick, 154

Bread Givers (Yezierska, 1925), 9–10, 35, 190, 212, 219–25

Bristow, Benjamin, 139

Brodhead, Richard, 64, 120

Brodkin, Karen, 13

Brooks, Elbridge Streeter, *A Son of Issachar; A Romance of the Days of Messias* (1890), 250n76

Brudno, Ezra, 188

"brute other," 160, 290n81

Bryant, William Cullen, 230–31, 302n13

Buelens, Gert, 135

Burr, Enoch, 250n7

Burroughs, John, 297n27

Cahan, Abraham, 3, 31–33, 37–91; Antin compared, 198; "Circumstances" (1897), 46; on Dreiser's *Hand of the Potter*, 160; Fisch on, 242n11; Hapgood's *The Spirit of the Ghetto* (1902) and, 250–51n82; Howells and, 42, 43–45, 47, 255nn19–20; Howells's *A Traveler from Altruria* (1893) translated into Yiddish by, 43; immigrant Jews, contemporary views of, 52–56; *Jewish Daily Forward*, as founding editor of, 42–43, 254n18, 257n49; on "Jewish Problem," 10, 11; local color writer, viewed as, 31–32, 39–41, 43–47, 49, 56, 58, 63–65, 68, 69, 79, 89, 214; Lower East Side in works of, 37–41, 42, 45, 47; memory and remembrance in fiction of, 39, 63–65, 68–69, 79, 80–81, 83, 85–91; New England literary culture and, 56–63, 64; in newspaper and periodical culture of late 19th/early 20th century, 31, 42–47, 56–63, 257n49; origins, family background, and early career, 41–42;

Cournos, John, 188

Cowen, Philip, 14, 189, 192, 193, 233, 296–97n27

Cox, Kenyon, 259n79

Craig, Alexander, *Ionia: Land of Wise Men and Fair Women* (1898), 23

Crane, Stephen, 45, 47, 51

credit and credit economy, 153–61, 177

Crèvecoeur, J. Hector St. John de, 108

Croswell, William, "The Synagogue" (1842), 230

cultural and travel cycloramas, 76, *77*, *78*

cultural pluralism versus melting pot model of assimilation, 208–10

Curtis, George W., 297n27

Custer's Last Stand cyclorama, *71*

cyclorama: as late 19th-century spectacle, 69–77, *71–75*, *77*, *78*, 89, 266n142, 266n144; as metaphor in Cahan's *Imported Bridegroom*, 40–41, 65–69, 76–79, 82, 83, 86, 87, 89, 90, 265n132

Danforth, Samuel, 18

Daniel Deronda (Eliot, 1876), 101–2, 104, 232, 234, 259n80, 273–74n30

Daughters of the American Revolution, 193

Davis, Fred, 66

Defoe, Daniel, 154, 289n66; *Robinson Crusoe* (1719), 203

Destruction of Temple, 81, 87, 269n178, 281n109

Dewey, John, 188, 189–90, 210–12, 214

"Dewey figures" in Yezierska's works, 189–90, 210–16, 222–23

Dickens, Charles, *Great Expectations* (1861), 164, 290n87

Dimock, Wai-Chee, 169, 175, 292n104; *Through Other Continents* (2006), 29

Diner, Hasia, 12, 191, 244n24, 247n45

dispensationalism, 247n46

Disraeli, Benjamin, 235

Dobkowski, Michael, 22, 63, 245n33, 262n100

Donovan, Josephine, 64

Douglas, Mary, 96

Douglass, Frederick, 29, 199

Dreiser, Theodore, 47; *An American Tragedy* (1925), 160; *The Hand of the Potter* (1916), 160; *Sister Carrie* (1900), 166, 215, 224, 290n91; *The Titan* (1914), 160

Dreyfus affair, 244, 297n30

Durkheim, Émile, 27, 121, 130, 156, 281n113, 287–88n58

Dutch colony, NYC as: Jews of, 60, 231, 262n100; Knickerbockers (original Dutch settlers), 59, 231

economic issues. *See* money and value

Edel, Leon, 93, 95

education: Antin on, 188, 198, 201–8; Dewey on, 210–11; Kallen on, 208–9; Yezierska on, 188, 210–12, 219–25

Edwards, Jonathan, 28

Eisen, Arnold, 196

Eliot, Charles W., 297n27

Eliot, George, 237, 303n22; *Daniel Deronda* (1876), 101–2, 104, 232, 234, 259n80, 273–74n30

Emerson, Ralph Waldo, 134, 212, 218, 225

Enlightenment, Jewish. *See Haskalah* and *maskilim*

ethnic labor patterns in NYC, 58, 261n91

ethnography, Jewish literature read as, 38

ethnonationalism and race-nations, rise of, 107, 282n122

eugenics, 193, 196–97, 214, 274n41

Ezrahi, Sidra Dekoven, 41, 68, 265–66n139

Fabian, Ann, 157, 158, 288n65

Fabian, Johannes, 147

Farish, Gerty, 169

farmers, populist, 158–59

Feiner, Shmuel, 243n21, 253n2, 269n186

Felsenstein, Frank, 25

feminist scholarship, 169, 291nn95–96

Fessenden, Tracy, 27

Fiddler on the Roof (musical, 1964), 254n7

financial issues. *See* money and value

Fireside Poets, 22, 36, 230–31

Fisch, Harold, 6, 242n11

Five Corners (NYC), 57

Fleissner, Jennifer, 175–76

Flower, B. O., 45

Follett, Danielle, 253n106

Follett, Wilson, 175, 285n36

Foote, Stephanie, 58, 64–65

Ford, Henry, antisemitism of, 133, 282n123

Foucault, Michel, 271–72n15

Franco, Dean, *Race, Rights, and Recognition* (2012), 26

Frank, Leo, lynching of (1915), 133

Franklin, Benjamin, 199, 288n61

Frederic, Harold, *The Market-Place* (1899), 34

Freedman, Jonathan, 97, 103, 271n15, 274n31; *Klezmer America* (2008), 26, 249n71

Freeman, Elizabeth, *Time Binds* (2010), 28–29

French Revolution, 10, 243n21, 253n2

Freneau, Philip, "The Jewish Lamentation at the Euphrates" (1779) and "Sketches in American History" (1784), 230

Friedman, Natalie, 190

Frontier Thesis, 264n129

Fuller, Melville W., 248n61

Gabirol, Solomon Ben Judah, 232; "Meditation on Death," 304n38

gambling: Henry Ward Beecher on, 120, 155, 262n102; Durkheim on, 287–88n58; late 19th-century economics and, 155–57; in Wharton's *House of Mirth*, 146–49, 161, 163, 165, 169, 177–79, 293n119

Garland, Hamlin, 32, 64, 65, 158–59, 264n123; "Local Color in Fiction" (1893), 264n122; *A Spoil of Office* (1892), 158–59

garment industry in NYC, 50–51, 58, 261n92

Geertz, Clifford, 264n19

Geismar, Maxwell, 273n23

gender issues: feminist scholarship, 169, 291nn95–96; Flora in Cahan's *Imported Bridegroom*, 86, 88–90,

Harvey, William H., *Coin's Financial School* (1894) and *A Tale of Two Nations* (1894), 289n72

Haskalah (Jewish Enlightenment) and *maskilim*: Antin and, 202; Cahan and, 37–38, 81, 86, 253n2, 269n186; cosmopolitanism and, 106–7; significance of, 11, 243n21

Haviland, Beverly, 101

Hay, John, 231

Hayes, Rutherford B., 7, 139

Hayot, Eric, 265n132

Hebraic myth of Jews as outside time, 1–36; antisemitism and philosemitism, binary framework of, 3, 9, 14–15; antisemitism as flip side of, 20–25; authors and works addressed on, 9–10, 13–14, 21–25, 31–36 (*See also specific authors and works*); Christian philosemitic typology of, 3–4, 6–7, 8, 9, 13, 15–16, 17–25; concept of philosemitism, 15–17; Henry James on, 1–3, 5–6; "Jewish Problem" or "Jewish Question," 4, 10–13, 38, 137, 140, 158, 188, 191–97, 235–37, 258n64; literary studies and, 25–31; newspaper and periodical culture of late 19th/early 20th century, 31–32; "noble Hebrew" versus "avaricious Jew" (*See* "noble Hebrew"); Protestant-centric notions of time and, 4–6, 159; Seligman-Hilton affair and, 7–10 (*See also* Seligman, Joseph, and Seligman-Hilton affair)

Hebraism, 24, 51, 55, 102, 215, 231, 248n53, 274n35

Hebrew Immigration Aid Society (HIAS), 189, 233

Hebrew literature, 38

Hegel, Georg Wilhelm Friedrich, 243n19, 272–73n21, 276n60

Heine, Heinrich, 232, 302n21; "Donna Clara," 232; "Hebrew Melodies," 36

Hendrick, Burton J., 194–96, 297n33; "The Great Jewish Invasion" (1907), 13, 194; *The Jews in America* (1922), 194, 195–96; "Will the Jews Disappear?" (1917), 195

Herrnstein Smith, Barbara, 97

Herzl, Theodor, 107, 237, 269n182

Herzog, Elizabeth, and Mark Zborowski, *Life Is with People: The Culture of the Shtetl* (1952), 38, 253–54n7

HIAS (Hebrew Immigration Aid Society), 189, 233

Higginson, Thomas Wentworth, Jr., 297n27

Higham, John, 159, 282n122

Hilton, Henry, and Seligman-Hilton affair. *See* Seligman, Joseph, and Seligman-Hilton affair

Hollinger, David, 107

Holmes, Oliver Wendell, 9, 193–94, 230, 231, 297n27; "At the Pantomime" (1874), 21–22; *Over the Teacups* (1890), 193–94; "The Pilgrim's Vision" (1895), 21

Holocaust and Final Solution, 37, 201, 248n62

The House of Mirth (Wharton, 1905), 9–10, 34–35, 139–82; *Chronos* and *Kairos* in, 149, 150, 166, 171,

177, 285n34; critical reception of, 174–75, 291–92n101; death of Lily in, 148, 162, 169, 172–75, 291n96; debt to Gus Trenor in, 169–71; determinism and chance in, 174–78; economic logic of credit/speculative economy and, 153–61, 177; gambling and, 146–49, 155–56, 157, 161, 163, 165, 169, 177–79, 293n119; James on, 174; James's *The American* compared, 119; "the Jew," Rosedale as, 145, 150, 151–52, 161, 180–81; as naturalist text, 34, 174–75, 292n104; negotiation of social and clock time in, 146–53, 161–74; old-money culture, decline of, 34, 145, 156–57, 160–61, 182, 285n33; parents of Lily Bart in, 164–65, 166–68; potential marriage between Lily Bart and Simon Rosedale, 33–34, 119, 145, 148–49, 151–53, 165–66, 172, 174, 178–80; "republic of the spirit" in, 34, 151, 163, 172, 180, 291n96; Rosedale as most sympathetic character in, 160, 179, 180–81, 293n111; Seligman as model for Simon Rosedale in, 139–46, 150, 152, 158, 181; *tableaux vivants* scene, 168–69; temporal hybridity in, 30; time-value linkage in, 145–46; trust, concept of, and economic/financial systems, 121, 122, 146, 148, 156–57, 161, 285n37, 286n46, 288nn63–64, 294n238; women, time as prison for, 146–48, 162, 163–65, 284n26, 284n29; Yezierska's novels and, 181, 219, 224

Howard, June, 175, 290n81
Howe, Irving, 56, 261n92; *The World of Our Fathers* (1976), 64, 258n68
Howells, Eleanor, 43
Howells, William Dean: Cahan and, 42, 43–45, 47, 255nn19–20; Cowen's survey, participation in, 297n27; Crane as protégé of, 47; Hapgood compared, 250–51n82; on man of letters as man of business, 103; money as fundamental realist concern for, 120; in newspaper and periodical culture of late 19th/early 20th century, 31; "New York Low Life in Fiction" (1896), 37; as Protestant realist, 32; shared history with other writers, 14; *A Traveler from Altruria* (1893) translated into Yiddish by Cahan, 43
How the Other Half Lives (Riis, 1891), 1, 53–56, 76, 258n67, 259n79
Huckabee, Mike, 16
Hull House, Chicago, 187, 190
Hunter, Robert, *Poverty* (1904), 53

An Illustrated History of the Holy Bible (1868), 20
immigrant Jews: ambivalence of Jewish writers regarding, 296n25; Antin on, 204–5; in Cahan's *Imported Bridegroom*, 85–91; James on, 99–105, 114, 272n16; Kallen on Americanism of, 209; late 19th-century American views on, 52–56; literary representations of Jewishness and peak of, 100; push and pull factors leading to immigration, 265–66n139, 265n134;

immigrant Jews (*continued*)
  statistics on Jewish immigration,
    11, 244–45n30, 244n24, 244n26,
    270n191, 273n24
immigration: Alien Contract Labor
    Laws (1885 and 1887), 244n26;
    Aliens Act (England), 244n29;
    arguments for and against restriction
    of, 193, 198; Chinese Exclusion Act
    (1882), 244n26, 270n191; Contract
    Labor Law (1886), 270n191
Immigration Act (1891), 12, 244n26
Immigration Restriction League, 193
The Imported Bridegroom (Cahan,
    1898), 9–10, 32–33, 49; cyclorama
    metaphor in, 40–41, 65–69, 76–79,
    82, 83, 86, 87, 89, 90, 265n132;
    film adaptation (1989), 269n185;
    on immigrant/diaspora Jews, 85–
    91; late 19th-century cyclorama
    spectacles, 69–77, *71–75, 77, 78,* 89,
    266n142, 266n144; *milieux
    de mémoire* (environments of mem-
    ory) in, 85–91; nostalgia critiqued
    in, 26, 32, 40, 41, 63, 64, 66, 68–70,
    76, 79, 82–85, 87–90, 263n117;
    racial hierarchy in, 268n174; Sholem
    Aleichem's "Tevye the Dairyman"
    stories compared, 67; on *shtetls* and
    shtetl life, 39–41, 79; World-to-
    Come and realist time in, 79–83,
    84–85, 87, 88; Yezierska's *Bread Giv-
    ers* compared, 225. *See also* Cahan,
    Abraham
Ingraham, Joseph Holt, 21, 249n67
intermarriage: Antin on, 35, 188, 200–
    201; assimilation, as means of, 13,

35, 137, 183–89, 195–97; "Jewish
    problem" and, 191–97; in late 19th-
    and early 20th-century fiction, 35,
    188–89; Sholem Aleichem's Tevye,
    daughters of, 67; Wharton's *House of
    Mirth*, potential marriage between
    Lily Bart and Simon Rosedale in,
    33–34, 119, 145, 148–49, 151–
    53, 165–66, 172, 174, 178–80; in
    Yezierska's works, 35, 188, 208, 210,
    212–19
Isabella Steward Gardiner museum,
    Boston, James on, 270–71n5

Jackson, Andrew, 158, 159
Jackson, George Anson, 250n7
Jackson, Gregory S., *The Word and Its
    Witness* (2008), 28, 53
Jacob, John, 231
Jacobson, Matthew Frye, 13
James, Henry, 33, 93–137; *The American*
    (1877), 95, 99, 114–19; "Ameri-
    cans Abroad" (1878), 277n73; *The
    American Scene* (1907), 1–3, 5–6, 31,
    33, 57, 100, 101, 114, 134–36, 204,
    241n2, 261n94, 261n97, 272n15;
    antisemite, viewed as, 100, 273n23;
    "The Art of Fiction" (1884), 102;
    "the cosmopolitan," in works of,
    98–99, 105–14, 125, 133–34, 136;
    "Daniel Deronda" (1876), 101–2,
    273–74n30; "Democracy and The-
    odore Roosevelt" (1898), 108; "The
    Figure in the Carpet" (1896), 108–9;
    Guy Domville (1895), theatrical
    failure of, 933; on immigrant Jews,
    99–105, 114, 181–82, 272n16; on

"intensity of Jewish aspect," 99–
105; on Isabella Steward Gardiner
museum, Boston, 270–71n5; "the
Jew," in works of, 97–105, 133–34,
136–37; avaricious view of Jews,
revision of, 98, 103–4, 133; narrative persona of, 57, 260n88; in
newspaper and periodical culture
of late 19th/early 20th century, 31;
New York Edition of works of, 93,
95, 281n115; pawnbrokers, writers
as, 94–95, 96–97, 99, 123, 134–36;
The Portrait of a Lady (1881), 93–95,
97, 131, 136; as Protestant realist,
32; "The Pupil" (1891), 99, 109–14;
"queerness" in, 110, 276n59; relationship between Jews and cosmopolitans in works of, 98–99, 103–4,
106–7, 109, 110, 112–13, 123, 133–
34, 136; shared history with other
writers, 14; *The Spoils of Poynton*
(1897), 271n5; vocabulary of value
created by, 90–91, 93–99, 119–23,
132–37; Wharton compared, 33,
153, 292n101; on Wharton's *House
of Mirth*, 174. *See also Golden Bowl*
James, William, 260n88
Jameson, Fredric, *The Antimonies
of Realism* (2013), 30–31, 176,
252n104, 253n106
Jefferson, Thomas, 159
Jennings, Mary Elizabeth, *Asa of
Bethlehem and His Household* (1895),
250n76
Jesus: Christian doctrine of atonement
and, 281n109; Crucifixion of, Jewish
guilt for, 20, 63, 192; Jewishness of,

16, 61, 197, 262n103; Jews as source
of, 17–18, 21, 22, 23, 24, 62–63, 144,
229; Messiah, Jewish failure to recognize as, 17, 20, 21, 25, 55, 237; as
"Nordic," 197; Renan's *Life of Jesus*,
60–61, 262n103; Second Coming of,
and return of Jews to Israel, 16, 237
Jewett, Sarah Orne, 63, 64
Jewish collective memory, concept of,
80–81
Jewish Daily Forward, Cahan as
founding editor of, 42–43, 254n18,
257n49
Jewish Enlightenment. *See Haskalah*
and *maskilim*
"Jewish Problem" or "Jewish Question,"
4, 10–13, 38, 137, 140, 158, 188,
191–97, 235–37, 258n64
Jewish women. *See* gender
Jews, Hebraic myth of. *See* Hebraic
myth of Jews as outside time
Jones, Jesse H., *Joshua Davidson*
(1903), 23
Joseph, Rabbi Jacob, 281n120
Joseph, Philip, 88
Judah Ben Ha-Levi, 232

Kabbalah, 19
Kairos and *Chronos,* in Wharton's *House
of Mirth*, 149, 150, 166, 171, 177,
285n34
Kallen, Horace, 208–10, 211, 234;
"Democracy Versus the Melting
Pot" (1915), 208
Kandiyoti, Dalia, 65
Kant, Immanuel, 40, 106, 107
Kaplan, Amy, 64, 120, 292n104

Garland's concept of, 158, 264n122; treated as genre, 64–65
Lodge, Henry Cabot, 193
Loeb, Solomon, 158
Logan, "Blackjack," 70
Longfellow, Henry Wadsworth, 5–6, 9, 56, 231; "The Jewish Cemetery at Newport" (1854), 21, 36, 227–29, 242n10
Lowell, James Russell, 22–23, 193, 230, 231
Lower East Side (NYC): in Cahan's work, 37–41, 42, 45, 47 (See also Cahan, Abraham); crowdedness of tenement living in, 59, 261nn94–95; James's American Scene on, 1–3, 5–6, 31, 33, 57, 99–105, 241n2, 261n94, 261n97; Shanley's "The Bowery at Night," 57–60; views of immigrant Jews of, 52–56; in Yezierska's Bread Givers, 219–20
Luciano, Dana, 28
Lukács, Georg, 28, 252n10
Luska, Sidney (Henry Harland), 188, 295n12

Maimonides, 19, 268n172
Malamud, Bernard, The Fixer (1966), 67
Marcus, Alfred A., 301n2
Marcus, Jacob Rader, 192–93
Marx, Karl, "Zur Judenfrage" (1844), 10, 243n19
maskilim. See Haskalah and maskilim
Mason, Caroline Atwater, The Quiet King: A Story of Christ (1895), 250n76
Mather, Cotton, 18; Magnalia Christi Americana (1702), 17

Mauss, Marcel, 27; The Gift (1950), 93, 96
McClanahan, Annie, 287n47
McClure, S. S., 297n33
McClure's Magazine, 44, 53, 256n35, 297n33
McCosh, James, 297n27
McKinley, William, 248n61
melting pot model of assimilation: Antin's Promised Land and, 198, 201; cultural pluralism versus, 208–10; in Yezierska's Salome of the Tenements, 35, 213, 218; Zangwill's The Melting Pot (1909), 35, 183–86, 187, 188, 213, 218, 258n64, 303n28
Melville, Herman, 287n50, 293n114; Clarel, 247n44; The Confidence Man (1857), 287n52; Redburn (1849), 121
memory and remembrance: in Cahan's fiction, 39, 63–65, 68–69, 79, 80–81, 83, 85–91; Destruction of Temple as focus of, 81, 87, 269n178, 281n109; Jewish collective memory, concept of, 80–81; lieux de mémoire (memory places), 63–64, 66, 68; milieux de mémoire (environments of memory), 66, 85–91; souvenirs as tokens of, 127, 128, 280n105; World-to-Come and, 79
Menassah ben Israel, 19
Mendele (S. Y. Abramovitsh; Mendele Moykher-Sforim), 38, 107
Mendelssohn, Moses, 11, 38
Menken, Adah Isaacs, 234, 239; "Judith" (1868), 303n29

Puritans and Puritanism: America as New Jerusalem for, 185, 186; assimilation and, 208; Cahan and New England literary culture, 56; Christian philosemitism of, 3, 4, 7, 13, 17–18, 20–22, 24, 247n51; economic logic of, 155, 159, 290n79; time as value for, 4–6, 159; in Yezierska's *Bread Givers*, 222

"queerness" in James, 110, 276n59
queer time, 28–29

Rabinowitz, Shalom. *See* Sholem Aleichem
race-nations and ethnonationalism, rise of, 107, 282n122
Ragozin, Madame Z. (Madame Zénaïde A.), 233; "Russian Jews and Gentiles: from a Russian point of view" (1882), 236–37
Rashi, 19
Ravage, M. E., 188
Reform Judaism, 7–8, 191–92, 195, 231, 242n15, 243n23, 302n17
Reigel, Christian, 180
Reinhard, Richard, *Der Tanz zum Tode* (1877), 233
remembrance. *See* memory and remembrance
Renan, Ernest, *The Life of Jesus* (1863), 60–61, 262n103
repentance versus atonement, 129, 281n109
"republic of the spirit," in Wharton's *House of Myth*, 34, 151, 163, 172, 180, 291n96

Ricoeur, Paul, 164
Riis, Jacob: *The Battle with the Slum* (1902), 53; Cahan apprenticed under, 46, 56; Christian philosemitic typology of, 25; dual Jewish images, difficulty reconciling, 102; on education, 208; *How the Other Half Lives* (1891), 1, 53–56, 76, 258n67, 259n79; on immigrant Jews, 51–52, 53–56, 181; on "Jewish Problem," 11; *Making of an American* (autobiography), 198; in newspaper and periodical culture of late 19th/early 20th century, 31, 45, 52; photography of, 259n79; "secularization thesis" and, 28; shared history with other writers, 14; tenement statistics of, 261n95
Ripley, William S., 193
Rischin, Moses, 250–51n82, 257n49, 261n91
Robbins, Bruce, 275n47
Rockefeller, John D., 248n61
Roosevelt, Theodore, 108, 186–87, 188, 194, 198, 208, 209, 272n16, 297n27; "True Americanism" (1894), 12, 35, 183, 187, 211
Roskies, David, 39
Ross, Edward Alsworth, 196–97, 208
Roth, Henry, 242n11
Rothschilds, 22, 106, 139, 140, 159, 282n4, 289n72
Rubin, Larry, 292n104

Salome of the Tenements (Yezierska, 1923), 9–10, 35, 190, 212–19

Sollors, Werner, 185

Sombart, Werner, 243n19

Southworth, E. D. E. N., *The Bridal Eve* (1864), 121

souvenirs, 127, 128, 280n105

Spargo, John, *The Bitter Cry of the Children* (1906), 53

speculative economy, 155–57, 177

Spengemann, William, 98, 119

Steffens, Josephine Bontecou, 49

Steffens, Lincoln: Cahan and, 46–52, 56, 257n49; S. S. McClure and, 297n33; in newspaper and periodical culture of late 19th/early 20th century, 31, 46–47, 52; philosemitism of, 47–49, 51–52; Riis compared, 56; "Schloma, Daughter of Schmuhl" (1896), 49–51; *The Shame of the Cities* (1904), 53, 259n71; shared history with other writers, 14; "Yom Kippur on the East Side" (1896), 49; Zangwill's *The Melting Pot* and, 258n64

Stewart, Susan, 85, 280n105

Stokes, Graham, 190

Stokes, Rose Pastor, 190

Storey, William Wetmore, 230

Stowe, Calvin Ellis, 60, 262n102; *The Origin and History of the Books of the Bible* (1867), 60; "The Talmud" (1868), 60–63

Stowe, Harriet Beecher, 60

Stuyvesant, Peter, 57, 60, 260n85, 261n98

Sundquist, Eric, 64, 120

Sutcliffe, Adam, 14, 15

symbolic capital, 149, 165, 285n31

Talmud, defined, 262–63n106

Taylor, Charles, 27, 64

Temple, Destruction of, 81, 87, 269n178, 281n109

Temple Emanu-El (NYC), 140, 231, 242n15

temporality. *See* time

the *shtetl*, 37–41, 63–64, 66–69, 79, 82, 199, 201, 253–54n7, 265–66n139

Thompson, E. P., 159

Timayenis, Telemachus T., 193, 233, 303n25

time: biblical, 16, 54, 242n11; Christian, 13, 15, 20; as commodity, 159–60; deep time, 29; historical, 32, 41, 66, 69, 78, 81–83, 96, 102, 228; homogeneous, 29, 31, 41, 83–85, 87, 89, 164, 171, 177; Jewish, 32, 80, 83, 89, 101, 191, 265n132; labor time, 26, 167; linear, 29, 30, 32, 33, 40, 64, 68, 70, 83–83, 145, 149, 151, 161, 164, 168, 173–78, 204; literary, 29–30; market time, 34, 59; messianic, 4–5, 10, 19, 26, 32, 81, 90, 191, 269n181; millennial/eschatological/end-time, 4–5, 18–20, 23, 29, 79–80, 191; modernity and, 4, 16, 25, 29, 31, 40, 146, 177, 181, 294n128; negotiation of social and clock time in Wharton's *House of Mirth*, 146–53, 161–74; nostalgia as nonsequential form of time in literature, 28; orders of, 16, 29, 33, 39, `45, 84, 85, 98, 149, 168, 204; pluralizing, 29–30, 83; as prison for women in Wharton's *House of Mirth*, 146–48, 162, 163–65, 284n26, 284n29;

time (*continued*)
Protestant notions of, 4–6, 159, 191; providential, 4, 6, 26, 79–82, 177; queer time, 28–29; realist time in Cahan's fiction, 79–85, 87, 88; redemptive, 83; religious, 27, 31; ritual, 32, 79–80, 84, 88, 90, 101, 146; sacred, 16, 27, 29, 31, 79–80, 83, 87, 149; secular, 16, 34, 41, 84, 85; time-value linkage in Wharton's *House of Mirth*, 145–46; typological, 4; usury as sale of, 1, 6, 151, 159–60, 169, 170. *See also* Hebraic myth of Jews as outside time
time-discipline and time-thrift, 152, 160
Tobenkin, Elias, 188
Touro Synagogue, Newport, 227, 301n2; Lazarus's "In the Jewish Synagogue at Newport" on, 227–30, 237, 304n38; Longfellow's "The Jewish Cemetery at Newport" on, 21, 36, 227–29, 242n10
Trachtenberg, Alan, 120, 241n2, 241n7, 264n129
Tracy, Benjamin V., 46
travel and cultural cycloramas, 76, 77, 78
Trump, Donald, 141
trust, concept of, and economic/financial systems, 121, 122, 146, 148, 156–57, 161, 285n37, 286n46, 288nn63–64, 294n238
Tuan, Yi-Fu, 269n178
Turner, Frederick Jackson, 264n129
Twain, Mark, 124; *The Gilded Age*, 102; *Innocents Abroad*, 247n44

typological aesthetic: Arnold's use of, 24; both fiction and nonfiction shaped by, 57; defined, 7, 16, 25, 53; in Hapgood's *Spirit of the Ghetto*, 24; in James, 101; Jewish literary figures and negotiation of, 10, 36; Lazarus and, 236; literary temporality and, 29–30; Longfellow and, 142, 229; Riis and, 55, 56; Seligman-Hilton affair and, 142; Steffens and, 42, 47, 48, 49, 56; theological basis of, 9, 16, 20, 21
typology: Christian, 3–4, 6–7, 8, 9, 13, 15–16, 17–25, 60–63, 143, 228; doubling logic of, 5, 18, 20, 23, 41; eugenics and, 197; fundamental paradox of, 62; James's use of language of, 102; Lazarus using Hebraic myth to disrupt, 235, 236; Protestant, 3, 7, 13, 28, 243n19

Ueda, Reed, 265n134
usury: economic logic of credit/speculative economy and, 156–59; Jews associated with, 21, 22, 99, 102, 122, 123, 152, 192, 235, 236; pawnbrokers associated with, 99, 102, 122, 279n93; time, as sale of, 1, 6, 151, 159–60, 169, 170

value. *See* money and value
Vance, Zebulon V., 297n27
Vanderbilt, William, 231
Veblen, Thorstein, 159
Verein für Kultur und Wissenschaft der Juden, 11
Very, Jones, 230

Vinchevsky, Morris, 269n186

Vizetelly, Frank H., 297n27

Wald, Priscilla, 52

Wallace, Lew, *Ben Hur* (1880), 23

Ward, Elizabeth Stuart Phelps, *The Story of Jesus Christ, An Interpretation* (1898), 250n7

Warner, Charles D., 297n27

Washington, Booker T., 199

Washington, George, 206–7, 221

Watt, Ian, 251n91, 274n39

Weber, Donald, 117

Weber, Max, 102, 120, 121, 160, 243n19, 290n79

Weinstein, Cindy, 28

Wharton, Edith, 3, 33–35; Antin and Yezierska compared, 35; *A Backward Glance* (1934), 148–49; Cahan compared, 153; "Getting on in New York Society" (1916), 293n119; James compared, 33, 153, 292n101; shared history with other writers, 14. *See also House of Mirth*

Wheatley, Phyllis, 199

Wheatly, Richard, 52

Whittier, John Greenleaf, 230–31; "The Rabbi Ishmael" and "The Two Rabbins" (1881), 302n13

Wilson, Anna May, 250n7

Winthrop, John, 18, 199

Wirth-Nesher, Hana, 64, 256n29

Wise, Isaac Meyer, 12, 243–44n23

Wolff, Cynthia Griffin, 169, 291n95, 291n100

women. *See* gender

"World-to-Come" (*ha-Olam ha-ba*), 5, 16, 26, 32, 39, 41, 79–85, 87, 88, 90, 220, 268n172; versus "this world" (*ha-Olam ha-ze*), 59, 81, 220

Wright, Harry J., 46

Wyckoff, Walter, 45

Yeazell, Ruth, 292n104

Yekl: A Tale of the New York Ghetto (Cahan, 1896), 39, 42, 44–45, 46, 65, 256n30. *See also* Cahan, Abraham

Yerushalmi, Joseph Hayim, 27

Yezierska, Anzia, 3, 183–225; *All I Could Never Be* (1932), 212; on assimilation, 188–91, 219–25; *Bread Givers* (1925), 9–10, 35, 190, 212, 219–25; Dewey and "Dewey figures" in works of, 189–90, 210–16, 222–23; on education, 188, 210–12, 219–25; on intermarriage, 35, 188, 208, 210, 212–19; Lazarus compared, 238; in newspaper and periodical culture of late 19th/early 20th century, 31; nostalgia for Jewish past, lack of, 197; *Salome of the Tenements* (1923), 9–10, 35, 190, 212–19; on settlement house movement, 189–90; shared history with other writers, 14; Wharton's *House of Mirth* and, 181, 219, 224

Yiddish literature, 38–39, 41, 66, 298n38; Cahan and, 42–43; Henry James and, 112–13; Lincoln Steffens and, 48–50, 56; Yiddish language and culture and, 2, 12, 31, 32, 80, 107, 196, 209, 251n82, 253n7

Yom Kippur, 48, 49, 129